SPELLING AND DICTION

18 sp
Spelling and Hyphenation
- **a** Pronunciation
- **b** Similar words
- **c** Prefixes, suffixes
- **d** *ei* and *ie*
- **e** Plural words
- **f** Hyphenation

19 g
Good Usage
- **a** Use of dictionary
- **b** Informal words
- **c** Slang, jargon
- **d** Regional words
- **e** Non-standard words
- **f** Archaic/obsolete words
- **g** Technical words
- **h** Overwriting
- **i** **Glossary of Usage**

20 e
Exactness
- **a** Exact words
- **b** Idiomatic words
- **c** Fresh expressions

21 w
Wordiness
- **a** Meaningless words
- **b** Eliminating wordiness
- **c** Needless repetition

22 ∧
Omission of Necessary Words
- **a** Articles, etc.
- **b** Verbs and auxiliaries
- **c** Incomplete comparisons
- **d** After *so, such, too*

EFFECTIV

23 u/log
Unity and Logical Thinking
- **a** Unrelated ideas
- **b** Excessive detail
- **c** Awkward constructions
- **d** Definition
- **e** Sound reasoning
- **f** Common fallacies

24 sub
Subordination
- **a** Short sentences
- **b** Unequal ideas
- **c** Excessive subordination

25 coh
Coherence
- **a** Misplaced parts
  - (1) Modifiers
  - (2) Phrases
  - (3) Clauses
  - (4) "Squinting" constructions
  - (5) Sentence bases, infinitives
- **b** Dangling modifiers

26 //
Parallelism
- **a** Balanced parts
- **b** Repeated words
- **c** Correlatives
- **d** *And who*, etc.

27 ns
Shifts
- **a** Tense, mood, voice
- **b** Person, number
- **c** Indirect/direct discourse
- **d** Tone, style
- **e** Perspective

28 ref
Reference of Pronouns
- **a** Ambiguous
- **b** Remote, obscure
- **c** Broad
- **d** Misuse of *it*

29 emp
Emphasis
- **a** Important words
- **b** Periodic sentences
- **c** Order of climax
- **d** Active voice
- **e** Repetition
- **f** Inversion
- **g** Balance
- **h** Sentence length

30 var
Variety
- **a** Sentence length
- **b** Sentence beginnings
- **c** Loose compound sentences
- **d** Subject–verb sequence
- **e** Series of statements

TS

The Paragraph
- **a** Coherence
- **b** Development
- **c** Unity
- **d** Transitions
- **e** Special types

32 comp
The Whole Composition
- **a** Choosing a topic
- **b** Collecting ideas
- **c** General pattern
- **d** Thesis statement
- **e** Audience
- **f** Rough outline
- **g** First draft
- **h** Second draft
- **i** Final draft

33 res
The Research Paper
- **a** Choosing a subject
- **b** Bibliography
- **c** Preliminary outline
- **d** Final outline
- **e** Note-taking
- **f** Writing the paper

34 bus
Business Writing
- **a** Business letters
- **b** The résumé

grt
Glossary of Grammatical Terms

HARBRACE COLLEGE HANDBOOK
For Canadian Writers

HARBRACE COLLEGE HANDBOOK For Canadian Writers

With the new MLA documentation style

Second Edition

John C. Hodges
Late of the University of Tennessee

and

Mary E. Whitten
North Texas State University

EDITORIAL CONSULTANT

Bruce R. Lundgren
Associate Professor of English
University of Western Ontario

With a Foreword by:

Peter Desbarats, Dean
Graduate School of Journalism
University of Western Ontario

Harcourt Brace Jovanovich, Canada
Toronto Orlando San Diego London Sydney

Canadian Cataloguing in Publication Data

Hodges, John C., 1892-1967.
Harbrace college handbook for Canadian writers

Includes index.
First ed. published under title: Harbrace college handbook. Canadian ed.
ISBN 0-7747-3046-3

1. English language — Grammar — 1950– 2. English language — Rhetoric. I. Whitten, Mary E. II. Title. III. Title: Harbrace college handbook. Canadian ed.

PE1112.H62 1986 808′.042 C85-099776-3

ISBN: 0-7747-3046-3

Printed and bound in Canada by John Deyell Company

1 2 3 4 5 6 90 89 88 87 86

Foreword

The rules of grammar begin and end, like all sciences, in the mystery and artistry of creation.

The first grammarian must have been preceded by the first poet. In our own time, the writer always has the last word about effective writing.

Grammar is a living science, forever trying to define rules for the ever-changing complexities of human expression. It never quite catches up with our delight in ingenuity and individuality. The rules always leave plenty of room for debate, for uncertainty, and for experimentation.

Even after 35 years of professional writing, I'm always challenged by the range of options that are available to me—whether, for instance, that dash I just used would have been more effective as a colon; whether that semi-colon might have been simply a comma, and whether trying to emphasize a word by using quotation marks like "this" is more effective than doing it in italics like *this*, or underlining it like this, or doing none of these and simply starting over again to write a much simpler sentence than this has been.

Grammar has to be a flexible instrument in the hand of a writer. On the other hand, it's also his/her starting point. A writer without a thorough, almost instinctive knowledge of grammar would be as handicapped—if one can imagine such an oddity at all—as a painter without an understanding of the elements of colour, or a composer without a knowledge of musical notation.

The study of the basic elements of language never ends. I always write for publication with a dictionary within reach.

"Don't you know how to spell?" one of my children once asked me in amazement.

Not always. Is there one "m" or two in accommodation? I often have to check. And on the way to the sought-after word, I usually stumble across the unexpected—the fact, for instance, that the colon in our abdomen is related to the colon in our grammar through the same Greek root. You never can tell when something like that will be useful.

Next to the dictionary, on the shelf over the terminal, are a few favourite guides to usage and style. Among them now, this second Canadian edition of the *Harbrace College Handbook*.

It isn't hard to tell why this has been an American classic for more than four decades. It covers a vast range of usage, from the simple sentence to the academic essay, in a logical, easily accessible structure.

In Canada, the publication of this revised edition could hardly be more timely. In the study and teaching of English, as in many other academic disciplines, educators and parents are scrambling back to "the basics" after several decades of "progressive" education. Many of us have felt that an entire generation—our children—have suffered from an excess of "doing your own thing" amid exaggerated claims that literacy in print was about to join the study of Latin and Greek among the discarded antiques in the attics of academia. Low levels of literacy in university students confirmed this. Now, with a renewed interest in such basic subjects as English grammar, this book should be welcomed not only by students and educators but by the many adults who feel the need for a "refresher course" in grammar, and for a quick reference to the basic rules of good Canadian English.

Peter Desbarats, *Dean*
Graduate School of Journalism
University of Western Ontario

Preface

The second Canadian edition of the *Harbrace College Handbook for Canadian Writers* is based on the 1984 printing of the American ninth edition of the *Harbrace College Handbook* by John C. Hodges, late of the University of Tennessee, and Mary E. Whitten of North Texas State University. In preparing the Canadian edition we have attempted to preserve the organization and methodology of the American original (which have been tested and refined over the course of several editions), while at the same time making the book more accurately reflect the needs of Canadian students and the Canadian cultural environment. In particular, we have included more examples chosen from the work of Canadian writers, expanded the use of Canadian names or terms to give selected examples the significance of a Canadian context, added still more Canadian works to the lists of reference books, and, as before, adopted metric units and Canadianized the spelling.

The *Harbrace College Handbook for Canadian Writers* is both a reference guide for the individual writer and a textbook for use in class. A comprehensive yet concise summary of the principles of effective writing, the *Harbrace Handbook* provides an easily-mastered system for the correction of student papers, and the directness and economy of its rules and examples make it a lasting resource for the writer. The endpapers provide a useful overview and handy guide for quick reference. The book begins with a review of the essentials of grammar to be used as needed to introduce the other sections; the book ends with a glossary, useful as a reference throughout the course. According to the requirements of a particular class, the book may be taught in any order. For example, some instructors may want to begin with Section **32, The Whole Composition**, others with Section **31, The Paragraph**, or with Sections **19–30**, which deal with diction and sentences. In every section, the large number and variety of exercises make it possible for instructors to select activities appropriate to the needs of their class.

The *Harbrace College Handbook for Canadian Writers* reflects the quality of the extensive revisions made for the ninth edition of the American *Harbrace College Handbook*. Section **31** includes expanded coverage of the topic sentence and methods of paragraph development, and Section **32** has been completely rewritten in terms of essay writing as a process—from choosing and limiting a topic, gathering ideas and formulating a thesis statement, to revising the second draft. Throughout the section, a single student essay is used to illustrate each step of the process. Section **33** describes and illustrates the new style of documentation adopted by the Modern Language Association. The sample research paper, accompanied by detailed annotations, adheres to the new MLA style. For the most part, Canadian references are used to illustrate the proper form to be used when following either the new 1984 MLA documentation style or the American Psychological Association's 1983 changes in reference format. Finally, in Section **34**, the four sample business letters and two résumés have been revised to reflect Canadian practices.

My thanks to all those associated with Harcourt Brace Jovanovich, Canada who have made this 1986 Canadian edition possible.

Bruce R. Lundgren
Associate Professor of English
University of Western Ontario

To the Student

Numbers or Symbols / A number or a symbol written in the margin of your paper indicates a need for correction or improvement and calls for revision. If a number is used, turn directly to the corresponding number at the top of the page in the handbook. If a symbol is used, first consult the alphabetical list of symbols inside the back cover to find the number of the section to which you should turn. An appropriate letter after a number or symbol (such as **2c** or **frag/c**) will refer you to a specific part of a section.

References / Your instructor will ordinarily refer you to the number or symbol (**2** or **frag, 9** or **cap, 18** or **sp, 28** or **ref**) appearing at the head of one of the thirty-four sections of the handbook. The rule given in colour at the beginning of each section covers the whole section. One of the more specific rules given within the section will usually be needed to guide you in revision. Study the section to which you have been referred—the whole of the section if necessary—and master the specific part of the section that applies to your writing.

Correction and Revision / After you have studied the rules called to your attention, revise your paper carefully, as directed by your instructor. One method of revision is explained and illustrated in Section **8**, page 104.

Contents

Foreword *by Peter Desbarats* v
Preface *by Bruce R. Lundgren* vii
To the Student ix

GRAMMAR

1 Sentence Sense **2**

a Recognizing verbs and subjects 5
b Recognizing objects and complements 9
c Recognizing all parts of speech 13
d Recognizing phrases and subordinate clauses 20
(1) Phrases used as nouns 22
(2) Phrases used as modifiers 23
(3) Subordinate clauses used as nouns 26
(4) Subordinate clauses used as modifiers 26
e Recognizing main clauses and types of sentences 28

2 Sentence Fragments **32**

TEST FOR SENTENCE COMPLETENESS 33
REVISION OF A SENTENCE FRAGMENT 34
a Phrases 35
b Subordinate clauses 36
c Other fragments 37

3 Comma Splice and Fused Sentence **40**

VARIOUS METHODS OF REVISION 41
a Co-ordinating conjunctions 41
b Conjunctive adverbs and transitional phrases 45

4 Adjectives and Adverbs — 50

a Adverbs 51
b Adjectives as subject or object complements 52
c Comparative and superlative forms 53
d Awkward use of a noun as an adjective 54

5 Case — 56

a Pronouns in compound constructions 59
b Use of a pronoun in its own clause 60
(1) *Who* or *whoever* as the subject of a clause 60
(2) *Who* or *whom* before *I think, he says*, etc. 61
(3) Pronoun after *than* or *as* 61
c *Whom* in formal writing 62
d Possessive case before a gerund 64
e Objective case with an infinitive 64
f Subjective case for the complement of *be* 65

6 Agreement — 66

a Subject and verb 68
(1) Intervening noun or pronoun; retention of *-s* suffix 68
(2) Subjects joined by *and* 68
(3) Singular subjects joined by *or*, etc. 69
(4) Inverted word order 70
(5) Relative pronoun as subject 70
(6) *Each*, etc., as subject 71
(7) Collective noun as subject 71
(8) Linking verbs 72
(9) Plural form, singular meaning 72
(10) Titles of works; words spoken of as such 73
b Pronoun and antecedent 74
(1) *Each, a person*, etc., as antecedent 74
(2) Antecedents joined by *and*; by *or/nor* 75
(3) Collective noun as antecedent 75

7 Verb Forms 78

TENSE, NUMBER AND PERSON, VOICE 78–79
MOOD 80
PROGRESSIVE FORMS 80
FORMS OF *BE* 81
a Misused principal parts; confused verbs 82
(1) Principal parts of verbs 82
PRINCIPAL PARTS OF VERBS 83
(2) *Set* and *sit*; *lay* and *lie* 85
b Sequence of tenses 87
(1) Meaning of tense forms 87
(2) Sequence of tense forms 89
VERBS, INFINITIVES, PARTICIPLES 89–90
c Subjunctive mood 91
d Needless shifts in tense and mood 92
e *Should* and *would* 94

MECHANICS

8 Manuscript Form 96

a Proper materials 96
b Arrangement 97
c Legibility 98
d Word division 99
e Revising and proofreading 101
(1) Before submitting the paper 101
PROOFREADER'S CHECKLIST 102
(2) After the paper has been marked 103
A PARAGRAPH MARKED BY AN INSTRUCTOR
THE SAME PARAGRAPH CORRECTED BY A STUDENT 104
INDIVIDUAL RECORD OF ERRORS 105

9 Capitals 108

a Proper names 109
(1) Proper names 109
(2) Words as part of proper names 110

(3) Derivatives 110
(4) Abbreviations 110
b Titles preceding proper names 111
c Titles of books, plays, etc. 111
d The pronoun *I* and the interjection *O* 112
e First word of the sentence 112
f Unnecessary capitals 113
STYLE SHEET FOR CAPITALIZATION 113

10 Italics 115

a Titles of books, etc. 115
b Foreign words and phrases 116
c Names of ships, aircraft, etc. 117
d Words, etc., spoken of as such 117
e Emphasized words 118

11 Abbreviations and Numbers 120

a *Mr., Dr.,* etc. 120
b Names of provinces, etc. 121
c *Street, Avenue,* etc. 121
d Courses of study 122
PERMISSIBLE ABBREVIATIONS 122
e Numbers 124
SPECIAL USAGE REGARDING NUMBERS 124

PUNCTUATION

12 The Comma 128

a Before *and*, etc., linking main clauses 129
b After introductory elements 132
(1) Adverb clauses 132
(2) Long phrases 133
(3) Transitional expressions and interjections 134

c Between items in series 135
(1) Words, phrases, and clauses 135
(2) Co-ordinate adjectives 136
d Non-restrictive and miscellaneous elements 137
(1) Non-restrictive clauses and phrases 137
(2) Non-restrictive appositives, contrasted elements, geographical names, and items in dates and addresses 140
(3) Parenthetical elements 142
e Prevention of misreading 143

13 Superfluous Commas **147**
a Subject and verb, verb and object 147
b Misuse with a co-ordinating conjunction 148
c Slightly parenthetical expressions 148
d Restrictive clauses, phrases, and appositives 148
e First and last items of a series 149

14 The Semicolon **151**
a Between main clauses not linked by *and*, etc. 152
b Between items in series 155
c Misuse with parts of unequal rank 156

15 The Apostrophe **159**
a Possessive case 159
(1) Singular nouns and indefinite pronouns 160
(2) Plural nouns 160
(3) Compounds or word groups 160
(4) Individual ownership 160
b Contractions 161
c Plurals of lower-case letters, etc. 162
d Misuse with pronouns and plural nouns 163

16 Quotation Marks 164

a Direct quotations 165
(1) Long prose quotations 165
(2) Poetry 166
(3) Dialogue 167
(4) Punctuation of dialogue 168
b Minor titles 169
c Words used in a special sense 169
d Overuse of quotation marks 170
e Placement with other marks of punctuation 170
(1) Period and comma 171
(2) Colon and semicolon 171
(3) Dash, question mark, and exclamation point 171

17 The Period and Other Marks 173

a The period 174
(1) Declarative and mildly imperative sentences; indirect questions 174
(2) Abbreviations 174
b The question mark 175
c The exclamation point 176
d The colon 177
(1) Explanations, appositives, series, and quotations 177
(2) Scriptural and time references; titles and subtitles 178
(3) Superfluous colons 178
e The dash 180
(1) Break in thought 180
(2) Explanation or illustration 180
(3) Between introductory series and main clause 181
(4) Parenthetical elements 181
f Parentheses 182
PUNCTUATION OF PARENTHETICAL MATTER 183
g Brackets 183
h The slash 184
i The ellipsis mark 185

SPELLING AND DICTION

18 Spelling and Hyphenation 190

a Pronunciation of problem words 191
b Words of similar sound and spelling 193
WORDS FREQUENTLY CONFUSED 194
c Prefixes and suffixes 195
(1) Addition of prefix to root 195
(2) Final *e* before suffix 196
(3) Addition of suffix to one-syllable word 197
(4) Final *y* before suffix 197
(5) Final *l* before *-ly* 198
d Confusion of *ei* and *ie* 198
e Forming the plural 199
(1) Nouns 199
(2) Nouns ending in *s*, etc. 199
(3) Nouns ending in *y* 199
A LIST OF WORDS FREQUENTLY MISSPELLED 200
f Hyphenation 207
(1) Two words as single adjective 207
(2) Compound numbers 208
(3) Prefix and root, suffix and root 209
(4) *Ex-*, etc.; prefix and proper name; *-elect* 209

19 Good Usage and Glossary 210

a Use of the dictionary 210
(1) Spelling, syllabication, and pronunciation 211
(2) Parts of speech and inflected forms 212
(3) Definitions and examples of usage 212
(4) Synonyms and antonyms 213
(5) Development of the language 214
(6) Special usage labels 218
b Informal words 219
c Slang and jargon 220
d Regional words 221

e Non-standard words and usages 222
f Archaic and obsolete words 222
g Technical words 222
h Overwriting; distracting sounds 223
i **Glossary of Usage** 224

20 Exactness 246

a Exact words 247
(1) Precise denotation 247
(2) Appropriate connotation 249
(3) Specific words 250
(4) Figurative language 253
b Idiomatic words 255
c Fresh expressions 257

21 Wordiness 261

a Meaningless words 262
(1) Avoiding tautologies 262
(2) Omitting unnecessary words 263
b Revising to avoid wordiness 265
c Careless or needless repetition 267

22 Omission of Necessary Words 271

a Articles, pronouns, conjunctions, and prepositions 272
(1) Omitted article or pronoun 272
(2) Omitted conjunction or preposition 272
b Awkward omission of verbs and auxiliaries 274
c Words necessary to complete comparisons 274
d Phrases and clauses after *so, such*, and *too* 275

EFFECTIVE SENTENCES

23 Unity and Logical Thinking 278

a Unrelated thoughts 279
b Excessive detail 280
c Mixed or awkward constructions 282
(1) Mixed metaphors 282
(2) Mixed constructions 282
(3) Awkward or obscure sentences 282
d Formal and informal definition 283
e Sound reasoning 285
f Common fallacies 287
(1) Non sequitur 287
(2) Self-contradiction 287
(3) Circular reasoning 287
(4) Facts and value judgments 288
(5) Hasty generalization 288
(6) Post hoc 288
(7) False analogy 289
(8) Ignoring the question 289
(9) Ad hominem 289
(10) Ad populum 289
(11) Bandwagon 290
(12) Appeal to authority or prestige 290
(13) Ambiguity 290
(14) Equivocation 290
(15) Oversimplification 291
(16) Either-Or 291

24 Subordination 293

a Related series of short sentences 295
b Ideas of unequal weight 296
c Excessive subordination 297

25 Coherence: Misplaced Parts, Dangling Modifiers 300

a Misplaced parts 301

(1) Placement of modifiers 301
(2) Placement of prepositional phrase 302
(3) Placement of adjective clause 303
(4) "Squinting" constructions 303
(5) Separation of sentence base; split infinitives 303
b Dangling modifiers 304
(1) Participial phrases 304
(2) Gerund and infinitive phrases 305
(3) Elliptical adverb clauses 305

26 Parallelism **308**

a Balanced parts 308
(1) Parallel words and phrases 309
(2) Parallel clauses 309
(3) Parallel sentences 309
b Repetition of a preposition, etc. 310
c Correlatives 311
d *And who, and which* constructions 312

27 Shifts **314**

a In tense, mood, and voice 314
b In person and number 315
c From indirect to direct discourse 316
d In tone or style 316
e In perspective or viewpoint 317

28 Reference of Pronouns **319**

a Ambiguous reference 320
b Remote or obscure reference 321
c Broad reference 322
(1) Reference to general idea of preceding clause 322
(2) Reference to implied word 323
(3) Indefinite *you* or *it* 323
d Placement of the pronoun *it* 324

29 Emphasis 325

a Placement of important words 326
b Periodic sentences 327
c Order of climax 329
d Active voice 330
e Repetition of important words 331
f Inversion 332
g Balance 332
h Sentence length 333

30 Variety 335

a Sentence length 336
b Sentence beginnings 338
(1) Adverb or adverb clause 338
(2) Prepositional or participial phrase 339
(3) Sentence connective 339
(4) Appositive or absolute 339
c Avoiding loose compound sentences 341
(1) Complex sentence 341
(2) Compound predicate 341
(3) Modifier or appositive 342
(4) Phrases 342
d Subject–verb sequence 343
e Question, exclamation, or command 343

LARGER ELEMENTS

31 The Paragraph 346

a Coherence 347
(1) Constructing the topic sentence 347
(2) Placing the topic sentence 349
(3) Organizing the paragraph 352
b Adequate development 356
(1) Narration 356
(2) Process 357
(3) Description 357

	(4) Classification	358
	(5) Analysis	359
	(6) Definition	360
	(7) Comparison/Contrast	361
	(8) Example	362
c	Unity	364
	(1) Relating sentences to main idea	364
	(2) Pronouns as links	365
	(3) Repetition of words or ideas	366
	(4) Transitional expressions	367
	(5) Parallel structure	368
d	Transitions between paragraphs	371
e	Special types of paragraphs	373
	(1) Opening paragraphs	373
	(2) Concluding paragraphs	374
	(3) Transitional paragraphs	375
	CHECKLIST FOR PARAGRAPH REVISION	374

32 The Whole Composition **379**

a	Choosing and limiting the subject	383
b	Collecting ideas	388
	(1) List-making	388
	(2) Asking the journalist's six questions	389
	(3) Asking questions based on paragraph-developing methods	390
c	Arranging ideas into a pattern	391
d	Shaping a thesis statement	393
e	Evaluating the audience	395
f	Developing a rough outline	400
	(1) Choosing a sequence for ideas	400
	(2) Preparing the rough outline	401
g	Writing and revising the first draft	405
h	Writing and revising the second draft	409
	REVISER'S CHECKLIST	414–15
i	Preparing the final draft	415

33 The Research Paper **420**

a	Choosing and limiting the subject	421

b	Preparing a bibliography	422
	(1) Library catalogues	422
	(2) Indexes to periodicals	425
	INDEXES TO PERIODICALS	427
	(3) Reference books	428
	REFERENCE BOOKS	428
	(4) Standard bibliographical form	432
	SAMPLE BIBLIOGRAPHICAL ENTRIES	433
	VARYING STYLES OF DOCUMENTATION	444
c	Developing the preliminary outline	446
d	Preparing the final outline	448
e	Taking notes	451
f	Writing the paper	459
	SAMPLE CITATIONS	460

Sample Research Paper **471**

34 Business Writing 513

a	Business letters	513
	(1) Business letter formats	513
	(2) Types of business letters	518
	(a) Thank-you letter	518
	(b) Claim and adjustment letter	518
	(c) Order letter	520
	(d) Application letter	522
	(3) Business envelopes	522
b	The résumé	524

Glossary of Grammatical Terms 529

Index 558

Acknowledgments 588

GRAMMAR

Sentence Sense 1

Sentence Fragments 2

Comma Splice and Fused Sentence 3

Adjectives and Adverbs 4

Case 5

Agreement 6

Verb Forms 7

Sentence Sense

1

Master the essentials of the sentence as an aid to clear thinking and effective writing.

A key to good writing is to possess or develop sentence sense. Sentence sense is the awareness of what *makes* a sentence—the ability to recognize its grammatical essentials and to understand the relationships between its parts.

Observing the positions, forms, and meanings of words can help you to understand the relationship between parts of sentences. Notice below how meaning is expressed by the arrangement and the forms of words:

> The hijacked plane has landed safely.

Note the importance of word order. Other arrangements of the same words are possible:

> The hijacked plane has safely landed. [no appreciable difference in meaning]
> Has the hijacked plane landed safely? [a change in meaning]

But not every arrangement of words is possible in an English sentence:

> NONSENSICAL Hijacked safely plane has landed the.

Note also that changing the forms of words affects sentence meaning:

The hijacked planes have landed safely. [a change in meaning]

Below are five simple sentences. In each, the vertical line separates the two basic grammatical parts of the sentence, the subject and the predicate. The first part functions as the complete subject (the subject and all words associated with it), and the second part functions as the complete predicate (the verb and all words associated with it). Most simple sentences follow this pattern:

Complete subject + complete predicate.

The hijacked **plane** | **has landed** safely.

Sandra | **gave** us three magnolia trees.

These **trees** | **should have been planted** in April.

The **tomato** | **is** a fruit. **It** | **tastes** good in salads.

In each of these sentences, the subject (or simple subject) and the verb are in boldface. The subject is the part of a sentence about which something is asserted in the predicate. The predicate is the part that asserts something about the subject.

Expanding Sentences

Below are examples of ways that a simple sentence may be expanded:

SENTENCE	The plane has landed. [subject + predicate]
EXPANSION	The hijacked plane | has landed safely.

The first hijacked plane to arrive at this airport | has landed safely in the south runway.

The first hijacked plane that we have ever seen at this airport | has landed safely in the south runway, which has been closed to traffic for a year.

The base of the expanded sentences may be isolated by striking out those words that have been added.

REDUCTION

The ~~first hijacked~~ plane ~~that we have ever seen at this airport~~ has landed ~~safely in the south runway, which has been closed to traffic for a year~~.

Combining Sentences

Speakers and writers combine sentences and in the process rearrange, add, delete, or substitute words:

The saying is old. It has a new meaning.

VARIOUS COMBINATIONS

The saying is old, but it has a new meaning.
Although it has a new meaning, the saying is old.
The saying, which is old, has a new meaning.
The old saying has a new meaning.
It is an old saying with a new meaning.

A close study of this section can help you to develop or sharpen your sentence sense. Sentence sense is prerequisite to the intelligent use of this handbook—especially Sections **2** (Sentence Fragment), **3** (Comma Splice), **6** (Agreement), **12** (The Comma), **14** (The Semicolon), **23** (Unity), **24** (Subordination), **25** (Coherence), **26** (Parallelism), **29** (Emphasis), and **30** (Variety). For explanations of any unfamiliar grammatical terms, see the **Glossary of Grammatical Terms** beginning on page 529.

1a

Learn to recognize verbs and their subjects.

You can learn to recognize verbs and the subjects of verbs by observing their meaning, their form, and their position in sentences.

VERBS

Meaning Verbs are words that express action, occurrence, or existence (a state of being).

Play ball!	The rain **stopped**.
They **exist**.	**Am I** right?

Function A verb functions as the predicate of a sentence or as an essential part of the predicate:

Subject + PREDICATE.

William	**drives**.
William	usually **drives** his car to work.

Form In the present tense, all verbs change form to indicate a singular subject in the third person (I *eat*—he *eats*). When converted from the present to the past tense, nearly all verbs change form (*eat—ate*).

PRESENT TENSE		PAST TENSE
I **ski**. Ray **skis**.		I **skied**.
You **win**. She **wins**.		You **won**.
We **quit**. He **quits**.	BUT	He **quit**.

In addition, certain suffixes, such as *-ize* and *-ify*, often indicate that a word is a verb (*legalize, classify*).

Verb phrases A verb may consist of two or more words (*may see, should have been eaten, will be helping*), a unit called a *verb phrase*. When used with *have, has*, or *had*, most verbs end in *-d* or *-ed* (*have moved, had played*), but some have a special ending (*has been eaten.*) Used with a form of *be*, all progressive verbs end in *-ing*, as in *was eating* (see page 80).

Tom **has moved**. They **have taken** the tests.
He **is moving**. We **had been taking** lessons.

Auxiliary verbs A verb phrase like *has moved* or *was taking* follows this pattern: **auxiliary verb + main verb**. The following words are commonly used as auxiliaries: *have, has, had, am, is, are, was, were, be, been, do, does, did, will, shall, can, may, must, would, should, could, might*. Word groups like *am going to, is about to, ought to, used to, had better*, and *have to* may function as auxiliary verbs:

He **had gone** to London.
We **were enjoying** the game. They **did** not **enjoy** it.
Ruth **is going to try**. [Compare: Ruth *will try*.]

Other words may intervene between the auxiliary and the main verb:

Television **will** never completely **replace** the radio. [The auxiliary *will* signals the approach of the verb *replace*.]

The contraction for *not* may be added to many auxiliaries: *haven't, doesn't, aren't, can't*.

Verbs with particles Many verbs are used with particles like *away, across, in, off, on, down, for, out*, and *up with*. Notice how meaning can be changed by the addition of one of these uninflected words.

SINGLE-WORD VERBS	VERBS WITH PARTICLES
She **called** me.	She **called on** me.
I **put** his picture on my desk.	I **put up with** his picture on my desk.

Other words may intervene between the verb and the particle:

We **looked** José **up**. Millie **handed** her report **in**.

SUBJECTS

Meaning To identify a subject, find the verb; then use the verb in a question beginning with *who* or *what*, as shown in the following examples:

The dog in the cage ate.
Verb: **ate**
WHO OR WHAT ate? **The dog** (not the cage) **ate**.
Subject: **dog**

The hut was built by Al.
Verb: **was built**
WHAT was built? **The hut** (not Al) **was built**.
Subject: **hut**

Form Although other words or word groups may function as subjects, nouns or pronouns are the most frequently used.

Many nouns (words used to name persons, places, things, ideas, animals, and so on) change their form to indicate number (*movement, movements; city, cities; woman, women*) and to indicate the possessive case (*John's* car, the *boys'* dogs, the *women's* vote). Such suffixes as *-ance, -ation, -ence, -ment, -ness,* and *-ship* frequently indicate that a word is a noun (*appearance, determination, reference, atonement, boldness, hardship*). The articles *a, an,* and *the* regularly signal that a noun is to follow (a *chair*, an *activity*, the last *race*).

Form makes it a simple matter to recognize some pronouns. Pronouns such as *I, we, she, he, they,* and *who* function as subjects; when used as objects, these words change to the forms *me, us, her, him, them,* and *whom*. Other pronouns—such as *you, it, mine, ours, yours, hers, his, theirs, that, which*—resemble nouns in that they function as either subjects or objects without a change in form.

Position Subjects usually come before verbs in sentences.

SUBJECT—verb.

They disappeared.
The youngest **boy** did not smile very often.

Common exceptions to the *subject—verb* pattern occur when subjects are used in questions and after the expletive *there* (which is never the subject).

Was the **statement** true? [verb—subject]
Did these **people survive?** [auxiliary—subject—verb]
There **were** no **objections.** [expletive—verb—subject]

Occasionally, verbs precede their subjects in sentences such as the following:

Over the door **were sprigs** of mistletoe.
Even more important **is** the **waste** of human resources.

Note: Subjects and verbs may be compound.

Cobras and **pythons** lay eggs. [compound subject]
We **sat** by the pool and **waited**. [compound verb]

■ **Exercise 1** Underline the verbs (including any auxiliaries and particles) and their subjects in the following sentences (selected from *Reader's Digest*).

1. Lasting friendships develop.
2. Secrecy was another problem.
3. Rodgers constantly courts trouble with his boat-rocking comments.
4. The fire gobbled up some of the most expensive real estate on earth.
5. Answers to such questions may never be found.
6. Are vitamins important for sudden bursts of energy?
7. There are now about two million television sets in China.
8. John's simplicity gave his actions the force of parables.
9. Gnats and small flies invade the sheath and pollinate the blossoms.
10. He straightened his glasses, breathed a prayer of thanks, and swung his hoe at a nearby weed.

1b

Learn to recognize objects of verbs, as well as complements of subjects and objects.

You can learn to recognize objects of verbs, subject complements, and object complements by observing their meaning, their form, and their position in sentences.

DIRECT AND INDIRECT OBJECTS OF VERBS

Meaning To identify a direct object, find the subject and the verb; then use them in a question ending with *whom* or *what* as shown in the following example:

> Karen graciously invited the reporters to lunch.
> Subject and verb: **Karen invited**
> Karen invited WHOM OR WHAT? **the reporters**
> Direct object: **reporters**

A verb that has a direct object to complete its meaning is called a *transitive* verb. Notice that a direct object in a sentence like the following is directly affected by the action of the verb:

> High winds levelled a *town* in Alberta. [The direct object is the receiver of the action.]

Some verbs (such as *give, offer, bring, take, lend, send, buy,* and *sell*) may have both a direct object and an indirect object. An indirect object states *to whom* or *for whom* (or *to what* or *for what*) something is done.

> Richard sent Audrey an invitation.
> Subject, verb, and direct object: **Richard sent invitation**
>
> Richard sent an invitation TO WHOM? **Audrey**
> Indirect object: **Audrey**

Form Like the subjects of verbs, direct and indirect objects of verbs are generally nouns or pronouns: see **1a**, page 7. See also **1c**, pages 15–16.

Two women hailed the **taxi driver**. They hailed **him**.
Sam bought **Ann** a new **watch**. He bought **her that**.

Position The following sentence patterns and examples show the usual word order of direct and indirect objects of verbs.

SUBJECT—VERB—OBJECT.

Mice frighten elephants.
Many **fans were hanging placards** in the stadium.

SUBJECT—VERB—INDIRECT OBJECT—DIRECT OBJECT.

Mary baked Timothy a **cake**.
The **company will** probably **send you** a small **refund**.

But in some sentences—especially questions—the direct object does not take the position indicated by the basic patterns.

What **placards did** the **fans hang** in the stadium?
[direct object—auxiliary—subject—verb]

A test for an object Knowing how to change an active verb to the passive voice can also help you to identify an object, since the object of an active verb can usually be made the subject of a passive verb:

ACTIVE The Leafs finally **defeated** the **Bruins**.
[*Bruins* is the direct object of *defeated*.]
PASSIVE The **Bruins were** finally **defeated** by the Leafs.
[*Bruins* is the subject of *were defeated*.]

Notice above that a form of *be* is added when an active verb is changed to the passive.

SUBJECT AND OBJECT COMPLEMENTS

Meaning A subject complement refers to, identifies, or qualifies the subject. Subject complements help to complete the meaning of intransitive linking verbs (*be, am, is, are, was, were, been, seem, become, feel, look, smell, sound, taste*, and so on). See also page 12.

> Diane is my **cousin**. [*Cousin* identifies *Diane*, the subject.]
> Several tourists became **homesick**. [*Homesick* describes or qualifies *tourists*, the subject.]

In the sentences above, the relationship between the subject and its complement is so close that the words used as subject complements can be placed next to the subject. They can then, in different sentences, serve as an appositive (an added noun explaining or identifying another noun) or as a regular adjective (rather than a predicate adjective).

> Diane, **my cousin**, dropped by. [appositive]
> Several **homesick** tourists did not enjoy the trip. [adjective]

An object complement refers to, identifies, or qualifies the direct object. Object complements help to complete the meaning of such verbs as *make, name, elect, call, find, consider*.

> We elected Phyllis **president**.
> [Compare: Because of our votes, Phyllis became president.]
> The dealer considered it **worthless**.
> [Compare: According to the dealer, it was worthless.]

Form Nouns, pronouns, and adjectives are used as subject and object complements. See **1a** for a discussion of the forms of nouns and pronouns. Adjectives (which modify or qualify a noun or pronoun) often change form to indicate comparison: *tall, taller, tallest*. In addition to *-er* and *-est*, such suffixes as *-al, -ful, -ish, -like, -ous*, and *-y* often indicate that a word is an adjective: *national, useful, greenish, childlike, famous, lumpy*.

Position Although word order varies (especially in questions or exclamations), a study of the following basic patterns and examples will help you learn to recognize subject and object complements.

SUBJECT—LINKING VERB—SUBJECT COMPLEMENT.

His **nickname** was **Skippy**.
The **pie tasted** too **sweet** for me.

SUBJECT—VERB—DIRECT OBJECT—OBJECT COMPLEMENT.

We called him Skippy.
I found the **pie** too **sweet**.

The ability to recognize objects of verbs and complements of subjects will help you to understand differences in the use of transitive and intransitive verbs. A transitive verb takes an object, and it may be made passive. See also page 10.

TRANSITIVE ACTIVE These statistics **deceive** many people. [The direct object is *people*.]

TRANSITIVE PASSIVE Many people **are deceived** by these statistics. [*People* is now the subject of the passive verb *are deceived*.]

Some intransitive verbs take a subject complement; some are complete without a complement.

INTRANSITIVE LINKING The data **seemed** reliable. [The subject complement is *reliable*.]

INTRANSITIVE COMPLETE They **did** not **listen**. [No complement is necessary.]

Note: Direct and indirect objects of verbs, subject complements and object complements may be compound.

She likes **okra** and **spinach**. [compound direct object]
They sent **Elyse** and **Mike** complimentary tickets. [compound indirect object]
The cathedrals are **old** and **famous**. [compound subject complement]
They will name the baby **Jude** or **Judith**. [compound object complement]

■ **Exercise 2** Underline all direct and indirect objects of verbs and the two subject complements in Exercise 1, page 8.

■ **Exercise 3** Label all subjects of verbs, subject complements, and object complements in the quotations below. Prepare for a class discussion of the basic sentence patterns (and any variations) and the types of verbs used.

1. Inventions are the hallmark of mankind. —JAKE PAGE
2. The multitude of books is making us ignorant. —VOLTAIRE
3. Scarcely anything awakens attention like a tale of cruelty. —SAMUEL JOHNSON
4. Down the lake, mile by mile over the calm water, steamed the Mariposa Belle. —STEPHEN LEACOCK
5. Only a moral idiot with a suicidal mania would press the button for a nuclear war. —WALTER LIPPMANN
6. On the south side of the highway, beyond the barn and the pastures, the South Mountain rose. —ERNEST BUCKLER
7. On his land there were three straw-stacks. —SINCLAIR ROSS
8. Sensible people find nothing useless. —LA FONTAINE

1c

Learn to recognize all the parts of speech.

Two methods of classifying words in a sentence are shown on the following page. The first method classifies words according to their function in a sentence; the second, according to their part of speech.

Waiters usually offer us free coffee at Joe's café.

	FUNCTION	PART OF SPEECH
Waiters	subject	noun
usually	modifier	adverb
offer	verb of predicate	verb
us	indirect object	pronoun
free	modifier	adjective
coffee	direct object	noun
at	preposition	preposition
Joe's	modifier	noun
café	object of preposition	noun

Notice here that one part of speech—the noun (a naming word with a typical form)—is used as a subject, a direct object, a modifier, and an object of a preposition.

Words are traditionally grouped into eight classes or parts of speech: *verbs, nouns, pronouns, adjectives, adverbs, prepositions, conjunctions*, and *interjections*. Verbs, nouns, adjectives, and adverbs (called vocabulary or content words) make up more than 99 per cent of all words listed in the dictionary. But pronouns, prepositions, and conjunctions—although small in number—are important because they are used over and over in our speaking and writing. Prepositions and conjunctions (called function or structure words) connect and relate other parts of speech.

Of the eight word classes, only three—prepositions, conjunctions, and interjections—do not change their form. For a summary of the form changes of the other parts of speech, see **inflection**, page 543.

Carefully study the forms, meanings, and functions of each of the eight parts of speech listed on the following pages. For additional examples or more detailed information, see the corresponding entries in the **Glossary of Grammatical Terms** beginning on page 529.

VERBS *notify, notifies, is notifying, notified*
write, writes, is writing, wrote, has written

A verb functions as the predicate of a sentence or as an essential part of the predicate: see **1a**.

> Herman **writes**.
> He **has written** five poems.
> He **is** no longer **writing** those dull stories.

One frequently used verb-forming suffix is *-ize*:

> *terror, idols* (nouns)—*terrorize, idolize* (verbs)

Note: Verb forms classified as participles, gerunds, or infinitives (verbals) cannot function as the predicate of a sentence: see **1d**.

PARTICIPLES	The man **writing** the note is Bill. [modifier] She gave him **written** instructions. [modifier]
GERUND	His **writing** all night long disturbed his whole family. [subject]
INFINITIVES	Herman wants **to write**. [direct object] The urge **to write** left him. [modifier]

NOUNS *man, men; kindness, kindnesses*
nation, nations; nation's, nations'
Carthage, Canada, William, RCMP
prudence, the *money,* an *understanding*

Nouns function as subjects, objects, complements, appositives, and modifiers, as well as in direct address and in absolute constructions. Nouns name persons, places, things, ideas, animals, and so on. See also **1a** and **1b** and pages 546-47.

> **Marilyn** drives a **truck** for the **Salvation Army**.

Endings such as *-ation, -ism, -ity, -ment,* and *-ness* are called noun-forming suffixes:

relax, starve (verbs)—*relaxation, starvation* (nouns)
kind, happy (adjectives)—*kindness, happiness* (nouns)

Compound nouns Words such as *father-in-law, Salvation Army, swimming pool, dropout*, and *breakthrough* are generally classified as compound nouns.

PRONOUNS *I, me, my, mine, myself; they, you, him, it this, these; who, whose, whom; which, that one, ones, one's; everybody, anyone*

Pronouns serve the function of nouns in sentences:

They bought **it** for **her**. **Everyone** knows **this**.

ADJECTIVES *shy, sleepy, attractive, famous*
three men, *this* class, *another* one
young, younger, youngest

The articles *a, an*, and *the* are variously classified as adjectives, determiners, or function words. Adjectives modify or qualify nouns and pronouns (and sometimes gerunds) and are generally placed near the words they modify:

The **beautiful** and **famous** cathedrals no longer interest **homesick** tourists.
Thrifty and **sensible**, he will be promoted soon.

Adjectives may function as complements of the subject or of the object: see **1b**.

The Rocky Mountains are most **beautiful** in the fall.
Her tennis serve made Joanne **famous**.

Suffixes such as *-al, -able, -ant, -ative, -ic, -ish, -less, -ous*, and *-y* may be added to certain verbs or nouns to form adjectives:

accept, repent (verbs)—*acceptable, repentant* (adjectives)
angel, effort (nouns)—*angelic, effortless* (adjectives)

ADVERBS *rarely* saw, call *daily, soon* left, left *sooner*
very short, *too* angry, *never* shy, *not* fearful
practically never loses, *nearly always* cold

As the examples show, adverbs modify verbs, adjectives, and other adverbs. In addition, an adverb may modify a verbal, a phrase, a clause, or even the rest of the sentence in which it appears:

> I noticed a plane **slowly** circling overhead.
> **Honestly**, Ben did catch a big shark.

The *-ly* ending nearly always converts adjectives to adverbs:

> *rare, honest* (adjectives)—*rarely, honestly* (adverbs)

PREPOSITIONS *on* a shelf, *between* us, *because of* rain
to the door, *by* them, *before* class

A preposition always has an object, which is usually a noun or a pronoun. The preposition links and relates its object to some other word in the sentence. The preposition with its object (and any modifiers) is called a *prepositional phrase*:

> Byron expressed **with great force** his love **of liberty**.

The preposition may follow rather than precede its object, and it may be placed at the end of the sentence:

> What are you selling it **for**? Faith is what we live **by**.

Words commonly used as prepositions:

about	before	by	in
above	behind	concerning	inside
across	below	despite	into
after	beneath	down	like
against	beside	during	near
along	besides	except	of
among	between	excepting	off
around	beyond	for	on
at	but	from	onto

out	round	to	up
outside	since	toward	upon
over	through	under	with
past	throughout	underneath	within
regarding	till	until	without

Phrasal prepositions (two or more words):

according to	by way of	in spite of
along with	due to	instead of
apart from	except for	on account of
as for	in addition to	out of
as regards	in case of	up to
as to	in front of	with regard to
because of	in lieu of	with respect to
by means of	in place of	with reference to
by reason of	in regard to	with the exception of

CONJUNCTIONS Amy *and* Bill, in *or* out
long *but* witty

She acts **as if** she really cares.
I worked, **for** my father needed money.

Conjunctions function as connectors of words, phrases, or clauses: see also **1d** and **1e**.

The co-ordinating conjunctions (*and, but, or, nor, for, so, yet*) and the correlatives (*both—and, either—or, neither—nor, not only—but also, whether—or*) connect sentence elements of equal grammatical rank.

The subordinating conjunctions (such as *after, as if, because, if, since, till, when, where, while*) connect subordinate clauses with main clauses: see **1d** and the list on page 25.

Conjunctive adverbs Words like *however, nevertheless, then*, and *therefore* (see the list on page 45) are used as conjunctive adverbs (or adverbial conjunctions):

Don seemed bored in class; **however**, he did listen and learn.

INTERJECTIONS *Wow!* *Oh*, that's a surprise.

Interjections are exclamations, which may be followed by an exclamation point or by a comma: see **12b** and **17c**.

A dictionary labels words according to their part of speech. Some words have only one classification—for example, *notify* (verb), *sleepy* (adjective), *practically* (adverb). Other words have more than one label. The word *living*, for instance, is first treated as a form of the verb *live* and is then listed separately and defined as an adjective and as a noun. The actual classification depends on the use of the word in a given sentence:

> They were **living** wretchedly. [verb]
> She is a **living** example of patience. [adjective]
> He barely makes a **living**. [noun]

Another example is the word *up*:

> Look **up**! [adverb]
> They dragged the sled **up** the hill. [preposition]
> The **up** escalator is jerking again. [adjective]
> He follows the **ups** and downs of the market. [noun]
> "They will **up** the rent again," he complained. [verb]

■ **Exercise 4** Using your dictionary as an aid if you wish, classify each word in the following sentences according to its part of speech:

1. He struts with the gravity of a frozen penguin. —TIME
2. Men are often taken, like rabbits, by the ears. And though the tongue has no bones, it can sometimes break millions of them. —F.L. LUCAS
3. Awesome is the tyranny of the fixed idea. —ERIC LARABEE
4. Of all persons, adolescents are the most intensely personal; their intensity is often uncomfortable to adults. —EDGAR Z. FRIEDENBERG
5. The presence of a North in man is even more critical than the presence of men in the North. —JACK WARWICK

1d

Learn to recognize phrases and subordinate clauses.

The sentences below consist only of the basic grammatical parts along with the articles *the* and *a*: see the sentence patterns in **1a** and **1b**.

> We explored the beach. We used metal detectors.
> We found a doubloon. It was battered.

Most sentences, however, contain groups of words used as single parts of speech. Such word groups are either phrases or subordinate clauses.

SENTENCES COMBINED

Exploring the beach with metal detectors, we found **a battered doubloon**. [phrases]

When we were exploring the beach with metal detectors, we found a battered doubloon. [subordinate clause preceding a main clause—see **1e**]

PHRASES

A phrase is often defined as a group of related words without a subject and a predicate. Phrases are generally classified as follows:

VERB PHRASES The rose **has wilted. Did** you **see** it? Mr. Kelly **may run up** the bill. The roof **used to leak**.

NOUN PHRASES **The severe drought** struck **all the prairie provinces**. I introduced Greer, **a very interesting speaker**.

PREPOSITIONAL PHRASES The oldest car **on campus** is mine. We were exploring the beach **with metal detectors**.

PARTICIPIAL PHRASES **Exploring the beach**, we found many sand dollars. The beach, **covered with seaweed**, looked uninviting.

GERUND PHRASES **Exploring the beach** is fun. They enjoyed **feeding the seagulls**.

INFINITIVE PHRASES We wanted **to explore the beach**. That is the problem **to be solved now**. Vernon and I went to Vancouver **to visit relatives**.

ABSOLUTE PHRASES **The van loaded**, we headed for the mountains. The Nobel Prize winner left the room, **reporters clustering around him**. [See also page 529.]

Notice in the examples above that *exploring*—a verb form ending in *-ing*—is used as an adjective and also as a noun. The grammatical classification is not based on form but on use in the sentence: the participle functions as an adjective and the gerund functions as a noun.

Participles, gerunds, and infinitives are derived from verbs. (See also the note on page 15 and **verbal** on page 556.) They are much like verbs in that they have different tenses, can take subjects and objects, and can be modified by adverbs. But they cannot serve as the only verb form in the predicate of a sentence. Participial, gerund, and infinitive phrases function as adjectives, nouns, or adverbs and are therefore only parts of sentences, as the following sentence combinations illustrate:

SENTENCES

Dr. Ford explained the process. He drew simple illustrations.

PHRASES IN SENTENCES

Explaining the process, Dr. Ford drew simple illustrations.
OR
Simple illustrations **drawn by Dr. Ford** explained the process. [participial phrases]

Dr. Ford explained the process by **drawing simple illustrations**. [gerund phrase]

Dr. Ford drew simple illustrations **to explain the process**. [infinitive phrase]

(1) Phrases used as nouns

Gerund phrases are always used as nouns. Infinitive phrases are often used as nouns (although they may also function as modifiers). Occasionally a prepositional phrase functions as a noun (as in "*After supper* is too late!").

NOUNS	PHRASES USED AS NOUNS
The **decision** is important.	**Choosing a major** is important. [gerund phrase—subject]
She likes the **job**.	She likes **to do the work**. [infinitive phrase—direct object]
His **action** prompted the **change**.	**His leaving the farm** prompted **her to seek a job in town.** [gerund phrase—subject; infinitive phrase—direct object]
He uses my room for **storage**.	He uses my room for **storing all his auto parts**. [gerund phrase—object of a preposition]
He wants two things: **money** and **power**.	He wants two things: **to make money** and **to gain power**. [infinitive phrases—a compound appositive]

■ **Exercise 5** Underline the gerund phrases and the infinitive phrases used as nouns in the following sentences (selected from *Time*). Be sure to underline any prepositional phrases modifying words in the gerund or the infinitive phrases.

1. Successfully merchandising a product is creative.
2. Angry and proud, Claire resolved to fight back.
3. They have also been getting tougher by enforcing strict new anti-litter laws.
4. Taking criticism from others is painful but useful.
5. Merely to argue for the preservation of park land is not enough.

6. "We just want to take some of the blindness out of blind dates," explains the founder of Operation Match.
7. After giving birth, most women lapse into some sort of melancholy.
8. Workers managed to pipe the gas through a purifying plant and into a pipeline.
9. All human acts—even saving a stranger from drowning or donating a million dollars to the poor—may be ultimately selfish.
10. This method of growing plants without soil has long been known to scientists but has only recently begun to attract amateurs' attention.

(2) Phrases used as modifiers

Prepositional phrases nearly always function as adjectives or adverbs. Infinitive phrases are also used as adjectives or adverbs. Participial phrases are used as adjectives. Absolute phrases are used as adverbs.

ADJECTIVES	PHRASES USED AS ADJECTIVES
It is a **significant** idea.	It is an idea **of significance**. [prepositional phrase]
Appropriate language is best.	Language **to suit the occasion** is best. [infinitive phrase]
Destructive storms lashed the Prairies.	**Destroying many crops of corn and oats**, storms lashed the Prairies. [participial phrase containing a prepositional phrase]
The **icy** bridge was narrow.	The bridge **covered with ice** was narrow. [participial phrase containing a prepositional phrase]

ADVERBS	PHRASES USED AS ADVERBS
Drive **carefully**.	Drive **with care on wet streets**. [prepositional phrases]

I nodded **respectfully**.

I nodded **to show respect**. [infinitive phrase]

ADVERBS

Consequently, we could hardly see the road.

PHRASES USED AS ADVERBS

The rain coming down in torrents, we could hardly see the road. [absolute phrase—see page 529]

The preceding examples demonstrate how phrases function in the same way as single-word modifiers. Remember, however, that phrases are not merely substitutes for single words. Many times phrases express more than can be packed into a single word:

> The gas gauge fluttered **from empty to full**.
> He telephoned his wife **to tell her of his arrival**.
> The firefighters **hosing down the adjacent buildings** had very little standing room.

■ **Exercise 6** Underline each phrase used as a modifier in the following sentences. Then state whether the phrase functions as an adjective or as an adverb.

1. A moment like that one should last forever.
2. The fans blinded by the sun missed the best plays.
3. Crawling through the thicket, I suddenly remembered the box of shells left on top of the truck.
4. The people to watch closely are the ones ruling behind the political scene.
5. A motorcycle racing along the beach zoomed over our big sand castle.
6. The number on that ticket indicates a seat in the balcony.
7. I came to college to get a liberal education and to learn a trade.
8. They worked fast, one man sawing logs and the other loading the truck.
9. Not wanting to appear in court, Pat decided to pay the fine.
10. All told, fame is fickle.

SUBORDINATE CLAUSES

A clause is often defined as a group of related words that contains both a subject and a predicate. Like a phrase, a subordinate (or dependent) clause is not a sentence. The subordinate clause functions as a single part of speech—as a noun, an adjective, or an adverb. Notice the relationship of the sentences below to the clauses that follow:

SENTENCES **That fact I must admit.**
Ralph was my first and only blind date.
I married him.

SUBORDINATE CLAUSES IN SENTENCES

I must admit **that Ralph was my first and only blind date**. [noun clause—direct object]
The first and only blind date **that I ever had** was Ralph. [adjective clause]
Ralph was my first and only blind date **because I married him**. [adverb clause]

In the examples above, *that* and *because* are used as *subordinators*: they subordinate the clauses they introduce, making these clauses dependent. The following words are commonly used to mark subordinate clauses:

RELATIVE PRONOUNS *that, what, which, who, whoever, whom, whomever, whose*

SUBORDINATING CONJUNCTIONS *after, although, as, because, before, if, once, since, that, though, till, unless, until, when, whenever, where, wherever, while*

Subordinators may consist of more than one word:

as if, as soon as, as though, even though, in order that, in that, no matter how, so that

No matter how hard I try, I cannot float with my toes out of the water.
We bought three dozen doughnuts **so that everyone would be sure to have enough**.

(3) Subordinate clauses used as nouns

NOUNS	NOUN CLAUSES
The **news** may be false.	**What the newspapers say** may be false. [subject]
I do not know his **address**.	I do not know **where he lives**. [direct object]
Give the tools to **Rita**.	Give the tools to **whoever can use them best**. [object of a preposition]
That fact—Karen's **protest**—amazed me.	The fact **that Karen protested** amazed me. [appositive]

The conjunction *that* before a noun clause may be omitted in some sentences:

I know **she is right**. [Compare: I know *that she is right.*]

(4) Subordinate clauses used as modifiers

Two types of subordinate clauses, the adjective clause and the adverb clause, are used as modifiers.

Adjective clauses Any clause that modifies a noun or a pronoun is an adjective clause. Adjective clauses, which nearly always follow the words modified, are most frequently introduced by a relative pronoun but may begin with such words as *when, where,* or *why*.

ADJECTIVES	ADJECTIVE CLAUSES
Everyone needs **loyal** friends.	Everyone needs friends **who are loyal**.
The **golden** window reflects the sun.	The window, **which shines like gold**, reflects the sun.
Peaceful countrysides no longer exist.	Countrysides **where one can find peace of mind** no longer exist.

If it is not used as a subject, the relative pronoun in an adjective clause may sometimes be omitted:

He is a man **I admire**.
[Compare: He is a man *whom I admire*.]

Adverb clauses An adverb clause usually modifies a verb but may modify an adjective, an adverb, or even the rest of the sentence in which it appears. Many adverb clauses can take various positions in a sentence: see **12b** and **12d**. Adverb clauses are ordinarily introduced by subordinating conjunctions.

ADVERBS	ADVERB CLAUSES
Soon the lights went out.	**When the windstorm hit**, the lights went out.
No alcoholic beverages are sold **locally**.	No alcoholic beverages are sold **where I live**.
The price is **too** high for me.	The price is higher **than I can afford**.
Speak **very** distinctly.	Speak as distinctly **as you can**.

Some adverb clauses may be elliptical. See also **25b**.

If I can save enough money, I'll go to Quebec next summer. **If not**, I'll take a trip to Edmonton. [Omitted words are clearly implied.]

■ **Exercise 7** Find each subordinate clause in the following sentences (selected from Catherine Ross's conversation with Jean Little which appeared in *Canadian Children's Literature*), and identify each as a subordinate noun clause, a subordinate adjective clause, or a subordinate adverb clause:

1. The idea for *Home from Far* came to me when I wondered what it was like for children who live in a foster home when they have a parent or parents still living.
2. *Look Through My Window* started with a magnificent house that we lived in when we were teenagers.
3. Once you've got the idea, there's the process of writing itself, which you have said goes slowly at first and then speeds up.

4. After I have an idea, I wait for a child to come into my mind who lives in that situation, and becomes real.
5. The books that I liked best were written from only one child's point of view, so that I was right inside that child's mind.
6. That was what I wanted and what I looked for in books: I liked fantasy only when it seemed real.
7. I realized then that I was having just as much fun writing as I did reading.
8. But, because of books, I knew exactly what kinds of friends I wanted.
9. But then I realized that if my characters read books that were still available, then my readers could find the books I mentioned.
10. In the book I'm working on now, *Mama's Going To Buy You a Mockingbird*, characters are reading Katherine Paterson's *The Great Gilly Hopkins*, Dennis Lee's *Alligator Pie*, and W.O. Mitchell's *Who Has Seen the Wind*?

1e

Learn to recognize main clauses and the various types of sentences.

A main clause can stand alone as a sentence, a grammatically independent unit of expression, although it may require other sentences to complete its meaning. Co-ordinating conjunctions (*and, but, or, nor, for, so, yet*) often connect and relate main clauses.

MAIN CLAUSES IN SENTENCES

I had lost my passport, but I did not worry about it. [A co-ordinating conjunction links the two main clauses.]

Although I had lost my passport, **I did not worry about it**. [A subordinate clause precedes the main clause.]

MAIN CLAUSES CONVERTED TO SENTENCES

I had lost my passport.
I did not worry about it. OR **But I did not worry about it**.

Unlike main clauses, subordinate clauses become fragments if isolated and written as sentences: see **2b**.

Sentences may be classified according to their structure as *simple*, *compound*, *complex*, or *compound-complex*.

1. A simple sentence has only one subject and one predicate (either or both of which may be compound):

   Dick started a coin collection. [**SUBJECT—VERB—OBJECT**. See also the various patterns of the simple sentence in **1a** and **1b**.]

2. A compound sentence consists of at least two main clauses:

   Dick started a coin collection, and his wife bought an album of rare stamps. [**MAIN CLAUSE, and MAIN CLAUSE**. See **12a**.]

3. A complex sentence has one main clause and at least one subordinate clause:

   As soon as Dick started a coin collection, his wife bought an album of rare stamps. [**ADVERB CLAUSE, MAIN CLAUSE**. See **12b**.]

4. A compound-complex sentence consists of at least two main clauses and at least one subordinate clause:

   As soon as Dick started a coin collection, his wife bought an album of rare stamps; on Christmas morning they exchanged coins and stamps. [**ADVERB CLAUSE, MAIN CLAUSE, MAIN CLAUSE**. See **14a**.]

Sentences may also be classified according to their purpose as *statements*, *commands* or *requests*, *questions*, or *exclamations* and are punctuated accordingly:

STATEMENT He refused the offer**.**

COMMAND OR REQUEST Refuse the offer**.**

QUESTIONS Did he refuse the offer**?** He refused, didn't he**?** He refused it**?**

EXCLAMATIONS What an offer**!** He refused it**!** Refuse it**!**

■ **Exercise 8** Underline the main clauses in the following sentences (selected from *Maclean's* and *Natural History*). Put subordinate clauses in brackets: see **1d**. (Noun clauses may be an integral part of the basic pattern of a main clause, as in the sixth sentence.)

1. Practice never really makes perfect, and a great deal of frustration invariably accompanies juggling.
2. The two clouds have a common envelope of atomic hydrogen gas, which ties them firmly together.
3. Agriculture is the world's most basic industry; its success depends in large part on an adequate supply of water.
4. There have been several attempts to explain this rhythm, but when each hypothesis was experimentally explored, it had to be discarded.
5. Allegiance to a group may be confirmed or denied by the use or disuse of a particular handshake, as Carl's experience indicates.
6. We know that innocent victims have been executed; fortunately, others condemned to death have been found innocent prior to execution.
7. So far in their campaign, none of the three national leaders has come up with an economic policy that would deal, in any real way, with the devastating effects of inflation.
8. In 1942 they rebelled against the combined will of federal and provincial governments and the church by voting against military conscription.
9. Later, the marketplace becomes a whirlpool of movement as performers and audience mingle and chase each other about.
10. Silt, the most widespread pollutant in North America, is one by-product of strip mining, but the general public remains unaware of the extent to which ecosystems are harmed by silt pollution.

■ **Exercise 9** Classify the sentences in Exercise 8 as *simple, compound, complex,* or *compound-complex*.

■ **Exercise 10** First identify the main and subordinate clauses in the sentences in the following paragraph; then classify each sentence according to structure.

[1] Jim angrily called himself a fool, as he had been doing all the way to the swamp. [2] Why had he listened to Fred's mad idea? [3] What did ghosts and family legends mean to him, in this age of computers and solar-energy converters? [4] He had enough mysteries of his own, of a highly complex sort, which involved an intricate search for values. [5] But now he was chasing down ghosts, and this chase in the middle of the night was absurd. [6] It was lunacy! [7] The legends that surrounded the ghosts had horrified him as a child, and they were a horror still. [8] As he approached the dark trail that would lead him to the old mansion, he felt almost sick. [9] The safe, sure things of every day had become distant fantasies. [10] Only this grotesque night—and whatever ghosts might be lurking in the shadows—seemed hideously real.

■ **Exercise 11** Observing differences in emphasis, convert each pair of sentences below to (*a*) a simple sentence, (*b*) a compound sentence consisting of two main clauses, and (*c*) a complex sentence with one main clause and one subordinate clause:

EXAMPLE

Male sperm whales occasionally attack ships. These whales jealously guard their territory.

a. *Jealously guarding their territory, male sperm whales occasionally attack ships.*
b. *Male sperm whales occasionally attack ships; these whales jealously guard their territory.*
c. *Since male sperm whales jealously guard their territory, they occasionally attack ships.*

1. The men smuggled marijuana into Spain. They were sentenced to six years in prison.
2. The council first condemned the property. Then it ordered the owner's eviction.
3. Uncle Oliver applied for a patent on his invention. He learned of three hundred such devices already on the market.
4. The border guards delayed every tourist. They carefully examined passports and luggage.

Sentence Fragments

2

As a rule, do not write sentence fragments.

A fragment is a non-sentence. It is a part of a sentence—such as a phrase or subordinate clause—written as if it were a sentence.

FRAGMENTS	SENTENCES
My father always planting a spring garden.	My father always plants a spring garden.
Because he likes to eat vegetables.	He likes to eat vegetables.
That help the body to combat infection. For example, yellow and green vegetables.	He eats foods that help the body to combat infection—for example, yellow and green vegetables.

Recognizing patterns of intonation may help you avoid some types of fragments in your writing. Read the following sentences aloud, and note how your voice indicates the end of each complete statement:

We saw that. We saw that movie.
We saw that movie on TV last summer.

The best way to avoid fragments, however, is to recognize the structural differences between sentences and non-sentences. Remember that a complete statement is an independent unit containing at least one subject and predicate.

Not all fragments are to be avoided. Some types of fragments are standard. Exclamations, as well as questions and their answers, are often single words, phrases, or subordinate clauses written as sentences:

> **Why? Because governments cannot establish heaven on earth.**
>
> Where does Peg begin a mystery story? **On the last page. Always!**

Written dialogue that mirrors speech habits often contains grammatically incomplete sentences or elliptical expressions within the quotation marks.

> "*So kind of you,*" fluted Miss Marple. "*Oh, yes, and my little blue muffler. Yes, as I say, so kind of you to ask me here.* I've been picturing, you know, just what your home was like, so that I can visualize dear Lucy working here."
>
> "*Perfect home conditions, with murder thrown in,*" said Cedric. —AGATHA CHRISTIE

Occasionally, professional writers deliberately use fragments for rhetorical effect:

> It spotted the boat and took to flight. A *slow unhurried takeoff, the vast wings spreading, the slender elongated legs gracefully folding up under the creature's body. Like a pterodactyl, like an angel, like something out of the word's dawn.*
>
> —MARGARET LAURENCE [The reader can readily supply omitted words in the italicized fragments. Note the use of repetition and parallel structure.]

Despite their suitability for some purposes, sentence fragments are comparatively rare in formal expository writing. In formal papers, sentence fragments are to be used—if at all—sparingly and with care. If you have difficulty recognizing fragments as you proofread your compositions, review **1d** and **1e**.

Test for Sentence Completeness

Before handing in a composition, proofread each word group written as a sentence. Test each one for completeness.

First, be sure that it has at least one subject and one predicate.

FRAGMENTS MISSING EITHER A SUBJECT OR A PREDICATE

And for days tried to change my mind. [no subject]
Water sparkling in the moonlight. [no predicate]

Next, be sure that the word group is not a dependent clause beginning with a subordinating conjunction or a relative pronoun (see page 25).

FRAGMENTS WITH SUBJECT AND PREDICATE

When he tried for days to change my mind. [subject and verb: *he tried*; subordinating conjunction: *When*]
Which sparkles in the moonlight. [subject and verb: *Which sparkles*; relative pronoun: *Which*]

Revision of a Sentence Fragment

Since a fragment is often an isolated, mispunctuated part of an adjacent sentence, one way to revise a fragment is to make it a part of the complete sentence. Another way to revise a fragment is to make it into a sentence. Revisions need not alter the meaning.

FRAGMENT Henry smiled self-consciously. **Like a politician before a camera**. [an isolated phrase]

REVISED Henry smiled self-consciously, like a politician before a camera. [phrase included in sentence]

OR

Henry smiled self-consciously—like a politician before a camera. [The use of the dash instead of the comma tends to emphasize the material that follows.]

OR

Henry smiled self-consciously. He looked like a politician before a camera. [fragment made into a sentence]

Caution: When revising fragments, do not misuse the semicolon between parts of unequal grammatical rank: see **14c**.

2a

Do not carelessly capitalize and punctuate a phrase as you would a sentence.

FRAGMENT Soon I began to work for the company. **First in the rock pit and later on the highway**. [prepositional phrases]

REVISED Soon I began to work for the company, first in the rock pit and later on the highway. [fragment included in the preceding sentence]

FRAGMENT He will have a chance to go home next weekend. **And to meet his new stepfather**. [infinitive phrase]

REVISED He will have a chance to go home next weekend and to meet his new stepfather. [fragment included in the preceding sentence]

FRAGMENT Astronauts venturing deep into space may not come back to earth for fifty years. **Returning only to discover an uninhabitable planet**. [participial phrase]

REVISED Astronauts venturing deep into space may not come back to earth for fifty years. They may return only to discover an uninhabitable planet. [fragment made into a sentence]

FRAGMENT The children finally arrived at camp. **Many dancing for joy, and some crying for their parents**. [absolute phrases]

REVISED The children finally arrived at camp. Many were dancing for joy, and some were crying for their parents. [fragment made into a sentence]

■ **Exercise 1** Eliminate each fragment below by including it in the adjacent sentence or by making it into a sentence:

1. They enjoy reading a few types of novels. Such as science fiction.
2. The pampered Dennis finally left home. Earnestly seeking to become an individual in his own right.

3. It is wise to ignore her sarcasm. Or to make a quick exit.
4. She did not recognize Gary. His beard gone and hair cut.
5. Louise likes to pretend that she is very old. And to speak of the "days of her youth."
6. They will visit our campus soon. Maybe next month.
7. These commercials have a hypnotic effect. Not only on children but on adults too.
8. A few minutes later. A news bulletin interrupted the show.
9. Eric just stood there speechless. His face turning redder by the minute.
10. He killed six flies with one swat. Against the law of averages but possible.

2b

Do not carelessly capitalize and punctuate a subordinate clause as you would a sentence.

FRAGMENT Thousands of young people became active workers in the community. **After this social gospel had changed their apathy to concern**. [subordinate clause]

REVISED Thousands of young people became active workers in the community after this social gospel had changed their apathy to concern. [fragment included in the preceding sentence]

FRAGMENT I didn't know where he came from. **Or who he was**. [subordinate clause]

REVISED I didn't know where he came from or who he was. [fragment included in the preceding sentence]

FRAGMENT I was trying to read the directions. **Which were confusing and absurd**. [subordinate clause]

REVISED I was trying to read the directions, which were confusing and absurd. [fragment included in the preceding sentence]

OR

I was trying to read the directions. They were confusing and absurd. [fragment made into a sentence]

OR

I was trying to read the confusing, absurd directions. [fragment reduced to adjectivals that are included in the preceding sentence]

■ **Exercise 2** Eliminate each fragment below by including it in the preceding sentence or by making it into a sentence:

1. I decided to give skiing a try. After I had grown tired of watching other people fall.
2. Pat believes that everyone should go to college. And that all tests for admission should be abolished.
3. Many students were obviously victims of spring fever. Which affected class attendance.
4. Paul faints whenever he sees blood. And whenever he climbs into a dentist's chair.
5. I am making a study of cigarette advertisements. That use such slogans as "less tar, more taste" and "the lowest in tar and nicotine."

2c

Do not carelessly capitalize and punctuate any other fragment (such as an appositive or a part of a compound predicate) as you would a sentence.

FRAGMENT Ms. Carter was looking for a new secretary. **A secretary with poise and experience**.

REVISED Ms. Carter was looking for a new secretary—a secretary with poise and experience. [The use of the dash tends to emphasize the material that follows.]

FRAGMENT He lost the gold watch. **The one which had belonged to his grandfather**.

REVISED He lost the gold watch, the one which had belonged to his grandfather. [fragment included in the preceding sentence]

OR

He lost the gold watch which had belonged to his grandfather.

FRAGMENT She studied cello at school. **And played in the orchestra at the Charlottetown Festival**. [detached part of a compound predicate]

REVISED She studied cello at school and played in the orchestra **at the Charlottetown Festival**.

■ **Exercise 3** Eliminate each fragment below by including it in the preceding sentence or by making it into a sentence:

1. My roommate keeps all her shoes, scuba gear, books, and clothes in one closet. The worst disaster area on campus.
2. According to Macaulay, half-knowledge is bad. Even worse than ignorance.
3. The group met during the summer and made plans. And decided on the dates for action in the fall.
4. The hydraulic lift raises the plows out of the ground. And lowers them again.
5. I had a feeling that some sinister spirit brooded over the place. A feeling that I could not analyze.

■ **Exercise 4** Find the nine fragments in the following paragraph. Revise each fragment by attaching it logically to an adjacent sentence or by rewriting the fragment so that it stands by itself as a sentence.

[1] The little paperback almanac I found at the news-stand has given me some fascinating information. [2] Not just about the weather and changes in the moon. [3] There are also intriguing statistics. [4] A tub bath, for example, requires more water than a shower. [5] In all probability, forty-five litres more, depending on how dirty the bather is. [6] And one of the Montezumas

downed fifty jars of cocoa every day. [7] Which seems a bit exaggerated to me. [8] To say the least. [9] I also learned that an average beard has thirteen thousand whiskers. [10] That, in the course of a lifetime, a man could shave off more than eight metres of whiskers, over eight hundred centimetres. [11] If my math is correct. [12] Some other interesting facts in the almanac. [13] Suppose a person was born on Sunday, February 29, 1976. [14] Another birthday not celebrated on Sunday until the year 2004. [15] Because February 29 falls on weekdays till then twenty-eight birthdays later. [16] As I laid the almanac aside, I remembered that line in *Slaughterhouse-Five:* "And so it goes."

Comma Splice and Fused Sentence

3

Do not carelessly link two sentences with only a comma (comma splice) or run two sentences together without any punctuation (fused sentence).

Carefully observe how three sentences have been linked to make the one long sentence below:

SENTENCES SEPARATED There is nothing men like so much as generalizing about women. All women are alike. Except the one they love.

SENTENCES LINKED There is nothing men like so much as generalizing about women; all women are alike, except the one they love. —ROBERTSON DAVIES

[MAIN CLAUSE; MAIN CLAUSE, *and* MAIN CLAUSE.]

When you connect the end of one sentence to the beginning of another, be especially careful about punctuation.

NOT The current was swift, he could not swim to shore. [comma splice—sentences are linked with only a comma]

NOT The current was swift he could not swim to shore. [fused sentence—sentences are run together with no punctuation]

VARIOUS METHODS OF REVISION

Because the current was swift, he could not swim to shore. [first main clause subordinated: see **12b**]

The current was so swift that he could not swim to shore. [second main clause subordinated]

Because of the swift current he could not swim to shore. [first clause reduced to an introductory phrase]

The current was swift. He could not swim to shore. [each main clause converted to a sentence]

The current was swift; he could not swim to shore. [main clauses separated by a semicolon: see **14a**]

The current was swift, so he could not swim to shore. [comma preceding the connective *so*: see **12a**]

He could not swim to shore, for the current was swift. [comma preceding the co-ordinating conjunction *for*]

When you revise carelessly connected sentences, choose a method that achieves the emphasis you want.

If you cannot always recognize a main clause and distinguish it from a phrase or from a subordinate clause, study **1d** and **1e**.

3a

Use a comma between main clauses *only* when they are linked by the co-ordinating conjunctions *and, but, or, for, nor,* or *yet*. See also **12a**.

COMMA SPLICE Our country observed its Centennial in 1967, my hometown celebrated its fiftieth anniversary the same year.

REVISED Our country observed its Centennial in 1967**, and** my hometown celebrated its fiftieth anniversary the same year. [the co-ordinating conjunction *and* added after the comma]
OR
Our country observed its Centennial in 1967**;** my hometown celebrated its fiftieth anniversary the same year. [A semicolon separates the main clauses. See **14a**.]

COMMA SPLICE Her first novel was not a best seller, it was not a complete failure either.

REVISED Her first novel was not a best seller**, nor** was it a complete failure. [Note the shift in the word order of subject and verb after the co-ordinating conjunction *nor*.]
OR
Her first novel was **neither** a best seller **nor** a complete failure. [a simple sentence with a compound complement]

COMMA SPLICE The old tree stumps grated against the bottom of our boat, they did not damage the propeller.

REVISED The old tree stumps grated against the bottom of our boat**, but** they did not damage the propeller. [the co-ordinating conjunction *but* added after the comma]
OR
Although the old tree stumps grated against the bottom of our boat**,** they did not damage the propeller. [Addition of *although* makes the first clause subordinate: see **12b**.]

Caution: Do not omit punctuation between main clauses not linked by *and, but, or, for, nor, so*, or *yet*.

FUSED SENTENCE She wrote him a love letter he answered it in person.

REVISED She wrote him a love letter**.** He answered it in person. [each main clause written as a sentence]

OR
She wrote him a love letter; he answered it in person. [main clauses separated by a semicolon: see **14a**]

Note 1: Either a comma or a semicolon may be used between short main clauses not linked by *and, but, or, for, nor, so*, or *yet* when the clauses are parallel in form and unified in thought:

School bores them, preaching bores them, even television bores them. —ARTHUR MILLER
One is the reality; the other is the symbol. —NANCY HALE

Note 2: The comma is used to separate a statement from a tag question:

He votes, doesn't he? [affirmative statement, negative question]
You can't change it, can you? [negative statement, affirmative question]

■ **Exercise 1** Connect each pair of sentences below in two ways, first with a semicolon and then with one of these co-ordinating conjunctions: *and, but, for, or, nor, so*, or *yet*:

EXAMPLE
I could have walked up the steep trail. I preferred to rent a horse.

a. *I could have walked up the steep trail; I preferred to rent a horse.*
b. *I could have walked up the steep trail,* ***but*** *I preferred to rent a horse.*

1. Dexter goes hunting. He carries his Leica instead of his Winchester.
2. The stakes were high in the political game. She played to win.
3. The belt was too small for him. She had to exchange it.
4. At the drive-in, they watched the musical comedy on one screen. We enjoyed the horror movie on the other.

■ **Exercise 2** Use a subordinating conjunction (see the list on page 25) to combine each of the four pairs of sentences in Exercise 1. For the use of the comma, refer to **12b**.

> EXAMPLE
> ***Although*** *I could have walked up the steep trail, I preferred to rent a horse.*

■ **Exercise 3** Proofread the following sentences (selected and adapted from *National Geographic*). Place a checkmark after a sentence with a comma splice and an X after a fused sentence. Do not mark correctly punctuated sentences.

1. The second-home craze has hit hard, everyone wants a piece of the wilderness.
2. The orchid needs particular soil microbes those microbes vanished when the virgin prairie was plowed.
3. Ty fought back the urge to push hard on the accelerator, which might have wrecked or disabled the van on the rough road.
4. Attempts to extinguish such fires have often failed some have been burning for decades.
5. Some of them had never seen an automobile, the war had bred familiarity with aircraft.
6. When the mining machines rumbled away, the ruined mountain was left barren and ugly.
7. The winds lashed our tents all night, by morning we had to dig ourselves out from under a snowdrift.
8. Man can easily unmake a wilderness he cannot make one.
9. The song that awakened me carried an incredible sense of mournfulness, it seemed to be the prolonged cry of a lone animal calling in the night.
10. Parting is an unsweet sorrow, for it connotes a lack of loyalty.

■ **Exercise 4** Use various methods of revision (see page 41) as you correct the comma splices or fused sentences in Exercise 3.

3b

Be sure to use a semicolon before a conjunctive adverb or transitional phrase placed between main clauses. See also **14a**.

COMMA SPLICE TV weather maps have various symbols, for example, a big apostrophe means drizzle.

REVISED TV weather maps have various symbols; for example, a big apostrophe means drizzle. [**MAIN CLAUSE;** ***transitional expression,*** **MAIN CLAUSE.**]

FUSED SENTENCE The tiny storms cannot be identified as hurricanes therefore they are called neutercanes.

REVISED The tiny storms cannot be identified as hurricanes; therefore they are called neutercanes. [**MAIN CLAUSE;** ***conjunctive adverb*** **MAIN CLAUSE.**]

Below is a list of frequently used conjunctive adverbs and transitional phrases; they function as both an adverb and a conjunctive:

CONJUNCTIVE ADVERBS

also	incidentally	nonetheless
anyway	indeed	otherwise
besides	instead	still
consequently	likewise	then
finally	meanwhile	therefore
furthermore	moreover	thus
hence	nevertheless	
however	next	

TRANSITIONAL PHRASES

after all	even so	in the second place
as a result	for example	on the contrary
at any rate	in addition	on the other hand
at the same time	in fact	
by the way	in other words	

Expressions such as *that is* and *what is more* also function as adverbials connecting main clauses:

> The new members have paid their dues; **what is more**, they are all eager to work hard for our organization.

Conjunctive verbs and transitional phrases are not grammatically equivalent to co-ordinating conjunctions. A co-ordinating conjunction has a fixed position between the main clauses it links, but many conjunctive adverbs and transitional phrases may either begin the second main clause or take another position in it:

> She doubted the value of daily meditation, **but** she decided to try it. [The co-ordinating conjunction has a fixed position.]
>
> She doubted the value of daily meditation; **however**, she decided to try it. [The conjunctive adverb begins the second main clause.]
>
> She doubted the value of daily meditation; she decided, **however**, to try it. [The conjunctive adverb appears later in the clause.]

Caution: Do not let a divided quotation trick you into making a comma splice.

COMMA SPLICE	''Marry her,'' Martin said, ''after all, she's very rich.''
REVISED	''Marry her,'' Martin said. ''After all, she's very rich.''
COMMA SPLICE	''Who won?'' Elizabeth asked, ''what was the score?''
REVISED	''Who won?'' Elizabeth asked. ''What was the score?''

Compare:

CORRECT	''The Argos led at the half,'' she said, ''by twenty-one points.'' [See **12d(3)**.]
CORRECT	''The Argos led at the half,'' she said. ''By twenty-one points.'' [See **9e**.]

■ **Exercise 5** Connect each pair of sentences below, following the pattern of the example:

EXAMPLE
At first the slogan shocked. After a year or two, however, it became a platitude.
At first the slogan shocked; however, after a year or two it became a platitude.

1. The art company sent a sample collection of famous Canadian paintings. The work of Robert Bateman, however, was carelessly omitted.
2. The loud arguments sounded convincing. The majority, therefore, voted for the motion.
3. I don't mind lending him money. He is, after all, my favourite cousin.
4. India is not poor. It has, as a matter of fact, a huge amount of coal and iron reserves.

■ **Exercise 6** Divide the following quotations without creating a comma splice, as shown in the example below:

EXAMPLE
W.L. Mackenzie King once said, "Some countries have too much history. Canada has too much geography."
"Some countries have too much history," W.L. Mackenzie King once said. "Canada has too much geography."

1. "I never saw her again. In fact, no one ever saw her again," wrote Kenneth Bernard.
2. W.C. Fields once said, "I am free of all prejudice. I hate everyone equally."
3. "To generalize is to omit. It is in the details of things where the truth lies," Dr. Peter Beter commented.
4. Irving Layton has observed, "You can sing about life or you can try to understand it. You can't do both."
5. The student asked ironically, "What use are credit cards? Who needs an accurate list of debts?"

Exercise 7 Correct the comma splices and fused sentences in the following paragraph. Do not revise a correctly punctuated sentence.

[1] "Nothing is impossible," Mr. Connell always tells us, "you can do anything if you want to badly enough." [2] We just look at him, an old man in a dingy store, and smile indulgently, at least we used to until we heard more about his life. [3] "I left the old country come seventy years ago," he told us, "I was only thirteen at the time." [4] He met his first wife, Nellie, while he was working as a longshoreman in Halifax, he was only eighteen then. [5] They were happily married for about three years however she died of typhus. [6] A couple of months later he pulled up roots, left the Maritimes, and headed out West. [7] "I'd heard there was work for men not afraid to work," he says, "I figured sweating in B.C. was better than crying in Nova Scotia." [8] He was on the road for twenty years, "I never made a fortune, but I never ate anything I didn't earn," he told us. [9] He met his second wife, Sarah, in Alberta, he farmed there for twenty years. [10] She died in the sixties, he got itchy feet again and headed back towards the Maritimes. [11] But he never got farther than Toronto. [12] He settled in Toronto, built up his hardware business from nothing, and lives very simply. [13] "I do it for a reason," he says, "you never know when I'll decide to move on again." [14] We don't smile when he says it, there's a lifetime of experience behind his words. [15] Maybe anything is possible if you want it badly enough.

Exercise 8 First review Section **2** and study Section **3**. Then proofread the following for sentence fragments, comma splices, and fused sentences. Make appropriate revisions. Put a check-mark after each sentence that needs no revision.

1. Juan first enrolled for morning classes only, then he went job-hunting.
2. The cabin was originally built to house four people a family of ten lives in it now. Not to mention all the dogs and cats.
3. Becky signed up for the swimming relay, however, she is not really interested in competitive sports.

4. The Optimists Club sponsors a flea market every year, it is not, however, an easy way to make money.
5. My daughter attended the National Ballet School, where she was not a success.
6. Mr. Jordan requires us clerks to be on time for work. The reason being that bargain hunters start shopping early, almost before the doors open.
7. Our choir will go to Holland in May, when the tulip gardens are especially beautiful.
8. A long article in the magazine describes botulism, this is just another name for food poisoning.
9. That is absurd. It's nonsense. An argument that is riddled with stupid assumptions.
10. After class, I often drop by the college bookstore. Usually buying best-selling paperbacks, then never getting around to reading any of them.

Adjectives and Adverbs

4

Distinguish between adjectives and adverbs and use the appropriate forms.

Adjectives and adverbs function as modifiers; that is, they qualify or restrict the meaning of other words. Adjectives modify nouns and pronouns. Adverbs modify verbs (or verbals), adjectives, and other adverbs.

ADJECTIVES	ADVERBS
the **sudden** change	changed **suddenly**
a **probable** cause	**probably** caused
an **unusual, large** one	an **unusually** large one

The *-ly* ending can be an adjective-forming suffix as well as an adverb-forming one.

NOUNS TO ADJECTIVES	earth—earthly, ghost—ghostly
ADJECTIVES TO ADVERBS	rapid—rapidly, lucky—luckily

A number of words ending in *-ly* (such as *deadly, cowardly*), as well as many not ending in *-ly* (such as *far, fast, little, well*), may function either as adjectives or as adverbs. Some adverbs have two forms (such as *loud, loudly; quick, quickly; slow, slowly).*

When in doubt about the correct form of a given modifier—such as *slow* or *slowly*—consult your dictionary. Look for the labels *adj.* and *adv.* and for examples of usage. Read any usage notes.

> I drove through the water **slowly**. Fry it **slowly**.
> Drive **slow**. Fry it **slow**. [incorrect]

Also consult your dictionary when in doubt about the forms of comparison and their spellings.

Present and past participles function as adjectives: "a *startling* comment," "the *startled* coach." Do not carelessly omit the *-d* or *-ed* of a past participle: "injure**d** players," "a prejudice**d** person," "the experience**d** driver."

Caution: Do not use the double negative. See also page 541.

NON-STANDARD	They don't have no home.
STANDARD	They don't have any home.
	OR They have no home.

4a

Use adverbs to modify verbs, adjectives, and other adverbs.

> His clothes fit him **perfectly**. [The adverb modifies the verb *fit*.]
> We have a **reasonably** secure future. [The adverb modifies the adjective *secure*.]
> Jean eats **exceptionally** fast. [The adverb *exceptionally* modifies the adverb *fast*.]

Avoid the following as informal or colloquial usage: *sure* for *surely*, *real* for *really*, and *good* for the adverb *well*.

COLLOQUIAL	I played **good**.
GENERAL	I played **well**.[appropriate in both formal and informal usage]

■ **Exercise 1** In the phrases below, convert adjectives into adverbs, following the pattern of the examples:

EXAMPLE
abrupt reply *replied abruptly* [OR *abruptly replied*]

1. vague answer
2. safe travel
3. fierce fight
4. quick refusal
5. hearty welcome
6. blind conformity

EXAMPLE
complete happiness *completely happy*

7. clear possibility
8. unusual anger
9. sudden popularity
10. strange sadness

■ **Exercise 2** In the following sentences, convert any non-standard or informal modifier into an adverb form. Put a check-mark after each sentence that needs no revision.

1. A pocket calculator sure does help.
2. He took the joke serious.
3. Our team played well but did not win.
4. He was lucky to escape as easy as he did.
5. I do not practise as regular as I should.
6. It all happened very sudden.
7. The price will probable come down eventually.
8. Last night Venus seemed exceptional bright.
9. He talks very loudly when he is not sure of himself.
10. My notes are hard to read when I have to write that rapid.

4b

Use adjectives (not adverbs) for complements modifying the subject or the object. See **1b.**

As subject complements (predicate adjectives), adjectives always modify the subject. Subject complements are used with such verbs as *feel, look, smell, sound*, and *taste*, which are called *linking verbs* when they connect a subject with its predicate adjective.

The soup tastes **different** with these herbs in it.
The speech sounded **bold**.

As object complements, adjectives always modify the object.

These herbs make the soup **different**.
He considered the speech **bold**.

Note: Both *bad* and *badly* are now standard when used with *feel* as a subject complement, but writers generally prefer *bad: They felt bad.*

Compare the meaning of the adjectives and adverbs below:

Jo looked **angry** to me. [adjective—subject complement]
Jo looked **angrily** at me. [adverb modifying *looked*]

He considered Jane **happy**. [adjective—object complement]
He considered Jane **happily**. [adverb modifying *considered*]

■ **Exercise 3** Using adjectives as complements, write two sentences that illustrate each of the following patterns:

Subject—linking verb—subject complement.

Subject—verb—direct object—object complement.

4c

Use the appropriate forms for the comparative and the superlative.

In general, the shorter adjectives (and a few adverbs) form the comparative degree by adding *-er* and the superlative by adding *-est*. The longer adjectives and most adverbs form the comparative by the use of *more (less)* and the superlative by the use of *most (least)*. A few modifiers have irregular comparatives and superlatives.

POSITIVE	COMPARATIVE	SUPERLATIVE
warm	warmer	warmest
warmly	more warmly	most warmly
helpful	less helpful	least helpful
good, well	better	best
bad, badly	worse	worst

Many writers prefer to use the comparative degree for two persons or things and the superlative for three or more:

COMPARATIVE Was Monday or Tuesday **warmer**?
James was the **taller** of the two.

SUPERLATIVE Today is the **warmest** day of the year.
William was the **tallest** of the three.

Caution: Do not use a double comparative or superlative: NOT more busier BUT busier; NOT least busiest BUT least busy.

Note: Current usage, however illogical it may seem, accepts comparisons of many adjectives or adverbs with absolute meanings, such as "a *more perfect* society," "the *deadest* campus," and "*less completely* exhausted." But many writers make an exception of *unique*—using "*more nearly* unique" rather than "more unique." They consider *unique* an absolute adjective—one without degrees of comparison.

Be sure to make your comparisons complete: see **22c**.

4d

Avoid awkward or ambiguous use of a noun form as an adjective.

Many noun forms are used effectively to modify other nouns (as in *boat* race, *show* business, *college* student and so on), especially when appropriate adjectives are not available. But such forms created by the compounding of nouns should be avoided when they are either awkward or confusing.

AWKWARD	Many candidates entered the leader race.
BETTER	Many candidates entered the leadership race.
CONFUSING	The Senator Landor recess manoeuvres led to victory.
BETTER	Senator Landor's manoeuvres during the recess led to victory.

■ **Exercise 4** Correct all errors in the use of adjectives or adverbs. Also eliminate any awkward use of nouns as adjectives. Put a checkmark after any sentence that needs no revision.

1. The repair estimates mechanic was out to lunch.
2. She was even more livelier than her daughter.
3. The class enjoyed writing autobiography compositions.
4. The magazine has been published continuous since 1951, but it does not sell good now.
5. Baseball is more easy followed than football.
6. The older of the two is doing well in school.
7. Maribeth lives in a reasonable exclusive Fredericton resident area.
8. That food, I thought, can't taste as bad as it looks.
9. That is the worse grade I have ever received.
10. The recession and inflation kept getting worser.

Case

5

Choose the case form that shows the function of pronouns or nouns in sentences.

Case refers to the form of a word that indicates its use in a sentence as the subject of a verb, the object of a preposition, and so on. The English language has three cases: subjective, possessive, objective. Most nouns, many indefinite pronouns, and the personal pronouns *it* and *you* have a distinctive case form only for the possessive: *Rebecca's* coat, *someone's* dog, *its* colour, *your* hands: see **15a**. But six common pronouns—*I, we, he, she, they, who*—have distinctive forms in all three cases:

Case forms

SUBJECTIVE	I	we	he, she	they	who
POSSESSIVE	my (mine)	our (ours)	his, her (hers)	their (theirs)	whose
OBJECTIVE	me	us	him, her	them	whom

SUBJECTIVE CASE *I, we, he, she, they, who*

Frank and **I** met in Paris. [subject of verb]
The only ones on stage were Lola and **she**. [subject complement]

Morris met the man **who** invented it. [subject in clause—see **5b**]
These people—**he** and **they**—remained silent. [appositives identifying the subject—see **5a**]

Subjects of verbs (but not of infinitives) are put in the subjective case.

POSSESSIVE CASE *my, our, his, her, their, whose, its, your, mine, ours, hers, theirs, yours*

Their dog finally learned to obey **its** master. [before a noun]
Theirs is better than **ours** is. [in the noun position]

Whose car did Terry drive? [before a noun]
His telling the story was a good idea. [before a gerund—see **5d**]

Note: The possessive forms *his* and *their* are non-standard when made a part of a *-self* pronoun. Use *himself, themselves*. (See also *myself*: **19i**, page 238.)

OBJECTIVE CASE *me, us, him, her, them, whom*

Fran likes Glenda and **me**. [direct object]
Weston sends **them** a package now and then. [indirect object]
The man did check the tires for **us**. [object of preposition]
Potter, for **whom** the party was given, did not want to make a speech. [object of preposition in clause—see **5c**]
The officer ticketed us both, Rita and **me**. [appositive identifying the object of the verb, the pronoun *us*—see **5a**]
Our guests expected **us** to entertain **them**. [subject and object of the verbal *to entertain*, an infinitive—see **5e**]
Ignoring Hank and **me**, the twins talked about old times. [object of the verbal *ignoring*, a participle]

Note: Use *who, whose,* or *whom* [NOT *which*] to refer to people: see page 245.

CASE IN COMBINED SENTENCES

Observe that the case (subjective or objective) of the italicized pronouns does not change when the following pairs of sentences are combined:

We need this. We are students.
We students need this.

Don told **us** that.
Don told **us** students that.

[The insertion of a plural noun after the boldface pronoun does not affect the form of the pronoun.]

My wife saw it. **I** saw it.
My wife and **I** saw it.

He wrote to Al. He wrote to **me**.
He wrote to Al and **me**.

[See also **5a**. Formal English does not accept *myself* as a substitute for *me* or *I*: see **19i**, page 238.]

I eat fast. She eats faster.
She eats faster than **I**.

I met Ed. I think **he** is shy.
I met Ed, **who** I think is shy.

[See also **5b**.]

Then I called on Warren. I can always depend on **him**.
Then I called on Warren, **whom** I can always depend on. [OR on whom I can always depend]

[See also **5c**.]

Observe the change in the case of the boldface pronouns in these sentences:

I grew up fast. New responsibilities caused this.
New responsibilities caused **me** to grow up fast.
[*I* is subject of *grew up* (verb with particle); *me* is subject of *to grow up* (an infinitive). See **5e**.]

He smokes a smelly pipe. She complains about it.
She complains about **his** smoking a smelly pipe.
[*He* is subject of *smokes* (a verb). *His* (the possessive case) is used before *smoking* (a gerund). See **5d** and page 542.]

In sentences such as the following, subjects and subject complements are interchangeable:

You and I are the losers. The losers are **you and I**.
[See also **5f**.]

5a

Take special care with pronouns in compound constructions (including compound appositives).

She and her brother played golf. [subject]
Clara may ask **you or me** about it. [object of verb]
They sat in front of **her and me**. [object of preposition]
My best friends are **Bob and he**. [subject complement—see **5f**]

Notice below that the form of the pronoun used as an appositive depends on the function of the noun that the appositive explains or identifies:

Two members of the cast, **he and I**, assist the director.
[Compare "*He and I*, members of the cast, assist the director."]

The director often calls on her assistants: **him and me**.
[Compare "The director often calls on *him and me*, her assistants."]

In general usage, *me* is the appropriate form in the expression *Let's you and me* (although *Let's you and I* is used informally). Compare "Let *us*—just you and *me*." Be sure to use objective pronouns as objects of prepositions:

between you and **me**
for you and **her**
except Elmer and **him**
like you and **me**
to her brother and **her**
with Carla and **him**

■ **Exercise 1** Choose the correct pronoun within the parentheses in each sentence below:

1. (He, Him) and (I, me) wrote and directed three one-act plays.
2. Joe and (I, me, myself) arrived an hour early.
3. It was Oliver and (they, them) who volunteered to address the envelopes.
4. (He, Him) and his brother are looking for part-time jobs.
5. Between Charlotte and (she, her) there is a friendly rivalry.
6. Mr. Rodriguez will hire a new engineer, either Williams or (he, him).
7. Leaving James and (he, him) at home, they went to the airport to meet the actor and (she, her).
8. My family and (I, me, myself) expected Frank and (she, her) to support (theirselves, themselves).
9. Two players on our team, Tom and (he, him), talked with the coach after the game.
10. After the game the coach talked with two players on our team, Tom and (he, him).

5b

Determine the case of each pronoun by its use in its own clause.

(1) *Who* or *whoever* as the subject of a clause

The subject of a verb in a subordinate clause takes the subjective case, even when the whole clause is used as an object:

I forgot **who** won the Grey Cup in 1980. [In its own clause, *who* is the subject of the verb *won*. The complete clause *who won the Grey Cup in 1980* is the object of the verb *forgot*.]

He has respect for **whoever** is in power. [*Whoever* is the subject of *is*. The complete clause *whoever is in power* is the object of the preposition *for*.]

(2) *Who* or *whom* before *I think, he says,* and so on

Such expressions as *I think, he says, she believes*, and *we know* may follow either *who* or *whom*. The choice depends on the use of *who* or *whom* in its own clause:

> Gene is a man **whom** we know well. [*Whom* is the direct object of *know*. Compare "We know him well."]
>
> Gene is a man **who** we know is honest. [*Who* is the subject of the second *is*. Compare "We know that Gene is a man *who* is honest."]

(3) Pronoun after *than* or *as*

In sentences such as the following, which have implied (rather than stated) elements, the choice of the pronoun form is important to meaning:

> She admires Kurt more than **I**. [meaning "more than I do"]
>
> She admires Kurt more than **me**. [meaning "more than she admires me"]
>
> He talks about food as much as **she**. [meaning "as much as she does"]
>
> He talks about food as much as **her**. [meaning "as much as he talks about her"]

Formal usage still requires the use of the subjective case of pronouns in sentences such as the following:

> Mr. Ames is older than **I**. [Compare "older than I am."]
>
> Aristotle is not so often quoted as **they**. [Compare "as they are."]

■ **Exercise 2** In sentences 1, 2, and 3 below, insert *I think* after each *who*; then read each sentence aloud. Notice that *who*, not *whom*, is still the correct case form. In sentences 4 and 5, complete each comparison by using first *they* and then *them*. Prepare to explain the differences in meaning.

1. George Eliot, who was a woman, wrote *Adam Bede*.
2. It was Elizabeth Holland who served as the eighth president of the university.
3. Maugham, who was an Englishman, died in 1965.
4. My roommate likes you as much as ________ .
5. The director praised her more than ________ .

5c

In formal writing use *whom* for all objects. See also **5b**.

In sentences:

> **Whom** do they recommend? [object of the verb *do recommend*]
> For **whom** did the board of directors vote? [object of the preposition *for*]
> Danny told Chet **whom** to call. Danny told Chet to call **whom**? [object of the infinitive *to call*—see also **5e**]

In subordinate clauses:

> The artist **whom** she loved has gone away. [object of the verb *loved* in the adjective clause]
> This is a friend **whom** I write to once a year. [object of the preposition *to* in the adjective clause]

Formal and informal English accept the omission of *whom* in sentences such as the following:

> The artist she loved has gone away.
> This is a friend I write to once a year.

Note: Informal English accepts *who* rather than *whom*, except after a preposition:

> Who do they recommend? She told me who to call.

■ **Exercise 3** Using the case form in parentheses, convert each pair of sentences below into a single sentence:

EXAMPLES

I understand the daredevil. He rafted down the Mackenzie River. (*who*)

I understand the daredevil who rafted down the Mackenzie River.

Evelyn consulted an astrologer. She had met him in Calgary. (*whom*)

Evelyn consulted an astrologer whom she had met in Calgary.

1. Hercule Poirot is a famous detective. Agatha Christie finally kills him off in *Curtain*. (*whom*)
2. Some parents make an introvert out of an only child. They think they are protecting their offspring. (*who*)
3. Does anyone remember the name of the Frenchman? He built a helicopter in 1784. (*who*)
4. One of the officials called for a severe penalty. The players had quarrelled with the officials earlier. (*whom*)

■ **Exercise 4** Formalize usage by changing *who* to *whom* when the pronoun functions as an object. Put a checkmark after sentences containing *who* correctly used as the subject of a verb or as a subject complement.

1. Who do they suspect?
2. Who could doubt that?
3. He knows who they will promote.
4. He knows who will be promoted.
5. The witness who the lawyer questioned next could remember nothing.
6. Guess who I ran into at the airport.
7. No one cares who they are or what they stand for.
8. In a crowded emergency room she knows exactly who to help first.
9. To find out who deceived who, be sure to tune in for the next episode.
10. During registration whoever I asked for directions gave me a map of the campus.

5d

As a rule, use the possessive case immediately before a gerund.

I resented **his** criticizing our every move. [Compare "I resented his criticism, not him."]
Harry's refusing the offer was a surprise. [Compare "Harry's refusal was a surprise."]

The *-ing* form of a verb can be used as a noun (gerund) or as an adjective (participle). The possessive case is not used before participles:

Caroline's radioing the Coast Guard solved our problem. [*Radioing* is a gerund. Compare "*Her action* solved our problem."]
The **man** sitting at the desk solved our problem. [*Sitting* is a participle. Compare "*He* solved our problem."]

Note: Do not use an awkward possessive before a gerund.

AWKWARD	The board approved of something's being sent to the poor overseas.
BETTER	The board approved of sending something to the poor overseas.

5e

Use the objective case for the subject or the object of an infinitive.

They expected Nancy and **me** to do the scriptwriting. [subject of the infinitive *to do*]
I did not want to challenge Victor or **him**. [object of the infinitive *to challenge*]

5f

Use the subjective case for the complement of the verb *be*.

> It was **she** who called. [Compare "She was the one who called."]
> The man who will get all the credit is no doubt Blevins or **he**. [Compare "Blevins or he is no doubt the man who will get all the credit."]

It's me (him, her, us, and *them)* is standard in informal speech or writing:

> If there had to be just one saved, I'm glad it was him.
> —JAMES HERRIOT

But many writers avoid this structure.

■ **Exercise 5** Find and revise in the sentences below all case forms that would be inappropriate in formal writing. Put a checkmark after each sentence that needs no revision.

1. I soon became acquainted with Ruth and her, whom I thought were agitators.
2. It was Doris and she who I blamed for me not making that sale.
3. Jack's racing the motor did not hurry Tom or me.
4. Between you and I, I prefer woodblock prints.
5. Who do you suppose will ever change Earth to Eden?
6. Since Joan eats less than I, I weigh more than she.
7. Let's you and I plan the curriculum of an ideal university.
8. The lawyer who I interviewed yesterday is going to make public the records of three men who she believes are guilty of tax evasion.
9. We players always co-operate with our assistant coach, who we respect and who respects us.
10. The librarian wanted us—Kurt Jacobs and I—to choose Newman's *The Canadian Establishment*.

Agreement

6

Make a verb agree in number with its subject; make a pronoun agree in number with its antecedent.

Verb and subject

In sentences such as those below, the forms of the verb and the subject (a noun or a noun substitute) agree grammatically:

SINGULAR The **list** of items **was** long.
PLURAL The **lists** of items **were** long.

Singular subjects take singular verbs (*list–was*), and plural subjects take plural verbs (*lists–were*).

The *-s* (or *-es*) suffix

Remember that *-s* (or *-es*) is (1) a plural-forming suffix for most nouns and (2) a singular-forming suffix for verbs—those present-tense verbs taking third-person singular subjects.

THIRD-PERSON SUBJECTS WITH PRESENT-TENSE VERBS

SINGULAR	PLURAL
The bell ring**s**.	The bell**s** ring.
The rope stretch**es**.	The rope**s** stretch.

SINGULAR	PLURAL
The church remains.	The church**es** remain.
A hero doesn't.	Hero**es** don't.

All present-tense verbs change form to agree with third-person singular subjects: *I remain, he remains; I do, it does; I have, she has*. (See also **person**, page 550). The verb *be* is the most irregular verb in the language: *I am, you are, she is* (present); *I was, you were, he was* (past). (See also **conjugation**, pages 535-36.)

Probably the best way for you to eliminate errors in subject-verb agreement in your writing is to proofread carefully. But if you find it difficult to distinguish verbs and relate them to their subjects, review **1a**.

Pronoun and antecedent

As a rule, a pronoun and its antecedent (the word the pronoun refers to) also agree in number:

SINGULAR Even an **animal** has **its** own territory.
PLURAL Even **animals** have **their** own territory.

Singular antecedents are referred to by singular pronouns (*animal* ← *its*); plural antecedents, by plural pronouns (*animals* ← *their*). See also Section **28**.

Note: A pronoun also agrees with its antecedent in person and in gender. Lack of agreement in person causes a shift in point of view: see **27b**.

NOT **One** reads for pleasure during **our** spare time. [shift from third person to first person]

BUT **We** read for pleasure during **our** spare time. [first person]

OR **You** read for pleasure during **your** spare time. [second person]

OR **People** read for pleasure during **their** spare time. [third person]

Agreement in gender is usually easy and natural: "the *boy* and *his* dog," "the *girl* and *her* dog." The masculine pronoun may be used to refer to common gender:

> **One** reads for pleasure if **he** has the time.

Two pronouns may refer to paired antecedents of different genders: "Every father and mother makes *his* or *her* mistakes." See also page 74

6a

Make a verb agree in number with its subject.

(1) Do not be misled by nouns or pronouns intervening between the subject and the verb or by subjects and verbs with endings difficult to pronounce.

> The **repetition** of the drumbeats **helps** to stir emotions.
> Every **one** of you **is invited** to the panel discussion.
>
> **Scientists sift** the facts.
> The **scientist asks** several pertinent questions.

As a rule, the grammatical number of the subject is not changed by the addition of expressions beginning with such words as *accompanied by, along with, as well as, in addition to, including, no less than, not to mention, together with.*

> **Unemployment** as well as taxes *influences* votes.
> **Taxes**, not to mention unemployment, **influence** votes.

(2) Subjects joined by *and* are usually plural.

> My **parents** and my **uncle do** not **understand** this.
> The **band** and the **team were leading** the parade.
> Her typewriter and my radio **were** stolen.
> The doctor and the teacher **have** much in common.

Exceptions: Occasionally, such a compound subject takes a singular verb because the subject denotes one person or a single unit.

My best friend and adviser **has changed** his mind again.

The flesh and blood of the world **was** dead.
—VIRGINIA WOOLF

Every or *each* preceding singular subjects joined by *and* calls for a singular verb:

Every member and officer in the club **was** upset.
Each cat and each dog **has** its own toy.

Placed after a plural subject, *each* does not affect the verb form. Some writers use a singular verb when *each* follows a compound subjet:

The cat and the dog each **have** their own toys.
[Or, sometimes, "The cat and the dog each *has* its own toy."]

(3) Singular subjects joined by *or, either . . . or,* or *neither . . . nor* usually take a singular verb.

Paula or her secretary **answers** the phone on Saturday.
Either the mayor or the premier **is** the keynote speaker.
Neither criticism nor praise **affects** them. [Informal "Neither criticism nor praise affect them."]

If one subject is singular and one is plural, the verb usually agrees with the nearer subject:

Neither the quality nor the prices **have** changed.
Neither the prices nor the quality **has** changed.
[Compare "The prices *and* the quality *have not* changed."]

The verb also agrees with the nearer subject in person in sentences like those below. (See also pages 67 and 550.)

Doesn't **he** or I deserve it? | Pat or **you were** supposed to call.
Don't **I** or he deserve it? | You or **Pat was** supposed to call.

(4) Do not let inverted word order (VERB + SUBJECT) or the structure *there* + VERB + SUBJECT cause you to make a mistake in agreement.

In the upper branches **was** a **nest** made of twigs and mud.
There **are** no poisonous **snakes** in the area.
There **remains** an unanswered **question**, as well as an unasked one.
Neither **do vegetarians** eat only vegetables.
—CONSUMER REPORTS
[Here *neither* is a conjunction meaning *nor yet*. See **6a(6)**.]
There **were anger** and **hatred** in that voice.
—JOHN CIARDI

Sometimes *there is* precedes a singular part of a plural compound subject:

There are the Clarks in *The Master of the Mill*. . . . **There is** John Elliott in *Our Daily Bread* and Abe Spaulding in *The Fruits of the Earth*. —MARGARET ATWOOD

(5) A relative pronoun (*who, which, that*) used as subject has the same number as its antecedent.

It is the **pharmacist who** often **suggests** a new brand.
Tonsillitis is among those **diseases that are** curable.
This is the only **one** of the local papers **that prints** a daily horoscope. [*That* refers to *one* because only one paper prints a daily horoscope; the other papers do not.]

(6) When used as subjects, such words as *each, either, neither, one, everybody,* and *anyone* regularly take singular verbs.

Neither likes the friends of the other.
Each of them **does have** political ambitions.
Everybody in the office **has** tickets.

Subjects such as *all, any, half, most, none*, and *some* may take a singular or a plural verb; the context generally determines the choice of the verb form.

Evelyn collects stamps; **some are** worth a lot. [Compare "Some of them are worth a lot."]

The honey was marked down because **some was** sugary. [Compare "Some of it was sugary."]

(7) Collective nouns (and phrases denoting a fixed quantity) take a singular verb when they refer to the group as a unit and take a plural verb when they refer to individuals or parts of the group.

Singular (regarded as a unit)

My **family has** its traditions.
The number is very small.
A **billion dollars is** a lot of money.
The **majority** of it **was** wasted.
Two-thirds of this **has** been finished.
The majority **has made** its decision.
A committee **was investigating** the charges.

Plural (regarded as individuals or parts)

A number were absent.
The **majority** of us **are** for it.
Two-thirds of these **have** been finished.

OPTIONS

Ten litres of gas is/are expensive.
A thousand tonnes of grain was/were crated.
The data is/are being studied.

(8) A linking verb agrees with its subject, not with its complement (predicate noun).

His **problem is** frequent headaches.
Frequent **headaches are** his problem.

Note: Because the number of the pronoun *what* depends on the number of the word (or word group) referred to, the verb does agree with its complement in sentences like these:

Of course, what you see in the final commercial **are** pretty pictures—the bear in a canoe, the bear in a Jeep, the bear padding behind the man. —JONATHAN PRICE
[Compare "Pretty pictures are what you see."]

What I do, at these times, **is** to change the way the system works. —LEWIS THOMAS
[Compare "That is what I do."]

(9) Nouns plural in form but singular in meaning usually take singular verbs. In all doubtful cases, consult a good dictionary.

Nouns that are regularly treated as singular include *economics, electronics, measles, mumps, news, physics*, and *tactics*.

News **is travelling** faster than ever before.
Physics **has fascinated** my roommate for months.

Some nouns ending in *-ics* (such as *athletics, politics*, and *statistics*) are considered singular when referring to an organized body of knowledge and plural when referring to activities, qualities, or individual facts:

Athletics **is required** of every student. [Compare "Participation in games *is required* of every student."]
Athletics **provide** good recreation. [Compare "Various games *provide* good recreation."]

(10) The title of a single work or a word spoken of as a word, even when plural in form, takes a singular verb.

Romeo and Juliet never **grows** old. [The play, not the characters, never grows old.]
"Rock of Ages" **is** an old song with a new sound.
They, a personal pronoun, **has** an interesting history.

■ **Exercise 1** The following sentences are all correct. Read them aloud, stressing the italicized words. If any sentence sounds wrong to you, read it aloud two or three more times so that you will gain practice in saying and hearing the correct forms.

1. The *timing* of these strikes *was* poorly planned.
2. There *are* a few *cookies* and *pickles* left.
3. A *wrench* and a *hubcap were* missing.
4. *Every one* of my cousins, including Larry, *has* brown eyes.
5. Sandy was the *only one* of the singers *who was* off-key.
6. *Does*n't *it* make sense?
7. *Each* of the episodes *is* exciting.
8. Every *one* of you *is* invited.
9. *A number* in this group *are* affected.
10. There *were* several *reasons* for this.

■ **Exercise 2** Choose the correct form of the verb within parentheses in each sentence below. Make sure that the verb agrees with its subject according to the rules of formal English.

1. Neither Anita nor Leon (feels, feel) that the evidence is circumstantial.
2. Tastes in reading, of course, (differs, differ).
3. Every one of the figures (was, were) checked at least twice.
4. A fountain and a hanging basket (adorns, adorn) the entrance.

5. Neither of them ever (asks, ask) for a second helping.
6. There (comes, come) to my mind now the names of the two or three people who were most influential in my life.
7. The booby prize (was, were) green apples.
8. A rustic lodge, as well as a game refuge and fishing waters, (is, are) close by.
9. Hidden cameras, which (invades, invade) the privacy of the unwary few, (provides, provide) entertainment for thousands.
10. The study of words (is, are) facilitated by breaking them down into prefixes, suffixes, and roots.

6b

Make a pronoun agree in number with its antecedent.

A singular antecedent (one that would take a singular verb) is referred to by a singular pronoun; a plural antecedent (one that would take a plural verb) is referred to by a plural pronoun:

SINGULAR An **actor** during early rehearsals often **forgets his** lines.

PLURAL **Actors** during early rehearsals often **forget their** lines.

(1) As a rule, use a singular pronoun to refer to such antecedents as *each, either, neither, one, anyone, everybody, a person*.

Each of these companies had **its** books audited. [NOT *their*]
One has to live with **oneself**. [NOT *themselves*]

Usage varies regarding the choice of pronoun referring to such antecedents as *everyone* or *a person* when the meaning includes both sexes or either sex (common gender):

A **person** needs to see **his** dentist twice a year. [OR *his or her*]
Every man and woman wants his/her dreams to come true.

So everybody gets married—unmarried—and married, but they're all married to somebody most of the time.
—MARGARET MEAD

In fact, the fear of growing old is so great that every aged person is an insult and a threat to the society. They remind us of our own death. . . . —SHARON CURTIN

(2) Two or more antecedents joined by *and* are referred to by a plural pronoun; two or more singular antecedents joined by *or* or *nor* are referred to by a singular pronoun.

Andrew and Roger lost **their** self-confidence.
Did **Andrew or Roger** lose **his** self-confidence?

If one of two antecedents joined by *or* or *nor* is singular and one is plural, the pronoun usually agrees with the nearer antecedent:

Neither the **package nor** the **letters** had reached **their** destination. [*Their* is closer to the plural antecedent *letters*.]
Stray **kittens or** even an abandoned grown **cat** has **its** problems finding enough food to survive long. [*Its* is closer to the singular antecedent *cat*.]

(3) Collective nouns are referred to by singular or plural pronouns, depending on whether the collective noun is used in a singular or plural sense. See also **6a(7)**.

Special care should be taken to avoid treating a collective noun as both singular and plural within the same sentence.

INCONSISTENT	The choir **is** writing **their** own music. [singular verb, plural pronoun]
CONSISTENT	The choir **is** writing **its** own music. [both singular]
CONSISTENT	The group of students **do** not agree on methods, but **they** unite on basic aims. [both plural]

■ **Exercise 3** Choose the correct pronoun or verb form within parentheses in each sentence below; follow the rules of formal English usage.

1. A number of people, such as Kate Swift and Warren Farrell, (has, have) offered (his, her and his, their) suggestions for a "human" singular pronoun, like *te* for *he or she* to refer to the antecedent *a person*.
2. If any one of the sisters (needs, need) a ride to church, (she, they) can call Trudy.
3. Neither the pilot nor the flight attendants mentioned the incident when (he, they) talked to reporters.
4. The Toronto team (was, were) opportunistic; (it, they) took advantage of every break.
5. If the board of directors (controls, control) the company, (it, they) may vote (itself, themselves) bonuses.

■ **Exercise 4** All the following sentences are correct. Change them as directed in parentheses, revising other parts of the sentence to secure agreement of subject and verb, pronoun, and antecedent.

1. Everyone in our Latin class thoroughly enjoys the full hour. (Change *Everyone* to *The students*.)
2. Every activity in that class seems not only instructive but amusing. (Change *Every activity* to *The activities*.)
3. Since the students eat their lunch just before the class, the Latin professor keeps coffee on hand to revive any sluggish thinkers. (Change *the students* to *nearly every student*.)
4. Yesterday one of the students was called on to translate some Latin sentences. (Change *one* to *two*.)
5. We were busily following the oral translation in our textbooks. (Change *We* to *Everyone else*.)
6. One or perhaps two in the class were not paying attention when the student, Jim Melton, said, "Who do you see?" (Use *Two or perhaps only one* instead of *One or perhaps two*.)
7. The Latin professor ordered, "Look at those inflections that indicate case! *Whom! Whom* do you see! Not *who!*" (Change *those inflections* to *the inflection*.)

8. Nobody in the room was inattentive as Jim translated the sentence again: "*Whom* do *youm* see?" (Change *Nobody* to *Few*.)
9. The students, who understood Jim's problem with inflections, were smiling as the professor exclaimed, "*Youm!* Whoever heard of *youm!*" (Change *The students* to *Everyone*.)
10. A student who sometimes poses questions that provoke thought about the nature of language, Jim politely replied, "But, sir, whoever heard of *whom?*" (Change *questions* to *a question*).

Verb Forms

7

Use the appropriate form of the verb. (See also **6a**.)

Verb forms indicate tense, number and person, voice, and mood.

Tense

Tense refers to the form of the verb that indicates time:

> We often **ask** questions. [present tense]
> After the lecture we **asked** questions. [past tense]
>
> I **see** the point now. [present tense]
> I finally **saw** the point. [past tense]

The suffix *-ed* or *-d* marks the past tense of regular verbs: *asked, hoped*. Irregular verbs do not form their past tense by the addition of *-ed* or *d: saw, went, gave, flew*.

Various auxiliary verbs indicate time in verb phrases:

will see	**had** asked	**do** hope	**were** going
can see	**have** asked	**did** hope	**has been** going

There are six tenses. Single-word verbs are used for two of these (the simple present and the simple past), and auxiliary verbs are used for the other four:

SIMPLE TENSES

present:	ask (asks)	see (sees)
past:	asked	saw
future:	will (shall) ask	will (shall) see

PERFECT TENSES

present:	have (has) asked	have (has) seen
past:	had asked	had seen
future:	will (shall) have asked	will (shall) have seen

The six tenses are based on primary forms called principal parts (*see, saw, seen*). See **7a**.

Number and Person

Verb forms also indicate the number of their subjects:

SINGULAR Only one question **was** asked.
PLURAL Many questions **were** asked.

In the present tense, all verbs change form to agree grammatically with third-person singular subjects: *I see, he sees*. See Section **6**, pages 66-67.

Voice

Voice is the form of a transitive verb that indicates whether or not the subject named performs the action denoted by the verb. There are two voices, active and passive. Only transitive verbs have voice. Transitive active verbs take direct objects (see **1b**).

ACTIVE Burglars often **steal** jewellery. [The subject acts. The object is *jewellery*.]

The object of a transitive active verb can usually be converted into the subject of a transitive passive verb. When an active verb is made passive, a form of *be* is used.

PASSIVE Jewellery **is** often **stolen** by burglars. [The prepositional phrase *by burglars* could be omitted.]

Compare the active and the passive forms of the verb *see* in the conjugation on pages 535-36. See also **29d**.

Note: Intransitive verbs do not take objects: see page 12.

> The rookies **did** not **go**.
> Carol **became** an engineer. [a linking verb with subject complement]

Mood

Verbs change form to indicate mood, or the way an assertion is conceived. There are three moods: indicative, imperative, and subjunctive.

INDICATIVE	She usually **rents** a car. [a factual statement] **Does** she usually **rent** a car? [a question]
IMPERATIVE	**Rent** a car. [a command or request]
SUBJUNCTIVE	If I **were** she, I **would rent** a car. [a condition contrary to fact] I suggested that she **rent** a car. [a recommendation]

See **7c** and **7d**.

Progressive Forms

The English language also has progressive verb forms, which are verb phrases consisting of a form of *be* plus an *-ing* verb (the present participle). These phrases denote an action in progress.

PRESENT	am (is, are) seeing
PAST	was (were) seeing
FUTURE	will be seeing
PRESENT PERFECT	have (has) been seeing
PAST PERFECT	had been seeing
FUTURE PERFECT	will have been seeing

Passive progressive forms include *am (is, are) being seen, was (were) being seen*, and so on.

Note: Infinitives, participles, and gerunds (verbals) also have progressive forms, as well as tense—but not all six tenses.

	Infinitives
PRESENT	to see, to be seen, to be seeing
PRESENT PERFECT	to have seen, to have been seen, to have been seeing
	Participles
PRESENT	seeing, being seen
PAST	seen
PRESENT PERFECT	having seen, having been seen
	Gerunds
PRESENT	seeing, being seen
PRESENT PERFECT	having seen, having been seen

Forms of *be*

Be is the most irregular verb in the English language. This verb has eight forms: *am, are, is, was, were, be, been, being*.

They ***are*** happy. That **may *be*** true.
We **will *be* leaving** soon. He ***was being*** difficult.
His shoulder **had *been* injured** before.

Below is a list of forms of *be* used with various subjects in the simple tenses.

PRESENT	I am	you are	he/she/it is	[singular]
	we are	you are	they are	[plural]
PAST	I was	you were	he/she/it was	[singular]
	we were	you were	they were	[plural]
FUTURE	will be OR shall be [all subjects, singular or plural]			

The perfect-tense forms are *have (has) been, had been*, and *will (shall) have been*.

7a

Avoid misusing the principal parts of verbs and confusing similar verbs.

(1) Avoid misusing the principal parts of verbs.

The principal parts of a verb include the *present* form (which is also the stem of the infinitive), the *past* form, and the *past participle*.

PRESENT STEM (INFINITIVE)	PAST TENSE	PAST PARTICIPLE
ask	asked	asked
begin	began	begun

Note: The *present participle* (the present form plus *-ing: asking, beginning*) is sometimes considered as a fourth principal part.

The *present* form may function as a single-word verb or may be preceded by words such as *will, do, may, could, have to, ought to,* or *used to.*

I **ask**, he **does ask**, we **begin**, it **used to begin**

The *past* form functions as a single-word verb.

He **asked** questions.
The show **began** at eight.

The *past participle*, when used as a part of a verb phrase, always has at least one auxiliary.

they **have asked**, she **was asked**, he **has been asked**
it **has begun**, the work **will be begun**, we **have begun**

Caution: Do not omit a needed *-d* or *-ed* because of the pronunciation. For example, although it is easy to remember a clearly pronounced *-d* or *-ed* (*faded, repeated*), it is sometimes difficult to remember to add a needed *-d* or *-ed* in such expressions as *hoped to* or *opened the*. Observe the use of the *-ed* or *-d* ending in these sentences:

> Yesterday I ask**ed** David. Then I talk**ed** to her.
> Perhaps we had price**d** our vegetables too high.
> It had happen**ed** before. She was not experience**d**.
> He use**d** to smoke. I am not suppose**d** to do it.
> A judge may be prejudice**d**. [Compare "a prejudic**ed** judge."]

When in doubt about the forms of a verb, consult a good dictionary. (If forms are not listed after an entry, the verb is generally a regular one, taking the *-d* or *-ed* ending.)

The following list gives the principal parts of a number of verbs that are sometimes misused. Give special attention to any forms unfamiliar to you.

Principal Parts of Verbs

PRESENT STEM (INFINITIVE)	PAST TENSE	PAST PARTICIPLE
become	became	become
begin	began	begun
blow	blew	blown
break	broke	broken
bring	brought	brought
burst	burst	burst
catch	caught	caught
choose	chose	chosen
cling	clung	clung
come	came	come
dive	dived OR dove	dived
do	did	done
draw	drew	drawn
drink	drank	drunk
drive	drove	driven
eat	ate	eaten
fall	fell	fallen

PRESENT STEM (INFINITIVE)	PAST TENSE	PAST PARTICIPLE
fly	flew	flown
forgive	forgave	forgiven
freeze	froze	frozen
give	gave	given
go	went	gone
grow	grew	grown
know	knew	known
ride	rode	ridden
ring	rang	rung
rise	rose	risen
run	ran	run
see	saw	seen
shake	shook	shaken
sing	sang OR sung	sung
sink	sank OR sunk	sunk
speak	spoke	spoken
spin	spun	spun
steal	stole	stolen
swear	swore	sworn
swim	swam	swum
swing	swung	swung
take	took	taken
tear	tore	torn
throw	threw	thrown
wear	wore	worn
write	wrote	written

Note: Mistakes with verbs sometimes involve spelling errors. Use care when you write troublesome verb forms such as the following:

PRESENT STEM (INFINITIVE)	PAST TENSE	PAST PARTICIPLE	PRESENT PARTICIPLE
lead	led	led	leading
loosen	loosened	loosened	loosening
lose	lost	lost	losing
pay	paid	paid	paying
study	studied	studied	studying

■ **Exercise 1** Respond to the questions in the past tense with a past tense verb; respond to the questions in the future tense with a present perfect verb (*have* or *has* + a past participle). Follow the pattern of the examples.

EXAMPLES Did she criticize Don? *Yes, she criticized Don.*
Will they take it? *They have already taken it.*

1. Did he give it away?
2. Will she surprise him?
3. Did the man drown?
4. Will they begin that?
5. Did the wind blow?
6. Will she choose it?
7. Did it really happen?
8. Will the river rise?
9. Did you do that?
10. Will they steal it?
11. Did you spin your wheels?
12. Will they freeze it?
13. Did he cling to that belief?
14. Will they go to the police?
15. Did she know them?
16. Will they go?
17. Did the sack burst?
18. Will he eat it?
19. Did you grow these?
20. Will Bert speak out?

(2) Do not confuse *set* with *sit* or *lay* with *lie*.

Sit means "be seated," and *lie down* means "rest in or get into a horizontal position." To *set* or *lay* something down is to place it or put it somewhere.

Learn the distinctions between the forms of *sit* and *set* and those of *lie* and *lay*.

PRESENT STEM (INFINITIVE)	PAST TENSE	PAST PARTICIPLE	PRESENT PARTICIPLE
(to) sit	sat	sat	sitting
(to) set	set	set	setting
(to) lie	lay	lain	lying
(to) lay	laid	laid	laying

As a rule, the verbs (or verbals) *set* and *lay* take objects; *sit* and *lie* do not.

She had **laid** the book aside. [*Book* is the object.]
I wanted to **lie** in the sun. [*To lie* has no object.]
After asking me to **sit** down, she seemed to forget I was there. [*To sit* has no object.]

Study the examples below, noting the absence of objects.

I did not sit down.	You should lie down.
Al sat up straight.	He lay down awhile.
She had sat too long.	It has lain here a week.
It was sitting here.	The coat was lying there.

Note: Because they take objects, the verbs *set* and *lay* may be passive as well as active.

Somebody **had set** the pup in the cart. [active]
The pup **had been set** in the cart. [passive]

We **ought to lay** our prejudices aside. [active]
Our prejudices **ought to be laid** aside. [passive]

■ **Exercise 2** Substitute the correct forms of *sit* and *lie* for the italicized word in each sentence. Follow the pattern of the example. Do not change the tense of the verb.

EXAMPLE I *remained* in that position for twenty minutes.
I ***sat*** *in that position for twenty minutes.*
I ***lay*** *in that position for twenty minutes.*

1. Jack doesn't ever want to *get* down.
2. The dog *stayed* near the luggage.
3. The toy soldier has been *rusting* in the yard.
4. He often *sleeps* on a park bench.
5. Has it *been* there all along?

■ **Exercise 3** Choose the correct verb form within the parentheses.

1. After lunch I wanted to (lie, lay) down for a few minutes.
2. Yesterday we (lay, laid) the rest of the tiles ourselves.
3. The garden hose has (lain, laid) there for weeks.
4. The money for the tickets was still (lying, laying) on my desk.
5. He had just (lain, laid) the child down.
6. Alice and Dawn were (sitting, setting) up watching a late movie.
7. Alice and Dawn were (sitting, setting) up chairs for the concert.

8. They came in and (sat, set) down for a chat.
9. How long had the visitors (sat, set) there?
10. Sometimes I just (sit, set) there and watch the tide come in.

7b

Learn the meaning of tense forms. Use logical tense forms in sequence.

The six tenses are based on the three principal parts of verbs: the *present* (stem of the infinitive—to *see*, to *use*); the *past* (*saw, used*); and the *past participle* (*seen, used*). See **7a**.

(1) Learn the meaning of the six tense forms.

Although tense indicates time (see pages 78-79), the tense forms of verbs do not always agree with division of actual time. The present tense, for example, is by no means limited to the present time.

PRESENT TENSE

I **see** what you meant by that remark. [now, present time]
He **uses** common sense. [habitual action]
Human beings **make** mistakes. [a timeless truth]
In the fall of 1939 Hitler **attacks** Poland. [historical present]
Officially winter **begins** next week. [present form (used with the adverbial *next week*) indicating future time]

Note: Auxiliaries indicate present tense in the following verb phrases:

He ***does*** **use** common sense. [emphatic present]
I ***am*** **learning** from my mistakes. [a progressive form indicating past, present, and (probably) future time]
Mistakes ***are*** often **made**. [passive form, habitual action]

PAST TENSE — past time, not extending to the present
I **saw** the accident. [at a definite time before now]
We **used** makeshift tools. [action completed in the past]

Note: Auxiliaries also indicate past tense:

I ***did*** **see** the accident. [emphatic]
We ***were*** **using** makeshift tools. [progressive]
The accident ***was*** **seen** by three people. [passive]
Talk shows ***used to*** **be** worse than they are now. [Compare "*were* worse then."]

FUTURE TENSE—at a future time, sometime after now
He **will see** his lawyer.
We **will use** a different strategy.

The auxiliary *will* also indicates future time in progressive and passive forms of the verb:

He **will be seeing** his lawyer. [progressive]
A different strategy **will be used**. [passive]

PRESENT PERFECT TENSE—sometime before now, up to now
I **have seen** the movie. [sometime before now]
He **has used** his savings wisely. [up to now]

PAST PERFECT TENSE—before an indicated time in the past
She **had seen** me before the game started.
When he **had used** his savings, he applied for a loan.

Note: Sometimes the simple past is used for the past perfect: "She *saw* me before the game started."

FUTURE PERFECT TENSE—after now and before an indicated time in the future.
They **will have seen** the report by next week.

Speakers and writers often substitute the simple future for the future perfect:

They **will see** the report by next week.

Examples of progressive and passive forms in the present perfect tense follow:

Kevin **has been using** the money wisely.
The Crawfords **have been seeing** deer in the woods.

The money **has been used** wisely.
Deer **have been seen** in the woods.

Again, the simple future usually replaces the future perfect:

By 1990 they **will have been seeing** their dreams in action. [USUAL: "they *will be seeing*"]

By 1990 their dreams **will have been seen** in action. [USUAL: "their dreams *will be seen* in action"]

■ **Exercise 4** Be prepared to explain the differences in the meaning of tense forms separated by slashes in the following sentences:

1. It *has rained* / *had rained* for days.
2. Mary *waxed* / *did wax* / *was waxing* the car.
3. Walter *teaches* / *is teaching* Spanish.
4. I *spoke* / *have spoken* to him about this.
5. The Bowens *had sold* / *will have sold* their house by then.
6. Time *passes* / *does pass* / *has passed* / *had been passing* rapidly.
7. In 1840 Thomas Carlyle *calls* / *called* time a great mystery, a miracle.

(2) Use logical tense forms in sequence.

Verbs

Notice in the examples below the relationship of each verb form to actual time:

When the speaker **entered**, the audience **rose**. [Both actions took place at the same definite time in the past.]

I **have ceased** worrying because I **have heard** no more rumours. [Both verb forms indicate action at some time before now.]

When I **had been** at camp four weeks, I **received** word that my application **had been accepted**. [The *had* before *been* indicates a time prior to that of *received*.]

Infinitives

Use the present infinitive to express action occurring at the same time as, or later than, that of the main verb; use the present perfect infinitive for action prior to that of the main verb:

I would have liked **to live** (NOT *to have lived*) in Shakespeare's time. [present infinitive—for the same time as that of the main verb]

She wanted **to win**. She wants **to win**. [present infinitives—for time later than *wanted* or *wants*]

I would like **to have won** that prize. [present perfect infinitive—for time prior to that of the main verb. Compare "I wish I *had won*."]

Participles

Use the present form of participles to express action occurring at the same time as that of the main verb; use the present perfect form for action prior to that of the main verb:

Walking along the streets, he met many old friends. [The walking and the meeting were simultaneous.]

Having climbed that mountain they felt a real sense of achievement. [The climbing took place first; then came their sense of achievement.]

■ **Exercise 5** Choose the verb form inside parentheses that is the logical tense form in sequence:

1. When the fire sale (ended, had ended), the store closed.
2. Fans cheered as the goal (had been made, was made).
3. The team plans (to celebrate, to have celebrated) tomorrow.
4. We should have planned (to have gone, to go) by bus.
5. (Having finished, Finishing) the test, Leslie left the room.
6. (Having bought, Buying) the tickets, Mr. Selby took the children to the circus.
7. The premier had left the meeting before it (had adjourned, adjourned).
8. It is customary for ranchers (to brand, to have branded) their cattle.

9. Marilyn had not expected (to see, to have seen) her cousin at the rally.
10. The pond has begun freezing because the temperature (dropped, has dropped).

7c

Use the subjunctive mood in the few types of expressions in which it is still appropriate.

Distinctive forms for the subjunctive occur only in the present and past tenses of *be* and in the present tense of other verbs used with third-person singular subjects.

INDICATIVE	I **am**, you **are**, he **is**, others **are** [present]
	I **was**, you **were**, he **was**, others **were** [past]
SUBJUNCTIVE	(with all subjects) **be** [present], **were** [past]
INDICATIVE	he **sees**, others **see** [present]
SUBJUNCTIVE	(that) he **see**, (that) others **see** [present]

The subjunctive has been largely displaced by the indicative. Compare the following optional usages:

Suppose he **were** to die.	Suppose he dies.
I will ask that he **do** this.	I will ask him to do this.
It is necessary that she **be** there on time.	She must be there on time.

Especially in formal English, however, the subjunctive is still used to express a contrary-to-fact condition.

Drive as if every other car on the road **were** out to kill you.
—ESQUIRE

The subjunctive is required (1) in *that* clauses of motion, resolution, recommendation, command, or demand and (2) in a few idiomatic expressions.

I move that the report **be** approved.
Resolved, that dues for the coming year **be** doubled.
I recommend (order, demand) that the prisoner **see** his lawyer.

I demand (request, insist) that the messenger **go** alone.
If need **be** . . . **Suffice** it to say . . . **Come** what may . . .
[fixed subjunctive in idiomatic expressions]

■ **Exercise 6** Prepare for a class discussion of the use of the subjunctive and of the indicative used informally in the following sentences:

1. If Linda was here, she would explain everything.
2. We insist that he be punished.
3. I wish that peace were possible.
4. Canadians now speak of Mexico as though it were just across the border.
5. Present-day problems demand that we be ready for any emergency.
6. If there was time, I could finish my report.
7. Come what may, we will never choose anarchy.
8. I demand that he make amends.
9. If I were you, I would apply tomorrow.
10. The man acts as though he were the owner.

■ **Exercise 7** Compose five sentences in which the subjunctive is required.

7d

Avoid needless shifts in tense or mood. See also **27a**.

INCONSISTENT He **walked** up to me in the cafeteria and **tries** to start a fight. [Tense shifts from past to present.]

BETTER He **walked** up to me in the cafeteria and **tried** to start a fight.

INCONSISTENT It is necessary to restrain an occasional foolhardy park visitor. If a female bear **were** to mistake his friendly intentions and **supposes** him a menace to her cubs, he would be in trouble. [Mood shifts from subjunctive to indicative.] But females with cubs **were** only one of the dangers. [a correct sentence if standing alone, but here inconsistent with present tense of preceding sentence and therefore misleading.] One **has** to remember that all bears **were** wild animals and not domesticated pets. [Tense shifts from present to past.] Though a bear **may seem** altogether peaceable and harmless, he **might** not **remain** peaceable, and he is never harmless. [Tense shifts from present to past.] It **is** therefore an important part of the park ranger's duty **to watch** the tourists and above all **don't** let anyone try to feed the bears. [Mood shifts from indicative to imperative.]

BETTER It is necessary to restrain an occasional foolhardy park visitor. If a female bear **were** to mistake his friendly intentions and **suppose** him a menace to her cubs, he would be in trouble. But females with cubs **are** only one of the dangers. One **has** to remember that all bears **are** wild animals and not domesticated pets. Though a bear **may seem** altogether peaceable and harmless, he **may** not **remain** peaceable, and he is never harmless. It **is** therefore an important part of the park ranger's duty **to watch** the tourists and above all not **to let** anyone try to feed the bears.

■ **Exercise 8** In the following passage correct all errors and inconsistencies in tense and mood as well as any other errors in verb usage. Put a checkmark after any sentence that is satisfactory as it stands.

[1] Charles Dickens creates many memorable characters in *David Copperfield*. [2] He give many of his characters names that suggest their personalities. [3] Mr. Murdstone is unfeeling, Little Emily is shy, and Dr. Strong is virtuous. [4] Dickens also tags his characters with recurring peculiarities of speech; these may even be call their trademarks. [5] For example, Barkis continues to have proposed marriage with these words: "Barkis is willin'." [6] The proud Uriah Heep, a hypocrite, keeps calling himself a humble man. [7] Over and over Mr. Micawber rambled on and then concludes, "In short—" [8] When he owed debts, this character shrugs off what he terms his "pecuniary difficulties." [9] With cheerful certainty, he repeats his favourite prophecy: "Something is bound to turn up." [10] Set down and read *David Copperfield* through to become acquainted with these interesting people.

7e

Observe such distinctions as exist between *should* and *would*.

(1) Use *should* to express a mild obligation or a condition.

I (You, He, We, They) **should** help the needy.
If I (you, he, we, they) **should** resign, the program would not be continued.

(2) Use *would* to express a customary action.

I (You, He, We, They) **would** spend hours lying on the beach every summer.

Caution: Do not use *would have* as a substitute for *had*.

If you **had** (NOT *would have*) arrived earlier, you would have seen the prime minister.

■ **Exercise 9** Revise any incorrect verb forms in the sentences below. Put a checkmark after any sentence that needs no revision. Prepare to explain the reason for each change you make.

1. If he would have registered later, he would have had night classes.
2. If Leslie enrolled in the class at the beginning, she could have made good grades.
3. A stone lying in one position for a long time may gather moss.
4. The members recommended that all delinquents be fined.
5. It was reported that there use to be very few delinquents.
6. After Douglas entered the room, he sat down at the desk and begins to write rapidly.
7. Until I received that letter, I was hoping to have had a visit from Marty.
8. Follow the main road for two kilometres; then you need to take the next road on the left.
9. The suspect could not deny that he had stole the tapes.
10. I would have liked to have been with the team on the trip to Yellowknife.

MECHANICS

Manuscript Form 8

Capitals 9

Italics 10

Abbreviations and Numbers 11

Manuscript Form

8

Put your manuscript in acceptable form. Divide words at the ends of lines according to standard practices. Revise and proofread with care.

8a

Use the proper materials.

Unless you are given other instructions, follow these general practices.

(1) Handwritten papers Use regular notebook paper, size 21 cm × 28 cm ($8^{1}/_{2}''$ × 11″), with widely spaced lines. (Narrow spaces between lines do not allow sufficient room for corrections.) Use black or blue ink. Write on only one side of the paper.

(2) Typewritten papers Use regular white typing paper (not sheets torn from a spiral notebook), size 21 cm × 28 cm ($8^{1}/_{2}''$ × 11″). Or use a good grade of bond paper (not onionskin). Use a black ribbon. Double-space between lines. Type on only one side of the paper.

8b

Arrange your writing in clear and orderly fashion on the page.

(1) Margins Leave sufficient margins—about 2.5 cm (1″) on all sides—to prevent a crowded appearance. The ruled vertical line on notebook paper marks the left margin.

(2) Indention Indent the first lines of paragraphs uniformly, about 2.5 cm (1″) in handwritten copy and five spaces in typewritten copy.

(3) Paging Use Arabic numerals—without parentheses or periods—in the upper right-hand corner to number all pages. After the first page, the author's name and initial should precede the page number.

(4) Title *Do not put quotation marks around the title or underline it* (unless it is a quotation or the title of a book), and use no period after the title. Capitalize the first and last words of the title and all other words except articles, short conjunctions, and short prepositions. See also **9c**. For proper placement of the title on the page, see **8b(7)**.

If you are instructed to use a separate title page, attractively space the following information: the title of your paper, each line of it, if more than one, centred above the middle of the page; in the lower right corner, your name, the course title and number, the instructor's name, and the date. See the example on page 473.

(5) Quoted lines When you quote over four lines of another's writing to explain or support your ideas, set the quotation off by indention: see **16a(1)** and **(2)** and Section **33**. Acknowledge the source of quotations: see Section **33**, pages 459-67.

(6) Punctuation Never begin a line with a comma, a colon, a semicolon, or a terminal mark of punctuation; never end a line with the first of a set of brackets, parentheses, or quotation marks.

(7) Identification Papers that follow MLA guidelines in not having a title page carry the name of the student, the course title and number, the instructor's name, and the date in the top left-hand corner of the first page of text. Double-space each line of the identification down to and including the title of the paper, which is centred on the width of the page. The first line of text begins four spaces below the title. See pages 476-77.

8c

Write or type your manuscript so that it can be read easily and accurately.

(1) Legible handwriting Form each letter clearly; distinguish between each *o* and *a, i* and *e, t* and *l, b* and *f*. Be sure that capital letters differ from lower-case letters. Use firm dots, not circles, for periods. Make each word a distinct unit. Avoid flourishes.

(2) Legible typing Before typing your final draft, check the quality of the ribbon and the cleanness of the type. Do not forget to double-space between lines. Do not strike over an incorrect letter; make neat corrections. Leave one space after a comma or a semicolon, one or two after a colon, two after a period, a question mark, or an exclamation point. To indicate a dash, use two hyphens without spacing before, between, or after. Use a pen to insert marks that are not on your typewriter, such as accent marks, mathematical symbols, or brackets.

8d

Whenever possible avoid the division of a word at the end of a line. When a division is necessary, make the break only between syllables and according to standard practices.

You will seldom need to divide words if you leave a reasonably wide right margin. Remember that the reader expects a somewhat uneven right margin but may be distracted or slowed down by a series of word divisions at the ends of consecutive lines.

When you do need to divide a word at the end of a line, use a hyphen to mark the separation of syllables. In college dictionaries, dots usually divide the syllables of words:

re · al · ly pre · fer pref · er · ence
sell · ing set · ting

But not every division between syllables is an appropriate place for dividing a word at the end of a line. The following principles are useful guidelines:

(1) **One-letter syllables** Do not put the first or last letter of a word at the end or beginning of a line. Do not divide:

o · mit a · ble spunk · y bo · a

(2) **Two-letter endings** Do not put the last two letters of a word at the beginning of a line. Do not divide:

dat · ed does · n't safe · ly grav · el tax · is

(3) **Misleading divisions** Do not make divisions that may cause a misreading. Do not divide:

sour · ces on · ions an · gel colo · nel

The red vertical line in the examples of the next three guidelines marks an appropriate end-of-the-line division.

(4) Hyphenated words Divide hyphenated words only at the hyphen.

mass-| produced
father-| in-law OR **father-in-| law**

(5) *-ing* words Divide words ending in *-ing* between those consonants that you double when adding *-ing*.

set-| ting **jam-| ming** **plan-| ning**
[Compare sell-| ing.]

(6) Consonants between vowels Divide words between two consonants that come between vowels—except when the division does not reflect pronunciation.

pic-| nic **dis-| cuss** **thun-| der**

(7) Abbreviations and acronyms Do not divide abbreviations, initials, or capitalized acronyms like

B.A. [degree], **Y.M.C.A.,** **CBC,** **RCMP,** **UNESCO.**

(8) Caution: Do not divide one-syllable words, such as *twelfth, through,* or *grabbed.*

■ **Exercise 1** First put a checkmark after the words below that should not be divided at the end of a line; then, with the aid of your dictionary, write out the other words by syllables and insert hyphens followed by a vertical line to indicate appropriate end-of-the-line divisions.

1. cross-reference
2. economic
3. fifteenth
4. Paris
5. combed
6. gripping
7. guessing
8. against
9. psychoanalyst
10. present (give)

11. seacoast
12. eventual
13. recline
14. H.R.H.
15. magical
16. CHUM-FM
17. matches
18. dissolve
19. cobwebs
20. stick-in-the-mud

8e

Revise and proofread your manuscript with care.

(1) Revise and proofread your paper before submitting it to the instructor.

When doing in-class papers, use the last few minutes for proofreading and making corrections. When doing out-of-class papers, write a first draft, put the paper aside for a few hours or a day, and then revise it. You will be able to see more objectively what parts need to be expanded or changed.

As you revise, focus your attention on content and style. Use the Reviser's Checklist in Section **32**, page 414. As you proofread, focus your attention on manuscript form—on mechanics, punctuation, spelling. Use the Proofreader's Checklist on the next page.

If only a few changes are needed, the paper may be handed in—after clear, legible corrections have been made—without rewriting. Changes may be made as follows:

(a) Deletion of words

Billboards ~~along the highway~~
can save travellers time.

(b) Addition of words

These samples ^often last for weeks.

They save ^the consumer money.

(c) Correction of misspellings, substitution of words

Those who damn advertising stress
~~Thoes~~ who ~~dam~~ advertising ~~talk~~
~~about~~ its disadvantages.

(d) Changes in capitalization and in punctuation

Consumers should appreciate
advertising, not condemn it.

Proofreader's Checklist

1. **Title** Is there any unnecessary punctuation in the title? Is it centred on the line? Are key words capitalized? See **8b(4)**.
2. **Indention** Is the first line of each paragraph indented? Is any lengthy quoted passage set off from the text? See **8b(2)** and **16a(1)-(2)**.
3. **Sentences** Does each sentence begin with a capital and end with the appropriate end mark? Are there any fragments, comma splices, or fused sentences? See **9e, 17a-c**, and Sections **2-3**.
4. **Spelling, mechanics** Are there any misspellings or mistakes in typing or handwriting? Are capitals and underlining (italics) used correctly? Should any abbreviations or numbers be spelled out? See **8c** and Sections **9-11** and **18**.
5. **Punctuation** Have any end marks been omitted? Are apostrophes correctly placed? Are there any superfluous commas? See Sections **12-17**.

Caution: Do not put words to be deleted in parentheses or make unsightly erasures. Do not forget to use a caret (‸) at the point in the line where an addition is made:

and ‸a present for Ma‸rtha

If extensive changes are necessary, make a full, clean copy to submit to the instructor.

(2) Revise your paper after the instructor has marked it.

One of the best ways to learn how to write is to revise returned papers carefully. Give special attention to any comment on content or style, and become familiar with the numbers or abbreviations used by your instructor to indicate specific errors or suggested changes.

Unless directed otherwise, follow this procedure as you revise a marked paper:

(a) Find in this handbook the exact principle that deals with each error or recommended change.

(b) After the instructor's mark in the margin, write the letter designating the appropriate principle, such as **a** or **c**.

(c) Rather than rewrite the composition, make the corrections on the marked paper. To make the corrections stand out distinctly from the original, use ink of a different colour or a no. 2 pencil.

The purpose of this method of revision is to help you not only to understand why a change is desirable but to avoid repetition of the same mistakes.

On the following page are examples of a paragraph marked by an instructor and the same paragraph corrected by a student.

A Paragraph Marked by an Instructor

Those who damn advertising stress its
3 disadvantages, however, it saves consumers time,
labour, and money. Billboards can save travellers
12 timo for many billboards tell where to find a meal
18 or a bed. TV commercials announce new labour-
2 saveing products. Such as a spray or a cleaner. In
addition, some advertisers give away free samples
19 of shampoo, toothpaste, soap flakes, and etc. These
24 samples often last for weeks. They save the
consumer money. Consumers should appreciate
advertising, not condemn it.

The Same Paragraph Corrected by a Student

Those who damn advertising stress its
3b disadvantages~~,~~; however, it saves consumers time,
labour, and money. Billboards can save travellers
12a time, for many billboards tell where to find a meal
18c or a bed. TV commercials announce new labour-
2c ~~saveing~~ saving products~~.~~, ~~Such~~ such as a spray or a cleaner. In
addition, some advertisers give away free samples
19i of shampoo, toothpaste, soap flakes, ~~and~~ etc. These
24a samples, which often last for weeks~~.~~, ~~They~~ save the
consumer money. Consumers should appreciate
advertising, not condemn it.

The method of revision shown opposite works equally well if your instructor uses abbreviations or other symbols instead of numbers. In that case, instead of putting **c** after **18**, for example, you would put **c** or **18c** after **sp**.

Individual Record of Errors

You may find that keeping a record of your errors will help you to check the improvement in your writing. A clear record of the symbols on your revised papers will show your progress at a glance. As you write each paper, keep your record in mind; avoid mistakes that have already been pointed out and corrected.

One way to record your errors is to write them down as they occur in each paper, grouping them in columns according to the seven major divisions of the handbook, as illustrated below. In the spaces for paper no. 1 are the numbers and letters from the margin of the revised paragraph on the opposite page. In the spelling column is the correctly spelled word rather than **18c**. You may wish to add on your record sheet other columns for date, grade, and instructor's comments.

RECORD OF ERRORS

Paper No.	Grammar 1–7	Mechanics 8–11	Punctuation 12–17	Words Misspelled 18	Diction 19–22	Effectiveness 23–30	Larger Elements 31–34
1	3 b 2 c		12 a	saving	19 i	24 a	

■ **Exercise 2** Proofread the following composition; circle mistakes. Prepare to discuss in class the changes that you would make.

Programmed People.

A lot of people in the workaday world is a machine—an insensitive, unhearing, unseeing, unthinking, unfeeling mechanism. They act like they are programmed, all their movements or responses triggered by clocks. Take, for example my brother. At 7:30 A.M. he automatically shuts off the alarm, then for the next hour he grumbles and sputter around like the cold, sluggish motor that he is.

On the way to work he did not see the glorious sky or notice ambulance at his neighbour's house. At 8:20 he unlocks his store and starts selling auto parts; however, all mourning long he never once really sees a customers' face. While eating lunch at Joe's cafe, the same music he spent a half dollar for yesterday is playing again. he does not hear it. At one o'clock my brother is back working with invoices and punching at a calculator; The clock and him ticks on and on.

When the hour hand hits five, it pushes the "move" button of my brother: lock store, take bus, pet dog at front door, kiss wife and baby, eat supper, read paper, watch TV, and during the 10-o'clock news he starts his nodding. His wife interrupts his light snoring to say that thier neighbour had a mild heart attach while mowing the lawn. My brother jerks and snorts. Then he mumbles, "Tell me tomorrow. I'm to tired now."

Capitals

9

Capitalize words according to standard conventions. Avoid unnecessary capitals.

A study of the principles in this section should help you use capitals correctly. When special problems arise with individual words or phrases, consult a good recent college dictionary. Dictionary entries of words that are regularly capitalized begin with capitals:

Satanism	Milky Way	Big Dipper
Halloween	National War Memorial	Wild Rose Country

Dictionaries also list capitalized abbreviations, along with options if usage is divided:

Dr., Mrs.	Ph.D.	A.M., a.m., AM
CMA, C.M.A.	M.A.	UHF, U.H.F., uhf, u.h.f.

A recent dictionary is an especially useful guide when a trademark (such as *Band-Aid, Frisbee*, or *Kleenex*) begins to function as a common noun (*bandaid, frisbee, kleenex*), and when a generally uncapitalized word is capitalized because of a specific meaning in a given sentence:

These are **mosaic** pictures. [having a certain design]
These are **Mosaic** laws. [of or pertaining to Moses]

Most capitalized words fall into three main categories: proper names, key words in titles, and the first words of sentences.

9a

Capitalize proper names, words used as an essential part of proper names, and, usually, derivatives and abbreviations of proper names.

Proper names begin with capitals, but names of classes of persons, places, or things do not:

T.H. Brady, Jr.	on Main Street	the Liberal Party
a graduate	a main street	a liberal person

(1) Proper names

Capitalize the names of specific persons, places, and things; peoples and their languages; religions and their adherents; members of national, political, racial, social, civic, and athletic groups; geographical names and regions; organizations and institutions; historical documents, periods, and events; calendar designations; trademarks; holy books and words denoting the god of a monotheistic religion.

Tom Evans, Europe, the Olympics, Jews, English
Christianity, a Christian, Canadians, New Democrat
a Presbyterian, an Albertan, Vancouver Canucks
Yellowknife, Arctic Ocean, the Prairies, the Red Cross
Newman Club, the U.S. Senate, McGill University
the Durham Report, the Middle Ages, the Winnipeg Strike
Monday, August, Canada Day, Masonite, Bible, Koran
God, Allah, Yahweh, the Supreme Being, the Deity

Note 1: Some writers still capitalize pronouns (except *who, whom, whose*) referring to the Deity. Many writers capitalize such pronouns only when the capital is needed to prevent ambiguity, as in the following sentence:

The Lord commanded the prophet to warn **His** people.

Note 2: Capitalize names of objects, animals, or ideas when they are personified. See also **20a(4)**.

> People in the Thirties, Forties, and Fifties were hardly likely to believe that life was a bowl of cherries when **War, Famine, Pestilence**, and **Depression** were staring them in the face so much of the time. —ANDREW SARRIS

(2) Words used as an essential part of proper names

Words like *college, river, park, memorial, street*, and *company* are capitalized only when they are part of proper names:

Trent University	Frobisher Bay	Kicking Horse Pass
Uranium City	Yonge Street	AVS Food Service

[Compare Norwegian elkhounds, a Honda hatchback, Parkinson's disease, Quaker guns.]

Note: In instances such as the following, capitalization depends on word placement:

on the Erie and Huron lakes   on Lakes Erie and Huron

(3) Derivatives

Words derived from proper names are usually capitalized:

Africanize   Torontonian   Darwinism   Orwellian

(4) Abbreviations

As a rule, capitalize abbreviations of (or acronyms formed from) capitalized words. See also **17a(2)**.

L.G. Savard   RMC   NATO   NDP   NASA

Note 1: Both *no.* and *No.* are correct abbreviations for *number*, as in *No. 444* or *no. 444*.

Note 2: When proper names and their derivatives become names of a general class, they are no longer capitalized:

malapropism [derived from *Mrs. Malaprop*]
chauvinistic [derived from *Nicholas Chauvin*]

9b

In ordinary writing, capitalize titles that precede a proper name, but not those that follow it.

Mayor Mike Stevens, Sergeant Bouchard, Aunt Edith
Mike Stevens, our mayor; Bouchard, the sergeant; Edith, my aunt

Note: Usage is divided regarding the capitalization of titles indicating high rank or distinction when not followed by a proper name, or of words denoting family relationship when used as substitutes for proper names.

Who was the Mayor (OR mayor) of Vancouver?
''Oh, Dad (OR dad)!'' I said. ''Tell Mother (OR mother).''

9c

In titles of books, plays, student papers, and so on, capitalize the first and last words and all other words except articles (*a, an, the*), short conjunctions, and short prepositions.

Crime and Punishment, Lives of Girls and Women
''The Canadian Poet's Predicament,'' ''A Code to Live By''

Note 1: In titles a conjunction or a preposition of five or more letters is usually capitalized.

The Man Without a Country, Coming Through the Rye

Note 2: In a title capitalize the first word of a hyphenated compound. As a rule, capitalize the word following the hyphen if it is a noun or a proper adjective or if it is equal in importance to the first word.

A Substitute for the H-Bomb [noun]
French-Canadian Music [proper adjective]
''Hit-and-Run Accidents'' [parallel words]

Usage varies with respect to the capitalization of words following such prefixes as *anti-*, *ex-*, *re-*, and *self-*:

The Anti-Poverty Program, "Re-covering Old Sofas"

9d

Capitalize the pronoun *I* and the interjection *O* (but not *oh*, except when it begins a sentence).

David sings, "Out of the depths I cry to thee, O Lord."

9e

Capitalize the first word of every sentence and the first word of directly quoted speech.

She asked me what time it was.

The reply is always "**N**ot today."

"**U**niversity is OK," I said. "**E**specially on weekends." [The first word of a fragment in dialogue is capitalized.]
COMPARE "University is OK," I said, "especially on weekends." [See also **12d(3)**.]

In the lobby we had a chance to get reacquainted. (It was a fifteen-minute intermission.) We talked about how much fun we had in high school. [a parenthetical sentence between sentences]
COMPARE In the lobby we had a chance to get reacquainted (it was a fifteen-minute intermission), and we talked about how much fun we had in high school. [a parenthetical main clause within a sentence]

Option:

One thing is certain: **w**e are still a free people. [regular usage]
One thing is certain: **W**e are still a free people. [used for emphasis] [See also **17d**.]

Note: Be sure to quote a written passage accurately, using the exact words, punctuation, and capitalization of the original.

> As Youth Cult continues to collapse all around us, Instant Historians will spring forth to examine this little fragment of Instant History. —MICHAEL HALBERSTAM

9f

Avoid unnecessary capitals.

If you have a tendency to overuse capitals, review **9a** through **9e**. Also keep in mind this rule: common nouns may be preceded by the indefinite articles (*a, an*) and by such limiting modifiers as *every* or *several.*

> **a** speech course in radio and television writing
> COMPARE Speech 245: Radio and Television Writing
>
> **every** university, **several** schools of medicine
> COMPARE the University of Toronto School of Medicine

When preceded by *a, an*, or modifiers like *every* or *several*, capitalized nouns name one or many of the members of a class: ***a** St. Bernard, **a** Haligonian, **several** Catholics.*

Study the following style sheet:

Style Sheet for Capitalization

CAPITALS	NO CAPITALS
Central High School	in high school
Dr. Freda E. Watts	my doctor
two Conservative MPs	a conservative approach
the Lord I worship	a lord among his peers
a Chihuahua, Saint Bernards	a beagle, fox terriers
Parkinson's disease	the flu, asthma, leukemia
the War of 1812	a space war in 1999
May, July, Friday, Sunday	summer, fall, winter, spring
the West, a Westerner	to fly west, a western wind
Zionism, Marxism	capitalism, socialism
the University Players	a university stadium

9f cap

■ **Exercise 1** Write brief sentences correctly using each of the following words:

(1) professor (2) Professor (3) university (4) University (5) south (6) South (7) avenue (8) Avenue (9) theatre (10) Theatre

■ **Exercise 2** Supply capitals wherever needed below.

1. Trying to raise my average in both english and history, i spent my winter break writing a paper entitled "the historical development of english-canadian literature."
2. the west offers grand sights for tourists: banff and jasper national parks, the canadian rockies, the fraser river, vancouver island, and the pacific ocean.
3. at the end of his sermon on god's social justice as set forth in the bible, he said, "materialism is undermining the true individualism which is at the heart of christianity."
4. robert sherrill wrote a book, the full title of which is *the saturday night special and other guns with which americans won the west, protected bootleg franchises, slew wildlife, robbed countless banks, shot husbands purposely and by mistake, and killed presidents—together with the debate over continuing same.*

Italics

10

To indicate italics, underline words and phrases (along with the punctuation) in accordance with customary practices. Use italics sparingly for emphasis.

In handwritten or typewritten papers, italics are indicated by underlining. Printers set underlined words in italic type.

TYPEWRITTEN	PRINTED
It was on The Journal.	It was on *The Journal*.

10a

Titles of separate publications (books, magazines, newspapers, pamphlets, long musical works) and titles of plays, films, radio and television programs, and long poems are underlined (italicized).

I skimmed through Timothy Findley's *The Wars*. [Note that the author's name is not italicized.]

According to the *Encyclopædia Britannica*, Arthur Miller wrote *The Misfits* for Marilyn Monroe. [An initial *a, an,* or *the* is italicized and capitalized when part of a title.]

Tickets to *Hey Rube!* were hard to find. [The italicized punctuation is part of the title.]

He subscribes to *Maclean's*, the *West Coast Review* and the *New York Times* (OR the New York *Times*). [An initial *the* in titles of periodicals is usually not italicized; the name of the city in titles of newspapers is sometimes not italicized.]

Occasionally quotation marks are used for titles of separate publications and of radio and television programs. The usual practice, however, is to reserve quotation marks for titles of the individual parts of longer works (such as short stories, essays, songs, short poems) and for titles of episodes of a radio or television series. See **16b**.

"Canada and Its Poetry" is the second essay in Northrop Frye's book *The Bush Garden*.

Exception: Neither italics nor quotation marks are used in references to the Bible and its parts or to legal documents.

The Bible begins with the Book of Genesis.
The Constitution Act, 1982, is the most important piece of legislation to be passed in Canada in many years.

10b

Foreign words and phrases are usually underlined (italicized) in the context of an English sentence.

Ceramic highrises look down over the tin shanties of some of Rome's 60 000 *baraccati*—the poor and displaced, many of them immigrants from the south, who live without water or electricity. —MACLEAN'S

Pauli studied the formulas carefully, frowned, looked up and said, "*Das ist falsch.*" —SCIENTIFIC AMERICAN

Genuine simplicity is always a technical *tour de force*.
—NORTHROP FRYE

Countless words borrowed from other languages are a part of the English vocabulary and are therefore not italicized:

amigo (Spanish)	dilemma (Greek)	karate (Japanese)
alumni (Latin)	disco (French)	pizza (Italian)

Dictionaries that label certain words and phrases as foreign are fairly dependable guides to the writer in doubt about the use of italics. The labels, however, are not always up-to-date, and writers must depend on their own judgment after considering current practices.

10c

Names of ships, aircraft, and spacecraft and titles of works of art are underlined (italicized).

Commander Marc Garneau has made many TV appearances since his historic flight in space aboard *Challenger 1*.

Alex Colville titled the sombre canvas *Tragic Landscape*.

Shelagh Delaney's *A Taste of Honey* was poorly received, as was Ibsen's *Wild Duck* and *Privates on Parade* (despite a delicious drag queen performance by Tom Kneebone).
—MATTHEW FRASER

10d

Words, letters, or figures spoken of as such or used as illustrations are usually underlined (italicized).

In no other language could a foreigner be tricked into pronouncing *manslaughter* as *man's laughter*. —MARIO PEI

The letters *qu* replaced *cw* in such words as *queen, quoth*, and *quick*. —CHARLES C. FRIES

The first *3* and the final *0* of the serial number are barely legible.

10e

Use underlining (italics) sparingly for emphasis. Do not underline the title of your own paper.

Writers occasionally use italics to show stress, especially in dialogue:

> Out comes the jeer-gun again: "Whose side are *you* on?"
>
> —GEORGE P. ELLIOTT

Sometimes italics are used to emphasize the meaning of a word, especially when the exact meaning might be missed without the italics.

> To *do* justice means to treat all men with respect and human dignity—Negroes, whites, cops, and all of creation.
>
> —DICK GREGORY

But overuse of italics for emphasis (like overuse of the exclamation point) defeats its own purpose. If you overuse italics to stress ideas, study Section **29**. Also try substituting more specific or more forceful words for those you are tempted to underline.

Note: Writers occasionally substitute all capitals for italics in order to gain emphasis.

> The symbol is NOT the thing symbolized; the word is NOT the thing; the map is NOT the territory it stands for.
>
> —S. I. HAYAKAWA

A title is not italicized when it stands at the head of a book or article. Accordingly, the title at the head of your paper (unless the title happens to be also that of a book) should not be underlined. See also **8b(4)**.

■ **Exercise** Underline all words in the following sentences that should be italicized.

1. While waiting for the dentist, I thumbed through an old issue of Saturday Night, and scanned an article on "The Education of Brian Mulroney."
2. On the Queen Mary from New York to London, Eleanor said she was so bored that she read all three books of Dante's The Divine Comedy!
3. Spelling errors involving the substitution of d for t in such words as partner and pretty reflect a tendency in pronunciation.
4. In Paris my young cousin attended a performance of Mozart's opera The Magic Flute, which she characterized in her letter as très magnifique.
5. Michelangelo's Battle of the Centaurs and his Madonna of the Steps are among the world's finest sculptures.

Abbreviations and Numbers

11

In ordinary writing use abbreviations only when appropriate, and spell out numbers that can be expressed simply.

Abbreviations and figures are desirable in tables, footnotes, and bibliographies (see the list on pages 441-43) and in some kinds of special or technical writing. In ordinary writing, however, only certain abbreviations are appropriate, and numbers that can be expressed in one word or two (like *forty-two* or *five hundred*) are usually spelled out.

All the principles in this section apply to ordinary writing, which of course includes the kind of writing often required in college and university.

Abbreviations

11a

In ordinary writing use the abbreviations *Mr., Mrs., Ms., Dr.,* and *St.* (for *Saint*). Spell out *doctor* and *saint* when not followed by proper names.

Mr. W.W. Kirtley, Mrs. Kay Gibbs, Dr. Bell, St. Francis
the young doctor, the early life of the saint

Note 1: The period is sometimes omitted after *Ms* (a shortened, combined form of *Miss* and *Mrs.*).

Caution: Do not use redundant titles: NOT Dr. E.T. Fulton, M.D. BUT Dr. E.T. Fulton OR E.T. Fulton, M.D. See also page 122.

Note 2: Such abbreviations as *Prof.*, *Sen.*, *Rev.*, *Gen.*, and *Capt.* may be used before full names or before initials and last names, but not before last names alone.

Sen. Anne Cools	Senator Cools
Capt. P.T. Gaines	Captain Gaines

11b

Spell out names of provinces, countries, months, days of the week, and units of measurement.

On Sunday, October 10, we passed through Guy, Alberta.
Slightly over a metre tall, Susan weighs forty-two kilograms.

Note: When using SI (*Système international d'unités*) metric units with numerals, SI abbreviations may be used. These are never pluralized and are written without a period. The standard reference on SI style is the *Canadian Metric Practice Guide* (Rexdale, Ontario: Canadian Standards Association, 1979).

The lake was 8.5 km long but only a few metres deep.

11c

In ordinary writing spell out *Street, Avenue, Road, Park, Mount, River, Company* and similar words used as an essential part of proper names.

College Street is south of Queen's Park.
The Ford Motor Company does not expect a strike soon.

Note: Avoid the use of & (for *and*) and such abbreviations as *Bros.* or *Inc.*, except in copying official titles.

11d

Do not abbreviate the names of courses of study and the words for *page, chapter,* and *volume.*

I registered for psychology, math, and chemistry. [Not an abbreviation, *math* is a clipped form of *mathematics*.]
The model sales chart is on page 46 of chapter 3.

Permissible Abbreviations

In addition to the abbreviations listed in **11a**, the following abbreviations and symbols are permissible and usually desirable.

1. *For titles and degrees after proper names*: Jr., Sr., Esq., D.D., Ph.D., M.A., M.D., C.P.A.

   Mr. Sam Jones, Sr.; Sam Jones, Jr.; Alice Jones, M.D.

2. *For words used with dates or figures*: A.D., B.C.; A.M. OR a.m., P.M. OR p.m.; no. OR No.; $

   The city of Jerusalem fell in 586 B.C. and again in A.D. 70.

   At 8 A.M. (OR 8:00 A.M.) he paid the manager $14.25. [Compare "At eight o'clock the next morning he paid the manager over fourteen dollars."]

3. *For such terms as* British Columbia *or* United States *used adjectivally, for the names of organizations or agencies and things usually referred to by their capitalized initials:* Washington D.C.; the B.C. government; NDP, NORAD, RCMP, CIA, WHO, JFK, CP Telecommunications, CRTC

5. *Certain common Latin expressions* (although the English term is usually spelled out in formal writing, as indicated in brackets below):

cf.	[compare]
e.g.	[for example]
et al.	[and others]
etc.	[and so forth]
i.e.	[that is]
vs. OR v.	[versus]

If you have any doubt about the spelling or capitalization of an abbreviation, consult a good dictionary.

Note: Periods are not used with acronyms such as CIDA or UNICEF. Before using an acronym, writers often spell out the phrase the acronym stands for to make the meaning of the acronym clear.

> Then there is the Canadian International Development Agency (CIDA). Consider CIDA's cost and value.

■ **Exercise 1** Strike out any form below that is not appropriate in formal writing. (In a few items two forms are appropriate.)

1. Ms. Janet Hogan; a dr. but not a saint
2. in the U.S. Senate; in the United States; in the U.S.
3. on TV; in B.C. and Alta.
4. on Barrington St.; on Barrington Street
5. Victoria, B.C.; Winnipeg, Man.
6. CBC; Canadian Broadcasting Corporation
7. on Aug. 15; on August 15
8. for Jr.; for John Evans, Jr.
9. e.g.; for example
10. before 6 A.M.; before six in the A.M.

Numbers

11e

Although usage varies, writers tend to spell out numbers that can be expressed in one word or two; they regularly use figures for other numbers.

after twenty-two years	after 124 years
only thirty dollars	only $29.99
five thousand voters	5261 voters
ten million people	10 402 317 people
over three litres	3.785 L

Special Usage Regarding Numbers

1. *Specific time of day*

   2 A.M. OR 2:00 A.M. OR two o'clock in the morning
   4:30 P.M. OR half-past four in the afternoon

2. *Dates*

   May 7, 1985 OR 7 May 1985 [NOT May 7th, 1985]
   May sixth OR the sixth of May OR May 6 OR May 6th
   the eighties OR the 1980's OR the 1980s
   the twentieth century
   in 1900 in 1981-1982 OR in 1981-82
   from 1980 to 1985 OR 1980-1985 OR 1980-85
   [NOT from 1980-1985, from 1980-85]

3. *Addresses*

   Apartment 1a, 633 Huron Street, Toronto, Ontario M5R 2R8
   Apt. 1a, 633 Huron St., Toronto, Ont. M5R 2R8

P.O. Box 14   Rural Route 2   Apartment 3   Room 19
16 Tenth Street 2 East 114 Street OR 2 East 114th Street

4. *Identification numbers*

   Channel 5   Highway 407   Henry VIII

5. *Pages and divisions of books and plays*

   page 30   chapter 6   part 4
   in act 3, scene 2 OR in Act III, Scene ii

6. *Decimals and percentages*

   a 2.5 average   12½ per cent   0.907 tonnes

7. *Numbers in series and statistics*

   two cows, five pigs, and forty-two chickens

   125 metres long, 20 metres wide, and 5 metres deep

   scores of 17 to 13 and 42 to 3 OR scores of 17-13 and 42-3

   The members voted 99 to 23 against it.

8. *Large round numbers*

   four billion dollars OR $4 billion OR $4 000 000 000
   [Figures are used for emphasis only.]

   12 500 000 OR 12.5 million

9. *Numbers beginning sentences*

   Six per cent of the students voted. [NOT 6 per cent of the students voted.]

10. *Repeated numbers (in legal or commercial writing)*

    The agent's fee will not exceed one hundred (100) dollars.
    OR
    The agent's fee will not exceed one hundred dollars ($100).

■ **Exercise 2** All items below are appropriate in formal writing. Using desirable abbreviations and figures, change each item to an acceptable shortened form.

EXAMPLES
Jude, the saint *St. Jude*
at two o'clock that afternoon *at 2* P.M.

1. on the fifteenth of June
2. Ernest Threadgill, a doctor
3. thirty million dollars
4. Louise Perreault, a chartered accountant
5. the United Nations
6. one o'clock in the afternoon
7. by the first of December, 1985
8. at the bottom of the fifteenth page
9. Association of Canadian Television and Radio Artists
10. four hundred years before Christ
11. in the second scene of the first act
12. a five-year plan (from 1985 to 1990)

PUNCTUATION

The Comma 12

Superfluous Commas 13

The Semicolon 14

The Apostrophe 15

Quotation Marks 16

The Period and Other Marks 17

The Comma

12

Use the comma (which ordinarily indicates a pause and a variation in voice pitch) where it is required by the structure of the sentence.

Just as pauses and variations in voice pitch help to convey the meaning of spoken sentences, commas help to clarify the meaning of written sentences.

> When the lightning struck, James Harvey fainted.
> When the lightning struck James, Harvey fainted.

The sound of a sentence can serve as a guide in using commas.

But many times sound is not a dependable guide. The use of the comma is primarily determined by the structure of the sentence. If you understand this structure (see Section **1**), you can learn to apply the basic principles governing comma usage. The following rules cover the usual practices of the best modern writers.

Commas—

a precede the co-ordinating conjunctions *and, but, or, nor, for* and the connectives *so* and *yet* between main clauses;
b follow certain introductory elements;

c separate items in a series (including co-ordinate adjectives);
d set off non-restrictive, parenthetical, and miscellaneous elements.

Between Main Clauses

12a

Use a comma before *and, but, or, nor, for, so,* and *yet* when they link main clauses. See also **1e.**

Study the sentence structure of the examples that follow the pattern below.

MAIN CLAUSE,	{ *and* / *but* / *or* / *nor* / *for* / *so* / *yet* }	MAIN CLAUSE.

> I am not one of those who thank God I am a Nova Scotian merely, for I am a Canadian as well. —JOSEPH HOWE
>
> Every man's religion is his own, and nobody else's business. —T.C. HALIBURTON
>
> Well, there's no explaining tastes, and ugliness is pretty nowadays. —MARGARET LAWRENCE
>
> No one watches the performance, for everybody is taking part. —JAN KOTT
>
> They are hopeless and humble, so he loves them. —E.M. FORSTER

The pattern and examples illustrate the punctuation of a compound sentence. The rule also applies to co-ordinating conjunctions that link the main clauses of a compound-complex sentence (that is, a sentence with at least two main clauses and one subordinate clause):

Men who are engaged in a daily struggle for survival do not think of old age, for they do not expect to see it.
—JOHN KENNETH GALBRAITH

Linking sentences with *nor* involves the omission of *not* as well as a shift in word order:

FROM A woman cannot hope to find a man who is free of sexist attitudes. She cannot make a man give up his privileges by arguing.

TO A woman cannot hope to find a man who is free of sexist attitudes, *nor* can she make a man give up his privileges by arguing. —ELLEN WILLIS

Exceptions to 12a

1. *Omission of the comma*

The comma may be omitted when there is no possibility of confusing the reader or when the comma is not needed to make reading easier.

The next night the wind shifted and the thaw began.
—RACHEL CARSON

Either the answer was true or it was false.

2. *Substitution of the semicolon or dash*

The semicolon or the dash may be substituted for the comma, especially when the main clauses reveal a striking contrast or have internal punctuation.

Historically, French Canadians have not really believed in democracy for themselves; and English Canadians have not really wanted it for others. —PIERRE ELLIOTT TRUDEAU

Hope springs eternal—but somehow or other troubles never stay long away. —ARTHUR MEIGHEN

A semicolon is often preferred when one of the main clauses contains commas. Sharply dividing the main clauses contributes to readability. See also **14a**.

Everyone there made allowances, of course; but being young is no excuse.

Note: When linking main clauses with co-ordinating conjunctions, be aware of the various meanings of these connectives as you relate the clauses:

> **and**—in addition, also, moreover, besides
>
> **but** OR **yet**—nevertheless, however, still
>
> **for**—because, seeing that, since
>
> **or**—as an alternative, otherwise
>
> **nor**—and not, or not, not either [used after a negative]
>
> **so**—therefore, as a result

When in doubt about the meaning of any connective, consult the dictionary. See also **3b** and **31c(4)**.

■ **Exercise 1** Following the punctuation pattern of **12a**, link the sentences in the items below with an appropriate *and, but, or, nor, for, so,* or *yet.*

> EXAMPLE
> We cannot win the battle. We cannot afford to lose it.
> *We cannot win the battle*, *nor can we afford to lose it.*

1. A crisis strikes. Another fact-finding Royal Commission is born.
2. The new leash law did not put all dogs behind bars. It did not make the streets safe for cats.
3. Motorists may admit their guilt and pay a fine immediately. They may choose to appear in court within thirty days and plead not guilty.
4. They decided not to take a vacation. They needed the money to remodel their kitchen.
5. The band leader can sing and dance and whistle. She cannot play the trombone.

■ **Exercise 2** Follow rule **12a** as you insert commas before connectives linking main clauses in the sentences below. (Remember that not all co-ordinating conjunctions link main clauses and that *but, for, so,* and *yet* do not always function as co-ordinating conjunctions.)

1. The students had finished taking the various tests and answering the long questionnaires and they had gone to lunch.
2. There are now special shoes for someone to fill for Bob has resigned and is going to business school.
3. I decided to withdraw from that eight-o'clock class so that I could sleep later but I plan to enroll again for the same class in January.
4. We had seen the stage play and the movie and the University Players' performance was the best of all.
5. Everyone in our group was invited to the party but Gary and Irene decided to go to the hockey game.

After Introductory Elements

12b

Use a comma after introductory elements such as adverb clauses, long phrases, transitional expressions, interjections, and an introductory *yes* or *no*.

(1) Introductory adverb clauses

Introductory adverb clauses begin with such subordinators as *after, although, as, as far as, as long as, as soon as, because, before, if, inasmuch as, insofar as, lest, no matter how, now that, once, provided, since, supposing, though, unless, until, when, whenever, where, wherever, whether or not, while.*

ADVERB CLAUSE, MAIN CLAUSE.

> If men could get pregnant**,** abortion would be a sacrament.
> —LAURA SABIA

> Where modern science has achieved its mastery**,** there is no place for local cultures. —GEORGE P. GRANT

(2) Long introductory phrases

Except for an overalled man with a bandage around his head and one ear, the waiting room was empty. —W.O. MITCHELL

In Canada with its hostile winters and its total dependence on transportation for survival, the energy crisis of the early seventies was not punitive but prophetic. —PELHAM DAVIS

Note 1: The comma may be omitted after an introductory adverb clause and a long introductory phrase if the omission does not make for difficult reading.

As soon as I saw the elephant I knew with perfect certainty that I ought not to shoot him. —GEORGE ORWELL

After months of listening for some meager clue he suddenly began to talk in torrents. —ARTHUR L. KOPIT

When we talk to people we always mean something quite different from what we say. —ANTHONY BURGESS

Note 2: When the adverb clause *follows* the main clause, there is usually no pause and no need for a comma.

They squatted down as if they belonged to the land. —FARLEY MOWAT

He stands amazed while she serenely twists her legs into the lotus position. —JOHN UPDIKE

Adverb clauses in this position, however, may be preceded by a comma if they are loosely connected with the rest of the sentence, especially if the subordinating conjunction seems equivalent to a co-ordinating conjunction.

Marine life is concentrated in about 4 per cent of the ocean's total body of water, whereas roughly 96 per cent is just about as poor in life as is a desert ashore. —THOR HEYERDAHL

Note 3: Introductory phrases, even though short, and introductory adverb clauses must sometimes be followed by a comma to prevent misreading. See also **12e**.

> As he spoke, a few heavy preliminary drops were already coming down. —MARGARET ATWOOD

> As we would expect, Freud's self-evaluation would hardly be agreed upon by everyone. —ERNEST BECKER

Note 4: Short introductory prepositional phrases, except when they are distinctly parenthetical expressions (such as *in fact* or *for example*), are usually not followed by a comma.

> Through the Middle Ages the Church was not an agent of oppression. —RICHARD N. GOODWIN

(3) Introductory transitional expressions, interjections, and an introductory *yes* or *no*.

Interjections, transitional expressions (such as *for example, in fact, on the other hand, in the second place*), and an introductory *yes* or *no* are generally considered parenthetical: see **12d(3)**. When used as introductory elements, they are ordinarily followed by commas:

> In fact, the most obvious fact about the rebellion is how strong and immediate the resistance to it was.
> —J.M.S. CARELESS

> Well, I could, and did, and that is the way I am made.
> —LOVAT DICKSON

■ **Exercise 3** In each of the following sentences, find the main clause and identify the preceding element as an adverb clause or as a phrase. Then determine whether or not to use a comma after the introductory element.

[1] In order to pay his way through university George worked at night in an iron foundry. [2] During this time he became acquainted with all the company's operations. [3] After four years of evaluating George's work the foundry owner offered George a position as manager. [4] Although George had planned to attend medical school and become a psychiatrist he found now that the kind of work he had been doing had a far greater appeal for him. [5] In fact he accepted the offer without hesitation. [6] When asked later if he thought he had made the right decision George smiled and nodded.

Between Items in a Series

12c

Use commas to separate items in a series (including co-ordinate adjectives).

The punctuation of a series depends on its form:

> The air was *raw*, *dank*, *gray*. [*a*, *b*, *c*]
> The air was *raw*, *dank*, and *gray*. [*a*, *b*, and *c*]
> The air was *raw* and *dank* and *gray*. [*a* and *b* and *c*]

(1) Words, phrases, and clauses in a series

> He should be large, combative, swift, cool, and crafty.
> —IRWIN SHAW

> Life at the top is financially rewarding, spiritually draining, physically exhausting, and short. —PETER C. NEWMAN

> What the camel is to desert tribes, what the horse is to the Arab, what the ship is to the colonizing Briton, what all modern means of locomotion are to the civilized world today, that the canoe was to the Indian. —WILLIAM WOOD

The comma before the conjunction may be omitted in the series *a, b, and c* if there is no danger of misreading:

> The only safe, legal way to reproduce, adapt or translate copyright material is to get written permission from the copyright holder. —CANADIAN WRITER'S GUIDE

(2) Co-ordinate adjectives

Use a comma between co-ordinate adjectives not linked by a co-ordinating conjunction:

> It is a waiting, silent, limp room. —EUDORA WELTY

> She was a frowsy, middle-aged woman with wispy, drab-brown hair. She sat behind a long wooden table on a high platform overlooking her disciples with her narrow, piercing eyes. —EVELYN KOSSOFF

Exception to 12c and a variation

If the items in a series contain internal punctuation, semicolons are used instead of commas for clarity: see **14b**. Occasionally the semicolon replaces the comma to mark a sharp separation of the items in a series, especially in a series of main clauses:

> Among scholars there are discoverers; there are critics; and there are teachers. —GILBERT HIGHET

■ **Exercise 4** Using commas as needed, supply co-ordinate adjectives to modify any six of the following twelve word groups.

EXAMPLE
metric system *the familiar, sensible metric system*

1. apple pie
2. social climbers
3. electronic music
4. pop art
5. minimum wage
6. traveller's cheques
7. Canada goose
8. rhetorical question
9. apartment buildings
10. major oil companies
11. blue cheese
12. secondary school

With Parenthetical and Miscellaneous Elements

12d

Use commas to set off non-restrictive clauses and phrases and other parenthetical and miscellaneous elements, such as transitional expressions, items in dates, words used in direct address, and so on. Restrictive clauses and phrases are not set off by commas.

To set off a word or a word group with commas, use two commas unless the element is placed at the beginning of the sentence or at the end:

> We need conscription, not only of bodies but of wealth, to strike a blow at war-lordism. —JOSEPH ATKINSON
>
> Socially, death is as taboo as Victorian sex. —OSBORN SEGERBERGER, JR.
>
> Just take a look around El Barrio, the section where so many Puerto Ricans live. —OSCAR LEWIS

Caution: When two commas are needed to set off an element, do not forget one of the commas:

CONFUSING	An experienced driver generally speaking, does not fear the open road.
CLEAR	An experienced driver, generally speaking, does not fear the open road.

(1) Non-restrictive clauses and phrases are set off by commas. Restrictive clauses and phrases are not set off.

Adjective clauses and phrases are classified as non-restrictive (parenthetical) or restrictive (not parenthetical).

NON-RESTRICTIVE CLAUSES AND PHRASES

Non-restrictive clauses and phrases are not essential to the meaning of the main clause and may be omitted. Such modifiers are parenthetical and are set off by commas.

> There are many Pygmalion-style directors**, who like to discover new people (even amateurs) and mould them into actors**. —ABE BURROWS
>
> [The *who* clause does not restrict or limit the meaning of directors (already identified) but does provide a parenthetical explanation of what is meant by *Pygmalion-style*.]
>
> Solar energy**, which is safe, renewable, environmentally benign,** has serious disadvantages, too. —STEPHEN CHAPMAN
>
> [The *which* clause is informative but non-essential.]
>
> Huge cranes**, delicate as a dinosaur's head,** moved over the street. —BELVA PLAIN
>
> [Compare "Huge cranes, *which looked as* delicate as a dinosaur's head, moved over the street."]
>
> He tossed the letter aside and pulled his apple pie**, topped with a melting scoop of vanilla ice cream,** toward him. —TRUMAN CAPOTE
>
> [The parenthetical phrase describes but does not identify the pie.]
>
> Claud got up**, groaning and growling,** and limped off. —FLANNERY O'CONNOR
>
> [Compare "Claud got up (*he was* groaning and growling) and limped off."]

RESTRICTIVE CLAUSES AND PHRASES

Restrictive clauses and phrases follow and limit the words they modify. They are essential to the meaning of the main clause and are not set off by commas.

> The Tories **who opposed responsible government** hurled a stream of insult and abuse at the Reform leaders. —RAMSAY COOK
>
> [The *who* clause is essential to the meaning of the sentence; not all Tories acted this way, but only those who were opposed to responsible government.]

Medical science has placed in their hands an instrument **that can determine the whole future of heredity**. —TORONTO LIFE

[An adjective clause beginning with *that* is retrictive.]

The poor live on a diet **heavy in bread**. —NOEL GRAVE
[The phrase identifies the kind of diet.]

The two things **most universally desired** are power and admiration. —BERTRAND RUSSELL
[The essential phrase can be expanded to a restrictive clause: "*that* (OR *which*) *are* most universally desired."]

Note: Although some writers prefer to use the connective *that* at the beginning of restrictive clauses, *which* is also acceptable.

Sometimes a clause or phrase may be either non-restrictive or restrictive. The writer signifies the meaning by using or by omitting commas:

NON-RESTRICTIVE He spent hours nursing the Indian guides, **who were sick with malaria**. [He cared for all the Indian guides. They were all sick with malaria.]

RESTRICTIVE He spent hours nursing the Indian guides **who were sick with malaria**. [Some of the Indian guides were sick with malaria. He cared only for the sick ones.]

■ **Exercise 5** Use commas to set off non-restrictive clauses and phrases in the following sentences. Put a checkmark after any sentence that needs no further punctuation.

1. I will interview Betty Lee who manages the bank.
2. I will interview the Betty Lee who manages the bank.
3. Freshmen who make a high verbal score are exempt from that English course.
4. The graduates of Clayton High School who always make a high verbal score are exempt from that English course.
5. My father always worrying about money wanted me to get a job.
6. The coach chewing gum and licking his fingers is George.
7. Venice which he visited next was torn by rival factions.
8. Venice is a city he likes to visit.

9. Red snapper fried in butter is better than baked red snapper.
10. The smoke that filled the room is now gone.

(2) Use commas to set off non-restrictive appositives, contrasted elements, geographical names, and most items in dates and addresses.

NON-RESTRICTIVE APPOSITIVES

But inertia**, the great minimizer,** provided them with the usual excuses. —MARY McCARTHY

The most visible victims of pollution, fish are only a link in a chain from microscopic life to man.
—GEORGE GOODMAN

[The appositive precedes rather than follows *fish*.]

The peaks float in the sky**, fantastic pyramids of flame**.
—ARTHUR C. CLARKE

[Notice that the appositive could be shifted to the beginning of the sentence.]

Was the letter from Frances Evans**, Ph.D.,** or from F.H. Evans**, M.D.**? [Abbreviations after names are treated like non-restrictive appositives.]

Note: Commas do not set off restrictive appositives.

His son *James* is sick. [*James*, not his son William]
The word *malapropism* is derived from Sheridan's *The Rivals*.
Do you refer to Samuel Butler *the poet* or to Samuel Butler *the novelist*?

CONTRASTED ELEMENTS

Racing is supposed to be a test of skill**, not a dice game with death**. —SONNY KLEINFIELD

His phrases dribbled off**, but not his memories**.
—JAMES A. MICHENER

The goal was achievement**, not adjustment**; the young were taught to work**, not to socialize**. —ALLEN WHEELIS
[Only one comma sets off an element before a semicolon.]

Note: Usage is divided regarding the placement of a comma before *but* in such structures as the following:

> Other citizens who disagree with me base their disagreement, not on facts different from the ones I know, but on a different set of values. —RENÉ DUBOS

> But I think I should prefer to go out laughing, not at death itself but at something irrelevantly funny enough to make me forget it. —JOSEPH WOOD KRUTCH

GEOGRAPHICAL NAMES, ITEMS IN DATES AND ADDRESSES

Sarajevo, Yugoslavia, was the site of the 1984 Winter Olympics.

The letter was addressed to Mr. R.K. Haines, Topsail, Newfoundland A0A 3Y0. [The postal code is not separated by a comma from the name of the province.]

Leslie applied for the job in October, 1984, and accepted it on Friday, March 8, 1985. OR

Leslie applied for the job in October 1984 and accepted it on Friday, 8 March 1985.
[Note that commas may be omitted when the day of the month is not given or when the day of the month precedes rather than follows the month.]

■ **Exercise 6** Combine each pair of sentences by reducing the second sentence to an appositive or to a contrasted element set off by commas. Insert commas where needed to set off items in dates or addresses.

EXAMPLES

Michael Roger was born on January 7 1982 in Corner Brook. He is my only son.

Michael Roger, my only son, was born on January 7, 1982, in Corner Brook.

Carla's social insurance number is 443 116 417. It is not 441 611 714.

Carla's social insurance number is 443 116 417, not 441 611 714.

1. Termites really are insects. Termites are distant cousins of roaches.
2. Those are pill bugs. They are not insects.
3. On April 1 1976 his divorced wife married his lawyer. His lawyer was Bill Wynne.
4. The publisher's address is 450 King Street West Toronto Ontario M5S 1R7. It is not 490 King Street West.
5. We moved to Banff Alberta on 30 September 1983. Alberta is one of the popular skiing provinces.

(3) Use commas to set off parenthetical elements.

The term *parenthetical* is correctly applied to all nonrestrictive elements discussed under **12d**. But it may also be applied to such transitional expressions as *however, first of all, in fact, to summarize*, or *that is* and to such expressions as *I believe* or *experts argue* (often called interrupters). Expressions that come at the beginning of a sentence are treated by both **12b** and **12d**.

PARENTHETICAL ELEMENTS

Finally, banks devise means of protecting the money.
—MALCOLM BRADBURY

Language**, then,** sets the tone of our society.
—EDWIN NEWMAN

Self-admissions or boasts like that**, I understand,** have special weight as testimony. —PAUL A. SAMUELSON

Well, global peace may be a dream. [mild interjection]

Animal lovers, write letters of protest. [direct address]

Science**, at its best,** is unifying. —STEPHEN JAY GOULD [parenthetical phrase]

No, the "characters" are vanishing in Velva**, just as they are vanishing in our cities**. —ERIC SEVAREID [introductory *no* and a parenthetical clause]

The Age of Television has dawned in China**, a generation later than in the West**. —LINDA MATHEWS [appended element]

He was thumping at a book**, his voice growing louder and louder**. —JOYCE CAROL OATES [absolute phrase]

Note 1: Expressions such as *also, too, of course, perhaps, at least, therefore,* and *likewise*, when they cause little or no pause in reading, are frequently not set off by commas.

"Involvement" is **perhaps** the key word to all that is happening in movies today. —ARTHUR KNIGHT

A great many people **therefore** think of me as being so vigorously concerned with technology that I lack humanist considerations. —R. BUCKMINSTER FULLER

Note 2: With direct quotations, such expressions as *he said, she asked, I replied,* and *we shouted* are set off by commas. See also **16a(4)**.

He said**,** "My opinion is really different."
"My opinion**,**" he said**,** "is really different."
"My opinion is really different**,**" he said.

12e

Occasionally a comma, although not called for by any of the major principles already discussed, may be needed to prevent misreading.

Use **12e** sparingly to justify your commas. In a general sense, nearly all commas are used to prevent misreading or to make reading easier. Your mastery of the comma will come through application of the more specific major principles (**a, b, c, d**) to the structure of your sentences.

CONFUSING Those who can pay and forego consumption of other essential goods.

BETTER Those who can**,** pay and forego consumption of other essential goods. —ERIK P. ECKHOLM

CONFUSING Those who can pay and forego consumption of other essential goods.

BETTER Those who can, pay and forego consumption of other essential goods. —ERIK P. ECKHOLM

■ **Exercise 7** All commas in the following paragraphs are correctly used. Explain the reason for each comma by referring to one of the principles discussed in this section (**12a, 12b, 12c,** or **12d**).

[1] Conflicts would not be restricted to conventional warfare. [2] True, we do have a treaty forbidding the use of "weapons of mass destruction" in outer space. [3] However, the treaty does not define "weapons of mass destruction," and although it does require inspection of all installations on celestial bodies, it says nothing about stations or space colonies in orbit. [4] In any case, the moral force of this treaty, all by itself, is hardly likely to deter the greedy ones, the bullies, the maniacs, the suicidal types, or the various champions of human "progress," "liberation," or "rejuvenation."

[5] Every colony, as well as the Earth itself, would be in danger from outer space at all times. [6] No matter how many problems we may have today, we can still look at the stars with fair assurance that they constitute no immediate threat to us. [7] But with millions of space colonies roaming the solar system, life could degenerate into a series of preparations for and recoveries from attacks—an updated version of the life-style of centuries past when raids of the Normans, Berbers and other seafaring people depopulated Europe's coastline—except that this time the weaponry would be a great deal more destructive.

—PAUL L. CSONKA, "Space Colonization: An Invitation to Disaster?"

■ **Exercise 8** Insert commas where needed in the following sentences (selected and adapted from the works of modern writers). Be prepared to explain the reason for each comma used. Also be prepared to point out where optional commas might be placed as a matter of stylistic preference.

1. Police action in arresting drunks will never prevent drunkenness nor can it cure an alcoholic. —RAMSEY CLARK
2. Fifty years ago *Hazel Beverly Marian Frances* and *Shirley* were all perfectly acceptable boys' names. —ALLEEN PACE NILSEN
3. Thus the ocean floors far from being the oldest features on earth were relatively young. —ALLISON R. PALMER
4. Even today in Communist Yugoslavia they assert their difference clinging ostentatiously to the Roman Catholic religion. —SATURDAY NIGHT
5. Hooper said "Look Chief you can't go off half-cocked looking for vengeance against a fish. That shark isn't evil." —PETER BENCHLEY
6. Thus expressed we need not offer love on command to people who are truly unlovable; we need not love others as much as ourselves which would be contrary to the laws of biology. —HANS SELYE
7. The crowd's answer was polite almost dainty applause the kind that has a lot of coughing at the end instead of a release of spirit. —ANTHONY TUTTLE
8. We do not always communicate with words. For instance when we are angry we can communicate our feelings physically—by hitting somebody. —AUSTIN REPATH
9. The earth breathes in a certain sense. —LEWIS THOMAS
10. December is the most violent month the time of murder robbery assault suicide and Christmas. —EARL SHORRIS
11. They can stand just so much eh Doctor? —E. B. WHITE
12. The temptation in describing a film like this one is to string together several adjectives—witless ugly brutal insensate stupid. —TIME
13. He disliked being categorized no matter what the category. —IRWIN SHAW
14. "I had to see where J.R. lived" said Mick Pattemore his accent revealing not Sweetwater Texas but Somerset England. —JANE HALL
15. Theirs has been described as a love/hate relationship smooth and pliable when they are of a mind and roof-shaking when they are not. —JOY G. SPIEGEL

■ **Exercise 9** For humorous effect, the writer of the following paragraph deliberately omits commas that can be justified by rules **12a, b,** or **d**. Be prepared for a discussion of the paragraph. Where could commas be inserted to contribute to ease in reading?

> The commas are the most useful and usable of all the stops. It is highly important to put them in place as you go along. If you try to come back after doing a paragraph and stick them in the various spots that tempt you you will discover that they tend to swarm like minnows into all sorts of crevices whose existence you hadn't realized and before you know it the whole long sentence becomes immobilized and lashed up squirming in commas. Better to use them sparingly, and with affection, precisely when the need for each one arises, nicely, by itself.
>
> —LEWIS THOMAS, *The Medusa and the Snail*

Superfluous Commas

13

Do not use superfluous commas.

Unnecessary or misplaced commas are false or awkward signals that may confuse the reader. If you tend to use too many commas, remember that although the comma ordinarily signals a pause, not every pause calls for a comma. As you read each sentence in the following paragraph aloud, you may pause naturally at places other than those marked by a period, but no commas are necessary.

> Springboard divers routinely execute manoeuvres in which their body rotates in space. The basic manoeuvres are the somersault and the twist. In the somersault the body rotates head over heels as if the athlete were rotating about an axis extending from his left side to his right side through his waist. In the twist the body spins or pirouettes in midair as if the athlete were rotating about an axis extending from his head to his toes.
>
> —CLIFF FROHLICH, "The Physics of Somersaulting and Twisting"

To avoid using unnecessary commas, first review Section **12** and then study and observe the following rules.

13a

Do not use a comma to separate the subject from its verb or the verb from its object.

The commas circled below should be omitted:

> Even people with unlisted telephone numbers(,) receive crank calls.
> [needless separation of subject and verb]
>
> The man said(,) that the old tires were guaranteed.
> [needless separation of verb and object (a noun clause)]

13b

Do not misuse a comma before or after a co-ordinating conjunction. See **12a.**

The commas circled below should be omitted:

> The facts were selected(,) and organized with care.
>
> The authorities debunked UFO sightings, but(,) millions of people didn't listen.

13c

Do not use commas to set off words and short phrases (especially introductory ones) that are not parenthetical or that are very slightly so.

The commas circled below should be omitted:

> E.J. Pratt was born(,) in Newfoundland(,) in 1883.
>
> Maybe(,) the battery cables needed cleaning.

13d

Do not use commas to set off restrictive (necessary) clauses, restrictive phrases, and restrictive appositives.

The commas circled below should be omitted:

> Everyone(,) who smokes cigarettes(,) risks losing about ten years of life. [restrictive clause: see **12d(1)**]

For years she has not eaten anything(,) seasoned with onions or garlic. [restrictive phrase: see **12d(1)**]

The word(,) *nope*(,) is an interesting substitute for *no*. [restrictive appositive: see **12d(2)**]

13e

Do not use a comma before the first item or after the last item of a series (including a series of co-ordinate adjectives).

The commas circled below should be omitted:

Field trips were required in a few courses, such as(,) botany, geology, and sociology.

The company hires talented, smart, ambitious(,) women.

■ **Exercise 1** Study the structure of the sentence below; then answer the question that follows by giving a specific rule number (such as **13a, 13d**) for each item. Be prepared to explain your answers in class.

> Now when you say "newly rich" you picture a middle-aged and corpulent man who has a tendency to remove his collar at formal dinners and is in perpetual hot water with his ambitious wife and her titled friends. —F. SCOTT FITZGERALD

Why is there no comma after (1) *Now,* (2) *say,* (3) *middle-aged,* (4) *man,* (5) *collar,* (6) *dinners,* or (7) *wife*?

■ **Exercise 2** Change the structure and the punctuation of the following sentences according to the pattern of the examples.

EXAMPLE

A motorcyclist saw our flashing lights**,** and he stopped to offer aid. [an appropriate comma: see **12a**]

A motorcyclist saw our flashing lights and stopped to offer aid. [second main clause reduced to a part of compound predicate—comma no longer needed]

1. The hail stripped leaves from trees, and it pounded early gardens.
2. Some science fiction presents newly discovered facts, and it predicts the future accurately.
3. Rob likes the work, and he may make a career of it.

EXAMPLE

If any students destroyed public property**,** they were expelled. [an appropriate comma: see **12b**]

Any students who destroyed public property were expelled. [introductory adverb clause converted to restrictive clause—comma no longer needed]

4. When people lead rather than demand, they often get good results.
5. If a boy is willing to work, he can get a job here.

■ **Exercise 3** In the following paragraph some of the commas are needed and some are superfluous. Circle all unnecessary commas. Be prepared to explain (see Section **12**) each comma that you allow to stand.

[1] There are, at least, three kinds of fishermen. [2] First, is the boat owner. [3] He usually gets up at 4 a.m., grabs a thermos of coffee, picks up his favourite, fishing buddy, and goes to the exact spot, where the trout or bass are striking. [4] Fishing for a certain kind of fish, is his specialty, and he, generally, gets exactly the kind he goes after. [5] Next is the person, who fishes with friends on a crowded pier, jetty, or barge. [6] He expects the fish to come to him, and is happy to catch anything, fit to eat, such as, perch or carp. [7] The third type is the loner, the one who fishes in some out-of-the-way place on the bank, by himself. [8] After he anchors one, great big, wad of bait on his hook, he throws his line out, and props up his pole, so that he doesn't have to hold it. [9] Then, he leans back, watches the cloud formations, or lazily examines a leaf or flower. [10] He, sometimes, dozes. [11] Also, he daydreams. [12] Lounging there with a kind of half smile on his face, he enjoys his solitude. [13] His fishing pole is merely an excuse for being there. [14] He forgets to watch his line, and, to rebait his hook.

The Semicolon

14

Use the semicolon (a) between main clauses not linked by *and, but, or, nor, for, so,* or *yet* and (b) between co-ordinate elements containing commas. Do not use the semicolon between parts of unequal grammatical rank.

Read aloud the following sentences; notice the way your voice reflects the differences in punctuation:

> The letters did not arrive until Thursday, although I had mailed them early Monday morning.
> The letters did not arrive until Thursday; however, I had mailed them early Monday morning.

A stronger mark of punctuation than the comma, the semicolon is sometimes called a weak period.

If you can distinguish between main and subordinate clauses and between phrases and clauses (see **1d** and **1e**), you should have little trouble using the semicolon. As you study the rules in this section, notice that the semicolon is used *only* between closely related co-ordinate elements.

14a

Use the semicolon between two main clauses not linked by *and, but, or, nor, for, so, yet.* See also **12a**.

MAIN CLAUSES LINKED WITHOUT A CONNECTIVE

MAIN CLAUSE; MAIN CLAUSE.

> He liked her very much; of that she was quite sure; she could always tell. —MORLEY CALLAGHAN
>
> A community cannot stand still; it must develop or decline. —CLINTON ROSSITER
>
> Landscapes in poems are often interior landscapes; they are maps of a state of mind. —MARGARET ATWOOD

Observe that each main clause above could be written as a separate sentence: see also **1d**, page 28.

Rule **14a** also applies in compound-complex sentences:

> A close friend of mine lived on a farm; I assumed he would always be there. —WILLIAM MUELLER [two main clauses and one subordinate clause]
>
> Curing is a process in which harvested tobacco is slowly dried; it removes excess starch and permits other chemical reactions, which lead to a milder smoke. —WILLIAM BENNETT [two main clauses and two subordinate clauses]

MAIN CLAUSES LINKED BY ADVERBIALS See also **3b**.

Be sure to use a semicolon before conjunctive adverbs (*however, therefore, then*, and so on) and transitional phrases (*for example, on the contrary*, and so on) when these adverbial connectives are placed between main clauses. See the lists on page 45.

MAIN CLAUSE;	{conjunctive adverb or transitional phrase}	**(,) MAIN CLAUSE.**

In the pattern the comma (in parentheses) is generally omitted after an adverbial connective when the connective is not considered parenthetical or when the comma is not needed to prevent misreading or to mark intonation. See also **12d(3)**.

> Many farms do not require a labour input every day; hence commuting could be lessened. —MARION CLAWSON

> We no longer confide in each other; in fact, there are many things I could not mention to her. —SAUL BELLOW

> They have not yet been moulded by experience; therefore, the immediate moment makes a great impression on them because that is all they know. —WILLIAM J. HARRIS

Caution: Do not overwork the semicolon. Often it is better to revise compound sentences according to the principles of subordination: see Section **24** and also **14c**.

Exceptions to 14a

1. A semicolon (instead of the usual comma) may precede *and, but, or, nor, for, so*, and *yet* when a main clause has internal commas or when the writer wishes to make a sharp division of the two main clauses. See also **12a**, page 130.

> I was, if anything, disintegrated; and I was puzzled. —WILLIAM GOLDING

> Food is obviously necessary for survival; so you might pay more for it than you would for almost anything else. —HARRY BROWNE

> Profound experiences stimulate thought; but such thoughts do not look very adequate on paper. —WALTER KAUFMANN

2. Sometimes a comma (instead of the usual semicolon) separates short main clauses like those below: see also **3a**, page 43.

   He isn't funny, he isn't romantic, he is neither urbane nor fancy free. —PHILIP TERIGAN

3. A colon (instead of the usual semicolon) appears between main clauses when the second main clause explains or amplifies the first. See also **17d**, page 178.

   This type of construction is like building a house of cards or of children's blocks: slabs of stone are set upright (orthostats) and other slabs are laid across the uprights as capstones.
   —GLYN DANIEL

■ **Exercise 1** Change each of the following items to conform to pattern **14a**, as shown in the examples below:

EXAMPLES

An engagement is not a marriage. Nor is a family quarrel a broken home.

An engagement is not a marriage; *a family quarrel is not a broken home.*

All members of my family save things they will never use. My sister, for example, saves old calendars and bent or rusty nails.

All members of my family save things they will never use; *for example, my sister saves old calendars and bent or rusty nails.*

1. The scientists did not accept this theory. Nor did they ridicule it.
2. Carol was hired as a design assistant. But in two years she was promoted to fashion designer.
3. He took a course in the art of self-defence. But later, during a class demonstration, he broke his wrist.
4. Tony himself cut and polished the turquoise. And it is a beauty.
5. The team kept on losing. And, as a result, the morale of the whole school was low.

14b

Use the semicolon to separate a series of items which themselves contain commas.

This use of the semicolon instead of the comma in a series is for clarity. The semicolon sharply separates the items so that the reader can distinguish the main divisions of the series at a glance.

> A board is elected or appointed from each of the three general categories of citizens: for example, a judge or lawyer of good repute; a professor of art, literature, or one of the humanities; and a social worker, psychologist, or clergyman.
>
> —GEORGE P. ELLIOTT

Note: Occasionally, for emphasis, semicolons may divide a series of items that do not contain internal punctuation—especially a series of main clauses.

> What results from this in the mind of the student? Facts, perhaps; ideas; information; the techniques of the present; the traditions of the past. —NORTHROP FRYE

■ **Exercise 2** Combine the following sentences by deleting words and using a series of items separated by semicolons. Use the colon to introduce each series, as in the example.

EXAMPLE

On stage all set to fight were three debaters. One was Eric Dunn, a zero-population advocate. Another was Susan Miles, a theologian. And the third was K.C. Osborn, president of the first-year committee.

On stage all set to fight were three debaters: Eric Dunn, a zero-population advocate; *Susan Miles, a theologian*; *and K.C. Osborn, president of the first-year committee.*

1. On the talk show were three guests. One was T.J. Ott, a psychic. Another was Charles Shelton, a local ufologist. And the third was Abbish Ludah, a guru.
2. We sold everything at our benefit flea market. We sold many dishes and vases, old and cracked. We also sold fishing gear, garden tools, and half-used tubes of lipstick.

14c

Do not use a semicolon between parts of unequal grammatical rank, such as a clause and a phrase or a main clause and a subordinate clause.

NOT Along came Harvey; the residence clown.
BUT Along came Harvey, the residence clown. [a parenthetical appositive phrase—see **12d(2)**]

NOT We took a detour; the reason being that the bridge was under construction.
BUT We took a detour, the reason being that the bridge was under construction. [a parenthetical phrase, an absolute—see **12d(3)**]

NOT Lucy has three topics of conversation; her courses, her career, and her travels.
BUT Lucy has three topics of conversation: her courses, her career, and her travels. [series—see **17d(1)**]

NOT If this report is true; then we should act now.
BUT If this report is true, then we should act now. [introductory adverb clause—see **12b**]

NOT We heard about the final decision; which really surprised us.
BUT We heard about the final decision, which really surprised us. [non-restrictive clause—see **12d(1)**]

NOT The truck needed a valve job; although it would still run.
BUT The truck needed a valve job, although it would still run. [parenthetical clause—see note 2 on page 133 and **12d(3)**]

■ **Exercise 3** Find the semicolons used between parts of unequal rank and substitute a correct mark of punctuation. Do not change properly placed semicolons.

1. Don went jogging one afternoon; never returning; then he was numbered among the tens of thousands who disappear every year.
2. Although the educational TV channel is sometimes a bore; at least tedious ads do not interrupt the programs.

3. I have two main pet peeves; jokes that are pointless and animals that get on furniture.
4. Before the derby she will take the motor apart and overhaul it; her supervisor will be an ace mechanic; her sister Alicia.
5. The tormented bull lowered his head in readiness for another charge; the one-sided contest not being over yet.

■ **Exercise 4** Compose four sentences to illustrate various uses of the semicolon.

General Exercise on the Comma and the Semicolon

■ **Exercise 5** First, review Sections **12** and **14**. Then, using the following examples as guides, punctuate sentences 1-10 appropriately.

12a Pat poured gasoline into the hot tank, for he had not read the warning in his tractor manual.

12b Since Pat had not read the warning in his tractor manual, he poured gasoline into the hot tank.
In very large print in the tractor manual, the warning is conspicuous.

12c Pat did not read the tractor manual, observe the warning, or wait for the tank to cool.
Pat was a rash, impatient young mechanic.

12d Pat did not read his tractor manual, which warned against pouring gasoline into a hot tank.
Pat, a careless young man, poured gasoline into the hot tank of his tractor.
First, warnings should be read.

12e A week before, he had glanced at the manual.

14a Pat ignored the warning in the tractor manual; he poured gasoline into the hot tank.
Pat poured gasoline into the hot tank; thus he caused the explosion.

14b At the hospital Pat said that he had not read the warning; that he had, of course, been careless; and that he would never again, under any circumstances, pour gasoline into a hot tank.

1. Many students were unhappy in the early 1980s for high unemployment threatened their future plans.
2. Dr. Felipe a visiting professor from Kenya says that often it is not fun to learn but that it is always fun to know.
3. The stalls of the open market along the wharf were filled with tray after tray of glassy-eyed fish slender stalks of pink rhubarb mounds of home-grown tomatoes and jars of bronze honey.
4. Two or three scrawny mangy-looking hounds lay sprawled in the shade of the cabin.
5. While Diana was unpacking the cooking gear and Grace was chopping firewood I began to put up our shelter.
6. Slamming the door of his four-wheel drive to cut short the argument with his wife Jerry grabbed the grocery list from her and stalked into the supermarket.
7. Still in high school we had to memorize dates and facts such as 1066 the Battle of Hastings 1914-1918 World War I 1939-1945 World War II and 1969 the first moon landing.
8. The dream home that they often talk about is a retreat in the Rockies to tell the truth however they seem perfectly happy in their mobile home on the outskirts of Saskatoon.
9. The criminal was asking for mercy his victim was pleading for justice.
10. Chris and I felt that our blustery argument would never end however my weather-watching roommate reminded us that thunderstorms are usually of short duration.

The Apostrophe

15

Use the apostrophe to indicate the possessive case (except for personal pronouns), to mark omissions in contracted words or numerals, and to form certain plurals.

15a

Use the apostrophe to indicate the possessive case of nouns and indefinite pronouns.

The possessive (or genitive) case shows ownership or a comparable relationship: *Donald's* car, two *weeks'* pay. The possessive case of nouns and of indefinite pronouns may be indicated by the use of *'s* (or by the apostrophe alone) or by an *of*-phrase.

everybody's friend OR the friend of everybody
the students' laughter OR the laughter of students

Occasionally, the possessive is indicated by the use of both an *of*-phrase and *'s*:

that pie **of** Al's [a double possessive]
COMPARE this description of Al [Al is described.]
this description of Al's [Al did the describing.]

A possessive noun or pronoun may be related to a word (or word group) that precedes it or that is clearly implied.

Is that old broken-down dune buggy **Frank's** or **Jane's**?

(1) For singular nouns and indefinite pronouns, add the apostrophe and *s*.

Laura's idea a week's work a dime's worth
anyone's guess somebody's coat one's choices

Option: If a singular noun ends in *s*, add the apostrophe and *s* or only the apostrophe.

Keats's poetry OR Keats' poetry
a waitress's tips OR a waitress' tips

When a singular word ends in *s*, many writers use the apostrophe and *s* to reflect pronunciation, but they prefer to use only the apostrophe when the word following begins with an *s* or a *z* sound.

Chris's enthusiasm BUT Chris' zeal
the hostess's idea BUT for the hostess' sake

(2) For plural nouns ending in *s*, add only the apostrophe. For plurals not ending in *s*, add the apostrophe and *s*.

boys' shoes (shoes for *boys*) two dollars' worth
babies' toes (toes of *babies*) the Joneses' reunion

BUT men's clothing women's job children's rights

(3) For compounds or word groups, add the apostrophe and *s* only to the last word.

my sister-in-law's shop someone else's turn
the Secretary of State's idea George Heming, Jr.'s reply

(4) To indicate individual ownership, add the apostrophe and *s* to each name.

Al's and Sue's cars [Note that *cars* is plural.]
the doctor's and the dentist's offices

Note: To indicate joint ownership, add the apostrophe and *s* only to the last name or to each name.

Al and Sue's car OR Al's and Sue's car

Variation to 15a

The use of the apostrophe or the possessive form varies with proper names (organizations, geographical designations, and so on).

Devil's Island Devils Tower Devil Mountain

■ **Exercise 1** Change the modifier after the noun to a possessive form before the noun, following the pattern of the examples.

EXAMPLES

the laughter of the crowd	*the crowd's laughter*
suggestions made by James	*James's suggestions* OR *James' suggestions*

1. the tape decks belonging to Johnny
2. the boat bought by the Weinsteins
3. the voices of Bess and Mary
4. the efforts of the editor-in-chief
5. the strategy that Doris uses
6. worth a quarter
7. ideas of somebody else
8. stories by Dickens
9. shoes for women
10. a song written by Henry and Ross

15b

Use an apostrophe to mark omissions in contracted words or numerals.

didn't he'll they're there's class of '85
o'clock [reduction of "of the clock"]

Note: Contractions in writing mirror speech. As a rule, they are avoided in formal writing: see **19d**. But they are common (and often preferable) both in informal writing and in dialogue.

INFORMAL

With all the books he reads, how come the guy is so illiterate? And why do people just naturally assume that you'll know what they're talking about? No, I don't know, and nobody knows. The planets don't, the stars don't, infinite space doesn't.
—SAUL BELLOW

DIALOGUE

"Well, Curley's pretty handy," the swamper said skeptically. "Never did seem right to me. S'pose Curley jumps a big guy an' licks him. Ever'body says what a game guy Curley is."
—JOHN STEINBECK

15c

Use the apostrophe and *s* to form the plural of lowercase letters and of abbreviations followed by periods. When needed to prevent confusion, use the apostrophe and *s* to form the plural of capital letters, of symbols, of abbreviations not followed by periods, and of words referred to as words.

His *a*'s look like *o*'s. [The '*s* is not italicized (underlined). See also **10d**.]

Over half of the Ph.D.'s were still looking for jobs.

Her *I*'s are illegible, and her *miss*'s appear to be *mess*'s.

Either '*s* or *s* may be used to form such plurals as the following:

the 1900's OR the 1900s his 7's! OR his 7s
two *B*'s OR two *B*s the &'s! OR the &s
her *and*'s! OR her *and*s the VON's OR the VONs

15d

Do not use the apostrophe with the pronouns *his, hers, its, ours, yours, theirs,* or *whose* or with plural nouns not in the possessive case.

> **His** parents sent money; **ours** sent food.
> A friend of **theirs** knows a cousin of **yours**.
> The **sisters** design **clothes** for **babies**

Caution: Do not confuse *its* with *it's* or *whose* with *who's*:

> **Its** motor is small. [the motor *of it*]
> **It's** a small motor. [*It is* a small motor.]
> **Whose** is that? [*Who owns* that?]
> **Who's** that? [*Who is* that?]

■ **Exercise 2** Insert apostrophes where needed in the following sentences. Put a checkmark after any sentence that needs no change in punctuation.

1. Many students attitudes changed completely in the mid-1970s.
2. Some students dropped these courses because of the stiff requirements.
3. Those newsstands sell Marian Rosss homemade candy.
4. Theyre not interested in hockey; its roughness repels them.
5. Snapshots of everyone in the class of 84 cover Jerrys bulletin board.
6. "It's just one R.N.s opinion, isnt it?" Otis commented.
7. Is that dog yours or theirs?
8. There are two *e*s and two *d*s in Hildegardes name, but not any *u*s.
9. The computer confused my account with somebody elses.
10. Marnie often quotes her Granddads favourite expression: "Everybodys useful, but nobodys indispensable!"
11. Its an expensive book, but its cover came unglued.
12. Theres nothing wrong with her attitude or idea, but theirs is not like hers.

Quotation Marks

16

Use quotation marks to set off all direct quotations, some titles, and words used in a special sense. Place other marks of punctuation in proper relation to quotation marks.

Quotations usually consist of passages borrowed from the written work of others or the direct speech of individuals, especially dialogue (conversation).

QUOTED WRITING Again Hopkins writes: “Take breath and read it with the ears, as I always wish to be read, and my verse comes all right.” And Joyce never tired of explaining how in *Finnegans Wake* “the words the reader sees are not the words that he will hear.” [The words and punctuation within quotation marks are exactly as they appear in Marshall McLuhan's *The Gutenberg Galaxy* (Toronto: University of Toronto Press, 1962), p. 104.]

QUOTED SPEECH “Sure enough, I'd like to own a slave,” Donna explained. “A compact, push-button robot!” [Within quotation marks are the exactly recorded words of the speaker; the punctuation is supplied by the writer.]

Remember that the speaker and the verb of saying (such as *Donna explained*) should be outside the quotation marks.

16a

Use double quotation marks to enclose direct (but not indirect) quotations; use single marks to enclose a quotation within a quotation.

Double quotation marks:

> Making fun of Cooper, Mark Twain said, "He saw nearly all things as through a glass eye, darkly." [a directly quoted sentence]
>
> According to Mark Twain, Cooper "saw nearly all things as through a glass eye, darkly." [part of a sentence quoted directly]
>
> Mark Twain said that Cooper saw nearly everything darkly, as if he were looking through a glass eye. [indirect quotation—no quotation marks]

Single quotation marks within double:

> She said, "Earl keeps calling my idea 'an impossible dream.' " [a quotation within a quotation]

Note: The double quotation marks enclosing a minor title (see **16b**) are reduced to single marks when the title appears within a direct quotation:

> "Edgar Allan Poe's 'A Predicament' is one of the funniest short stories I've ever read!" Chet exclaimed. [a title within a quotation]

(1) Long prose quotations (not dialogue) In printed matter, quoted material of ten or more lines is usually set off from the rest of the text by the use of smaller type, indention, or both. Quotation marks are used only if they appear in the original. In typewritten papers, lengthy quoted passages (more than four lines) are either single-spaced and indented from the left margin five spaces (as shown below) or double-spaced and indented ten spaces (see Section **33**). The first line is indented an additional three spaces when it marks the beginning of a paragraph.

In a published extract of the CBC program, "Journey Without Arrival: A Personal Point of View from Northrop Frye," this critic credits Ned Pratt with being the "landmark figure" in a changing perspective of the Canadian imaginative identity:

> We came into this century without any agreement on what kind of people we were—or even, whether a Canadian could be identified.... All that is beginning to change.
>
> And Pratt is the symbol of the change ... the people who have followed Pratt, the Earle Birneys, the Margaret Atwoods, and James Reaneys, they're the mapmakers of the Canadian imagination. They're putting us in possession of our past and our shared responses.

(The Globe and Mail 6 Apr. 1976, 7)

For the proper documentation of sources in a research paper, see Section **33**.

(2) Poetry In both printed matter and typewritten papers, except for very special emphasis, a single line of poetry or less is handled like other short quotations—run in with the text and enclosed in quotation marks. A two-line quotation may be run in with the text, with a slash marking the end of the first line. Or it may be set off from the text like longer quotations and quoted line by line exactly as it appears in the original:

The poet asks, "If there were dreams to

sell, / What would you buy?"

OR

The poet asks,

If there were dreams to sell,
  What would you buy?

In printed matter, longer passages (sometimes italicized) are usually set off by smaller type. In typewritten papers, they are single-spaced and indented from the left five spaces. (The numbers in parentheses indicate the line numbers of the poem.)

Siberia was a natural prison. Its bleak

landscape, described in James Mangan's poem

"Siberia," offered little comfort to those

exiled there:

In Siberia's wastes
  Are sands and rocks.
Nothing blooms of green or soft,
But the snowpeaks rise aloft
  And the gaunt ice-blocks. (21–25)

(3) Dialogue (conversation) Written dialogue represents the directly quoted speech of two or more persons talking together. Standard practice is to write each person's speech, no matter how short, as a separate paragraph. Verbs of saying, as well as closely related bits of narrative, are included in the paragraph along with the speech:

> Through an interpreter, I spoke with a Bedouin man tending nearby olive trees.
> “Do you own this land?” I asked him.
> He shook his head. “The land belongs to Allah,” he said.
> “What about the trees?” I asked. He had just harvested a basket of green olives, and I assumed that at least the trees were his.
> “The trees, too, are Allah's,” he replied.
> I marvelled at this man who seemed unencumbered by material considerations . . . or so I was thinking when, as if in afterthought, he said, “Of course, I own the *olives!*”
>
> —HARVEY ARDEN, "In Search of Moses"

(4) Punctuation of dialogue Commas are used to set off expressions such as *he said* and *she asked* in quoted dialogue: see **12d(3)**.

He said, “Pro football is like nuclear warfare.”
“Pro football,” he said, “is like nuclear warfare.”
“Pro football is like nuclear warfare,” he said.

When the quoted speech is a question or an exclamation, the question mark or exclamation point replaces the usual comma.

“Pro football?” she asked. “Like nuclear warfare!” she added.

When an expression such as *he said* introduces a quotation of two or more sentences, it is often followed by a colon: see **17d(1)**.

It is as Frank Gifford said: “Pro football is like nuclear warfare. There are no winners, only survivors.”

■ **Exercise 1** In the following sentences, change each indirect quotation to a direct quotation and each direct quotation to an indirect one.

1. Doris said that she had a theory about me.
2. Allen announced that he had read "The Sunless Sea."

3. An ardent Weight Watcher, Laura explained that she could eat as much as she wanted—of foods like spinach, rhubarb, and celery!
4. Clyde asked, "Will you go to the opera with me?"
5. Last night Faez said that he thought that Amanda's favourite quotation was "Tomorrow belongs to me."

16b

Use quotation marks for minor titles (short stories, essays, short poems, songs, episodes of a radio or television series, articles in periodicals) and subdivisions of books.

“The Panther and the Jaguar” was part of the CBC *Morningside* program.

Ross Laver's “The Slow Death of Afghanistan,” in the December 24, 1984 issue of *Maclean's*, is about the devastation caused by the continuing warfare in that country.

Max Shulman's *Guided Tour of Campus Humor* contains numerous poems and short stories, including “Tears from One Who Didn't Realize How Good He Had It” and “Love Is a Fallacy.”

Note: Quotation marks are sometimes used to enclose titles of books, periodicals, and newspapers, but italics are generally preferred: see **10a**.

16c

Words used in a special sense are sometimes enclosed in quotation marks.

Such “prophecy” is intelligent guessing.
His “castle” was in reality a cozy little rat-trap.

Note: Either quotation marks or italics may be used in definitions such as the following. See also **10d**.

> "Puritanical" means "marked by stern morality."
> *Puritanical* means "marked by stern morality."
> *Puritanical* means *marked by stern morality*.

16d

Do not overuse quotation marks.

Do not use quotation marks to enclose the title of your composition: see **8b(4)**. In general, do not enclose in quotation marks common nicknames, bits of humour, technical terms, or trite or well-known expressions. Instead of using slang and colloquialisms within quotation marks, use more formal English. Do not use quotation marks for emphasis.

> NEEDLESS PUNCTUATION "Kitty" will not "cop out."
> BETTER Kitty will not quit.

■ **Exercise 2** Add correctly placed quotation marks below.

1. In a poem entitled 2001, scientists turn one Einstein into three Einsteins.
2. Here, stoked means fantastically happy on a surfboard.
3. David enjoyed reading the short story A Circle in the Fire.
4. *Learning to Live Without Cigarettes* opens with a chapter entitled Sighting the Target.
5. Bernice replied, my grandfather once said, Never spend your money before you have it.

16e

When using various marks of punctuation with quoted words, phrases, or sentences, observe the following conventions.

(1) Place the period and the comma within the quotation marks.

"Jenny," he said, "let's have lunch."
She replied, "OK, but first I want to finish 'The Machine Stops.' "

Exception:

The author states: "Time alone reveals the just" (471). [The period follows the reference to the source of the direct quotation. The new MLA conventions (see Section **33**) omit the **p.**, so (p. 471) becomes (471).]

(2) Place the colon and the semicolon outside the quotation marks.

She spoke of "the protagonists"; yet I remembered only one in "The Tell-Tale Heart": the mad murderer.

(3) Place the dash, the question mark, and the exclamation point within the quotation marks when they apply only to the quoted matter; place them outside when they apply to the whole sentence.

Pilate asked, "What is truth?" [The question mark applies only to the quoted matter.]

What is the meaning of the term "half truth"? [The question mark applies to the whole sentence.]

Why did he ask, "What is truth?" [Both the quoted matter and the sentence as a whole are questions, but a second question mark does not follow the quotation marks.]

Gordon answered, "No way!" [The exclamation point applies only to the quoted matter.]

Stop whistling "All I Do Is Dream of You"! [The whole sentence, not the song title, is an exclamation.]

■ **Exercise 3** Insert quotation marks where they are needed in the following sentences:

1. Helen's really out of it, I commented to Carl as we sat down to lunch in the cafeteria. Too bad she saw *The Rivals*. She's been acting like Mrs. Malaprop ever since.
2. Oh, cut it out about Helen! Carl snapped as he unrolled his napkin and sorted his silverware. I actually like Helen's bad jokes. Her word play—
3. Please pass the salt, I interrupted.
4. Ignoring my frown, Carl continued: I'll grant you that Helen's puns are usually as old and as bad as the joke ending with Huck'll bury Finn; but here she comes. Start talking about something else.
5. Clearing my throat noisily, I took his advice and said, Perhaps your parents should buy a perambulator.
6. A perambulator! Helen happily took up my cue as she plopped down in the chair near Carl. My parents bought me an eight-cup perambulator for my birthday. Just plug it in, and coffee is ready in four minutes!
7. Aren't you thinking of a percolator? I asked her in mock seriousness. An electric percolator heats quickly.
8. Sure, Helen replied, winking at Carl. It's the same thing as an incubator.
9. You don't mean *incubator!* I said sharply, and then I added a bit of my own nonsense. You mean *incinerator*. After a moment of silence, I yawned and said, Incinerator bombs are really fiery weapons.
10. As though admitting defeat at her own game, Helen grinned and said, with a blasé sigh, Oh, let's forget this game. It's time we had a new aversion.

The Period and Other Marks

17

Use the period, the question mark, the exclamation point, the colon, the dash, parentheses, brackets, the slash, and the ellipsis mark according to standard practices. (For the use of the hyphen, see **18f**.)

Read the following sentences aloud. Observe how the punctuation in colour signals intonation (pitch, stress, stops) and helps to reveal sentence meaning:

> Think—just think! Who controls everything?
>
> —SAUL BELLOW
>
> In *Lady Windermere's Fan* (1892) is this famous line: "I [Lord Darlington] can resist everything except temptation."
>
> Still he listened . . . and it seemed that all that would speak, in this world, was listening. —EUDORA WELTY
>
> No day / night cycle exists there. The inhabitants have no way of measuring time—even years—by our standards.
>
> —JOHN A. KEEL

This section covers the main principles of usage of these punctuation marks in ordinary (rather than technical or special) writing.

The Period

17a

Use the period after declarative and mildly imperative sentences, after indirect questions, and after most abbreviations.

(1) Use the period to mark the end of a declarative sentence, a mildly imperative sentence, and an indirect question.

Everyone should drive defensively. [declarative]

Learn how to drive defensively. [mild imperative]

She asks how drivers can cross the city without driving offensively. [indirect question]

"What is that?" she asked. [declarative containing a direct question]

"Get with it!" he hollered. [declarative containing an exclamation]

(2) Use periods after most abbreviations.

Mrs. an M.D. R.S.V.P. No. 444 etc. 1:10 p.m.

In current usage the period is frequently omitted after many abbreviations: see also Section **11**, page 122.

CBC CNIB DSO CRTC LSD kg km

Do not use periods after shortened or clipped forms:

2nd 10th math premed gym lab psych

When in doubt about the punctuation of an abbreviation, consult a good college dictionary. Dictionaries often list a range of choices (for example, *A.W.O.L.*, *a.w.o.l.*, *AWOL*, *awol*).

Caution: When an abbreviation ending in a period appears last in the sentence, do not add a second period:

Someday I hope to be an R.N.

The Question Mark

17b

Use the question mark after direct (but not indirect) questions.

Who started the rumour?
Did he ask **who started the rumour?** [The sentence as a whole is a direct question despite the indirect quesion at the end.]
Did you hear her ask, "Are you accusing me of starting the rumour?" [double direct question followed by a single question mark]

Declarative sentences may contain direct questions:

"Who started the rumour?" he asked. [No comma follows the question mark.]
He asked, "Who started the rumour?" [No period follows the question mark.]
She told me—did I hear her correctly?—who started the rumour. [interpolated question]

A declarative or an imperative sentence may be converted into a question:

He drove to Baie Comeau?
Drive to Baie Comeau?

Question marks may be used between the parts of a series:

Did he rent the house? buy the house? buy the adjoining land? [Question marks cause full stops and emphasize each part. Compare "Did he rent the house, buy the house, and buy the adjoining land?"]

Note: A question mark within parentheses is used to express the writer's uncertainty as to the correctness of the preceding word, figure, or date:

> Chaucer was born in 1340 (?) and died in 1400.

Caution: Do not use a comma or a period after a question mark.

> "Are *gobbledygook* and *Jabberwocky* synonyms?" he asked.
> He asked, "Are *gobbledygook* and *Jabberwocky* synonyms?"

The Exclamation Point

17c

Use the exclamation point after an emphatic interjection and after a phrase, clause, or sentence to express a high degree of surprise, incredulity, or other strong emotion.

> Wow! What a desperation pass!
> "Man! We've been conned!" he said.
> Act now! Get involved!

Caution 1: Avoid overuse of the exclamation point. Use a comma after mild interjections, and end mildly exclamatory sentences and mild imperatives with a period. See also **17a(1)**.

> Oh, don't get involved.
> How quiet the lake was.

Caution 2: Do not use a comma or a period after an exclamation point.

> "Get off the road!" he yelled.
> He yelled, "Get off the road!"

■ **Exercise 1** Illustrate the chief uses of the period, the question mark, and the exclamation point by composing and correctly punctuating brief sentences of the types specified:

EXAMPLE
a declarative sentence containing a quoted direct question
"*What does fennel taste like*?" she asked.

1. a direct question
2. a mild imperative
3. a declarative sentence containing a quoted exclamation
4. a declarative sentence containing an indirect question
5. a declarative sentence containing an interpolated question

The Colon

17d

Use the colon as a formal introducer to call attention to what follows and as a mark of separation in scriptural and time references and in certain titles.

(1) The colon may direct attention to an explanation or summary, an appositive, a series, or a quotation.

For in her heart of hearts, Isabelle-Marie was like her brother: a creature of innate purity. —MARIE-CLAIRE BLAIS

Three times he drags me over to the bulletin board to show me his team's enviable record: five straight league titles. —HAROLD BRODKEY

So this was her kingdom: an octagonal house, a roomful of books, and a bear. —MARIAN ENGEL

Ruth-Anne waits for Dorothy in the cloakroom. She delivers the highest accolade a listener can receive: "I'm sorry I didn't invite you, Dorothy. I didn't know you half as well then as I do now." —SYLVIA FRASER

The colon may separate two main clauses or sentences when the second explains or amplifies the first:

> The scientific value of even the most recent contributions to this literature, however, is seriously qualified: The sole witness to the dream is the dreamer himself.
> —SCIENTIFIC AMERICAN

> I write poems like spiders spin webs, and perhaps for much the same reason: to support my existence. —ALFRED PURDY

Note: After the colon, quoted sentences regularly begin with a capital, but other sentences (as the preceding examples show) may begin with either a capital letter or a lower-case letter, although the latter is generally preferred.

(2) Use the colon between figures in scriptural and time references and between titles and subtitles.

The text of the sermon was Matthew 6:10.
At 2:15 A.M. the phone rang.
I had just read *On Being Funny: Woody Allen and Comedy* by Eric Lax.

Note: The colon is also used after the salutation of a business letter and in bibliographical data: see **33b(4)** and **34a(3)**.

(3) Do not use superfluous colons.

As a rule, superfluous or unnecessary colons interrupt the sentence base. Sometimes they follow *such as*.

SUPERFLUOUS These handicapped people can repair almost anything, such as: old lawnmowers, broken clocks, frayed wires, cracked vases.

REVISED These handicapped people can repair almost anything, such as old lawnmowers, broken clocks, frayed wires, cracked vases. [colon omitted]

OR These handicapped people can repair almost anything: old lawnmowers, broken clocks, frayed wires, cracked vases. [*such as* omitted]

SUPERFLUOUS The six survivors were: one man, two women, and three children.

REVISED The six survivors were one man, two women, and three children.

OR There were six survivors: one man, two women, and three children.

OR The six survivors were as follows: one man, two women, and three children. [Although *survivors* is plural, *as follows* (not *as follow*) is standard usage.]

■ **Exercise 2** Punctuate the following sentences by adding colons. Put a checkmark after any sentence that needs no change.

1. At 1230 A.M. he was still repeating his favourite quotation "TV is the opiate of the people."
2. The downtown streets are narrow, rough, and junky.
3. Even people in rural areas were not safe many criminals had left the cities and the suburbs.
4. Dr. Morris recommended three magazines *Books in Canada*, the *Malahat Review*, and the *Dalhousie Review*.
5. All their thoughts were centred on equal pay for equal work.

■ **Exercise 3** Decide whether to use a colon or a semicolon between the main clauses of the following sentences. See also **14a**.

1. These laws all have the same purpose they protect us from ourselves.
2. Some of these laws have an obvious purpose others seem senseless.
3. Few things in life are certain perhaps we could name them all on one hand.
4. One thing is certain the future looks bright.

The Dash

17e

Use the dash to mark a sudden break in thought; to set off (for emphasis or clarity) an added explanation, or illustration, or parenthetical element; and to mark the end of an introductory series.

On the typewriter, the dash is indicated by two hyphens without spacing before, between, or after. In handwriting, the dash is an unbroken line about the length of two or three hyphens.

(1) Use the dash to mark a sudden break in thought, an abrupt change in tone, or faltering speech.

> A hypocrite is a person who—but who isn't?
>
> —DON MARQUIS

> And we gathered together all the spades and buckets and towels, empty hampers and bottles, umbrellas and fishfrails, bats and balls and knitting, and went—oh, listen, Dad!—to the Fair in the dusk on the bald seaside field.
>
> —DYLAN THOMAS

> Quickly regaining speech, but still in a state of disbelief, I stammered: "No. Uh, yes. Uh—it's all right."
>
> —DOROTHY K. DUFFEY

(2) Use the dash to set off (for emphasis or clarity) an added explanation or illustration.

> Lightning is an electrical discharge—an enormous spark.
>
> —RICHARD E. ORVILLE

> "Of course," I come back at her quickly. "I'm well aware of that. I only meant—"
> "You must have dozed," she says. —MARGARET LAURENCE

''Would—would you mind telling me—'' he said to the guide, much deflated, ''what was so stupid about that?''
—KURT VONNEGUT, JR.

She did not have a particularly light touch with flavours and textures—her roasts were dredged with flour, her seasonings heavily dependent on cayenne, parsley, and tomato.
—LAURA SHAPIRO

[A colon, which might be used here instead of the dash, would be more formal.]

(3) Use the dash to set off a parenthetical element for emphasis or (if it contains commas) for clarity.

It had been for Nancy—unreservedly loving one day, withdrawn and sullen the next—to pronounce.
—MORDECAI RICHLER

His mother and the lady—whom Moses, had he been pressed, would have identified as Mrs. Pyopyo—hovered about the bed, their attitudes intent. —ADELE WISEMAN

Isn't it strange how people—not people in universities, like you and me, but just people—keep forgetting that ''crisis'' is Greek for ''judgement.'' —ROBERTSON DAVIES

(4) Use the dash between an introductory series and the main part of the sentence that explains or amplifies the series.

Items in an introductory series are often referents of *all, everything, none, such*, or *these* in the main part of the sentence.

Patience, diligence, painstaking attention to detail—these are the requirements. —MARK TWAIN

She was fair-haired, discreet, wanly solicitous—already an old maid. —ALICE MUNRO

Marble-topped tables, two Singer sewing machines, a big vase of pampas grass—everything was rich and grand.
—CARSON McCULLERS

Caution: Use the dash carefully in formal writing. Do not use dashes as substitutes for commas, semicolons, or end marks.

Parentheses

17f

Use parentheses to set off parenthetical, supplementary, or illustrative matter and to enclose figures or letters when used for enumeration within a sentence.

The *Bentely* spent the entire night at it and arrived at Gravely Bay (Port Colbourne on Lake Erie) the following morning.
—EDITH FOWKE

She caters mainly to people who have had (or thought they needed) psychotherapy and who live (or dream of living) in an opulent, sophisticated world. —ROBERT FULFORD

When confronted with ambiguities we are not certain as to how we should interpret (1) single words or phrases, (2) the sense of a sentence, (3) the emphases or accents desired by the writer or speaker, or (4) the significance of a statement.
—LIONEL RUBY

Each entry will be judged on the basis of (*a*) its artistic value, (*b*) its technical competence, and (*c*) its originality.

Note: In sentences such as the following, the commas and periods are placed after the closing parenthesis, not before the opening parenthesis:

According to Herbert J. Muller (1905-1967), instability is one of the conditions of life. [no comma before the first parenthesis]

Avanthea Swan taught at Dalhousie (although she was there for only seven years).

If a whole sentence beginning with a capital is in parentheses, the period or other end mark is placed just before the closing parenthesis. See also **9e**.

> Chance entered into things when a North York controller died. (Controllers are elected borough-wide.)
> —THE FINANCIAL POST

> Whatever else may be happening, Madame Colette is never *really* unaware, never *really* confused, never *really* afraid. (She can get mighty irritated sometimes.) —STEPHEN KOCH

Punctuation of Parenthetical Matter

Dashes, parentheses, commas—all are used to set off parenthetical matter. Dashes set off parenthetical elements sharply and usually emphasize them:

> Man's mind is indeed—as Luther said—a factory busy with making idols. —HARVEY COX [See **17e(3)**.]

Parentheses generally minimize the importance of the elements they enclose:

> Man's mind is indeed (as Luther said) a factory busy with making idols. [See **17f**.]

Commas are the most commonly used separators:

> Man's mind is indeed, as Luther said, a factory busy with making idols. [See **12d**.]

Brackets

17g

Use brackets to set off interpolations in quoted matter and to replace parentheses within parentheses.

> The *Home Herald* printed the beginning of the mayor's speech: "My dear fiends [sic] and fellow citizens." [A bracketed *sic*—meaning "thus"—tells the reader that the error appears in the original.]

Perhaps Marshall McLuhan's book should be required reading for prospective teachers (*City as Classroom* [Agincourt: The Book Society of Canada Limited, 1977]).

Deems Taylor has written: "Not for a single moment did he [Richard Wagner] compromise with what he believed, with what he dreamed."

The Slash

17h

Use the slash between terms to indicate that either term is applicable and to mark the end of a line of quoted poetry. See also **16a(2).**

Note that the slash is used unspaced between terms, but with a space before and after it between lines of poetry.

> Today visions of the checkless/cashless society are not quite as popular as they used to be. —KATHRYN H. HUMES

> Equally rare is a first-rate adventure story designed for those who enjoy a smartly told tale that isn't steeped in blood and/or sex. —JUDITH CRIST

> We are taught by ubiquitous custom to smile, "How was your Christmas (Easter/Hanukkah/vacation)?" in the knowledge that no other answer is possible except "Wonderful (Great/Just fine/Good)."
>
> —EDMOND G. ADDEO AND ROBERT E. BURGER

■ **Exercise 4** Correctly punctuate each of the following sentences by supplying commas, dashes, parentheses, brackets, or the slash. Be prepared to explain the reason for all marks you add, especially those you choose for setting off parenthetical matter.

1. Gordon Gibbs or is it his twin brother? plays the drums.
2. Joseph who is Gordon's brother is a lifeguard at the Beachfront Hotel.

3. "I admit that I" he began, but his voice broke; he could say no more.
4. This organization needs more of everything more money, brains, initiative.
5. Some of my courses for example, French and biology demand a great deal of work outside the classroom.
6. In the TV version of *The Lone Ranger*, Jay Silverheels 1918-1980 played the role of Tonto.
7. This ridiculous sentence appeared in the school paper: "Because of a personal fool sic the Cougars failed to cross the goal line during the last seconds of the game."
8. The word *zipper* once a trademark like Polaroid is now a common noun.
9. Gently rolling hills, rich valleys, beautiful rivers these things impress the tourist in New Brunswick.
10. Some innovations for example the pass fail system did not contribute to grade inflation.

The Ellipsis Mark

17i

Use three spaced periods (the ellipsis mark) to indicate an omission within a quoted passage and to mark a reflective pause or hesitation.

It is generally considered unnecessary to use the ellipsis mark at the beginning or the end of a quoted passage.

OMISSION WITHIN A QUOTED PASSAGE

> Clinton Rossiter writes: "My own answer to the question 'What is liberty?' is essentially this: Liberty . . . cannot be defined but can be understood." [Note the use of single quotation marks: see **16a**.]

Compare the quoted passage above with the original:

> My own answer to the question ''What is liberty?'' is essentially this: Liberty, like truth and justice and all the other great abstractions, cannot be defined but can be understood, and the first step toward understanding is to identify the most important uses of the word. —CLINTON ROSSITER

If a complete sentence in the quotation precedes the omission, use a period before the ellipsis mark:

> ''Nevertheless, inflation really is a horror,'' Martin Mayer contends, ''because it demeans work. In a developed economy, people necessarily work for money. . . . If the money they receive in return for their labours is continually diminishing in value, they feel an insult to themselves and to their function in society, even if as installment debtors they benefit by it.'' [Note that no space precedes the period before the ellipsis mark.]

Compare the quotation with the original:

> Nevertheless, inflation really is a horror, because it demeans work. In a developed economy, people necessarily work for money. Obviously, they want money to buy something, but at the time of work, and of thinking about work, they do not normally have in their heads the idea of what they are going to buy with the proceeds. If the money they receive in return for their labours is continually diminishing in value, they feel an insult to themselves and to their function in society, even if as installment debtors they benefit by it. —MARTIN MAYER

The ellipsis mark indicates that a part of a sentence, one or more sentences, or (sometimes) a full paragraph or more has been left out. Spaced periods covering a whole line mark the omission of at least one paragraph in prose or a full line in poetry.

> All I can say is—I saw it!
> . . . .
> Impossible! Only—I saw it! —ROBERT BROWNING

A REFLECTIVE PAUSE OR HESITATION

The ellipsis mark is also used to indicate a pensive or thought-filled pause, deliberate hesitation, or an intentionally unfinished statement (not an interruption).

> Love, like other emotions, has causes . . . and consequences. —LAWRENCE CASLER

> "It's well for you . . ." began Lucille. She bit the remark off. —ELIZABETH BOWEN
> [a deliberately unfinished statement]

The ellipsis mark may come after a period marking the end of a sentence:

> All channels are open. The meditation is about to begin. . . .
> —TOM ROBBINS

■ **Exercise 5** Beginning with *According to John Donne*, or with *As John Donne has written*, quote the following passage, omitting the words placed in brackets. Use three or four periods as needed to indicate omissions.

> No man is an island [entire of itself;] every man is a piece of the continent, a part of the main. [If a clod be washed away by the sea, Europe is the less, as well as if a promontory were, as well as if a manor of thy friend's or of thine own were.] Any man's death diminishes me because I am involved in mankind [and therefore never send to know for whom the bell tolls; it tolls for thee].
> —JOHN DONNE

■ **Exercise 6** First, observing differences in meaning and emphasis, use an ellipsis mark in place of the dash, commas, and the italicized words below. Then write two sentences of your own to illustrate the use of the ellipsis mark to indicate a pause or hesitation.

1. My father was dying—*and, I wondered*, what would happen to us?
2. Our lives would have been different if *he had lived*.

■ **Exercise 7** Punctuate the following sentences (the first five were selected and adapted from *Canadian Geographic*; the next four, from *Horizon Canada*) by supplying appropriate internal and end marks—commas, semicolons, colons, dashes, parentheses, and apostrophes. Do not use unnecessary punctuation. Be prepared to explain the reason for each mark you add, especially when you have a choice of correct alternatives (for example, commas, dashes, or parentheses).

1. The ravines stretched right across Metro rivers running north south tributaries branching east west Mimico Black Etobicoke and Highland creeks the Humber Don and Rouge rivers.
2. After all mammals with pouches have lived on this planet for over 70 million years and although seldom seen Canadas only marsupial isnt playing possum it is playing Natures deadly game of survival in a cold land for which it is barely suited.
3. They do not spawn naturally in BC waters except in a few secluded spots where condition temperature salinity nutrients etc are just right.
4. Though the best poles were removed in 1957 the site has been declared a World Heritage cultural site see Anthony Island Totems The Last Big Stand Canadian Geographic Oct Nov 1981.
5. Dr. Trudel declared it Nova Scotia appears on maps long before Cartier crossed the Atlantic.
6. Author of many scientific papers on railways among other subjects Sir Sandford Fleming was one of the founders of the Canadian Institute the publisher of the first large scale surveyors map in Canada the designer of the first usable chart of Toronto harbour the creator and promoter of the trans Pacific submarine telegraph cable and apart from his functions as chief engineer of the CPR the chancellor of Queens University for thirty five years.
7. Lawren Harris A Y Jackson Arthur Lismer J E H MacDonald Frederick Varley Frank Jonston and Franklin Carmichael the youngest persisted in remembering Tom Thomson who died in 1917 before the Group formed as a member the movement was due to him if it was due to anyone they felt.

SPELLING AND DICTION

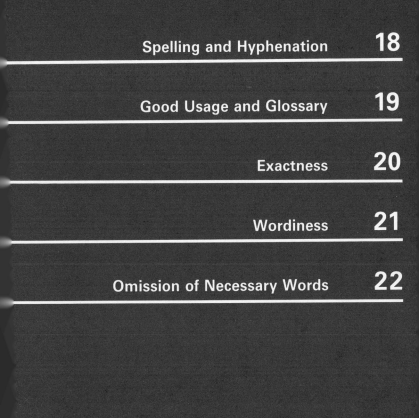

Spelling and Hyphenation **18**

Good Usage and Glossary **19**

Exactness **20**

Wordiness **21**

Omission of Necessary Words **22**

Spelling and Hyphenation 18

Spell every word according to established usage as shown by your dictionary. Hyphenate words in accordance with current usage.

Spelling

Spelling is a highly individual problem. You can improve your spelling by following these six suggestions:

1. Proofread to detect misspellings. Many misspellings are a result of mistakes in typing or in handwriting. Below are samples of a proofreader's corrections of typical misspellings:

   ```
   a/lot   dosen't   durring   therefore
   what ever   worldly
   ```

2. Make good use of your dictionary. When you consult the dictionary for a correct spelling, give attention to syllabication, pronunciation, and (when helpful) etymology. Check meaning to be sure that you have found the exact word you have in mind. Check for labels like *obsolete* or *archaic* (*compleat* for *complete*), *regional* or *dialectal* (*heighth* for *height*), *slang* (*weirdo*), or *informal* (*kids* for children).

   If your dictionary lists unlabelled optional spellings—such as *likable*/*likeable* or *tornados*/*tornadoes*—either form is correct.

Where labels like *British* or *Also, esp. Brit.* appear in an American dictionary, Canadian usage is not likely to be indicated, but the *Gage Canadian Dictionary* suggests the following generally preferred Canadian usages:

	BRITISH	AMERICAN	PREFERRED CANADIAN
1.	*-our*	*-or*	*-or* (honor, labor, humor)
2.	*-re*	*-er*	*-re* (centre, theatre)
3.	*-ise*	*-ize*	*-ize* (harmonize, recognize)
4.	*-ae*	*-e*	*-ae* (aesthetic, encyclopaedia)
5.	*-ce*	*-se*	*-ce* (defence, licence)
6.	*-ll-*	*-l-*	*-ll-* (woollen, traveller, jeweller)

Note that practices are changing, particularly in government publications and journalism, toward a standard American spelling. With the exception of *-our*, the preferences of the *Gage Canadian Dictionary* have been adopted in this book.

3. Study in context pairs of spellings (like *device, devise*) that you confuse. Visualize the words as you pronounce them. Practise writing them in phrases that bring out their denotations.
4. Spell by rule. Take time to analyze the structure of a word. Learn regular patterns of spellings (as well as exceptions) to avoid repetition of similar errors.
5. Study word lists. The lists in this section consist of hundreds of frequently misspelled words. Single out for special study those words that you find troublesome.
6. Keep an individual spelling list. List for study those words that you have misspelled or tend to misspell. Be sure that each word on your list is correctly written.

18a

Do not allow pronunciation (whether incorrect or correct) to cause you to misspell words by omitting, adding, or transposing letters.

Mispronunciation often leads to the misspelling of such words as those listed below. To avoid difficulties resulting from mispronunciation, pronounce problem words aloud several times, clearly and distinctly, in accordance with the pronunciation shown by a dictionary. Be careful not to omit, add, or transpose any letter or syllable.

athlete	drowned	modern	quantity
barbarous	escape	pertain	recognize
candidate	everything	prescribe	represent
disastrous	gratitude	probable	umbrella

A word that is difficult to spell may have two correct pronunciations. Of these, one may be a better guide to spelling. For example, the person who correctly leaves out the first /n/ when saying *government* or the first /r/ when saying *surprise* may be more likely to omit the *n* or *r* when writing these words than one who, again correctly, pronounces these sounds.

Each word in the following list has more than one correct pronunciation. If you tend to misspell any of these words because of the way you say them, then depend on your vision and memory to learn their correct spellings.

arctic	hundred	sophomore
boundary	interest	temperature
February	literature	veteran
generally	perhaps	where

As you check pronunciations in the dictionary, give special attention to /ə/, the symbol for a neutral vowel sound in unaccented syllables, usually an indistinct *uh* sound (as in *confidence*). Be especially careful not to omit letters representing /ə/. (The term *schwa* is used to refer to the vowel sound or to its phonetic symbol.)

Caution: Do not misspell words like *and, have*, or *than* because they are not stressed in context.

We had ham and [NOT *an*] eggs.
I should have [NOT *of*] won.
The movie is even more exciting than [NOT *then*] the book.

18b

Distinguish between words of similar sound and spelling; use the spelling required by the meaning.

Words such as *forth* and *fourth* or *sole* and *soul* sound alike but have vastly different meanings. Always be sure to choose the right word for your context.

A number of frequently confused spellings may be studied in groups:

Contractions and possessive pronouns:

It's best to wait.	The team did **its** best.
You're required to attend.	**Your** attendance is required.
There's a change in plans.	**Theirs** have changed.

Single words and two-word phrases:

It's an **everyday** event.	It happens nearly **every day**.
Maybe that is true.	That **may be** true.
I ran **into** trouble.	I ran **in to** get it.
Nobody cared.	The ghost had **no body**.

Singular nouns ending in ***nce*** *and plural nouns ending in* ***nts***:

not much **assistance**	too many **assistants**
for **instance**	just **instants** ago
even less **patience** with	several **patients**

As you study the list of words below, use your dictionary to check the meaning of words not thoroughly familiar to you. You may find it helpful to devise examples of usage such as these:

breath—a deep breath	**breathe**—to breathe deeply
passed—had passed	**past**—in the past

Words Frequently Confused

accept, except
access, excess
advice, advise
affect, effect
aisle, isle
alley, ally
allude, elude
already, all ready
altar, alter
10 altogether, all together
always, all ways
angel, angle
ascent, assent
assistance, assistants
bare, bear
birth, berth
board, bored
born, borne
breath, breathe
20 canvas, canvass
Calvary, cavalry
capital, capitol
censor, censure
choose, chose
cite, sight, site
clothes, cloths
coarse, course
complement, compliment
conscience, conscious
30 council, counsel
dam, damn
descent, dissent
desert, dessert
device, devise
dominant, dominate
dyeing, dying
envelop, envelope
fair, fare
formerly, formally
40 forth, fourth
gorilla, guerrilla
hear, here
heard, herd
hole, whole
holy, wholly
human, humane
its, it's
later, latter
lead, led
50 lesson, lessen
lightning, lightening
lose, loose
maybe, may be
minor, miner
moral, morale
of, off
passed, past
patience, patients
peace, piece
60 personal, personnel
plain, plane
precede, proceed

presence, presents
principle, principal
prophecy, prophesy
purpose, propose
quiet, quite, quit
respectfully, respectively
reverend, reverent
70 right, rite, -wright, write
sense, since
stationary, stationery
statue, stature, statute
straight, strait
taut, taunt
than, then
their, there, they're
through, thorough
to, too, two
80 tract, track
weather, whether
were, where
who's, whose
your, you're

18c

Apply the rules for spelling when adding prefixes and suffixes to the root.

The root is the base to which the prefix or the suffix is added.

PREFIXES

(1) Add the prefix to the root without doubling or dropping letters.

Do not double the last letter of the prefix when it is different from the first letter of the root (as in *disappear*). Do not drop the last letter of the prefix when the root begins with the same letter (as in *immortal*).

dis + agree = disagree	dis + satisfied = dissatisfied
un + usual = unusual	un + noted = unnoted
mis + used = misused	mis + spent = misspent
re + do = redo	re + elect = re-elect [OR reelect]

SUFFIXES

(2) Drop an unpronounced final *e* before a suffix beginning with a vowel but not before a suffix beginning with a consonant.

like → liking BUT likely, likeness, likelihood
use → usage, using BUT useful, useless

Dropped **-*e*** *before vowel:*		*Retained* **-*e*** *before consonant:*	
age	aging	care	careful
combine	combination	entire	entirely
desire	desirable	manage	management
fame	famous	rude	rudeness
scarce	scarcity	safe	safety

Caution: To keep the sound /s/ of *-ce* or /j/ of *-ge*, do not drop the final *e* before *-able* or *-ous*:

noticing BUT noticeable
changing BUT changeable
raging BUT outrageous
engaging BUT courageous

Similarly, keep the *e* before *-ance*, as in *vengeance*.

Other exceptions:

acreage hoeing lineage mileage [-e kept before vowel]
argument ninth truly wholly [-e dropped before consonant]

■ **Exercise 1** Practise adding suffixes to words ending in an unpronounced *e*.

EXAMPLES

-ing: rise, lose, guide *rising, losing, guiding*
-ly, -er, -ness: late *lately, later, lateness*

1. -ly: like, safe, sure
2. -able, -ing, -ment: excite
3. -ful: care, hope, use
4. -ing, -ment, -able: argue

5. -ing: come, notice, hope
6. -ing, -less: use
7. -ous: continue, courage
8. -ly, -ing: complete
9. -able: desire, notice
10. -ing, -ment: manage

(3) Double a final single consonant before a suffix beginning with a vowel (*a*) if the consonant ends a stressed syllable or a word of one syllable and (*b*) if the consonant is preceded by a single vowel. Otherwise, do not double the consonant.

One-syllable words:		*Words stressed on last syllable:*	
drag	dragged	abhor	abhorrent
hid	hidden	begin	beginning
shop	shoppers	occur	occurrence
stun	stunning	regret	regrettable
wet	wettest	unwrap	unwrapped

Compare: benefited, reference [stressed on first syllable]

■ **Exercise 2** Write the present participle (*-ing* form) and the past tense of each verb: *rob*—robbing, robbed.

admit	conceal	hope	plan	stop
brag	grip	jog	rebel	audit

(4) As a rule, change final *y* to *i* before adding a suffix, but keep the *y* before *-ing*.

apply → applies, applied, appliance BUT applying
study → studies, studied BUT studying
happy → happily, happiness, happier, happiest

Exceptions: Verbs ending in *y* preceded by a vowel do not change the *y* before *-s* or *-ed: stay, stays, stayed*. Following the same pattern of spelling, nouns like *joys* or *days* have *y* before *s*. The following irregularities in spelling are especially troublesome:

lays, laid pays, paid [*Compare*: says, said.]

(5) Do not drop a final *l* when you add *-ly*.

formal	formally	usual	usually
real	really	wool	woolly

■ **Exercise 3** Add the designated suffixes to the following words:

1. -able: vary, ply
2. -er: funny, carry
3. -ous: vary, luxury
4. -ly: easy, final
5. -ed: supply, stay
6. -ing: study, worry
7. -d: pay, lay
8. -hood: lively, likely
9. -ness: friendly, lonely
10. -ly: usual, cool

18d

Apply the rules for spelling to avoid confusion of *ei* and *ie*.

When the sound is /ē/ (*ee*), write *ie* (except after *c*, in which case write *ei*).

				(after *c*)	
chief	grief	pierce	wield	ceiling	deceive
field	niece	relief	yield	conceit	perceive

When the sound is other than /ē/ (*ee*), usually write *ei*.

counterfeit	foreign	heifer	heir	sleigh	vein
forfeit	freight	height	neighbour	stein	weigh

Exceptions: friend, mischief, seize, sheik

■ **Exercise 4** Fill in the blanks with the appropriate letters: *ei* or *ie*:

1. p ____ ce
2. ach ____ ve
3. rec ____ ve
4. n ____ gh
5. fr ____ ght
6. ap ____ ce
7. bel ____ f
8. conc ____ ve
9. th ____ r
10. dec ____ t
11. n ____ ce
12. sh ____ ld
13. w ____ rd
14. shr ____ k
15. pr ____ st

18e

As a rule, form the plural of nouns by adding *s* or *es* to the singular.

(1) Form the plural of most nouns by adding *s* to the singular:

two boy**s**	many nation**s**	a few scientist**s**
several safe**s**	three cupful**s**	all the radio**s**

both sister**s**-in-law [chief word pluralized]
the Dudley**s** and the Berry**s** [proper names]

Note: To form the plural of some nouns ending in *f* or *fe*, change the ending to *ve* before adding the *s: a thief, two thieves; one life, our lives.*

(2) Add *es* to singular nouns ending in *s, ch, sh,* or *x*.

many loss**es**	these mailbox**es**	the Rogers**es**
two approach**es**	a lot of ash**es**	two Doris**es**

[Note that each plural above makes an extra syllable.]

(3) Add *es* to singular nouns ending in *y* preceded by a consonant, after changing the *y* to *i*.

eighty—eighti**es**
strawberry—strawberri**es**
company—compani**es**
industry—industri**es**

Note: Although *es* is often added to a singular noun ending in *o* preceded by a consonant, usage varies:

echo**es**	hero**es**	potato**es**	veto**es**	[-*es* only]
auto**s**	memo**s**	pimento**s**	pro**s**	[-*s* only]
no**s**/no**es**	motto**s**/motto**es**	zero**s**/zero**es**		[-*s* or -*es*]

Exceptions: Irregular plurals (including retained foreign spellings) are not formed by adding *s* or *es*.

SINGULAR	woman	goose	analysis	alga	species
PLURAL	women	geese	analyses	algae	species

■ **Exercise 5** Supply plural forms (including any optional spelling) for the following words, applying rule **18e**. (If a word is not covered by the rule, use your dictionary.)

1. belief
2. theory
3. church
4. genius
5. Kelly
6. bath
7. hero
8. story
9. wish
10. forty
11. radius
12. scarf
13. wife
14. speech
15. tomato
16. phenomenon
17. halo
18. child
19. handful
20. rodeo

A List of Words Frequently Misspelled

Like the words discussed in Section **18b**, the following list may be studied in groups of ten or twenty at a time. Blank spaces are provided at the end of the list for the addition of other words which you may wish to master (possibly those from your special field of interest) or which your instructor may recommend.

absence
acceptable
accessible
accidentally
accommodate
accompanied
accomplish
accordion
accuracy
10 accustomed
achievement
acquainted
acquire
acreage
across
actually
address
admission
adolescent
20 advice
advised
affected
affectionately
aggravate
aggression
aisles
alcohol
all right
a lot of
30 always

amateur
among
analysis
ancestry
angel
annihilate
announcement
anywhere
apiece
40 apology

apparent
appearance
appoint
appreciate
appropriate
approximately
arguing
argument
arrest
50 article

aspirin
assassination
associate
atheist
athletics
attached
attacked
attendance
authentic
60 average

barbarous
bargain
basically
beautiful
beginning
belief
believed
beneficial
benefited
70 biggest

birthday
boundary
breath
breathe
bulletin
bureaucracy
business
cafeteria
calculator
80 calendar

carrying
category
cemetery
census
certain
challenge
changeable
changing
channel
90 characteristic

chief
children
chocolate
chosen
Christianity
coarsely
commercial
commitment
committee
100 competent

competition
completely
conceited
conceive
concentrate
condemn
confident
conscience
conscientious
110 consensus

consistent
continuous
contradict
controlled
controversial
convenient
coolly
courses
courteous
120 criticism

criticize
crowd
cruelty
curiosity
curious
dealt
deceive
decision
decorate
130 definitely

delicate
descend
description
desirable
despair
desperate
despicable
destroy
develop
140 different

disagree
disappear
disappoint
disapprove
disastrous
discipline
discussion
disease
dispel
150 distinct

disturb
divide
divine
doctor
dormitory
easily
ecstasy
effect
efficient
160 eighth

elaborately
embarrass
empty
enemy
entirely
environment
equipment
equipped
escape
170 especially

everything
evidently
exaggerate
excellent
except
exercise
exhaust
existence
expense
180 experience

experiment
explanation
extremely
familiar
family
fascinate
favourite
February
finally
190 financially

fluorine
foreign
foresee
foretell
forty
forward
friend
fulfill
gauge
200 generally

government
governor
grammar
group
gruesome
guaranteed
guard
guerrilla
guidance
210 happened

happily
harass
heard
height
here
heroes
hindrance
holiday
hoping
220 human

humane
humorous
hundred
hungry
hurriedly
hypocrisy
hypocrite
ideally
idiosyncrasy
230 ignorant

illogical
imaginary
imagine
imitate
immediately
immensely
incalculable
incidentally
incredible
240 independent

indispensable
individually
influential
initiative
innocuous
instead
insurance
intelligent
interest
250 interference

integrate
interrupt
introduce
involve
irrelevant
irresistible
irritated
jealousy
jewellery
260 knowledge

laboratory
laid
led
leisure
length
lenient
liable
library
licence (n.)
270 lightning

likelihood
listening
liveliest
lose
luxury
lying
magazine
magnificent
maintenance
280 manageable

management
manoeuvre
manual
marriage
material
mathematics
meanness
meant
medicine
290 mere

miniature
minor
minutes
mirror
mischievous
missile
morale
morals
mortgage
300 morning

muscle
mysterious
narrative
naturally
necessary
nevertheless
nickel
niece
nineteen
310 ninety

ninth
noticeable
noticing
nowadays
nuclear
nuisance
numerous
occasion
occasionally
320 occurred

occurrence
occurring
off
official
omission
omit
omitted
omitting
opponent
330 opportunity

opposite
oppression
optimism
ordinarily
originally
paid
pamphlet
parallel
parallelled
340 parole

particle
particularly
past
pastime
peaceable
peculiar
penetrate
perceive
performance
350 perhaps

permanent
permissible
persuade
pertain
phase
physical
pigeon
pitiful
planned
360 pleasant

poison
politician
pollute
possession
possibly
practical
practically
precede
predominant
370 preferred

prejudice
prepare
preparation
pretty
prevail
prevalent
principle
prisoner
privilege
380 probably

procedure
proceed
processes
professor
prominent
pronunciation
propaganda
prophecy
prophesy
390 psychology

publicly
pumpkin
purpose
pursue
pursuing
pursuit
quandary
quantity
questionnaire
400 quiet

quite
quizzes
rarity
reality
realize
really
rebel
receipt
receive
410 recession

recipe
recognize
recommend
referring
regular
regulate
rehearsal
relief
relieve
420 religious

remember
remembrance
reminisce
repetition
representative
reproduce
resemblance
resistance
resources
430 restaurant

review
rhythm
ridiculous
roommate
sacrifice
safety
sandwich
satellite
Saturday
440 saxophone

scarcity
scenery
schedule
secede
secretary
seize
senseless
sentence
separate
450 sergeant

several
sheriff
shining
shoulder
shrubbery
significant
similar
simply
since
460 sincerely

ski
skiing
sophomore
source
souvenir
speak
speeches
specimen
sponsor
470 statistics

stayed
stepped
stopped
straight
strategy
strength
strenuous
stretch
strict
480 stubbornness

studies
studying
suburban
succeed
succession
sufficient
suicide
summary
superintendent
490 supersede

suppose
suppress
surely
surprise
surround
suspicious
susceptible
swimming
symbol
500 technical

technique
temperature
temporary
tendency
than
their
theirs
themselves
then
510 therefore

thorough
though
thought
through
till
tobacco
together
tomorrow
too
520 tragedy

transferred
tremendous
trouble
truly
twelfth
typical
tyranny
unanimous
unconscious
530 undoubtedly

until
usage
using
usually
vacuum
valuable
various
vegetable
vengeance
540 vice

view
villain
violence
visible
vitamins
warrant
warring
weather
Wednesday
550 weird

where
wherever
whether
whichever
wholly
whose
without
woman
women
560 writing

written
yield

Hyphenation

18f

Hyphenate words chiefly to express the idea of a unit and to avoid ambiguity. For the division of words at the end of a line, see **8d**.

Words forming a compound may be written separately, written as one word, or connected by hyphens. For example, three modern dictionaries all have the same listings of these compounds:

hair stylist   hairsplitter   hair-raiser

Another modern dictionary, however, lists *hairstylist*, not *hair stylist*. Compounding is in such a state of flux that authorities do not always agree.

(1) Use the hyphen to join two or more words serving as a single adjective before a noun.

the bluish-green sea   chocolate-covered peanuts
peace-loving natives   his know-it-all glance
the twenty-two-year-old laboratory technician

[Note the singular form of the noun *year* after the numeral in the hyphenated modifier.]

Notice that in the examples below the modifiers after the noun are not hyphenated:

The sea was bluish green.
The peanuts, which were chocolate covered, tasted stale.
The laboratory technicians was twenty-two years old.

[Numbers like *twenty-two* are hyphenated wherever they appear in a sentence.]

More than one hyphenated adjectival, of course, may precede the noun modified:

> The ethic of the Chamber of Commerce, do-it-yourself, my-way-is-as-good-as-yours, who-are-you-anyway-to-prefer-brains-to-what-I-have, is artlessly turned into a hippie slogan.
> —J. BRONOWSKI

"Suspension" hyphens are used in such series as the following:

two-, three-, and four-hour classes

Note: The hyphen is generally omitted after an adverb ending in *-ly* in such phrases as the following:

a hopelessly lost cause   a frequently used example

■ **Exercise 6** Convert the following word groups according to the pattern of the example:

EXAMPLES

an initiation lasting two months	*a two-month initiation*
ideas that shake the world	*world-shaking ideas*

1. an apartment with six rooms
2. examinations that exhaust the mind
3. fingers stained with ink
4. a voter who is eighteen years old
5. shoppers who are budget minded
6. tents costing a hundred dollars
7. peace talks that last all night
8. a program that trains teachers
9. a hitchhiker who was waving a flag
10. ponds covered with lilies

(2) Use the hyphen with compound numbers from twenty-one to ninety-nine (or twenty-first to ninety-ninth).

forty-six, fifty-eighth   BUT   three hundred twenty

Note: Usage varies regarding the hyphenation of fractions. The hyphen is required, however, only when the fraction functions as a compound modifier. See also **18f(1)**.

almost one-half full   BUT   eating only one half of it
a two-thirds vote   BUT   two thirds of the voters

(3) Use the hyphen to avoid ambiguity or an awkward combination of letters or syllables between prefix and root or suffix and root.

a dirty movie-theatre [Compare "a dirty-movie theatre."]
to re-sign a petition [Compare "to resign a position."]
semi-independent, shell-like BUT semifluid, childlike

(4) Use the hyphen with the prefixes *ex-* ("former"), *self-*, *all-*; with the suffix *-elect*; and between a prefix and a capitalized word.

ex-wife self-help all-inclusive mayor-elect
mid-September non-Biblical anti-Semitic

Note: The hyphen is also used with figures or letters such as *mid-1980s* or *T-shirt*.

■ **Exercise 7** Refer to **18f** and to your dictionary as you convert each phrase (or words within each phrase) to a compound or to a word with a prefix. Use hyphens when needed.

EXAMPLES

glasses used for water	*water glasses* OR *waterglasses*
not Communistic	*non-Communistic*
a man who makes $75 000 a year	*a $75 000-a-year man*

1. respect for oneself
2. persons keeping the score
3. bacon cured with sugar
4. a plan for sharing the profit
5. a latch used at night
6. four and twenty
7. a cleaner for all purposes
8. a woman who is ninety-two years old
9. in the shape of a V
10. fences that are covered with snow
11. the flight from Montreal to Vancouver
12. a sale lasting two or three days

Good Usage and Glossary

19

Use a good dictionary to help you select the words that express your ideas exactly.

You can find valuable information about words by referring to a good college dictionary, such as one of the following:

Gage Canadian Dictionary
The Concise Oxford Dictionary
The American Heritage Dictionary
The Random House Dictionary
Webster's New Collegiate Dictionary
Webster's New World Dictionary

Occasionally you may need to refer to an unabridged dictionary or to a special dictionary: see the two lists on pages 428-29.

19a

Use a good dictionary intelligently.

Intelligent use of a dictionary requires some understanding of its plan and of the special abbreviations given in the introductory matter. Knowing how the dictionary arranges and presents material will enable you to interpret much of the information provided in its entries.

Below is a sample dictionary entry. First, note the various definitions of *empty* as an adjective, as a transitive verb, as an intransitive verb, as a noun, and as part of an idiomatic phrase (with *of*). Next, observe the examples of usage. Finally, note the various other kinds of information (labelled in colour) that the dictionary provides.

Pronunciation
Syllabication
Adjective forms
Spelling
Etymology
Special usage (*Colloquial*)
Verb forms
Other forms (noun plural, idiom, adverb, derived word)
Synonyms with definitions and distinctions
Antonym

emp·ty (emp′tē) *adj.* **-ti·er, -ti·est** [ME. *emti* & (with intrusive -*p*-) *empti* < OE. *æmettig*, unoccupied, lit., at leisure < *æmetta*, leisure (< *æ*-, without + base of *motan*, to have to: see MUST[1]) + -*ig*, -Y[2]] **1.** containing nothing; having nothing in it **2.** having no one in it; unoccupied; vacant [an *empty* house] **3.** carrying or bearing nothing; bare **4.** having no worth or purpose; useless or unsatisfying [*empty* pleasure] **5.** without meaning or force; insincere; vain [*empty* promises] **6.** [Colloq.] hungry —*vt.* **-tied, -ty·ing 1.** to make empty **2.** *a*) to pour out or remove (the contents) of something *b*) to transfer (the contents) *into*, *onto*, or *on* something else **3.** to unburden or discharge (oneself or itself) —*vi.* **1.** to become empty **2.** to pour out; discharge [the river *empties* into the sea] —***n.***, *pl.* **-ties** an empty freight car, truck, bottle, etc. —**empty of** lacking; without; devoid of —**emp′ti·ly** *adv.* —**emp′ti·ness** *n.*

SYN.—**empty** means having nothing in it [an *empty* box, street, stomach, etc.]; **vacant** means lacking that which appropriately or customarily occupies or fills it [a *vacant* apartment, position, etc.]; **void**, as discriminated here, specifically stresses complete or vast emptiness [*void* of judgment]; **vacuous**, now rare in its physical sense, suggests the emptiness of a vacuum. See also VAIN —*ANT.* **full**

(1) Spelling, syllabication, and pronunciation. As a writer, use your dictionary not only to check spelling but also to find where words may be divided at the end of a line: see **8d**. As a speaker, check the pronunciation of unfamiliar words in your dictionary. Keys to the sound symbols are at the bottom of each two-page spread as well as in the introductory matter at the front of the dictionary. A primary stress mark (′) normally follows the syllable that is most heavily accented. Secondary stress marks follow lightly accented syllables.

Exercise 1 With the aid of your dictionary, write out the following words using sound symbols and stress marks to indicate the correct pronunciation (or a correct one if options are given).

1. harass
2. incongruous
3. performance
4. Mozart
5. pica
6. interest
7. egalitarian
8. advertisement
9. pogonip
10. oceanography

(2) Parts of speech and inflected forms Your dictionary provides labels indicating the possible uses of words in sentences—for instance, *adj*. (adjective), *adv*. (adverb), *v.t.* (verb, transitive). It also lists ways that nouns, verbs, and modifiers change form to indicate number, tense, or comparison or to serve as another part of speech (for example, under *repress, v.t.*, many appear *repressible, adj.*).

Exercise 2 With the aid of your dictionary, classify each of the following words as a verb (transitive or intransitive), a noun, an adjective, an adverb, a preposition, or a conjunction. Give the principal parts of each verb, the plural (or plurals) of each noun, and the comparative and superlative of each adjective and adverb. (Note that some words are used as two or more parts of speech.)

1. permit
2. lonely
3. sweet-talk
4. tattoo
5. subtle
6. for
7. late
8. bring
9. crisis
10. fine

(3) Definitions and examples of usage Observe how your dictionary arranges the definitions of a word: whether the most common meaning is given first or whether the definitions are listed in historical order. Notice also that an illustration of the usage of a word often clarifies a definition.

Exercise 3 Study the definitions of any five of the following pairs of words, paying special attention to any examples of usage in your dictionary; then write sentences to illustrate the shades of difference in meaning.

1. rot—putrefy
2. sensual—sensuous
3. viable—practicable
4. yukking—guffawing
5. mercy—clemency
6. charisma—charm
7. burgoo—gumbo
8. free—liberate
9. jaded—a jade
10. draw—draft

(4) Synonyms and antonyms Lists and discussions of synonyms in dictionaries often help to clarify the meaning of closely related words. By studying the denotations and connotations of words with similar meanings, you will find that you are able to choose your words more exactly and to convey more subtle shades of meaning. Lists of antonyms can help you to find a word that is the direct opposite of another in meaning.

Note: For more complete lists of synonyms, antonyms, related and contrasted words, refer to a special dictionary or thesaurus. Below is a sample thesaurus entry.

empty *adj* **1** lacking contents that could or should be present <an *empty* apartment> <the whole book is *empty* of meaning>

Synonyms —— ***syn*** bare, clear, stark, vacant, vacuous, void

Related words —— ***rel*** barren, blank; abandoned, deserted, emptied, forsaken, godforsaken, unfilled, unfurnished, uninhabited, untenanted, vacated; destitute, devoid; depleted, drained, exhausted

Contrasted words —— ***con*** complete, replete; filled, occupied, packed, teeming

Antonym —— ***ant*** full

2 ***syn*** VAIN 1, hollow, idle, nugatory, otiose

rel paltry, petty, trifling, trivial; banal, flat, inane, ineffectual, insipid, jejune, vapid; dumb, fatuous, foolish, ignorant, silly, simple

con meaningful, pregnant, significant; authentic, bona fide, genuine, veritable

3 ***syn*** EXPRESSIONLESS, blank, deadpan, inexpressive, unexpressive, vacant

4 ***syn*** DEVOID, innocent, void

Before choosing a synonym or closely related word from such a list, look it up in the dictionary to make sure that it expresses your meaning exactly. Although *stark, idle*, and *inexpressive* are all listed above as synonyms of *empty*, they have vastly different connotations.

■ **Exercise 4** With the aid of your dictionary or thesaurus, list two synonyms and one antonym for each of the following words. (1) hatred (2) pleasure (3) false (4) oppose (5) stingy

(5) Origin: development of the language In college dictionaries the origin of the word—also called its *derivation* or *etymology*—is shown in square brackets. For example, after *expel* might be this information: "[<L *expellere* < *ex-* out + *pellere* to drive, thrust]." This means that *expel* is derived from (<) the Latin (L) word *expellere*, which is made up of *ex-*, meaning "out," and *pellere*, meaning "to drive or thrust." Breaking up a word, when possible, into *prefix—root—suffix* will often help to get at the basic meaning of a word.

	prefix		*root*		*suffix*
dependent	**de-** down	+	**pend** to hang	+	**-ent** one who
interruption	**inter-** between	+	**rupt** to break	+	**-ion** act of
preference	**pre-** before	+	**fer** to carry	+	**-ence** state of

The bracketed information given by a good dictionary is especially rich in meaning when considered in relation to the historical development of our language. English is one of the Indo-European (IE) languages, a group of languages apparently derived from a common source.* Within this group of languages, many of the more familiar words are

*The parenthetical abbreviations for languages here and on the next few pages are those commonly used in bracketed derivations in dictionaries.

remarkably alike. Our word *mother*, for example, is *mater* in Latin (L), *meter* in Greek (Gk.), and *matar* in ancient Persian and in the Sanskrit (Skt.) of India. Words in different languages that apparently descend from a common parent language are called *cognates*. The large number of cognates and the many correspondences in sound and structure in most of the languages of Europe and some languages of Asia indicate that they are derived from the common language that linguists call Indo-European, which it is believed was spoken in parts of Europe about six thousand years ago. By the opening of the Christian era the speakers of this language had spread over most of Europe and as far east as India, and the original Indo-European had developed into eight or nine language families. Of these, the chief ones that influenced English were the Hellenic (Greek) group on the eastern Mediterranean, the Italic (Latin) on the central and western Mediterranean, and the Germanic in northwestern Europe. English is descended from the Germanic.

Two thousand years ago the Hellenic, the Italic, and the Germanic branches of Indo-European each comprised a more or less unified language group. After the fall of the Roman Empire in the fifth century, the several Latin-speaking divisions developed independently into the modern Romance languages, chief of which are Italian, French, and Spanish. Long before the fall of Rome the Germanic group was breaking up into three families: (1) East Germanic, represented by the Goths, who were to play a large part in the history of the last century of the Roman Empire before losing themselves in its ruins; (2) North Germanic, or Old Norse (ON), from which modern Danish (Dan.), Swedish (Sw.), Norwegian (Norw.), and Icelandic (Icel.) derive; and (3) West Germanic, the direct ancestor of English, Dutch (Du.), and German (Ger.).

The English language may be said to have begun about the middle of the fifth century, when the West Germanic Angles, Saxons, and Jutes began the conquest of what is now England and either absorbed or drove out the Celtic-speaking inhabitants. (Celtic—from which Scots Gaelic, Irish Gaelic, Welsh, and other languages later developed—is another member of the Indo-European family.) The next six or seven hundred years are known as the Old English (OE) or Anglo-Saxon (AS) period of the English language. The fifty or sixty thousand words then in the language were chiefly Anglo-Saxon, with a small mixture of Old Norse words as a result of the Danish (Viking) conquests of England beginning in the eighth century. But the Old Norse words were so much like the Anglo-Saxon that they cannot always be distinguished.

The transitional period from Old English to Modern English—about 1100 to 1500—is known as Middle English (ME). The Norman Conquest began in 1066. The Normans, or "Northmen," had settled in northern France during the Viking invasions and had adopted Old French (OF) in place of their native Old Norse. Then, crossing over to England by the thousands, they made French the language of the king's court in London and of the ruling classes—both French and English—throughout the land, while the masses continued to speak English. Only toward the end of the fifteenth century did English become once more the common language of all classes. But the language that emerged at that time had lost most of its Anglo-Saxon inflections and had taken on thousands of French words (derived originally from Latin). Nonetheless, it was still basically English, not French, in its structure.

The marked and steady development of the English language (until it was partly stabilized by printing, introduced in London in 1476) is suggested by the following passages, two from Old English and two from Middle English.

Hē ǣrest scēop   eorðan bearnum
He first created   for earth's children

heofon tō hrōfe,   hālig Scyppend.
heaven as a roof,   holy creator.

From the "Hymn of Cædmon"
(middle of the Old English period)

Ēalā, hū lēas and hū unwrest is þysses middan-eardes wēla.
Alas! how false and how unstable is this midworld's weal!

Sē þe wæs ǣrur rīce cyng and maniges landes hlāford,
He that was before powerful king and of many lands lord,

hē næfde þā ealles landes būton seofon fōt mæl.
he had not then of all land but seven foot space.

From the *Anglo-Saxon Chronicle*, A.D. 1087
(end of the Old English period)

A knight ther was, and that a worthy man,
That fro the tyme that he first bigan
To ryden out, he loved chivalrye,
Trouthe and honour, fredom and curteisye.

From Chaucer's Prologue to the
Canterbury Tales, about 1385

Thenne within two yeres king Uther felle seke of a grete maladye. And in the meane whyle hys enemyes usurpped upon hym, and dyd a grete bataylle upon his men, and slewe many of his peple.

From Sir Thomas Malory's *Morte d'Arthur*,
printed 1485

A striking feature of Modern English (that is, English since 1500) is its immense vocabulary. As already noted, Old English used some fifty or sixty thousand words, very largely native Anglo-Saxon; Middle English used perhaps a hundred thousand words, many taken through the French from Latin and others taken directly from Latin; and unabridged dictionaries today list over four times as many. To make up this tremendous word hoard, we have borrowed most heavily from Latin, but we have drawn some words from almost every known language. English writers of the sixteenth century were especially eager to interlace their works with words from Latin authors. And, as the English pushed out to colonize and to trade in many parts of the globe, they brought home new words as well as goods. Modern science and technology have drawn heavily from the Greek. As a result of all this borrowing, English has become one of the richest and most cosmopolitan of languages.

In the process of enlarging our vocabulary we have lost most of our original Anglo-Saxon words. But those that are left make up the most familiar, most useful part of our vocabulary. Practically all our simple verbs, our articles, conjunctions, prepositions, and pronouns are native Anglo-Saxon; and so are many of our familiar nouns, adjectives, and adverbs. Every speaker and writer uses these native words over and over, much more frequently than the borrowed words. Indeed, if every word is counted every time it is used, the percentage of native words runs very high—usually between 70 and 90 per cent. Milton's percentage was 81, Tennyson's 88, Shakespeare's about 90, and that of the King James Bible about 94. English has been enriched by its extensive borrowings without losing its individuality; it is still fundamentally the *English* language.

■ **Exercise 5** With the aid of your dictionary, give the etymology of each of the following words:

1. aspirin
2. ecology
3. gardenia
4. geriatrics
5. guerrilla
6. helicopter
7. laser
8. OK
9. polyester
10. Teflon

(6) Special usage labels Dictionaries ordinarily carry no usage labels for the bulk of English words. Unlabelled, or general, words range from the learned words appropriate in the most formal situations to the words used every day in both formal and informal situations.

Most dictionaries, however, provide a variety of special usage labels for words or for particular definitions of words. These labels indicate varieties of usage that differ from the general. Here is a sampling of labelled definitions, each of them found in two or more college dictionaries.

unalienable	*Archaic, Obsolete*	inalienable
lift	*Informal, Colloquial*	plagiarize
nowheres	*Non-standard, Dialect, Colloquial*	not anywhere, nowhere
stink	*Slang*	to be of low quality

As the examples above indicate, the classification of words is often difficult and controversial because our language is constantly changing. Good writers try to choose the words, whatever their labels, that exactly fit the audience and the occasion, informal or formal.

■ **Exercise 6** Classify the following words and phrases according to the usage labels in your dictionary. If a word has no special usage label, classify it as *General*. If a given definition of a word has a usage label, give the meaning after the label.

EXAMPLES
tote bag—general
aholt—dialectal
nutty—informal for *silly*, slang for *insane*

1. doll
2. dude
3. funky
4. holler
5. irregardless
6. junk
7. macho
8. rube
9. snigger
10. unto

19b

Avoid informal words in formal writing.

Words or expressions labelled *Informal* or *Colloquial* in college dictionaries are standard English and are used by speakers and writers every day. These words are thus appropriate in informal writing, especially in dialogue. But informal words or expressions are usually inappropriate in formal expository compositions. In formal writing, use instead the general English vocabulary, the unlabelled words in your dictionary.

INFORMAL In class the teacher gave a definition of *polyunsaturated*, but I didn't **get it**.

FORMAL In class the teacher gave a definition of *polyunsaturated*, but I did not **understand it**.

Contractions are common in informal English, especially in dialogue: see the examples on page 162. But contracted forms (like *won't* or *there's*) are usually written out (*will not, there is*) in a formal composition—which is not as casual or spontaneous as conversational English is.

■ **Exercise 7** Make a list of ten words that you would consider informal in your writing. Then check your dictionary to see how (or if) each definition you have in mind is labelled.

19c
Use slang and jargon only when appropriate to the audience.

Slang words, including certain coinages and figures of speech, are variously considered as breezy, racy, extremely informal, non-standard, facetious, taboo, off-beat, or vigorous. On occasion, slang can be used effectively, even in formal writing. Below is an example of the effective use of the word *spiel*, still labelled by dictionaries as *Slang*:

> Here comes election year. Here come the hopefuls, the conventions, the candidates, the spiels, the postures, the press releases, and the TV performances. Here comes the year of the hoopla. —JOHN CIARDI

A few years ago the word *hoopla* was also generally considered as slang, but now dictionaries disagree: one classifies this word *Standard* (unlabelled); another, *Colloquial* (*Infor-*

mal); still another, *Slang*. Like *hoopla*, words such as *spiel, uptight, paddy wagon, raunchy, schlep*, and *party pooper* have a particularly vivid quality; they soon may join former slang words such as *sham* and *mob* as part of the general English vocabulary.

But much slang is trite, tasteless, and inexact. For instance, when used to describe almost anything disapproved of, *gross* becomes inexact, flat.

Caution: As you avoid the use of ineffective slang in your writing, remember that many of the most vivid short words in our language are general, standard words. Certain long words can be as inexact and as drab as trite slang. For examples of the ineffective use of big words, see Exercise 9, page 223.

■ **Exercise 8** Replace the italicized words in the following sentences with more exact words or specific phrases:

1. After dress rehearsal the whole cast *goofed off*.
2. Lately the weather has been *lousy* on weekends.
3. Jean's new haircut is *dynamite*.
4. That *wisecrack ticked* him *off*.

19d

Use regional words only when appropriate to the audience.

Regional, or *dialectal*, words (also called *localisms* or *provincialisms*) should normally be avoided in speaking and writing outside the region where they are current. Speakers and writers may, however, safely use regional words known to the audience they are addressing.

REGIONAL Monty was **fixing to** feed his steak to the **critter**.
GENERAL Monty was **about to** feed his steak to the **dog**. [OR *animal* OR *creature*]

19e

Avoid non-standard words and usages.

Words and expressions labelled by dictionaries as *Non-standard* or *Illiterate* should be avoided in most writing and speaking. Many common illiteracies are not listed in college dictionaries.

NON-STANDARD	**They's** no use asking them.
STANDARD	**There's** no use asking them.

19f

Avoid archaic and obsolete words.

All dictionaries list words (and meanings for words) that have long since passed out of general use. Such words as *ort* (fragment of food) and *yestreen* (last evening) are still found in dictionaries because these words, once the standard vocabulary of great authors, occur in our older literature and must be defined for the modern reader.

A number of obsolete or archaic words—such as *worser* (for *worse*) or *holp* (for *helped*)—are still in use but are now non-standard.

19g

Use technical words only when appropriate to the audience.

When you are writing for the general reader, avoid all unnecessary technical language. Since the ideal of good writing is to make one's thought clear to as many people as possible, the careful writer will not describe an apple tree as a *Malus pumila* or a high fever as *hyperpyrexia*. (Of course, technical language, with its greater precision, is highly desirable when one is addressing an audience that can understand it, as when a physician addresses a group of physicians.)

19h

Avoid overwriting, an ornate or flowery style. Do not needlessly combine distracting sounds.

Overwriting, as well as the combination of distracting sounds, calls attention to words rather than to ideas. Such writing is generally fuzzy and repetitious, or carelessly indifferent to the importance of sound and its relationship to meaning.

ORNATE	Since the halcyon days of my early youth I have always anticipated with eagerness and pleasure the exciting vistas of distant climes and mysterious horizons.
BETTER	Since childhood I have looked forward to seeing the world.
DISTRACTING	The use of catalytic converters is just one contribution to the solution of the problem of air pollution.
BETTER	The use of catalytic converters is just one way to help solve the problem of air pollution.

Equally unpleasing to the average reader is the overuse of alliteration (repetition of the same consonant sound), as in "Some people *sh*un the *s*ea*sh*ore."

■ **Exercise 9** Using simple, formal, straightforward English, rewrite the following sentences (from Stuart Chase's *Power of Words*):

1. It is obvious from the difference in elevation with relation to the short depth of the property that the contour is such as to preclude any reasonable developmental potential for active recreation.
2. Verbal contact with Mr. Blank regarding the attached notification of promotion has elicited the attached representation intimating that he prefers to decline the assignment.
3. Voucherable expenditures necessary to provide adequate dental treatment required as adjunct to medical treatment

being rendered a pay patient in in-patient status may be incurred as required at the expense of the Public Health Service.

4. I hereby give and convey to you, all and singular, my estate and interests, right, title, claim and advantages of and in said orange, together with all rind, juice, pulp and pits, and all rights and advantages therein.
5. I prefer an abbreviated phraseology, distinguished for its lucidity.
6. Realization has grown that the curriculum or the experiences of learners change and improve only as those who are most directly involved examine their goals, improve their understandings and increase their skill in performing the tasks necessary to reach newly defined goals.

Glossary of Usage

19i

Consult the following glossary to determine the standing of a word or phrase and its appropriateness to your purpose.

The entries in the following glossary are authoritative only to the extent that they describe current usage. The usage labels included do not duplicate the descriptions in any one dictionary, but justification for each can usually be found in at least two of the leading dictionaries.

For a discussion of the special usage labels used in dictionaries, see **19a(6)**. The following labels appear most frequently in this glossary:

General Words in the standard English vocabulary, listed in dictionaries without special usage labels and appropriate in both formal and informal writing and speaking.

Informal Words or expressions labelled *Informal* or *Colloquial* in dictionaries—words widely used by educated as well as uneducated writers and speakers but not appropriate in a formal context. See also **19b**.

Standard All general and informal words or expressions.

Non-standard Words or expressions labelled in dictionaries as *Archaic, Illiterate, Non-standard, Obsolete, Slang,* or *Substandard*—words not considered a part of the standard English vocabulary. See also **19c, e**, and **f**.

Of course, the following glossary can include only a few of the words likely to cause difficulty. If the word you are looking for is not included, or if you need more information about any word in the list, consult a good college dictionary.

a, an Use *a* before a consonant sound, *an* before a vowel sound.

a history	**a** union	**a** one-dollar bill	**a** new dress	**a** C
an hour	**an** uncle	**an** only child	**an** NHL game	**an** F

accept See **except, accept**.

accidentally, incidentally When using these adverbs, remember that *-ly* is added to the adjective forms *accidental* and *incidental*, not to the noun forms *accident* and *incident*.

> NON-STANDARD Mr. Kent **accidently** overheard the report.
> STANDARD Mr. Kent **accidentally** overheard the report.

adapt, adopt Do not confuse. To *adapt* is to adjust or make suitable. To *adopt* is to select as one's own or to choose to use or follow.

> We **adapted** the guidelines to our needs. [made them fit]
> The company **adopted** new guidelines. [chose to use]

advice, advise Pronounced and spelled differently, *advice* is a noun, *advise* a verb.

> Patients should follow their doctors' **advice**.
> Patients should do what their doctors **advise**.

affect, effect Do not confuse the verb *affect* with the noun *effect*. To *affect* is to rouse the emotions or to influence, change. An *effect* is a result, an outcome. (When used as a verb, *effect* means "bring about" or "accomplish": "The medicine *effected* a complete cure.")

His tears **affected** her deeply.	The **effect** surprised me.
The drug **affects** one's appetite.	The drug has side **effects**.

aggravate Informally *aggravate* means "to annoy or to irritate." In general usage it means "to make worse" or "to intensify."

> INFORMAL Undisciplined children **aggravate** babysitters.
> GENERAL Lack of water **aggravated** the suffering.

a half a Informal for *half a* or *a half.*

ain't A non-standard contraction generally avoided in writing, unless used in dialogue or for humorous effect.

all the farther, all the faster Regional, or dialectal, for *as far as, as fast as.*

> NON-STANDARD A mile is all the farther Mae can jog.
> STANDARD A mile is **as far as** Mae can jog.

allude, elude See **elude, allude**.

allusion, illusion Do not confuse. An *allusion* is a casual or indirect reference. An *illusion* is a false idea or an unreal image.

> The author's **allusion** to a heaven on earth amused me.
> The author's concept of a heaven on earth is an **illusion**.

almost, most See **most**.

a lot Sometimes misspelled as *alot.*

already, all ready *Already* means "before or by the time specified." *All ready* means "completely prepared."

> The theatre was **already** full by seven o'clock.
> The cast was **all ready** for the curtain call.

alright Not yet a generally accepted spelling of *all right.*

altogether, all together *Altogether* means "wholly, thoroughly." *All together* means "in a group."

> That law is **altogether** unnecessary.
> They were **all together** in the lobby.

A.M., P.M. (OR **a.m., p.m.**) Use only with figures.

NOT The wedding begins at ten thirty in the **a.m.**
BUT The wedding begins at 10:30 **A.M.** [OR at ten thirty in the morning]

among, between Prepositions with plural objects (including collective nouns). As a rule, use *among* with objects denoting three or more (a group), and use *between* with those denoting only two (or twos).

walked **among** the crowd, quarrelling **among** themselves
a choice **between** war and peace, reading **between** the lines

amount of, number of *Amount of* is followed by singular nouns; *number of*, by plural nouns.

an **amount of** money, light, work, or postage [singular]
a **number of** coins, lights, jobs, or stamps [plural]

See also **a number, the number**.

an See **a, an**.

and etc. Omit the redundant *and. Etc.* is an abbreviation of *et* ("and") *cetera* ("other things"). See also **etc**.

ante-, anti- Do not confuse these prefixes. *Ante-* means "before, in front of." The more frequently used *anti-* means "against, opposite to" or "hostile to."

antedate, anteroom, antenatal, antebellum, antecedent
antiwar, anticlimax, antichrist, anti-Semitic, antidote, antibiotic

a number, the number As subject, *a number* is generally plural and *the number* is singular. Make sure that the verb agrees with the subject.

A number of options **are** available.
The number of options **is** limited.

anyone, any one *Anyone* means "any person at all." *Any one* refers to a specific person or thing in a group. Similar forms are *everyone, every one; someone, some one.*

Anyone can wax a floor.
Any one of those men can wax a floor.

anyways, anywheres Dialectal or colloquial for *anyway, anywhere*.

as (1) Do not use *as* in place of the preposition *like* in making a comparison.

NOT Natalie, as her mother, stands tall.
BUT Natalie, **like** her mother, stands tall.
See also **like**.

(2) In your formal writing, do not use *as* in place of *whether, if*, or *that* after such verbs as *feel, know, say*, or *see*.

INFORMAL I do not know as the Prime Minister's adviser is right.
GENERAL I do not know **whether** the Prime Minister's adviser is right.

(3) If there is even a slight chance of ambiguity, many writers prefer not to use *as* for *because, since*, or *while*.

GENERAL As it was raining, we watched TV. [probably clear in context but possibly not]
PREFERRED **While** it was raining, we watched TV.
OR **Because** it was raining, we watched TV.

at Redundant after *where*. See **where at, where to**.

awful An overworked word for *ugly, shocking, very bad*. Informal as a substitute for *very*, as in "awful pretty" or "awful important."

awhile, a while Distinguish between the adverb *awhile* and the article and noun *a while* (ordinarily used as an object of a preposition).

After our long swim, we rested **awhile**.
After our long swim, we rested for **a while**.

bad, badly The adverb *badly* is preferred after most verbs. But either *bad* or *badly* is now standard in the sense of "ill" or "sorry," and writers now usually prefer *bad* after such verbs as *feel* or *look*.

The organist plays **badly**.
Charles feels **bad**.

be sure and Write *be sure to* in such sentences as "*Be sure to* consult a lawyer."

because See **reason . . . because**.

being as, being that Non-standard for *since, because.*

beside, besides Always a preposition, *beside* usually means "next to," sometimes "apart from." As a preposition meaning "in addition to" or "other than," *besides* is now more common in writing than *beside*. When used adverbially, *besides* means "also" or "moreover."

> Marvin was sitting **beside** Jessica.
> **Besides** countless toys, these children have their own TV set.
> The burglars stole our silver—and my stereo **besides**.

better, had better In the sense of an emphatic "ought to," *better* is an informal shortening of *had better.*

INFORMAL	He better watch out!
GENERAL	He **had** better watch out! [OR He'**d** better watch out!]

between See **among, between**.

boys See **girls, boys**.

broke Archaic for *broken.*

STANDARD	Only my little finger was **broken** [NOT broke].

bug Slang if used as a verb. As a noun, *bug* is slang in the sense of "fan, enthusiast."

SLANG	Loud noises bug her.	I am a tennis bug.
STANDARD	Loud noises bother her.	I love tennis.

bunch Informal if used to refer to people.

bust, busted, bursted The principal parts of *burst* are *burst, burst, burst. Bursted* is archaic. *Bust* and *busted* are still considered slang. When *burst* does not fit the context, use a different verb, such as a form of *break* (NOT "busted the record" BUT "*broke* the record").

but what Informal after *no* or *not* following such expressions as "no doubt" or "did not know."

INFORMAL	There was no doubt but what they would win.
GENERAL	There was no doubt **that** they would win.

can, may Formal English still distinguishes between *can* referring to ability and *may* referring to permission.

> **Can** student nurses give injections? [Are they able to?]
> **May** student nurses give injections? [Are they permitted to?]

can't hardly, can't scarcely Double negatives in implication. Use *can hardly, can scarcely*. See also **hardly, scarcely**.

case, line Often used in wordy expressions.

WORDY	In the case of Jones there were good intentions.
CONCISE	Jones had good intentions.
WORDY	Buy something in the line of fruit.
CONCISE	Buy some fruit.

cause of . . . on account of, due to Redundant. Omit the *on account of* or *due to*; or recast to avoid wordiness.

WORDY	One cause of misunderstandings is on account of lack of communication.
BETTER	One cause of misunderstanding is lack of communication.
CONCISE	Lack of communication causes misunderstandings.

centre on, revolve around Do not mix these terms.

WRONG	The discussion centred around justice.
STANDARD	The discussion centred on justice.

compare to, compare with Formal English prefers *compare to* for the meaning "regard as similar" and *compare with* for the meaning "examine to discover similarities or differences."

> The speaker **compared** the earth **to** a lopsided baseball.
> Putting one under the other, the expert **compared** the forged signature **with** the authentic one.

complementary, complimentary Do not confuse. *Complementary* means "completing" or "supplying needs." *Complimentary* means "expressing praise" or "given free."

> His talents and hers are **complementary**.
> Admiring the performance, he made several **complimentary** remarks.

conscious, conscience Do not confuse. An adjective, *conscious* means "aware, able to feel and think." A noun, *conscience* means "the sense of right and wrong."

> After the accident, when I became **conscious** of my guilt, my **conscience** started bothering me.

considerable Used generally as an adjective, informally as a noun. Non-standard as an adverb.

NON-STANDARD	Prices have dropped considerable.
INFORMAL	**Considerable** has been donated to the civic fund.
GENERAL	A **considerable** amount has been donated to the civic fund.

could of Non-standard for *could have*. See **of**.

couple, couple of Informal for *two* or for *several* in such phrases as "a couple aspirin," "a couple more litres of paint," or "in just a couple of seconds."

data, criteria, phenomena The plurals of *datum* (rarely used), *criterion*, and *phenomenon*. *Criterion* and *phenomenon* have alternate plurals: *criterions, phenomenons*. The plural *data* is often construed as a collective noun: "This *data has* been verified."

differ from, differ with *Differ from* means "to stand apart because of unlikeness." *Differ with* means "to disagree."

disinterested, uninterested Often used interchangeably. Some authorities, however, do not accept *disinterested* ("impartial") as a substitute for *uninterested* ("indifferent").

done Standard as an adjective and as the past participle of the verb *do*. Non-standard as an adverb and as a substitute for *did*.

NON-STANDARD	Do the police know who done it?
STANDARD	Do they know who **did** it? Who **has done** it?

don't A contraction of *do not* rather than of *does not*.

NON-STANDARD	He don't smoke. (He do not smoke.)
STANDARD	He **doesn't** smoke. (He *does not* smoke.)
STANDARD	They **don't** smoke. (They *do not* smoke.)

each and every Redundant.

effect See **affect, effect**.

elicit, illicit A verb, *elicit* means "bring out or evoke," as in "to *elicit* information." An adjective, *illicit* means "illegal or improper," as in "an *illicit* sale."

elude, allude To *elude* is to escape the notice of. To *allude* is to refer to casually or indirectly. The corresponding adjectives are *elusive* and *allusive*.

> Exact dates often **elude** me.
> Carol likes to **allude** to the ghost of Hamlet's father.

See also **allusion, illusion**.

emigrate from, immigrate to The prefix *e-* (a variant of *ex-*) means "out of"; *im-* (a variant of *in-*) means "into." To *emigrate* is to go out of one's own country to settle in another. To *immigrate* is to come into a different country to settle there. The corresponding adjective or noun forms are *emigrant* and *immigrant*. (Compare: *export, import*.)

> Many workers **emigrated from** Italy. The number of **emigrants** increased during the 1970s.
> Many Italians **immigrated to** Canada. These **immigrant** workers contributed to the growth of our economy.

eminent, imminent *Eminent* means "distinguished." *Imminent* means "about to happen, threatening."

> Charlotte is an **eminent** scientist.
> Bankruptcy seemed **imminent**.

enthuse, enthused *Enthuse* is informal as a verb meaning "to show enthusiasm." *Enthused* is informal as a synonym for *enthusiastic*.

> INFORMAL We were all **enthused** about the new club.
> GENERAL We were all **enthusiastic** about the new club.

etc. Appropriate informally but used sparingly in formal writing. Many writers prefer to substitute *and so on* or *and so forth*. (Since *etc.* means "and other things," *and etc.* is redundant.)

> NEEDLESS Ordinary games like Monopoly, backgammon, etc., did not interest these electronics hobbyists.

REVISED Ordinary games like Monopoly and backgammon did not interest these electronics hobbyists.

ever so often, every so often Do not confuse. *Ever so often* means "very often, frequently." *Every so often* means "every now and then, occasionally."

everyone, every one See **anyone, any one**.

except, accept Do not confuse. To *except* is to exclude or make an exception of. To *accept* is to approve of or receive.

These laws **except** juveniles.	Present company **excepted!**
These schools **accept** juveniles.	I **accepted** their apologies.

explicit, implicit *Explicit* means "expressed directly or precisely." *Implicit* means "implied or expressed indirectly."

The advertisement was **explicit**: "All sales final."
Reading between the lines, I understood the **implicit** message.

farther, further Used interchangeably. Some writers, however, prefer *farther* in references to geographic distance (as in "six kilometres *farther*"). *Further* is used as a synonym for *additional* in more abstract references (such as "without *further* delay," "*further* proof").

fewer, less Informally used interchangeably in the sense of "not many." Formally, *fewer* refers to numbers (how many), and *less* refers to amount, extent, or collective quantity (how much).

fewer seeds	fewer hours	fewer than twenty students
less seed	less time	less than $7,500 a year

fine Informal for *very well*, as in "did fine on that test." Use sparingly as a vague word of approval.

fit, fitted When used in the sense of adapted to a person or occasion, *fitted* is preferable to *fit*, in the past tense.

Her words **fitted** the occasion.
His suit **fitted** him well.

folks Informal for *parents, relatives*.

former Refers to the first named of two. If three or more items are named, use *first* and *last* instead of *former* or *latter*.

> The Folger and the Huntington are two famous libraries: the **former** is in Washington, D.C., and the latter is in San Marino, California.

fun Informal if used adjectivally, as in "a fun person," "a fun car."

further See **farther, further**.

get Useful in numerous idioms but not appropriate formally in such expressions as "get with the times," "always gets in with his instructors," and "a stubborn attitude that gets me."

good Informal if used adverbially.

> INFORMAL Watson plays good under pressure.
> GENERAL Watson plays **well** under pressure.

great Overworked informally for *skillful, good, clever, enthusiastic*, or *very well*, as in "really great at guessing the answers" or "with everything going great for us."

guy(s) Informal for *any person(s)*.

had of, had have Non-standard for *had*.

> NON-STANDARD I wish I had of [OR had have] said that.
> STANDARD I wish I **had** said that.

had ought, hadn't ought Non-standard for *ought, ought not* or *oughtn't*.

hang Useful in numerous idioms but slang in such expressions as "his hang-up about marriage" and "to hang out in discos."

hanged, hung Informally interchangeable in the sense of "put to death by hanging." Formally, it is *hanged* (often used figuratively nowadays) that refers to such an act.

> Whenever my parents supplied enough rope, I usually **hanged** myself—but not always.

hardly, scarcely Words with negative force, usually considered non-standard if used with an unnecessary negative like *not*, *nothing*, or *without*.

NOT I couldn't hardly quit then.
BUT I **could hardly** quit then.

NOT Hardly nothing was in order.
BUT **Hardly anything** was in order.

NOT The motion passed without scarcely a protest.
BUT The motion passed **with scarcely** a protest.

hisself Non-standard for *himself*.

hooked on Slang for *addicted to* or *obsessed with*.

hopefully Still questionable for *it is hoped*.

how come Informally used as a substitute for *why*.

INFORMAL I do not know how come they did that.
GENERAL I do not know **why** they did that.

illusion See **allusion, illusion**.

immigrate See **emigrate from, immigrate to**.

imply, infer Used interchangeably as synonyms for *hint at, intimate, suggest*. Most writers, however, carefully distinguish between *infer* (meaning "draw a conclusion based on evidence") and *imply* ("suggest without actually stating").

His attitude **implies** that money is no problem.
I **infer** from his attitude that money is no problem.

incredible, incredulous *Incredible* means "unbelievable, improbable." *Incredulous* means "skeptical, doubting."

The witness's story was **incredible**.
The judge gave the witness an **incredulous** look.

inferior than Use *inferior to* or *worse than*.

ingenious, ingenuous *Ingenious* means "clever, resourceful"; *ingenuous* means "open, frank," "artless."

This electric can opener is an **ingenious** device.
Don's **ingenuous** smile disarms the critics.

in regards to Non-standard for *in regard to* or *as regards.*

irregardless Non-standard for *regardless.*

is when, is where Do not use *when* or *where* after *is* in giving definitions.

> NOT Begging the question is when [OR is where] a person argues by taking the conclusion for granted.
> BUT Begging the question is taking the conclusion for granted in an argument.
> OR A person begs the question by taking the conclusion for granted in an argument.

its, it's *Its* is a possessive pronoun ("for *its* beauty"). *It's* is a contraction of *it is* ("*It's* beautiful!") or of *it has* ("*It's* been a beautiful day!").

kick Slang or very informal in such expressions as "to kick in my share," "on another kick," "just for kicks," "always kicking about grades," "gets kicked out of class," "just kicking around town."

kind, sort Singular forms, which may be modified by *this* or *that*. The use of *these* or *those* is increasingly common but is still questionable.

> QUESTIONABLE These kind of arguments are deceptive.
> PREFERRED **These kinds** of arguments are deceptive.
> OR **This kind** of argument is deceptive.

kind of, sort of Informal when used adverbially in the sense of "to a degree, somewhat, a bit" or "in a way" (as in "kind of silly," "sort of hesitated," or "kind of enjoying it").

kind of a, sort of a Omit the *a* in your formal writing: NOT "this kind of a tour," BUT "this *kind of* tour."

later, latter Comparative forms of *late* often confused in writing. In modern English, *later* (like *sooner*) refers to time; *latter* (like *former*) refers to one of two—to the second one (but not to the last of several).

> We set a **later** date. They arrived **later** than usual.
> She wrote a song and a play. The **latter** won a prize.

See also **former**.

lay (laying, laid) Non-standard for *lie* (*lying, lay, lain*) meaning "to rest or recline." See also **7a(2))**.

NON-STANDARD	I did lay down awhile. Had he laid down? The truck was laying on its side.
STANDARD	I did **lie** down awhile. Had he **lain** down? The truck was **lying** on its side.
NON-STANDARD	After lunch, I laid down awhile.
STANDARD	After lunch, I **lay** down awhile. [past of *lie*]

learn Non-standard for *teach, instruct, inform*.

NOT That'll learn him!
BUT That'll **teach** him!

leave Non-standard for *let* except when followed by an object and *alone*, as in "*Leave* [OR Let] them alone."

NON-STANDARD	He won't leave me go now.
STANDARD	He won't **let** me go now. [OR let me leave]
NON-STANDARD	Leave us not protest too much.
STANDARD	**Let** us not protest too much.

less See **fewer, less**.

let's us Redundant. Use *let's* or *let us*.

liable to Informally used in place of *likely to* in reference to mere probability. Formally, *liable to* not only denotes likelihood or possibility but also suggests the idea of harm or danger.

INFORMAL	It's liable to be cooler soon. [mere likelihood]
GENERAL	The roof is **liable** to collapse. [likelihood + danger]

lie (lying, lay, lain) Non-standard for *lay (laying, laid)* in the sense of "put, place." See also **7a(2)**.

NON-STANDARD	Onion slices are then lain on the fillets.
STANDARD	Onion slices are then **laid** on the fillets.
NON-STANDARD	Last night I lay my homework aside.
STANDARD	Last night I **laid** my homework aside.

like Widely used as a conjunction (in place of *as, as if*, or *as though*) in conversation and in public speaking. Formal English, however, still rejects the use of *like* as a conjunction.

FORMAL He drives **as** [NOT like] I did before my accident. OR He drives **the way** I did before my accident.
FORMAL They acted **as though** [NOT like] they owned the town.

line See **case, line**.

lose, loose Do not confuse. *Lose* is a verb: *to lose, did lose, will lose*. *Loose* is chiefly an adjective: "a *loose* sentence," "to become *loose*," "at *loose* ends."

lousy Slang, overworked informally, for *mean, bad, painful, inferior, nasty, messy*.

may be, maybe Do not confuse the verb phrase *may be*, with the adverb *maybe*.

The story **may be** [OR might be] true.
Maybe [OR Perhaps] the story is true.

me and Non-standard as part of a compound subject. See also **5a**.

NON-STANDARD Me and Drake took an early flight.
STANDARD Drake and I took an early flight.

mighty Informal for *very* or *extremely* (as in "mighty fine" or "mighty big").

morale, moral Do not confuse. *Morale* (a noun) refers to mood or spirit. *Moral* (chiefly an adjective) refers to right conduct or ethical character.

the **morale** of our team, affecting **morale**, low **morale**
a **moral** person, **moral** judgments, an im**moral** act

most Informal if used in place of *almost*.

INFORMAL Most everyone needs to take a daily walk.
GENERAL **Almost** everyone needs to take a daily walk.

myself Standard as an intensive or a reflexive pronoun: "I *myself* saw a UFO" (intensive). "Momentarily I hated *myself*" (reflexive). Not acceptable formally and still questionable informally as a replacement for the subjective form *I* or the objective *me*.

My sister and **I** [NOT myself] prefer soccer.
He confided in Hayden as well as **me** [NOT myself] .

neither Non-standard for *either* in double negatives such as "I don't like spinach neither." See **not . . . no/none/nothing**.

no-account, no-count, no-good Informal for *worthless, good-for-nothing*.

nohow Non-standard for *not at all, in no way, anyway*.

no such a Omit the *a*: NOT "no such a place" BUT "no such place."

not . . . no/none/nothing A non-standard construction when the two negatives have a negative meaning.

NON-STANDARD	He did not keep no records. [double negative]
STANDARD	He did not keep any records. [one negative: *not*]
	OR He kept no records. [one negative: *no*]
NON-STANDARD	We needed gas but couldn't buy none.
STANDARD	We needed gas but couldn't buy any.
	OR We needed gas but could buy none.
NON-STANDARD	I cannot do nothing about it.
STANDARD	I cannot do anything about it.
	OR I can do nothing about it.

nowheres Non-standard or regional for *nowhere*.

number See **amount of, number of; a number, the number**.

of Do not write *of* for an unstressed *have*.

COMPARE	I could have it done. [stressed]
	I could have done it. [unstressed]
NON-STANDARD	I might of [may of, could of, would of, must of, should of, ought to of] said that.
STANDARD	I might **have** [may *have*, could *have*, would *have*, must *have*, should *have*, ought to *have*] said that.

See also **had of**.

off of In formal writing, omit the *of* after *off* in such phrases as "fell off of the ladder."

OK, O.K., okay All three are accepted as standard forms expressing general approval. However, a more specific word usually replaces *OK* in a formal context.

per Used especially in commercial writing. Many authors prefer to use *per* only in Latinisms ("per capita," "per se," or "per cent/percent").

COMMERCIAL	over $1.50 per litre	as per regulations
PREFERRED	over $1.50 **a** litre	**according to** regulations

phenomena See **data**.

plenty Informal when used adverbially to mean *quite* or *sufficiently* (as in "plenty good enough") or adjectivally for *plenty of* ("in plenty time").

plus Informal if used as a substitute for *and* between main clauses or if used as a conjunctive adverb (for *moreover, besides, in addition*) between main clauses or sentences. See also **12a** and **14a**.

INFORMAL Barbara is taking five courses, plus she has to work three hours a day.

GENERAL Barbara is taking five courses, **and** she has to work three hours a day.

INFORMAL Barbara is taking five courses; plus, she has to work three hours a day. [OR . . . courses. Plus, she has to work . . .]

GENERAL Barbara is taking five courses; **moreover**, she has to work three hours a day. [OR . . . courses. *Moreover,* she has to work. . . .]

P.M., A.M. See **A.M., P.M.**

practical, practicable *Practical* means "useful, sensible" or "not theoretical." *Practicable* means "feasible, capable of being put into practice."

The sponsors are **practical** people. These plans are **practicable**.

practice, practise *Practice* is a noun; *practise* is a verb.

principal, principle Distinguish between *principal*, an adjective or noun meaning "chief" or "chief official," and the noun *principle*, meaning "fundamental truth."

A **principal** factor in his decision was his belief in the **principle** that human beings are born equal.

quote Still considered chiefly informal for *quotation* (as in "a quote from Chaucer").

raise, rise Do not confuse. *Raise*(*raised, raising*) means "to lift or cause to move upward, to bring up or increase." *Rise* (*rose, risen, rising*) means "to get up, to move or extend upward, ascend." *Raise* (a transitive verb) takes an object; *rise* (an intransitive verb) does not.

Retailers **raised** prices. Retail prices **rose** sharply.

rap Informal for *chat, discuss*, or *talk*. Slang in such expressions as "to beat a murder rap" or "took the rap for cheating."

rarely ever In formal writing, either omit the *ever*, or use *hardly* instead of *rarely*.

NOT He rarely ever mentioned money.
BUT He **rarely** mentioned money.
OR He **hardly ever** mentioned money.

real Informal when used as an adverb meaning "very, extremely."

INFORMAL The victorious team was **real** tired.
GENERAL The victorious team was **extremely** tired.

reason . . . because Informal redundancy. Use *that* instead of *because* or recast the sentence.

INFORMAL The reason why he missed his class was because he overslept.
GENERAL The **reason** why he missed his class was **that** he overslept.
OR He missed his class **because** he overslept.

reckon Informal for *guess, think*.

respectively, respectfully Do not confuse. *Respectively* means "in the order given." *Respectfully* means "in a courteous manner."

I considered becoming a farmer, a landscape artist, and a

florist, **respectively**.
I considered the rabbi's suggestion **respectfully**.

right Archaic or dialectal for *very* (as in "a right nice apartment").

rise See **raise, rise**.

said Except in legal writing, questionable as an adjectival meaning "already specified or mentioned before." Substitute a demonstrative like *this* or *these* for *the said*.

LEGAL The said machines were defective.
GENERAL **These** machines were defective.

same Used as a pronoun without *the* chiefly in commercial or legal writing. General usage prefers *it, this*, or *that*.

COMMERCIAL I had a service policy but did not renew same.
GENERAL I had a service policy but did not renew **it**.

says Avoid the use of *says* for *said* after a past-tense verb: NOT "stood up and says" BUT "stood up and *said*." See also **27a**.

scarcely See **hardly, scarcely**.

seldom ever Omit the *ever* in your formal writing.

set, setting Non-standard for *sit* or *sat, sitting*. It is the verb *sit* (NOT *set*) that means "be seated or be situated." See also **7a(2)**.

NON-STANDARD I didn't even set down. He yawned and set up.
Some cabins were setting in two metres of water.

STANDARD I didn't even **sit** down. He yawned and **sat** up.
Some cabins were **sitting** in two metres of water.

show up Informal for *arrive* or *come* and for *outdo* (as in "might show up at the party" and "trying to show me up").

sit Occasionally misused for *set* (*put, place*): NOT "to sit something" BUT "to *set* something." See also **7a(2)**.

so Often overworked as an intensive (as in "so very pleased") and as a connective between main clauses (see **24b**).

some Informal for *remarkable, extraordinary* and for *somewhat,* *a little* (as in "was some dog," "is some better," and "was talking some").

someone, some one See **anyone, any one**.

somewheres Non-standard for *somewhere*.

sort See **kind, sort**.

sort of a Omit the *a* in your formal writing.

stationary, stationery *Stationary* means "in a fixed position"; *stationery* means "writing paper and envelopes."

superior than Non-standard. Use *superior to* or *better than*.

suppose to Be sure to add the *-d*.

Who is **supposed to** be in charge?
You were **supposed to** read this chapter.

sure Informal for *surely* or *certainly*.

INFORMAL The sunrise **sure** was beautiful.
GENERAL The sunrise **certainly** was beautiful.

sure and See **be sure and**.

their, there, they're Do not confuse. *Their* is the possessive form of *they; there* is ordinarily an adverb or an expletive; *they're* is a contraction of *they are*.

There is no explanation for **their** refusal.
They're installing a traffic light **there**.

theirself, theirselves Non-standard for *themselves*.

them Non-standard when used adjectivally: NOT them apples BUT *those* [OR *these*] apples.

then Sometimes incorrectly used for *than*. See also page 192-93. Unlike *then, than* does not relate to time.

Last summer, we paid more **than** that. [Compare "We paid more *then*."]
Other **than** a welfare cheque, they had no income.

these kind, these sort, those kind, those sort See **kind, sort**.

thing Often used in wordy constructions.

WORDY One thing that we need is a map.
CONCISE We need a map.

this here, that there, these here, them there Non-standard expressions. Use *this, that, these, those.*

thusly Grammatically redundant. Write *thus* (already an adverb without the *-ly*).

to, too, two Distinguish the preposition *to* from the adverb *too* and the numeral *two*.

> If it isn't **too** cold, I will take my **two** poodles **to** the park.

try and Informal for *try to.*

type Informal for *type of* (as in "that type program").

use to, used to Be sure to add the *-d* to *use* unless the auxiliary is accompanied by *did* in questions or in negative constructions.

> NOT Our coins use to contain silver.
> BUT Our coins **used to** contain silver.
> NOT Did he used to smoke? He didn't used to smoke.
> BUT Did he **use to** smoke? He didn't **use to** smoke.

used to could Non-standard for *used to be able.*

very Omit when superfluous (as in "very unique" or "very terrified"). If you tend to overuse *very* as an intensifier, try using more exact words; in place of "very strange," for example, try *outlandish, grotesque,* or *bizarre.*

wait on Informal for *wait for.*

> INFORMAL The taxi was waiting on him.
> GENERAL The taxi was **waiting for** him.

want for Omit the non-standard *for* in such sentences as "I want for you to quit."

want in, out, down, up, off, through Informal or regional for *want to get in, out, down, up, off, through.*

want that Non-standard when a *that* clause is the object of *want.*

> NON-STANDARD I want that he should have a chance.
> STANDARD I **want** him to have a chance.

ways Informal for *way* when referring to distance.

INFORMAL It's a long ways to Labrador City.
GENERAL It's a long **way** to Labrador City.

what Non-standard for *who* or *that*.

NOT The man what did it got away.
BUT The man **who** did it got away.

where Informal for *that*.

INFORMAL I saw in the newspaper where the strike had been settled.
GENERAL I saw in the newspaper **that** the strike had been settled.

where . . . at, where . . . to Omit the superfluous *at, to*.

NOT	Where is she at?	Where is she going to?
BUT	Where is she?	Where is she going?

which, who Use *who* or *that* instead of *which* to refer to persons.

while Do not overuse as a substitute for *and* or *but*. The conjunction *while* usually refers to time.

would of Non-standard for *would have*. See **of**.

Xmas Standard for *Christmas* but used chiefly in commercial or informal writing.

you was Non-standard for *you were*.

your, you're Do not confuse. *You're* is a contraction: "You're [*You are*] always right!" *Your* is the possessive form of *you*: "*Your* idea is a good one."

Exactness

20

Select words that are exact, idiomatic, and fresh.

Note: Sections **20** and **21** of this handbook deal with diction, the term used to refer to a writer's or speaker's choice of words.

Especially when writing, you should strive to choose words which express your ideas and feelings exactly. The choice of a right word will depend on your purpose, your point of view, and your reader.

If you can make effective use of the words you already know, you need not have a huge vocabulary. In fact, as shown by the following example, good writing often consists of short, familiar words.

> The ball was loose, rolling free near the line of scrimmage. I raced for the fumble, bent over, scooped up the ball on the dead run, and turned downfield. With a sudden burst of speed, I bolted past the line and past the linebackers. Only two defensive backs stood between me and the goal line. One came up fast, and I gave him a hip feint, stuck out my left arm in a classic straight-arm, caught him on the helmet, and shoved him to the ground. The final defender moved toward me, and I cut to the sidelines, swung sharply back to the middle for three steps, braked again, and reversed my direc-

tion once more. The defender tripped over his own feet in confusion. I trotted into the end zone, having covered seventy-eight yards on my touchdown run, happily flipped the football into the stands, turned and loped casually toward the sidelines. Then I woke up.

—JERRY KRAMER, *Farewell to Football*

Of course, as you gain experience in writing, you will become increasingly aware of the need to add to your vocabulary. When you discover a valuable new word, make it your own by mastering its spelling, meaning, and exact use.

20a

Select the exact word needed to express your idea.

(1) Select the word that precisely denotes what you have in mind.

WRONG A loud radio does not detract me when I am reading a good novel. [*Detract* means "to subtract a part of" or "to remove something desirable."]

RIGHT A loud radio does not **distract** me when I am reading a good novel. [*Distract* means "to draw the attention away."]

INEXACT Arnold was willing to pay the bill, and his wallet was empty. [*And* adds or continues.]

EXACT Arnold was willing to pay the bill, **but** his wallet was empty. [*But* contrasts.]

WRONG What they did was unjustful.

RIGHT What they did was **unjust**.

WRONG He never reverts to himself as an expert.

RIGHT He never **refers** to himself as an expert.
OR He never **reminds** anyone that he is an expert.

■ **Exercise 1** The italicized words in the following sentences are wrong or inexact. Correct the errors in diction and replace inexact words with exact ones.

1. Every gardener should have a *compote* bin.
2. Bo was interested in photography, *and* I bought her a new camera.
3. They did not do anything about this *disjustice*.
4. The lyrics are perfectly *adopted* to the music.
5. Strangers on campus are *awfully nice*.
6. Perhaps she just missed getting that job by some *misfortunate* chance.
7. I frequently consult the classified ads, *and* I can seldom find what I want.
8. She didn't say but she *intimidated* it.
9. Hurricanes are *seasonable*.
10. Liquor *effects* the brain and nervous system.

■ **Exercise 2** With the aid of your dictionary, give the exact meaning of each italicized word in the quotations below. (Italics have been added.)

1. Ignorance of *history* is dangerous. —JEFFREY RECORD

   Those who cannot remember *the past* are condemned to repeat it. —GEORGE SANTAYANA

2. The capacity for rage, spite and aggression is part of our endowment as *human beings*. —KENNETH KENISTON

   Man, all down his history, has defended his uniqueness like a point of honor. —RUTH BENEDICT

3. Travel is no cure for melancholia; space-ships and time machines are no *escape* from the human condition. —ARTHUR KOESTLER

   Well, Columbus was probably regarded as an *escapist* when he set forth for the New World. —ARTHUR C. CLARKE

4. Once, a full high school education was the best achievement of a minority; today, it is the *barest minimum* for decent employment or self-respect. —ERIC SEVAREID

   Study and planning are an *absolute prerequisite* for any kind of intelligent action. —EDWARD BROOKE

5. We had a *permissive* father. He *permitted* us to work. —SAM LEVENSON

■ **Exercise 3** Prepare for a class discussion of diction. After the first quotation below are several series of words that the author might have used but did not select. Note the differences in meaning when an italicized word is substituted for the related word at the head of each series. Be prepared to supply your own alternatives for each of the words that follow the other four quotations.

1. Creeping gloom hits us all. The symptoms are usually the same: not wanting to get out of bed to start the day, failing to smile at ironies, failing to laugh at oneself.

   —CHRISTOPHER BUCKLEY

   a. gloom: *sadness, depression, dismals* (hit), *melancholy*
   b. hits: *strikes, assaults, infects, zaps*
   c. usually: *often, frequently, consistently, as a rule*
   d. failing: *too blue, unable, neglecting, too far gone*
2. Our plane rocked in a rain squall, bobbed about, then slipped into a patch of sun. —THEODORE H. WHITE

   a. rocked b. bobbed c. slipped d. patch
3. She stood on the riverbank quite still, conscious that every motion made a foreign sound, even her hands rubbing in her pockets for warmth. —MARIAN ENGEL

   a. still b. conscious c. foreign d. warmth
4. How is it that the same work can create stress or distress?

   —HANS SELYE

   a. stress b. distress
5. Believing the program to be true, people drove into the country to escape; others barricaded themselves in their cellars, prepared to die fighting. —AUSTIN REDPATH

   a. escape b. barricaded c. prepared d. die

(2) Select the word with the connotation, as well as the denotation, appropriate to the idea you wish to express.

The denotation of a word is what the word actually signifies. According to the dictionary, the word *hair* denotes "one of the fine, threadlike structures that grow from the skin of most mammals." The connotation of a word is what the word suggests or implies. *Hair*, for instance, may connote beauty, fertility, nudity, strength, uncleanliness, temptation, rebellion, or primitivism.

The connotation of a word includes the emotions or associations that surround it. For instance, *taxi, tin lizzie, limousine, dune buggy, station wagon, dump truck, hot rod*—all denote much the same thing. But to various readers, and in various contexts, each word may have a special connotation. *Taxi* may suggest a city rush hour; *tin lizzie*, a historical museum; *limousine*, an airport; *dune buggy*, a seaside vacation; *station wagon*, children and dogs; *dump truck*, highway construction; *hot rod*, noise and racing. Similarly, *hatchback, bus, clunker, bookmobile, moving van, ambulance, squad car*—all denote a means of transportation, but each word carries a variety of connotations.

A word may be right in one situation, wrong in another. *Female parent*, for instance, is a proper expression in a biology laboratory, but it would be very inappropriate to say "John wept because of the death of his female human parent." *Female human parent* used in this sense is literally correct, but the connotation is wrong. The more appropriate word, *mother*, conveys not only the meaning denoted by *female human parent* but also the reason why John wept. The first expression simply implies a biological relationship; the second includes emotional suggestions.

■ **Exercise 4** Give one denotation and one connotation for each of the following words:

1. blue
2. mountain
3. astrology
4. Tuktoyaktuk
5. conservative
6. law
7. dog
8. tennis shoes
9. technology
10. Saudi Arabia

(3) Select the specific and concrete word rather than the general and abstract.

A *general* word is all-inclusive, indefinite, sweeping in scope. A *specific* word is precise, definite, limited in scope.

GENERAL	SPECIFIC	MORE SPECIFIC / CONCRETE
food	dessert	apple pie
prose	fiction	short stories
people	Canadians	the Singhs

An *abstract* word deals with concepts, with ideas, with what cannot be touched, heard, or seen. A *concrete* word has to do with particular objects, with the practical, with what can be touched, heard, or seen.

ABSTRACT WORDS	democracy, loyal, evil, hate, charity
CONCRETE WORDS	mosquito, spotted, crunch, wedding

All writers must sometimes use abstract words and must occasionally resort to generalizations, as in the following sentence:

> I still believe that a liberal education, even if it will not solve the problems of individuals or the world, will help us to understand those problems. —CONRAD A. BALLIET

In a case like this, abstractions and generalizations are vital to the communication of ideas and theories. To be effective, however, the use of these words must be based upon clearly understood and well-thought-out ideas.

Experienced writers may have little difficulty handling general and abstract words. Many inexperienced writers, however, tend to use too many such words, leaving their writing drab and lifeless due to the lack of specific, concrete words. As you select words to fit your context, be as specific as you can. For example, instead of the word *bad*, consider using a more precise adjective (or adjectival) in phrases such as the following:

bad planks: rotten, warped, scorched, knotty, termite-eaten

bad children: rowdy, rude, ungrateful, selfish, perverse

bad meat: tough, tainted, overcooked, contaminated

To test whether or not a word is specific, ask one or more of these questions about what you want to say: Exactly who? Exactly what? Exactly when? Exactly where? Exactly how? As you study the examples below, notice what a difference specific, concrete words can make in the expression of an idea. Notice, too, how specific details can be used to expand or develop ideas.

VAGUE I always think of a good museum as one that is very big.

SPECIFIC I always think of a good museum as one I get lost in. —EDWARD PARKS

VAGUE The discontented people debated the matter and finally found a suitable leader in William Lyon Mackenzie.

SPECIFIC The malcontents argued on the platforms and in the end they found a leader to their hearts in William Lyon Mackenzie, a Scot, arrived in 1820, editing the *Colonial Advocate*, as honest as daylight, and as uncompromising as the Westminster Catechism. —STEPHEN LEACOCK

VAGUE I remember my pleasure at discovering new things about language.

SPECIFIC I remember my real joy at discovering for the first time how language worked, at discovering, for example, that the central line of Joseph Conrad's *Heart of Darkness* was in parentheses. —JOAN DIDION

VAGUE The hero must be a character with flaws but he must also have virtues.

SPECIFIC Traditionally the hero must have a tragic flaw or two; he may be a man destroyed by his own pride, like Oedipus, or by his own indecisiveness, like Hamlet, but he must also have great virtues. Above all he must be central, significant. —MARGARET ATWOOD

■ **Exercise 5** Replace the general words and phrases in italics with specific ones.

1. I always think of a pawn shop as *very small.*
2. *A lot of people* are threatened by *pollution.*
3. The *movie* was *great.*
4. Every Monday he has *the same thing* in his lunch box.
5. Our history professor suggested that we subscribe to *some magazines.*
6. Backpacking has *numerous advantages.*
7. The *dog walked* over to his *food.*
8. My father looked at my grade in science and said *what I least expected to hear.*
9. *Various aspects of the television show* were criticized *in the newspaper.*
10. *Cities* have their *problems.*

(4) Use appropriate figurative language to create an imaginative or emotional impression.

A figure of speech is a word or words used in an imaginative rather than in a literal sense. The two chief figures of speech are the *simile* and the *metaphor*. A *simile* is an explicit comparison between two things of a different kind or quality, usually introduced by *like* or *as*. A *metaphor* is an implied comparison of dissimilar things. In a metaphor, words of comparison, such as *like* or *as*, are not used.

SIMILES

The first thing people remember about failing at math is that it felt like sudden death. —SHEILA TOBIAS

The trench was *like a tunnel with a black heavy layer of smoke as its roof.* —TIMOTHY FINDLEY

Canadians have taken to ballet *as happily as the Russians have taken to hockey.* —MALCOLM ROSS

METAPHORS

Dress is language. —LANCE MORROW

The sun was a distant blowtorch. —DON BAILEY

Language is not a tough plant that always grows toward the sun, regardless of weeds and trampling feet.
—DOUGLAS BUSH

> We are born princes and the civilizing process turns us into frogs. —ERIC BERNE
>
> Wolf pups make a frothy ribbon of sound like fat bubbling. —EDWARD HOAGLAND [a metaphor and a simile]

Single words are often used metaphorically:

> These roses must be **planted** in good soil. [literal]
>
> A man's feet must be **planted** in his country, but his eyes should survey the world. —GEORGE SANTAYANA [metaphorical]

Similes and metaphors are especially valuable when they are concrete and tend to point up essential relationships that cannot otherwise be communicated. (For faulty metaphors, see **23c**.) Sometimes writers extend a metaphor beyond a sentence:

> Some women have managed to shape up and ship out into the mainstream of life, handling the currents and the rapids and the quiet pools with a gracious, confident ease. Others are trapped in one eddy after another, going nowhere at all, hung up in swirling pockets of confusion. Everyone gets sidetracked once in a while, and requires a rescue operation. That's the way life is. But some have been caught in an eddy or a piece of dead wood for so long that they have forgotten that life was meant to be lived in the mainstream.
>
> —GLADYS HUNT, *Ms. Means Myself*

Two other frequently used figures of speech are *hyperbole* and *personification*. *Hyperbole* is deliberate overstatement or fanciful exaggeration. *Personification* is the attribution to the non-human (objects, animals, ideas) of characteristics possessed only by the human.

> HYPERBOLE
>
> I, for one, don't expect till I die to be so good a man as I am at this minute, for just now I'm fifty thousand feet high—a tower with all the trumpets shouting. —G. K. CHESTERTON
>
> PERSONIFICATION
>
> Time talks. It speaks more plainly than words. . . . It can shout the truth where words lie. —EDWARD T. HALL

■ **Exercise 6** Complete each of the following sentences by using a simile, a metaphor, hyperbole, or personification. Use vivid and effective figures of speech.

EXAMPLES

It was a voice like *a stream of crystal water fighting to reach the sea.* —AUSTIN CLARKE

The utopia of Karl Marx, like all utopias before or since, was *an image in a rearview mirror.* —MARSHALL McLUHAN

1. Sightseers flocked around the commune like ________.
2. A revolutionary idea in the 1980s, like a revolutionary idea in any age, is ________ .
3. The mosquitoes in the Yukon ________ .
4. The worst blizzard in living memory slashed through Manitoba ________ .
5. Death in a hovel or in a penthouse is ________ .
6. Like ________ , the class sat speechless.
7. The lecture was as ________ .
8. Her eyes looked like ________ .
9. Surging forward, the rioters ________ .
10. The opinions of politicians with vested interests are as predictable as ________ .
11. She was as self-confident as ________ .
12. The alarm sounded like ________ .

20b

Select words that are idiomatic.

An idiomatic expression—such as *many a man, Sunday week,* or *hang fire*—means something beyond the simple combination of the definitions of its individual words. An idiom may be metaphorical: *He gets under my skin.* Such expressions cannot be meaningfully translated word for word into another language. Used every day, they are at the very heart of the English language.

Be careful to use idiomatic English, not unidiomatic approximations. *Many a man* is idiomatic; *many the man* is not. Ordinarily, native speakers use idiomatic English naturally and effectively, but once in a while they may have difficulty choosing idiomatic prepositions. When you are in doubt about what preposition to use after a given word, look up that word in the dictionary. For instance, *agree* may be followed by *about, on, to*, or *with*. The choice depends on the context. Below is a list of troublesome idioms for study.

FAULTY	IDIOMATIC
according with	according to
accuse with	accuse of
adverse against	adverse to
comply to	comply with
conform in	conform to/with
desirous to	desirous of
die with	die of
in accordance to	in accordance with
independent from	independent of
inferior than	inferior to
jealous for	jealous of
prior than	prior to
superior than	superior to

■ **Exercise 7** Using your dictionary, classify the following expressions as idiomatic or unidiomatic. Revise any expressions that are unidiomatic. Classify idiomatic expressions according to the usage labels in your dictionary, using *General* as the classification for unlabelled expressions.

EXAMPLES
similar with *Unidiomatic—similar to*
to let on *Idiomatic, Informal*

1. oblivious about
2. to go at
3. to dress down
4. capable to
5. in search for
6. to compare against
7. to break with
8. prior than
9. to drop in
10. plan on going

20c

Select fresh expressions instead of trite, worn-out ones.

Such trite expressions as *to the bitter end, get it all together,* and *clean as a whistle* were once striking and effective. Excessive use, however, has drained them of their original force and made them clichés. Some euphemisms (pleasant-sounding substitutions for more explicit but possibly offensive words) are not only trite but wordy—for example, *laid to rest* for *buried* or *sanitary engineer* for *janitor*. Many political slogans and the catchy phraseology of advertisements soon become hackneyed. Faddish or trendy words—like *impacted on, viable, upbeat*, or *be into* (as in "I am into dieting")—are so overused (or misused) that they quickly become trite and lose their force.

Nearly every writer uses clichés from time to time because they are so much a part of the language, especially of spoken English, and do contribute to the clear expression of ideas in written English.

> We feel free when we escape—even if it be but **from the frying pan into the fire**. —ERIC HOFFER

It is not unusual for a professional writer to give a new twist to an old saying or a well-known literary passage.

> If a thing is worth doing, it is worth doing badly. —G. K. CHESTERTON

> Into each life a little sun must fall. —L. E. SISSMAN

> He is every other inch a gentleman. —REBECCA WEST

Many writers use familiar lines from literature or the Bible and quote proverbs.

> Our lives are empty of belief. They are **lives of quiet desperation**. —ARTHUR M. SCHLESINGER, JR. [Compare Thoreau's *Walden*: "The mass of men lead lives of quiet desperation."]

> Slowly but steadily, in the following years, a new vision began gradually to replace the dream of political power—a powerful movement, the rise of another ideal to guide the unguided, another **pillar of fire by night** after a clouded day.
>
> —W.E.B. DU BOIS [Compare Exodus 13:21: "And the Lord went before them . . . by night in a pillar of fire, to give them light."]

Good writers, however, do not rely heavily on the phraseology of others; they choose their own words to communicate their own ideas.

■ **Exercise 8** Below is a list of trite expressions—only a sampling of the many in current use. Select ten that you often use or hear, and rewrite them in carefully chosen words.

EXAMPLES
a bolt from the blue *a shock*
beyond the shadow of a doubt *undoubtedly*

1. a brilliant performance
2. a chip off the old block
3. a crying shame
4. a good Samaritan
5. abreast of the times
6. after all is said and done
7. as cold as ice
8. as happy as a lark
9. at a complete loss for words
10. at the crack of dawn
11. at one fell swoop
12. beating around/about the bush
13. bite the bullet
14. bored to tears/death
15. few and far between
16. follow in the footsteps of
17. hightailed/hotfooted it out of there
18. hoping against hope
19. in the last analysis
20. in this day and age
21. it goes without saying
22. like a bull in a china shop/hog on ice
23. like water off a duck's back
24. little bundle of joy
25. makes my blood boil
26. nipped in the bud
27. stick to your guns

■ **Exercise 9** Choose five of the ten items below as the basis for five original sentences. Use language that is exact, idiomatic, and fresh.

EXAMPLES
the appearance of her hair

Her hair, which she wore in two braids around her head, was the same colour as her skin, pallid. —SHIRLEY FAESSLER

OR *Her dark hair was gathered up in a coil like a crown on her head.* —D.H. LAWRENCE

1. the look on his face
2. her response to fear
3. the way she walks
4. the condition of the streets
5. spring in the air
6. the noises of the city
7. the appearance of the room
8. the scene of the accident
9. the final minutes of play
10. the approaching storm

■ **Exercise 10** Following are two descriptions, one of bounty, the other of terror. Read each selection carefully in preparation for a class discussion of the authors' choice of words, their use of concrete, specific language, and their use of figurative language.

[1] The days were short, and often sombre, but we kept a good fire going in the house, we ate pumpkin pie, we sorted walnuts and corn. [2] We also set tomatoes to ripen on the window sills, and on certain days the whole house was permeated with the odour of pickles cooking over a gentle fire in large pans. [3] The saw could be heard singing in the yard; its two-toned song, first clear, then deeper and heavier as it bit into the wood, seemed to me to promise us joyfully, "I'm cutting you fine logs, fine logs for the whole winter." [4] All this time the house, like a ship ready to weigh anchor or a city about to undergo a siege, was being filled with provisions—sauerkraut, maple syrup from Quebec, red apples from British Columbia, plums from Ontario. [5] Soon also we began to receive from our uncles in the country fat geese and turkeys, dozens of chickens, hams and salt bacon, cases of fresh eggs and farm butter. [6] To help ourselves we only had to go into our summer kitchen, now transformed into a storehouse, where the frost preserved our stock. [7] Such were the joys of autumn, based upon abundance and a feeling of security that I think I appreciated even then.

—GABRIELLE ROY

[1] They say, too, that nature did its best to co-operate. [2] A wind came up from somewhere, bending trees, shaking the house. [3] You could hear the screech of giant trunks grinding against each other. [4] You could hear the squeal of nails wrenched in the lumbered walls and the cedar roof above you. [5] The water in the strait was churned up into waves that smashed against the cliff, and leapt upwards high enough to spray the windows and toss driftwood logs like sticks across the yard. [6] A door flew open in the wind, crashed against the wall, and was forced shut again by someone whose face was streaming with rain and salt water and strips of kelp. [7] Sticks and bits of limbs were flying across the floor. [8] Dead pine needles clotted like hairballs in the corner. [9] Keneally's voice rose above the tumult to include it.

[10] He would be transformed, Keneally said, his voice suddenly heavy with importance. [11] He would be transformed from flesh into spirit this night. [12] He would, in fact, be dead. [13] The organ music spiralled upward into a final impossible note that lay across the sudden silence like a clear metallic lid, though frightened Kathleen's feet kept pumping madly still and her forehead pressed against the elaborately carved wood of the instrument like a cyclist against the wind. [14] Logs crashed on the verandah; men whimpered; bladders weakened; a light in the ceiling dimmed.

—JACK HODGINS

■ **Exercise 11** Choose the word inside parentheses that best suits the context of each item below.

1. Driving east to Regina the wind is blowing, a heavy gusting wind that (scoops, lifts) topsoil off the farmland. —AL PURDY
2. The creeks were (foaming, rushing) as brown as vat-run lager. —DENNIS T. PATRICK SEARS
3. A poem is an Alka-Seltzer tablet: orthodoxies begin to (fizz, complain) when one is dropped into their midst. —IRVING LAYTON
4. Every evening at the rush hour the subway (unveils, disgorges) its millions. —JACQUES BARZUN
5. There was a roaring in my ears like the rushing of (music, rivers). —STEPHEN VINCENT BENÉT

Wordiness

21

To avoid wordiness, use direct, economical diction. Repeat a word or phrase only when it is needed for emphasis or clarity.

The use of more words than necessary to express meaning is an offence against exact diction: see Section **20**. As you proofread and revise your compositions, delete unneeded words but keep or add exact ones. In this way, you can say more in fewer words.

WORDY FIRST DRAFT

In the early part of the month of February there was a really mean blizzard with very high winds that was moving threateningly toward Halifax.

FIRST REVISION

In ~~the~~ early ~~part of the month of~~ February ~~there was~~ a really mean blizzard with very high winds ~~that~~ was moving threateningly toward Halifax.

SECOND REVISION

```
                          vicious
In early February, a ^ really mean blizzard with
150-kilometre-per-hour          threatening
^ very high winds was ^ moving threateningly
toward Halifax.
```

FINISHED COPY

```
In early February a vicious blizzard with
150-kilometre-per-hour winds was threatening
Halifax.
```

21a

Make every word count; omit words or phrases that add nothing to the meaning.

(1) Avoid tautology (the use of different words to say the same thing).

WORDY Commuters going back and forth to work or school formed carpools.

CONCISE Commuters formed carpools.

WORDY Each writer has a distinctive style, and he or she uses this in his or her own works.

CONCISE Each writer has a distinctive style.

Notice below that the useless words in brackets serve only to echo meaning. Avoid such wordiness in your own writing.

yellow [in colour]
at 9:45 P.M. [that night]
[basic] essentials
bitter [-tasting] salad
but [though]
connect [up together]
circular [in shape]
return [back]
rich [and wealthy] nations
small [-size] potatoes
to apply [or utilize] rules
[true] facts

Caution: Be sure to avoid double comparisons, the double subject (subject + nominative pronoun referring to the subject), and the double negative.

> [more] easier than, the [most] farthest
> my sister [she] is, the victims [they] are
> could[n't] hardly, did[n't do] nothing [See also *not . . . no,* **19i**.]

(2) Do not use many words when a few will express the idea well. Omit the unnecessary words.

WORDY **In the event that** the grading system is changed, expect complaints **on the part of** the students.
CONCISE **If** the grading system is changed, expect complaints **from** the students. [Two words take the place of eight.]

WORDY **As far as sexism is concerned, it seems to me that** a woman can be as guilty of sexism as a man.
CONCISE A woman can be as guilty of sexism as a man. [Unnecessary words are deleted.]

One or two words can replace such expressions as these:

at this point in time	**now**
bring all this to a conclusion	**conclude**
during the same time that	**while**
has a tendency to break	**breaks easily**
has the ability to sing	**can sing**
in a great many instances	**often**
made contact by personal visits	**visited**
on account of the fact that	**because**
situated in the vicinity of	**near**
was of the opinion that	**believed**

Note: One exact word can say as much as many. (See also **20a**.)

spoke in such a low and hard-to-hear voice	**mumbled**
persons who really know their particular field	**experts**

Notice below that the words in brackets are not necessary.

because [of the fact that]	was [more or less] hinting
[really and truly] fearless	by [viture of] his authority
fans [who were] watching TV	the oil [that exists] in shale

■ **Exercise 1** Revise the following sentences to eliminate wordiness:

1. As a usual rule, politicians express concern about public interest, but though it takes a crisis to get them to act.
2. Good health is essential. This is one of the most important things.
3. During the last two innings, many senseless mistakes occurred without any apparent reason for them.
4. When combined together, these ingredients they make a nutritious one-dish meal.
5. The exact date has not been set and is not known to us.
6. Long lines of starving refugees in need of food were helped by Red Cross volunteer people.
7. Alex delights in giving parties; he really likes to be a host.
8. Perhaps maybe the chief cause of or reason for obesity in people who are overweight is lack of exercise.
9. Only beginners, those who are inexperienced, can enter that contest.
10. The tall skyscraper buildings form a dark silhouette against the evening sky.

■ **Exercise 2** Substitute one or two words for each item below:

1. prior to the time that
2. in this day and age
3. did put in an appearance
4. has the capability of working
5. passed away OR met his maker
6. in the not too distant future
7. similar in character to
8. involving a great deal of expense
9. in a more or less serious manner
10. somewhere in the neighbourhood of $2,500

Exercise 3 Strike out unnecessary words in the following sentences:

1. In the year 1985, Uncle Vance was close to the point of bankruptcy.
2. The editorial gave reasons why the Chinese citizens in East Asia cannot leave their home towns that they live in unless they have a permit from the government giving them permission to leave town.
3. The award-winning English playwright made ruthless murder and flagrant blackmail the absurd hobbies of his heroes.
4. One reason why Canadians are well informed is because of the fact that books of all sorts on a great variety of subjects are available to them as inexpensive paperbacks.
5. The backlash that followed as a result of the Supreme Court ruling was stronger than I myself had expected that it would be.

21b

Eliminate needless words by combining sentences or by simplifying phrases and clauses.

Note differences in emphasis as you study the following examples:

WORDY	He has a special way of telling a story. He makes a big to-do over little details. They sound like they are very important.
CONCISE	When telling a story, he makes little details sound important.
WORDY	A few of the listeners who had become angry called in so that they would have the opportunity of refuting the arguments set forth by Ian.
CONCISE	A few angry listeners called in to refute Ian's arguments.
WORDY	It is within the realm of possibility that what is earned by individual persons, the part that is surplus, will be subject to special taxation as a windfall.
CONCISE	Perhaps an individual's surplus earnings will be subject to a windfall-profits tax.

■ **Exercise 4** Following the pattern of the examples, condense the sentences below:

EXAMPLE
These were theories which were, in essence, concerned with politics.
These were political theories.

1. These are pitfalls that do, of course, pose a real danger.
2. This is an act which, in truth, partakes of the nature of aggression.

EXAMPLE
It was a house built with cheap materials.
It was a cheaply built house.

3. It was a garden planned with a great deal of care.
4. It was a speech delivered with a lot of passion.

EXAMPLE
The stories written by Carson McCullers are different from those composed by Flannery O'Connor.
Carson McCullers' stories are different from Flannery O'Connor's.

5. The dishes prepared by her husband are not as good as those fixed by her father.
6. The ideas shared by the students were different from those promoted by the advertiser.

EXAMPLE
It is unfortunate. A few come to college so that they can avoid work.
Unfortunately, a few come to college to avoid work.

7. It is inevitable. Corporations produce goods so that they can make a profit.
8. It is predictable. Before an election politicians reduce taxation so that they can win the approval of voters.

EXAMPLE
The forces that were against abortion ran an advertisement that covered two pages.
The anti-abortion forces ran a two-page advertisement.

9. A group that is in favour of labour wants vacations that last two months.
10. One editorial against "nukes" stressed the need for plants that are state controlled.

■ **Exercise 5** Restructure or combine sentences to reduce the number of words.

1. There is one opera singer who works with mentally retarded children. He teaches them songs and games.
2. When the Indians made tools, they used flint and bones.
3. Ken McCoy strutted into the room, and as he did so he tripped over a briefcase.
4. A deep blue grass covered the lawn. It looked like a carpet.
5. Being in junior high school was like being in a circus having three rings.

21c

Avoid careless or needless repetition of a word or phrase.

Sometimes a repeated word or phrase, by calling attention to itself rather than to its meaning, can be distracting.

> FAULTY This interesting instructor knows how to make an uninteresting subject interesting.

Such repetition is not always easy to avoid or eliminate. But as a rule, you can quickly revise awkward repetition of words by making judicious substitutions or omissions.

> REVISED This instructor knows how to make a dull subject interesting.

At times, however, synonyms can be clumsy, needlessly repeating an idea. It may be necessary to rewrite sentences to avoid repetition that weakens your writing.

Note: For the effective use of repetition in parallel structures, for emphasis, and as a transitional device, see **26b**, **29e**, and **31c(3)**.

Avoid careless or needless repetition of a word.

CARELESS	We had problems solving those problems.
REVISED	We had a hard time solving those problems.
NEEDLESS	I think that he knows that that girl is not the one for him to marry.
REVISED	I think he knows he should not marry that girl.
NEEDLESS	His uncle is not like her uncle. Her uncle takes more chances than his uncle does.
REVISED	Their uncles are different. Hers takes more chances than his.

Avoid carelessly repeating a root or a word base.

CARELESS	I got the impression that his expression of sympathy was insincere.
REVISED	I felt that his expression of sympathy was insincere.

Do not unintentionally use the same word or root in different senses.

CARELESS	Even at the graveside services, the brothers kept quarrelling. It was a grave situation.
BETTER	. . . It was a **serious** situation.

Eliminate careless jingles (like "compared the fares there") and other distracting repetition of sounds: see **19h**.

Use a pronoun instead of needlessly repeating a noun. As long as the reference remains clear, several pronouns in succession, even in successive sentences, may refer to the same antecedent noun. In the following paragraph, for example, the italicized pronouns refer clearly to the noun *Robert*, which is not once repeated. See also **31b(2)**.

Twenty feet away, Robert sat on his haunches watching them. *His* pistol hung down from *his* fingers between *his* knees. *He* still wore *his* uniform with its torn lapels and burned sleeves. In the firelight, *his* eyes were very bright. *His* lips were slightly parted. *He* could not breathe through *his* nose. It was broken. *His* face and the backs of *his* hands were streaked with clay and sweat. *His* hair hung down across *his* forehead. *He* was absolutely still. *He* had wandered now for over a week. —TIMOTHY FINDLEY

■ **Exercise 6** Revise the following sentences to eliminate wordiness and useless repetition.

1. In the last act of the play there is the explanation of the title of the play.
2. Statistics show that in the decade from 1950 to 1960, enrolments at universities doubled; in 1960 there were twice as many students as in 1950.
3. *Fantabulous* is a blend of the words *fantastic* and *fabulous*; *galumph* is a blend of *gallop* and *triumph*.
4. The National Gallery of Art, which is in Washington, D.C., and which houses the Mellon, Kress, and Widener collections, is one of the largest marble structures in the entire world.
5. The radio announcer repeatedly kept saying, "Buy Peterson's Perfect Prawns," over and over and over again.
6. Leslie likes to go to the mountains to ski, Marcia enjoys going there to fish, and Joseph likes to go to the same type of high country to meditate.
7. Numerous products can be made from tobacco. The nicotine from this plant is used in pesticides. A sugar extracted from tobacco helps control blood pressure.
8. There were fifty people in the hospital ward who were among those who received great benefit from the new drug.
9. I had an advantage over the other contestants because of the fact that I had just looked up the word myself in a dictionary.

10. In this day and time, it is difficult today to find in the field of science a chemist who shows as much promise for the future as Joseph Blake shows.
11. He found the problem of discovering the legal status of the refugees an almost insoluble problem.
12. In order that immigrants may apply to become citizens of Canada they must make out an application stating their intention to become citizens.

Omission of Necessary Words

22

Do not omit a word or phrase necessary to the meaning of the sentence.

In many instances a word or a phrase is optional; a writer may use it or omit it without changing the meaning of the sentence. In the following example, optional words are in brackets:

> It seems [that] the security force on [the] campus overreacted.

In other instances a word like *that* or *the* is necessary or desirable for clarity:

> I know **that** the security force on **the** other campus overreacted.

If you omit necessary words in your compositions, your mind may be racing ahead of your pen, or your writing may reflect omissions in your spoken English.

> The analyst talked about the tax dollar goes. [The writer thought "talked about where" but did not write *where*.]
>
> You better be there on time! [When speaking, the writer omits *had* before *better*.]

To avoid omitting necessary words, proofread your compositions carefully and study **22a-c**.

22a

Do not omit a necessary article, pronoun, conjunction, or preposition. See also **26b.**

(1) Omitted article or pronoun

INCOMPLETE Feelings of inferiority are at bottom of person's jealousy.
COMPLETE Feelings of inferiority are at **the** bottom of **a** person's jealousy.

INCOMPLETE Al knows a man had a lawyer like that.
COMPLETE Al knows a man **who** had a lawyer like that.

To avoid ambiguity, it is often necessary to repeat a pronoun or an article before the second part of a compound.

AMBIGUOUS A friend and helper stood nearby. [One person or two?]
CLEAR A friend and **a** helper stood nearby. [two persons clearly indicated by repetition of *a*]
ALSO CLEAR My mother and father were there. [clearly two persons—repetition of *my* before *father* not necessary]

(2) Omitted conjunction or preposition

CONFUSING Fran noticed the passenger who was sleeping soundly had dropped his wallet in the aisle. [The reader may be momentarily confused by "noticed the passenger."]
BETTER Fran noticed **that** the passenger who was sleeping soundly had dropped his wallet in the aisle.

INFORMAL I had never seen that type movie before.
GENERAL I had never seen that type **of** movie before.

INCOMPLETE Such comments neither contribute nor detract from his reputation.
COMPLETE Such comments neither contribute **to** nor detract from his reputation.
[When two verbs requiring different preposi-

tions are used together, do not omit the first preposition. See also **20b**.]

In sentences such as the following, if you omit the conjunction, use a comma in its place:

> The English used the paints chiefly on churches at first, then later on public buildings and the homes of the wealthy. —E.M. FISHER [Compare "on churches at first *and* then later on public buildings."]

> The fact is, very few people in this society make a habit of thinking in ethical terms. —HARRY STEIN [Compare "The fact is *that* very few people. . . ."]

■ **Exercise 1** Insert needed words below:

1. Gary reminded Sheila Richard might not approve.
2. What kind course to take is the big question.
3. Winter and spring breaks the campus is dead.
4. The trouble was my good pair shoes got stolen.
5. Boynton will not ask nor listen to any advice.
6. Fires had burned for weeks were still not out.
7. She lent me a dollar then decided to take it back.
8. The book which the professor referred was not in stock.
9. The recipe calls for a variety spices.
10. She saw the boy finally obeyed her.

■ **Exercise 2** Fill in the blanks below with appropriate articles, pronouns, conjunctions, or prepositions:

1. _____ good are not always rewarded; _____ evil often prosper. Life is not _____ morality play. —MICHAEL NOVAK
2. The battle left him untouched: it was the peace _____ undid him. —VIRGINIA WOOLF
3. Quarrelling means trying to show _____ the other man is in the wrong. —C. S. LEWIS
4. To me, there are two kinds of liberals: the type _____ fellow _____ would take off his coat in a snowstorm and put it around my shoulders, and the type _____ fellow _____ would caution me to wear a coat against the snow. —JAMES ALAN McPHERSON

22b

Avoid awkward omission of verbs and auxiliaries.

AWKWARD Preston has never and cannot be wholly honest with himself.

BETTER Preston has never **been** and cannot be wholly honest with himself.

INCOMPLETE Since I been in college, some of my values have changed.

COMPLETE Since I **have** been in college, some of my values have changed.

Usage is divided regarding the inclusion or the omission of verbs in such sentences as the following:

> The Lions are overwhelming; the evént is unavoidable.
> —E.B. WHITE [Plural *are* is used with *Lions*, and singular *is* with *event*.]

> The sounds were angry, the manner violent.
> —A.E. VAN VOGT [Plural *were* is used with *sounds*, but singular *was* after *manner* is omitted.]

22c

Do not omit words needed to complete comparisons.

INCOMPLETE Broken bottles around a swimming area are more dangerous than picnic tables.

COMPLETE Broken bottles around a swimming area are more dangerous than **around** picnic tables.

INCOMPLETE Snow here is as scarce as Miami.

COMPLETE Snow here is as scarce as **it is in** Miami.

INCOMPLETE The equipment of a soldier is heavier than a sailor.

COMPLETE The equipment of a soldier is heavier than **that of** a sailor.

OR A **soldier's** equipment is heavier than a **sailor's**.

CONFUSING Sometimes a counsellor helps an alcoholic less than the rest of the family.

CLEAR Sometimes a counsellor helps an alcoholic less than he or she **does** the rest of the family. OR Sometimes a counsellor helps an alcoholic less than the rest of the family **does**.

INCOMPLETE The amateur's performance was as good, possibly even better than, the professional's.

COMPLETE The amateur's performance was as good **as**, possibly even better than, the professional's.

In a comparison such as the following, the word *other* may indicate a difference in meaning:

O'Brien runs faster than any player on the team. [O'Brien is apparently not on the team. In context, however, this may be an informal sentence meaning that O'Brien is the fastest of the players on the team.]

O'Brien runs faster than any **other** player on the team. [*Other* clearly indicates that O'Brien is on the team.]

■ **Exercise 3** Supply needed words in verb phrases and in comparisons.

1. They been trying to make small cars safe.
2. The consumers better listen to these warnings.
3. Ed's income is less than his wife.
4. Bruce admires Cathy more than Aline.
5. Fibreglass roofs are better.
6. The scenery here is as beautiful as any place.
7. I always have and always will like to read the comics.
8. One argument was as bad, maybe even worse than, the other.
9. The ordinance never has and never will be enforced.
10. The crusty old man irritates his roommate more than the cranky young nurse.

22d

When used as intensifiers in formal writing, *so, such,* and *too* are generally (but not always) followed by a completing phrase or clause.

Elizabeth has **such** beautiful hands **that nearly everyone she meets comments on them**.

Many a man is praised for his reserve and so-called shyness when he is simply **too** proud **to risk making a fool of himself**.

—J.B. PRIESTLEY

■ **Exercise 4** Supply needed words in the following sentences:

1. I had my senior year a strange type virus.
2. As far as Quebec City, I could see the people were proud of their history.
3. The group is opposed and angered by these attempts to amend the bill.
4. I wish I been able to play football at university.
5. It's good to talk with a person has a similar problem.
6. His assistant and close friend considered only themselves.
7. The trouble is a good water-purifier costs so much.
8. He entered the Department of External Affairs 1949.
9. Mr. Carter paid me more than Jim.
10. Nick announced the winner of the debate had not yet been voted on.
11. In our province the winter is as severe as Saskatchewan.
12. The mystery of the stolen jewels reminds me of mysteries like Sherlock Holmes.
13. Here is the hole which the rabbit escaped.
14. If Jack goes into a profession which he is not trained, he will fail.
15. The lawyer had to prove whatever the witness said was false.
16. I been concerned because the tuition is too high.
17. These trainees know they better study.
18. The large stadium was already filled with people and still coming.
19. Nobody interested their problems.
20. Elizabeth saw Nell was not in room.

EFFECTIVE SENTENCES

Unity and Logical Thinking 23

Subordination 24

Coherence: Misplaced Parts, Dangling Modifiers 25

Parallelism 26

Shifts 27

Reference of Pronouns 28

Emphasis 29

Variety 30

Unity and Logical Thinking

Unity, coherence, emphasis, variety—these are fundamental qualities of effective writing. Unity and coherence in sentences help to make ideas clear. Emphasis makes them forceful. Variety lends interest. But the final test of effective writing is the soundness of its reasoning.

23

Write unified sentences. Base your writing on sound logic.

A study of this section should help you write sentences that are neither cluttered with unrelated ideas or excessive detail, nor marred by mixed or awkward constructions. It should also help you avoid faulty definitions and illogical arguments, two very common mistakes in reasoning.

Unity

A sentence is unified when all its parts contribute to making one clear idea or impression. The parts of an ideal sentence form a perfect whole, so that a clause, a phrase, or even a word cannot be changed without disturbing the clarity of the thought or the focus of the impression.

23a

Bring into a sentence only related thoughts; use two or more sentences for thoughts not closely related.

Unrelated ideas should be developed in separate sentences. If the ideas in a sentence are related, they should be expressed in such a way that the relationship is immediately clear to the reader.

UNRELATED Yesterday Ted sprained his ankle, and he could not find his chemistry notes anywhere.

RELATED Accident-prone all day yesterday, Ted not only sprained his ankle but also lost his chemistry notes. [The relationship of the two ideas is made clear by the addition of the opening phrase.]

■ **Exercise 1** All the sentences below contain ideas that are apparently unrelated. Adding words when necessary, rewrite each of the sentences to indicate clearly a relationship between ideas. If you cannot establish a close relationship, put the ideas in separate sentences.

1. Although the visiting professor has different and refreshing views, I played badminton on September 20.
2. I hate strong windstorms, and pecans pelted my bedroom roof all night.
3. The fence and barn need repairs, and why are property taxes so high?
4. There are many types of bores at social gatherings, but personally I prefer a quiet evening at home.
5. A telephone lineperson who works during heavy storms can prove a hero, and cowards can be found in any walk of life.
6. Jones was advised to hire a tutor in French immediately, but the long hours of work at a service station kept his grades low.

7. Macbeth was not the only man to succumb to ambition, and Professor Stetson, for example, likes to draw parallels between modern men and literary characters.
8. Brad sent his sister a dozen red roses, and she sang on a fifteen-minute program over CKFM.
9. The food in the cafeteria has been the subject of many jokes, and most of the students do not look underfed.
10. Birds migrate to the warmer countries in the fall and in summer get food by eating worms and insects that are pests to the farmer.

23b

Do not allow excessive detail to obscure the central thought of the sentence.

If the detail of an overloaded sentence is important, it should be developed in separate sentences; otherwise it should be omitted.

> EXCESSIVE DETAIL In 1867, Sir John A. Macdonald, who was born in Glascow in 1815, the third child of Hugh Macdonald, a native of Sutherlandshire, and who had worked in a law office in Kingston, then a very small but thriving town, from the age of fifteen, six years before he volunteered for military service during the 1837 rebellion, became the first Premier of the Dominion of Canada.
>
> BETTER In 1867, Sir John A. Macdonald, a one-time legal clerk, became the first Premier of the Dominion of Canada.

As you strive to eliminate excessive detail, remember that length alone does not make a sentence ineffective. Good writers can compose very long sentences, sometimes of paragraph length, without loss of unity. Parallel structure, balance, rhythm, effectively repeated connectives, and careful punctuation can bind a sentence into an emphatic unit, as in the following example:

I would often invent this dream for myself at the edge of sleep, and then it was strange how content it would make me, how it would make peace and consolation flow, and I would close my eyes and float on it into my real dreams which were never so kind, but full of gritty small problems, lost socks, not being able to find the Grade eight classroom, or terrors, such as dancing on the hall stage and finding I had forgotten to put my headdress on. —ALICE MUNRO "Changes and Ceremonies," *Lives of Girls and Women*

■ **Exercise 2** Recast the following sentences to eliminate excessive detail:

1. During the first period last Monday in room 206 of the English building, we students enjoyed discussing the implications of language in various advertisements.
2. The fan that Joan bought for her brother, who frets about any temperature that exceeds twenty and insists that he can't stand the heat, arrived today.
3. When I was only four, living in a house built during the Edwardian period, little of which remains today, I often walked alone the four kilometres between my house and the lake.
4. Four cars of various designs and makes piled up on the highway, which cost the province over $2 million.
5. In a firm voice and in a straight chair, the member of Parliament advocated drastic reforms, occasionally taking time out for a sip of water.
6. The dilapidated boat, seaworthy ten years ago but badly in need of repairs now, moved out into the bay.
7. Flames from the gas heater that was given to us three years ago by friends who were moving to Australia licked at the chintz curtains.
8. After finishing breakfast, which consisted of oatmeal, toast, and coffee, Sigrid called the tree surgeon, a cheerful man approximately fifty years old.
9. A course in business methods helps undergraduates to get jobs and in addition helps them to find out whether they are fitted for business and thus to avoid postponing the crucial test, as so many do, until it is too late.

23c

Avoid mixed or awkward constructions.

(1) Do not mix metaphors by changing rapidly from one to another. See also **20a(4)**.

MIXED Playing with fire can get a person into deep water.
BETTER Playing with fire can result in burned fingers.

MIXED Her plans to paint the town red were nipped in the bud.
BETTER Her plans to paint the town red were thwarted. OR Her plans for a gala evening were nipped in the bud.

(2) Do not mix constructions. See also Section **1**.

MIXED When Howard plays the hypochondriac taxes his wife's patience. [adverb clause + predicate]
CLEAR When Howard plays the hypochondiac, **he** taxes his wife's patience. [adverb clause, main clause]
CLEAR Howard's playing the hypochondriac taxes his wife's patience. [subject + predicate]

(3) Avoid awkward or obscure sentences. Complete every construction clearly and sensibly.

OBSCURE An example of discrimination is a café owner, especially after he has refused to serve foreigners. [It is the refusal, not the café owner, that is an example of discrimination.]
CLEAR An example of discrimination is a café owner's refusal to serve foreigners.

In defining words, careful writers tell *what* a thing is, not when it is or where it is. See also **23d**.

AWKWARD A sonnet is when a poem has fourteen lines.
BETTER A sonnet is a poem of fourteen lines.

AWKWARD Banishing a man is where he is driven out of his country.
BETTER Banishing a man is driving him out of his country.

Often a sentence is flawed by a confusion of singular and plural words.

AWKWARD Hundreds who attended the convention drove their own car.

BETTER Hundreds who attended the convention drove their own cars.

■ **Exercise 3** Revise the following sentences to eliminate mixed or awkward constructions:

1. For Don, money does grow on trees, and it also goes down the drain quickly.
2. Because his feet are not the same size explains the difficulty he has finding shoes that fit.
3. Friction is when one surface rubs against another.
4. Several of the applicants brought their résumé with them.
5. One example of a ripoff would be a butcher, because he could weigh his heavy thumb with the steak.
6. Like a bat guided by radar, Mark never skated on thin ice.
7. To be discreet is where a person carefully avoids saying or doing something tactless.
8. Does anyone here know why George resigned or where did he find a better job?
9. Tourists are not permitted to bring their camera indoors.
10. When children need glasses causes them to make mistakes in reading and writing.

Logical Thinking

Be sure that your sentences are well thought out and contain no slips or weaknesses of logic. The following principles of sound thinking may help you avoid the most common errors.

23d

Formulate definitions with care. See also **31b(6).**

Errors and misunderstanding result when meanings of words and concepts are not clear. The two main types of definition are *formal* and *informal*. Either type can extend to the length of a paragraph, an essay, or even a book.

Formal definition. In formal writing you may sometimes need to use a technical or unfamiliar term to express your thought precisely. If the exact meaning of such a term is essential to your reader's understanding or interpretation, it may be necessary for you to define it formally. In a formal definition the essential nature of the term to be defined is expressed first by saying what the term *is* and then, implicitly or explicitly, what it is *not*. That is, first the class or category to which the word belongs is identified. Then the term being defined is distinguished from other members of that class or category. The first process is called *classification*, and the second is called *differentiation*.

TERM	An *invertebrate* is
CLASSIFICATION	an animal
DIFFERENTIATION	with no spinal column, ranging in size from minute protozoans to giant squids, and accounting for more than 90 per cent of all living animal species.

TERM	A *sonnet* is
CLASSIFICATION	a lyric poem
DIFFERENTIATION	written in a single stanza, consisting of fourteen iambic pentameter lines linked by an intricate rhyme scheme.

As a rule, you can strengthen a definition by sharply restricting the classification. For example, "A sonnet is a lyric poem" is better than "A sonnet is a poem."

Informal definition. The demands of clarity and precision in writing are frequently satisfied by informal definition, in which synonyms or examples are commonly used.

SYNONYMS

Magendo, or black-market corruption, is flourishing.
—KEN ADELMAN [a lexical definition of a foreign term]

The Musical Instrument Digital Interface, or MIDI, is a specification for a protocol of communication between diverse music hardware. —GREGORY STEPHEN [an explanatory definition of an acronym and a denotative definition by function]

If you press your forefinger gently against your closed eyelid for a minute or less, you will probably start to see phosphenes: shapes and colors that march and swirl across your darkened field of view. —JEARL WALKER [word substitutions with restrictive details]

EXAMPLES

Many homophones (*be* and *bee*, *in* and *inn*, *see* and *sea*) are not common problems for spellers.

For the most part, the "external" arts, such as judo and karate, emphasize the acquisition of physical skills—speed, balance, accuracy, co-ordination, power.
—DON ETHAN MILLER

23e

Base your arguments on sound reasoning.

In compositions an argument is a group of statements that present evidence in support of a thesis. Each argument thus consists of a set of propositions, or premises, offered as justification for the thesis, or conclusion. A valid argument has two characteristics that must always be present: (a) all premises must be true; and (b) the form (or pattern) of the argument must itself be valid. If the premises are true and the form of the argument is valid, the conclusion must be true. Conclusions derived in this way are based on *deductive logic*.

IF	all dogs have four legs and	[premise]
IF	Bruno is a dog	[premise]
THEN	Bruno must have four legs.	[conclusion]

If a premise is false or only partially true, the conclusion does not necessarily follow. If the form is invalid, then the argument is also faulty.

FALSE PREMISE All dogs have four ears, and Bruno is a dog; therefore, Bruno has four ears.

INVALID FORM All cats have four legs, and Bruno has four legs; therefore, Bruno is a cat.

Note: *Inductive logic* goes from specific observations or particular instances to a general conclusion that is probably—but not necessarily—valid. You should carefully state such generalizations (avoiding qualifiers like *all, never, always*) and should support them with sufficient and relevant evidence. See Fallacies of Induction, pages 287-89.

■ **Exercise 4** Be prepared for a class discussion of the premises and the conclusions in the following items:

1. First, many situations in real life have unhappy endings; therefore, if fiction is to illuminate life, it must present defeat as well as triumph. —LAURENCE PERRINE

2. The media can create fear in others without feeling it themselves. —ROBERT FULFORD

3. You can command any response—you can even command people to die—but you cannot command love. —ERIC BERNE

4. The notion that advertising can somehow "manipulate" people into buying products which they should not buy is both arrogant and naive. —MARTIN MAYER

5. If one wishes to have a career outside Canada one has to be known outside. No one will come and get you here even if you have the most marvellous talent in the world. —MONIQUE MERCURE

23f

Avoid common fallacies or mistakes in reasoning.

FALLACIES OF DEDUCTION OR INFERENCE (See also 23e.)

(1) **Non sequitur ("It does not follow"):** an argument in which the conclusion is not a necessary consequence of the premises.

FAULTY Billy Joe is honest; therefore, he will get a good job.

BETTER Billy Joe is honest; this characteristic should help him get a good job.

(2) **Self-contradiction:** an argument that contains mutually exclusive premises.

FAULTY The government should control this unmanageable situation.

BETTER We cannot expect government to control the uncontrollable, but it should try to do something about this situation.

(3) **Circular Reasoning, or Begging the Question:** a deductive argument in which the conclusion is contained in one of the premises.

FAULTY I believe that this is an evil because society has always condemned it; society has always condemned it because it is evil.

BETTER Society has always condemned this as an evil, and I believe society's judgment is correct.

FALLACIES OF INDUCTION

The following fallacies contain patterns of reasoning that misuse evidence or fail to support the general conclusion. See also the note on page 286.

(4) **Confusion of Fact and Value Judgment.** What can be observed, measured, and tested is a fact. Whether we like the fact or not, whether we believe it should be changed or not, these are value judgments—opinions or personal preferences. Both value judgments and facts are important, but they should not be confused.

FACT AND VALUE CONFUSED Your hair is too long. ["Too" indicates a personal preference, not a fact.]

FACT Your hair is long.

VALUE I don't like your hair long.

(5) **Hasty Generalization:** a generalization offered on the basis of too little evidence or evidence that is exceptional or biased in some way. *Enough* evidence must be gathered to warrant generalizing, and the evidence must not be exceptional or unusual.

INSUFFICIENT EVIDENCE None of the children in my family drink coffee; therefore, children don't like coffee. [More evidence is needed before this generalization is warranted.]

EXCEPTIONAL OR UNUSUAL EVIDENCE The increasing number of subway riders in Toronto and Montreal shows that urban dwellers in this country prefer mass transit to the automobile. [These two cities are unique in that their geographic area favours mass transit. Other cities whose geographic area is very large and whose population density is sparse might not favour mass transit.]

(6) **Post hoc, ergo propter hoc ("After this, therefore because of this"):** the mistake of assuming that because one event followed another, the first must be the cause of the second.

FAULTY Liz got wet and cold in the rain, so now she has a cold. [Many people become cold and wet in the rain and do not catch a cold.]

BETTER Liz came in contact with and was susceptible to cold germs, so now she has a cold.

(7) False Analogy: a weak, far-fetched comparison.

FAULTY The new mayor is not even the head of his own household, so I do not expect him to be a good civic leader or to have much influence on the city council.

BETTER Because he was indecisive during his campaign, I do not expect the new mayor to be a good civic leader or to have much influence on the city council.

FALLACIES OF IRRELEVANCE

(8) Ignoring the Question, or Rambling: presenting details or facts that are off the point and do not support the thesis.

FAULTY We should do more to help the poor help themselves. Of course, the Bible says we'll always have the poor with us, even though it does not say we should give them everything we have. [The writer loses sight of the main point: "We should help the poor help themselves."]

(9) Ad hominem ("To the person"): an attempt to disprove an argument by attacking the person who presents it. Do not evade the facts by attacking your opponent's economic, social, philosophical, or ethnic background.

FAULTY That merchant is allegedly a thief and a liar; his arguments against sales tax are worthless. [The merchant might steal and lie and yet have excellent views on economic matters such as sales tax. The evidence is not relevant to the assertion.]

(10) Ad populum ("To the people"): an appeal to popular emotions, prejudices, or beliefs.

FAULTY The majority of Canadians today are a generous, compassionate, and freedom-loving people; to reflect the will of the people, immigration laws should not be changed but abolished.

(11) **Bandwagon, or Join the Crowd:** an argument saying, in effect, "Everyone's doing or saying or thinking this, so you should too."

FAULTY This novel has been No. 1 on the best-seller list for weeks. You must read it!

(12) **Appeal to Authority, or Appeal to Prestige:** an argument relying not on facts but on opinions, beliefs, or theories of experts or on testimonials of famous people.

FAULTY Both the *Globe and Mail* and the *Montreal Gazette* have predicted his re-election, so he will represent us again. [Predictions, even by experts, may or may not be accurate.]

FAULTY One of the greatest athletes eats this cereal, so it is probably more nutritious than the others.

BETTER A comparison of nutrition information printed on the boxes indicates that this cereal is probably more nutritious than the others.

FALLACIES OF IMPRECISION

(13) **Ambiguity:** a statement or argument in which the meaning is unclear; two or more different interpretations are therefore possible.

AMBIGUOUS "John is a poor mechanic." [This statement could be interpreted as "John is not a competent mechanic" or as "John's financial resources are limited."]

(14) **Equivocation:** a statement or argument in which an expression or word is used in two different senses.

FAULTY We Canadians have the right to pursue happiness, and we should want to do what is right. So let's make happiness our goal in life. [The word *right* is used in two different senses.]

FALLACIES OF MISREPRESENTATION

(15) Oversimplification: a statement or argument that leaves out relevant considerations about an issue.

FAULTY People who pass tests are usually lucky.
BETTER People who pass tests are usually lucky, although they are prepared to answer most questions well.

FAULTY World War I was caused by the assassination of Archduke Francis Ferdinand in June, 1914.
BETTER World War I had many causes, but the immediate precipitating event was the assassination of Archduke Francis Ferdinand in June, 1914.

(16) False Division, or Either-Or: any attempt to eliminate the middle ground by drawing a sharp distinction between parts of a complex whole when the facts show a gradation between the parts.

FAULTY All living things are either plants or animals.
FAULTY A nation is either at war or at peace.

■ **Exercise 5** Prepare for a class discussion of the faulty logic in the sentences below:

1. Everyone goes to Florida in the winter.
2. Breaking a mirror brings seven years of bad luck.
3. Young people today do not obey their parents.
4. Jacqueline will be a good class president because all her classmates like her.
5. The other car was at fault, for the driver was a teenager.
6. All Germans like opera; I have never met a German who did not.
7. Gertrude has a migraine headache because she ate popcorn last night and got that phone call.

8. These razor blades give the smoothest shave; all the baseball players use them.
9. After that oil spill, the fish I caught tasted greasy. The report from the marine lab is wrong. Those fish are contaminated!
10. It is a fact that travelling by air is not safe. Within forty-eight hours eleven persons have been killed in air crashes.
11. If you do not lock your car, someone may steal it. Since someone stole your car, it must not have been locked up.
12. When an automobile accident occurs in the city, the police are never on hand.
13. Either the train is late or my watch is wrong. Since the train is on time, my watch must be accurate.
14. Susan is not qualified to talk about honesty in government because only last year she was accused of bribery and extortion.
15. A successful politician must be either a lion or a fox.

Subordination

24

Use subordination to relate ideas concisely and effectively; use co-ordination only to give ideas equal emphasis.

One of the marks of a mature writing style is the ability to connect and relate ideas effectively, either by co-ordination or by subordination. *Co-ordination* means "being of equal structural rank." Co-ordination gives equal grammatical emphasis to two or more ideas. See also Section **26**.

CO-ORDINATE ELEMENTS

tactless, abrasive language [co-ordinate adjectives]
not only **sings** but also **dances** [verbs]
chicken livers **slowly fried in butter** and **heavily seasoned with garlic** [participial phrases]
a person **whose last name I do not know** and **whom I have never met** [co-ordinate adjective clauses]
If they do get to the Super Bowl, **they will lose the game**, or **they will win it because of lucky breaks**. [main clauses]
These kindnesses did not go unnoticed. Nor were they unappreciated. [simple sentences]

Notice in these examples that co-ordinating conjunctions and correlatives link words, phrases, clauses, and sentences of equal grammatical rank.

24 sub

Subordination means "being of lower structural rank." It is the use of dependent elements—such as modifiers—that are of less importance grammatically than independent elements. Clauses functioning as nouns, adjectives, or adverbs are called subordinate because they are grammatically secondary to main clauses. Subordinate elements are parts of sentences, not sentences.

SUBORDINATE ELEMENTS

It was **tactless, abrasive** language. [The modifiers are of less importance grammatically than the sentence base: *It was language*.]

Chicken livers **slowly fried in butter and heavily seasoned with garlic** are good with rice. [The compound phrase functions as modifier.]

Gail is a person **whose last name I do not know and whom I have never met**. [The adjective clauses (linked by the co-ordinating conjunction *and*) are secondary to the main clause: *Gail is a person*.]

In the following sentence, the main clause (*subject* + *compound predicate*) is in boldface. All other elements in the sentence are grammatically subordinate to the main clause.

> Since I was sixteen years old at the time and had been graduated from high school, **I knew a great deal and had opinions** on a variety of subjects that I thought anyone else in the office would consider it a privilege to hear.
>
> —EDWIN NEWMAN

As this example shows, grammatically subordinate structures may contain very important ideas.

Inexperienced writers tend to use too much co-ordination—too many short simple sentences or stringy compound ones. To express relationships between ideas, do not overwork co-ordinating connectives like *so* or *and* or conjunctive adverbs like *then* or *however*. Use relative pronouns (*who, which, that*) appropriately as subordinators. Also use subordinating conjunctions to indicate such relationships as cause (*because, since*), concession (*although, though*), time (*after, as, before, since, when, whenever, while, until*), place (*where, wherever*), condition (*if, unless*), and comparison (*as if*). Notice the differences in emphasis in the following sentences:

> **Clem had finished the pre-employment course**, *and* **he was ready for an on-the-job experience**.
> **Clem**, *who* had finished the pre-employment course, **was ready for an on-the-job experience**.
> *Because* Clem had finished the pre-employment course, **he was ready for an on-the-job experience**.

If you cannot distinguish between phrases and clauses and between subordinate and main clauses, study **1d** and **1e**.

24a

Use subordination to combine a related series of short sentences into longer, more effective units.

When combining a series of related sentences, first choose one complete idea for your sentence base; then use subordinate structures (such as modifiers, parenthetical elements, and appositives) to relate the ideas in the other simple sentences to the base.

As you study the following examples of combined sentences, notice that the use of subordinate elements contributes to the concise expression of ideas. See also Section **21**.

CHOPPY Douglas wrote a quick note. It was to Nora. She is his former employer.

BETTER Douglas wrote a quick note to Nora, his former employer.

CHOPPY Two days passed. Then helicopters headed for the mountaintop. The blizzard had stranded several climbers.

BETTER After two days, helicopters headed for the mountaintop because the blizzard had stranded several climbers.

CHOPPY The limbs were covered with ice. They sparkled in the sunlight. They were beautiful.

BETTER Sparkling in the sunlight, the ice-covered limbs were beautiful.

■ **Exercise 1** Combine the following short sentences into longer sentences by using effective subordination as well as co-ordination. (If you wish, keep one short sentence for emphasis: see **29h**.)

[1] I have just read "The Idea of a University" by John Henry Newman. [2] I am especially interested in his views regarding knowledge. [3] He says that knowledge is its own reward. [4] It is not just a means to an end. [5] Newman says knowledge is a treasure in itself. [6] I had looked upon knowledge only in terms of practical results. [7] One result would be financial security. [8] But that was before I read this essay. [9] Now I accept Newman's definition of knowledge. [10] Such knowledge is worth pursuing for its own sake.

24b

Do not string main clauses together with *and, so,* or *but* when ideas should be subordinated. Use co-ordination only to give ideas equal emphasis. See also **30c**.

AWKWARD I wanted to go to college, so I mowed and trimmed lawns all summer, and that way I could earn enough money to pay my tuition.

BETTER Because I wanted to go to college, I mowed and trimmed lawns all summer to earn enough money for my tuition.

AWKWARD Burns won, and it was a landslide vote, but he had rigged the election.

BETTER Burns, who had rigged the election, won by a landslide vote.

OR

Having rigged the election, Burns won by a landslide vote.

CO-ORDINATION	The offer was tempting, but I did not accept it. [equal grammatical stress on the offer and the refusal]
SUBORDINATION	Although the offer was tempting, I did not accept it. [stress on the refusal] OR Although I did not accept it, the offer was tempting. [stress on the offer]

■ **Exercise 2** To improve sentence unity, revise the following sentences by using effective subordination and, when needed, co-ordination:

1. First she selected a lancet and sterilized it, and then she gave the patient a local anesthetic and lanced the infected flesh.
2. Yesterday I was taking a shower, so I did not hear the telephone ring, but I got the message in time to go to the party.
3. Two ambulances tore by, and an oncoming bus crowded a truckload of labourers off the road, but nobody got hurt.
4. Jean Henri Dunant was a citizen of Switzerland, and he felt sorry for Austrian soldiers wounded in the Napoleonic Wars; therefore, he started an organization, and it was later named the Red Cross.
5. The administrators stressed career education, and not only did they require back-to-basics courses, but they also kept students informed about job opportunities.

24c
Avoid excessive or overlapping subordination.

AWKWARD	I have never before known a man like Ernie, my friend who is always ready to help anybody who is in trouble that involves finances.
BETTER	I have never before known a man like my friend Ernie, who is always ready to help anybody in financial trouble.

AWKWARD These were the voters who were concerned about unemployment that kept rising, who were worried about the dollar, which was diminishing in value.

BETTER These were the voters concerned about rising unemployment and the diminishing value of the dollar.

■ **Exercise 3** Prepare to contribute to a class discussion of the subordination and the co-ordination of ideas in the following paragraph, including the punctuation used:

[1] Though it means moving two and three miles to their one, the best trail to confuse them in the foothill ravines was a spiral zigzag. [2] West of the mountains he has not seen them; he has outrun them so far in crossing the Richardson Mountains during the blizzard that when he reaches a river he thought it must be the Porcupine because he seems at last to be inside something that is completely alone. [3] But the creeks draining east lay in seemingly parallel but eventually converging canyons with tundra plateaus glazed under wind between them, and when he paused on one leg of his zag he sometimes saw them, across one plateau or in a canyon, labouring with their dogs and sleds as it seems ahead of him. [4] In the white scream of the mountain pass where no human being has ever ventured in winter he does not dare pause to sleep for two days and the long night between them, one toe and perhaps another frozen beyond saving and parts of his face dead, but in the east he had seen the trackers up close, once been above them and watched them coming along his trails towards each other unawares out of two converging canyons with their sleds and drivers trailing, and suddenly round the cliff to face each other in cursing amazement. [5] He was far enough not to hear their words as they heated water for tea, wasting daylight minutes, beating their hands to keep warm.

—RUDY WIEBE, "The Naming of Albert Johnson"

■ **Exercise 4** Combine choppy sentences and tighten loose ones. Use exact conjunctions (see pages 294-95) as you make a main clause subordinate or convert a sentence into a main clause.

1. I was walking across the campus. I found a twenty-dollar bill.
2. I was musing on the pleasures of loafing, and the idea struck me: complete idleness is hard work.
3. Growth stops. Insects eat the plant off. They do their eating just below the soil.
4. The little boy slept through it all, and so he was unconscious of our worries and fears.
5. I felt bad. I didn't tell anybody. I didn't want to go to the hospital again.
6. The yearbook had predicted it. Within a year the twins were married. They married twins.
7. The price of peace may be high. The price of war is higher.
8. An intention is not the deed. A blueprint is not a home.
9. The battle is worth fighting, and success is inevitable, or so the optimist believes.
10. Oliver is a bantam boxer, and he likes to throw his weight around, and so he keeps on picking fights.

■ **Exercise 5** Relating your ideas precisely, use each connective below in a sentence. When necessary, consult the dictionary for exact meanings.

as	once	whether
besides	since	where
except for	so	whereas
like	thus	till/until

Coherence: Misplaced Parts, Dangling Modifiers

25

Avoid needless separation of related parts of the sentence. Avoid dangling modifiers.

Since the meaning of most English sentences depends largely on word order, the position of the parts of a sentence is especially important to clear communication.

MISPLACED The doctor said that there was nothing seriously wrong **with a smile**.

BETTER **With a smile** the doctor said that there was nothing seriously wrong.

OR

The doctor said **with a smile** that there was nothing seriously wrong.

DANGLING **When discussing creativity**, a person's ability to finish a pun is stressed by John E. Gibson.

BETTER **When discussing creativity, John E. Gibson** stresses a person's ability to finish a pun.

The parts of a sentence should be placed to convey the precise emphasis or meaning desired. Note how the meaning of the following sentences changes according to the position of the modifiers:

Rex **just** died with his boots on.
Rex died with **just** his boots on.
Just Rex died with his boots on.

The man **who drowned** had tried to help the child.
The man had tried to help the child **who drowned**.

Normally the modifier should be placed as near the word modified as idiomatic English will permit.

Misplaced Parts

25a

Avoid needless separation of related parts of the sentence.

(1) In standard written English, modifiers such as *almost, only, just, even, hardly, nearly,* and *merely* are regularly placed immediately before the words they modify.

In speech such modifiers are often put before the verb.

SPOKEN The hut only costs $450. [OR costs *only* $450]
WRITTEN The hut costs **only** $450.

SPOKEN Stacey will not even write us a postcard. [OR write us *even* a postcard]
WRITTEN Stacey will not write us **even** a postcard.

■ **Exercise 1** Revise the following sentences, placing the modifiers in correct relation to the words they modify:

1. The bomb of the terrorists only killed one student.
2. Bruce polished his silver dollars almost until they looked like new.
3. The transistor nearly cost fifty dollars.
4. He even works during his vacation.

5. Some contemporary poets hardly show any interest in making their poems intelligible.
6. On Thanksgiving Day the guests almost ate all the turkey.
7. I barely had enough to pay my tuition.

(2) The position of a modifying prepositional phrase should clearly indicate what the phrase modifies.

A prepositional phrase used as an adjective nearly always comes immediately after the word modified. (When used as an adjectival before the noun modified, a prepositional phrase is hyphenated: "on-the-job training." See **18f**.)

MISPLACED A garish poster attracts the visitor's eye **on the east wall**.

BETTER A garish poster **on the east wall** attracts the visitor's eye.

Adverb phrases may be placed near the word modified or at the beginning or end of a sentence. Sometimes, however, the usual placement can be awkward or unclear.

MISPLACED One student said that such singing was not music but a throat ailment **in class**.

BETTER **In class** one student **said** that such singing was not music but a throat ailment. OR One student **said in class** that such singing was not music but a throat ailment.

■ **Exercise 2** Revise the following sentences to correct undesirable separation of related parts:

1. Newspapers carried the story of the quarterback's fumbling in every part of the country.
2. Lucille bakes date muffins just for her friends with pecans in them.
3. At the picnic Gertrude served sundaes to hungry guests in paper cups.
4. The professor made it clear why plagiarism is wrong on Monday.

(3) Adjective clauses should be placed near the words they modify.

MISPLACED	We bought gasoline in the States at a small country store **which cost $10.25**.
BETTER	At a small country store in the States, we bought gasoline **which cost $10.25**.

(4) Avoid "squinting" constructions—modifiers that may refer to either a preceding or a following word.

SQUINTING	Jogging **often** relaxes her.
BETTER	**Often, jogging** relaxes her. OR It relaxes her **to jog often**.

(5) Avoid the awkward separation of the sentence base and the awkward splitting of an infinitive.

AWKWARD	I **had** in spite of my not living in a neighbourhood as fine as Jane's **pride**. [awkward separation of a verb from its object]
BETTER	In spite of my not living in a neighbourhood as **fine as Jane's, I had pride**.
AWKWARD	Hawkins is the man **to**, whether you are a Liberal, Conservative, or New Democrat, **vote for**. [awkward splitting of an infinitive]
BETTER	Whether you are a Liberal, Conservative, or New Democrat, Hawkins is the man **to vote for**.

Note: Sometimes splitting an infinitive seems natural; however, eliminating the split infinitive is preferable in formal writing.

INFORMAL	For her to **never** complain seems unreal.
FORMAL	For her **never** to complain seems unreal.

■ **Exercise 3** Revise the following sentences to eliminate squinting modifiers or needless separation of related sentence parts:

1. An official warned the hunter not to carry a rifle in a car that was loaded.
2. Selby said in the evening he would go.
3. Marvin wanted to, even during the 6:15 P.M. sports news, finish our game of checkers.
4. Harriet promised when she was on her way home to stop at the library.
5. The car was advertised in last night's paper which is only two years old and is in excellent condition.

Dangling Modifiers

25b

Avoid dangling modifiers.

Although any misplaced word, phrase, or clause can be said to dangle, the term *dangling* is applied primarily to verbal phrases that do not refer clearly and logically to another word or phrase in the sentence.

To correct a dangling modifier, rearrange the words in the sentence to make the modifier clearly refer to the right word, or add words to make the meaning clear and logical.

(1) Avoid dangling participial phrases.

DANGLING **Discouraged by low grades**, dropping out made sense.

REVISED **Because I was discouraged by low grades**, dropping out made sense. OR
Discouraged by low grades, I thought dropping out made sense.

The second revision above follows this pattern:

PARTICIPIAL PHRASE, SUBJECT—PREDICATE.

In the following sentence, the participial phrase is placed after the sentence base.

DANGLING The evening passed very pleasantly, **playing backgammon and swapping jokes**.

REVISED **They** passed the evening very pleasantly, **playing backgammon and swapping jokes**.

In the revision above, the participial phrase refers to the subject, as the following pattern illustrates:

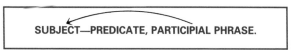

SUBJECT—PREDICATE, PARTICIPIAL PHRASE.

(2) Avoid dangling phrases containing gerunds or infinitives.

DANGLING **Instead of watching *The National***, a novel was read.

REVISED **Instead of watching *The National***, **Nancy** read a novel.

DANGLING **Not able to swim that far**, a lifeguard came to my rescue.

REVISED **I was not able to swim that far**, so a lifeguard came to my rescue.

OR **Because I was not able to swim that far**, a lifeguard came to my rescue.

(3) Avoid dangling elliptical adverb clauses.

Elliptical clauses have words that are implied rather than stated.

DANGLING **When confronted with these facts**, not one word was said.

REVISED **When confronted with these facts, nobody** said a word.

OR **When they were confronted with these facts**, not one word was said.

DANGLING **Although only a small boy**, my father expected me to do a man's work.

REVISED **Although I was only a small boy**, my father expected me to do a man's work.

Note: Verbal phrases such as the following (often called *sentence modifiers* because they qualify a whole clause or the rest of the sentence) are not classified as dangling modifiers but are considered standard usage.

To judge from reports, all must be going well.
His health is fairly good, **considering his age**.

■ **Exercise 4** Revise the following sentences to eliminate dangling modifiers. Put a checkmark after any sentence that needs no revision.

1. While wondering about this phenomenon, the sun sank from view.
2. By standing and repeating the pledge, the meeting came to an end.
3. Once made, you must execute the decision promptly.
4. Prepare to make an incision in the abdomen as soon as completely anesthetized.
5. After sitting there awhile, it began to snow, and we went indoors.
6. Darkness having come, we stopped for the night.
7. Having taken his seat, we began to question the witness.
8. Ready to pitch camp, the windstorm hit.
9. The convicts did not yield, thinking they could attract the support of the press.
10. Burned to the ground, the Welches had to build a new house.

■ **Exercise 5** Combine the two sentences in each item below into a single sentence. Use an appropriately placed verbal phrase or elliptical clause as an introductory parenthetical element.

EXAMPLES

We were in a hurry to leave Bonavista. The dented fender was not noticed.

Being in a hurry to leave Bonavista, we did not notice the dented fender.

A person may sometimes be confused. At such times he ought to ask questions.

When confused, a person ought to ask questions.

1. The statue has a broken arm and nose. I think it is an interesting antique.
2. James sometimes worried about the world situation. At such times joining CUSO seemed to him a good idea.
3. I read the first three questions on the test. The test covered materials that I had not studied.
4. Larry was only twelve years old. His teachers noticed his inventive abilities.
5. I turned on the flashers and lifted the hood. A passing motorist, I thought, might see my predicament, slow down, and offer me a ride.

Parallelism

26

Use parallel structure as an aid to coherence.

Parallel (grammatically equal) sentence elements regularly appear in lists, series, and compound structures. Connectives like *and, or, but, yet* link and relate balanced sentence elements. (See also Section **24**.) Faulty parallelism disrupts the balance.

AWKWARD What do the super-rich know about disease, those who are hungry, and poverty?

PARALLEL What do the super-rich know about **disease, hunger**, and **poverty**? [nouns in series]

PARALLEL What do the super-rich know about those who are **sick, hungry, and poor**? [adjectives in series]

If you cannot readily distinguish between parts of speech and between types of phrases and clauses, study Section **1**.

26a

For parallel structure, balance nouns with nouns, prepositional phrases with prepositional phrases, main clauses with main clauses, and so on.

As you study the parallel words, phrases, clauses, and sentences that follow, notice that repetition can be used to emphasize the balanced structure.

(1) Parallel words and phrases

She had || **no time to be human,**
|| **no time to be happy.** —SEAN O'FAOLAIN

A millionaire by inheritance, Trudeau had used his wealth to secure an enviable array of cosmopolitan experiences including

|| **university** || **degrees** in the
|| **social sciences**
and || **law**
from || **Canadian**
|| **American**
and || **European** universities,
wide and adventurous travel,
active social-democratic participation in the militant trade union revival that led to the Quiet Revolution in Quebec,
independent || **legal practice**
and || **university lecturing,**
and || **the writing of powerful analytical articles**
for || **academic journals**
and || ***Cité Libre.*** —KENNETH McNAUGHT

(2) Parallel clauses

|| **What we say**
and || **what we do**
somehow seem out of joint. —NORMAN COUSINS

Where

|| **Creighton was a scholar and an artist, the bardic singer celebrating and creating a nation by giving it a past,**
|| **Underhill was an intellectual, a Socratic teacher, and a Shavian wit.** —WILLIAM KILBOURN

(3) Parallel sentences

|| **When I breathed in, I squeaked.**
|| **When I breathed out, I rattled.** —JOHN CARENEN

■ **Exercise 1** Underline the parallel structures in the following sentences:

1. In English, there are countless situations, moods, and relationships for which there is no single word.
   —THOMAS H. MIDDLETON
2. Imagine America without baseball, Europe without soccer, England without cricket, the Italians without bocci, China without Ping-Pong, and tennis for no one.
   —BARBARA W. TUCHMAN
3. We are all sick, all lonely, all in need of love.
   —JEAN VANIER
4. Montreal has something of American luxury, the sagacity of London, the briskness of New York, the gaiety of Europe.
   —V.S. PRITCHETT
5. Tufts of hair sprouted from his ears, from his nose; his jowls were grey with afternoon beard, and his handshake almost furry. —TRUMAN CAPOTE
6. Broadly speaking, human beings may be divided into three classes: those who are toiled to death, those who are worried to death, and those who are bored to death.
   —WINSTON CHURCHILL
7. To say that some truths are simple is not to say they are unimportant. —WILLIAM J. BENNETT
8. Reading through *The Origin* is like eating Cracker Jacks and finding an I O U note at the bottom of the box.
   —JOHN FLUDAS
9. She completed her page, ornamented the foot of it with a rattling row of fancy lines and dots, threw over the release, spun the roller, twitching the foolscap sheets from under it in vicious haste, flung the carbons into the basket, shuffled the copies into order, slapped them vigorously on all four edges to bring them into symmetry, and bounced with them into the inner office. —DOROTHY SAYERS

26b

To make the parallel clear, repeat a preposition, an article, the *to* of the infinitive, or the introductory word of a phrase or clause.

The reward rests not || **in** the task
but || **in** the pay. —JOHN K. GALBRAITH

Life is || **a** mystery
and || **an** adventure
which he shares with all living things.
—JOSEPH WOOD KRUTCH

It is easier || **to love humanity as a whole**
than || **to love one's neighbor**. —ERIC HOFFER

It is the things we think we know—
|| **because** they are so elementary
or || **because** they surround us—
that often present the greatest difficulties when we are actually challenged to explain them. —STEPHEN JAY GOULD

■ **Exercise 2** Insert words needed to bring out the parallel structure in the following sentences:

1. They would lie on the battlefield without medical attention for an hour or day.
2. Two things I intend to do: to try and succeed.
3. I told him politely that I could not go and I had reasons.
4. I finally realized that one can learn much more by studying than worrying.
5. On the safari Eva took photographs of a tiger and elephant.

26c

Correlatives (*both . . . and; either . . . or; neither . . . nor; not only . . . but also; whether . . . or*) usually connect parallel structures.

AWKWARD We judge our friends both by what they say and actions.

PARALLEL We judge our friends
both || **by their words**
and || **by their actions**.

PARALLEL We judge our friends
both || **by what they say**
and || **by how they act**.

AWKWARD Not only practising at 6 a.m. during the week, but the team also scrimmages on Sunday afternoons.

PARALLEL The team
not only || **practises at 6 a.m. during the week**
but also || **scrimmages on Sunday afternoons**.

OR Not only does the team practise at 6 a.m. during the week, but it also scrimmages on Sunday afternoons. [The *also* may be omitted.]

AWKWARD Either they obey the manager or get fired.

PARALLEL Either || **they obey the manager**
or || **they get fired.**

PARALLEL They either || **obey the manager**
or || **get fired**.

AWKWARD Whether drunk or when he was sober, he liked to pick a fight.

PARALLEL Whether || **drunk**
or || **sober**,
he liked to pick a fight.

26d

Be sure that a *who, whom,* or *which* clause precedes *and who, and whom,* or *and which.*

AWKWARD Inez Santos is a woman with an open mind and who is seeking office. [A *who* clause does not precede the *and who.*]

PARALLEL Inez Santos is a woman || **who has an open mind**
and || **who is seeking office**.

■ **Exercise 3** Revise the following sentences by using parallel structure to express parallel ideas. Put a checkmark after any sentence that needs no revision.

1. It is a rare disease and which is hard to diagnose.
2. Shirley likes to play tennis and watching basketball.

3. Our personalities are shaped by both heredity and what type of environment we have.
4. Someone has said that Canadians cannot enjoy life without a TV set, an automobile, and a summer cottage.
5. My friend told me that the trip would be delayed but to be ready to start on Friday.
6. William is a man with the best intentions and who has the highest principles.
7. A seal watches carefully the way his fellows act and how they obey their trainer.
8. He was quiet and in a serious mood after the talk.
9. The secretary must attend all meetings, call the roll, and keep the minutes.
10. People fall naturally into two classes: the workers and those who like to depend on others.

■ **Exercise 4** First study the parallelism in the sentences below. Then use one of the sentences as a structural model for a sentence of your own.

1. All peoples, past and present, civilized and barbarian, share at least one thing in common: when the need arises, or the humour is upon them, they swear. —EDWARD C. ECHOLS
2. In the ghetto everybody gets a piece of the action: those who are Jews and those who are Christians; those who are white and those who are black; those who run the numbers and those who operate the churches; those—black and white—who own tenements and those—black and white—who own businesses. —BAYARD RUSTIN
[Note that semicolons sharply divide the long, compound items in the series and contribute to clarity.]
3. Finally to laugh, to chatter, to smile and know the warmth of responding smiles, to feel somebody's arm on one's shoulder, to put one's arm through another's in walking along, to have allies, supporters, to be wanted, sought, joined gratefully, left regretfully, to be liked, to be loved: with such a rich experience suddenly proffered, why should earlier solitude be a barrier? —SALLY CARRIGHAR
[Note that the colon here is used (instead of the dash) to call attention to the question that follows.]

Shifts

27

Avoid needless shifts in grammatical structures, in tone or style, and in viewpoint.

Abrupt, unnecessary shifts—for example, from past to present, from singular to plural, from formal diction to slang, from one perspective to another—tend to obscure a writer's meaning and thus to cause needless difficulty in reading.

27a

Avoid needless shifts in tense, mood, and voice. See also Section **7**.

SHIFT During their talk Harvey **complained** about the idiocy of overkill while his father **discusses** the dangers of overlive. [shift from past to present tense]

BETTER During their talk Harvey **complained** about the idiocy of overkill while his father **discussed** the dangers of overlive. [both verbs in the past tense]

SHIFT If I **were** rich and if my father **was** still alive, my life would be different. [shift from subjunctive to indicative mood]

BETTER If I **were** rich and if my father **were** still alive, my life would be different. [verbs in the subjunctive mood]

SHIFT The old man finally **had to enter** a nursing home, but it **was** not **liked** by him. [The voice shifts from active to passive.]

BETTER The old man finally **had to enter** a nursing home, but he **did** not **like** it. [Both verbs are active.]

When the literary present is used, as in summarizing plots of novels and plays, care should be taken to avoid slipping from the present tense into the past tense.

Romeo and Juliet fall in love at first sight, marry secretly, and die (NOT *died*) together in the tomb within the same hour.

27b

Avoid needless shifts in person and in number. See also **6b**.

SHIFT A man has to expect criticism when you succeed. [shift in person]

BETTER A **man** has to expect criticism when **he** succeeds.

OR

You have to expect criticism when **you** succeed.

OR

One has to expect criticism when **one** [OR he OR he or she] succeeds.

OR

Successful people have to expect criticism.

SHIFT Every **student** in favour of the legalization of marijuana **was** asked to sign **their names** on a master ditto sheet. [shift in number]

BETTER All **students** in favour of the legalization of marijuana **were** asked to sign **their names** on a master ditto sheet.

■ **Exercise 1** Correct all needless shifts in tense, mood, voice, person, and number in the following sentences:

1. After his easy victory, Kurt strutted over to me and asks a smart-aleck question.

2. Martínez recommended that property taxes be raised and spend wisely for the poor.
3. Marvin added meat to the frozen pizza, and then it was baked fifteen minutes by him.
4. Every bystander was suspect, so they were taken away for questioning.
5. I was told that billions of germs live on one's skin and that you should bathe often.

27c

Avoid needless shifts from indirect to direct discourse. See also **26a**.

SHIFT The Gordons wonder **how the thief got the car keys** and **why didn't he or she steal the tapes**? [shift from indirect to direct discourse—a mixture of indirect and direct questions]

BETTER The Gordons wonder **how the thief got the car keys** and **why he or she didn't steal the tapes**. [two indirect questions]

OR

The Gordons asked, "**How did the thief get the car keys**? **Why didn't they steal the tapes**?" [The shift in number from *thief* to *they* is typical of conversational English.]

SHIFT The secretary said **that he was sick** and **would I please read the minutes**. [shift from indirect to direct discourse]

BETTER The secretary said **that he was sick** and **asked me to read the minutes**. [indirect discourse]

27d

Avoid needless shifts in tone or style throughout the sentence (as well as throughout the larger elements of the composition).

INAPPROPRIATE Journalists who contend that the inefficiency of our courts will lead to the total elimination of the jury system are **nuts**. [a shift from formal to colloquial diction; replace *nuts* with a word like *wrong, uninformed,* or *alarmists*.]

INAPPROPRIATE After distributing the grass seed evenly over the lawn, rake the ground at least twice and then **gently bedew it with fine spray**. [The boldfaced expression is too "poetic" in a sentence with a prosaic purpose. Substitute something like *water it lightly*.]

27e

Avoid needless shifts in perspective or viewpoint throughout the sentence (as well as throughout the larger elements of the composition).

FAULTY PERSPECTIVE The underwater scene was dark and mysterious; the willows lining the shore dipped gracefully into the water. [The perspective abruptly shifts from beneath the surface of the water to above it.]

BETTER The underwater scene was dark and mysterious; **above**, the willows lining the shore dipped gracefully into the water.

■ **Exercise 2** Correct all needless shifts in the following sentences. Put a checkmark after any sentence that needs no revision.

1. A woman stepped forward, grabs the mugger's belt, snatches the purses, and got lost in the crowd.
2. A vacation is enjoyed by all because it refreshes the mind and the body.
3. Aunt Leila spent her summers in Alberta but flew to British Columbia for the winters.
4. Jim wondered whether Jack had left and did he say when he would return?
5. Every cook has their own recipes for making chili.

6. He told his aunt that there is someone in the room.
7. If she really likes someone, she would make any sacrifice for them.
8. Take your raincoat. They will be needed.
9. The outside of the building looks like a fortress; the comfortable furnishings seem out of place.
10. The darkness of the auditorium, the monotony of the ballet, and the strains of music drifting sleepily from the orchestra aroused in me a great desire to sack out.

■ **Exercise 3** Revise the following paragraph to eliminate all needless shifts:

[1] He was a shrewd businessman, or so it had always seemed to me. [2] He has innocent-looking eyes, which are in a baby face, and swaggered when he walks. [3] When questioned about his recent windfall, he up and says, "I'm lucky enough to have the right contacts." [4] Not one name was mentioned by him; moreover, his reluctance to discuss his business transactions was evident. [5] Take these comments for what they are worth; they may help one in your dealings with this big shot.

Reference of Pronouns

28

Make a pronoun refer unmistakably to its antecedent. See also **6b**.

Each boldfaced pronoun below clearly refers to its italicized antecedent, a single word or a word group:

> *Languages* are not invented; **they** grow with our need for expression. —SUSANNE K. LANGER

> There is no *country* in the world **whose** population is stationary. —KENNETH BOULDING

> Thus, *being busy* is more than merely a national passion; **it** is a national excuse. —NORMAN COUSINS

A pronoun may clearly refer to a whole clause:

> Some people think that the fall of man had something to do with sex, but **that**'s a mistake. —C.S. LEWIS [Compare "*To think this* is a mistake."]

As you proofread your compositions, check to see that the meaning of each pronoun is immediately obvious. If there is any chance of confusion, repeat the antecedent, use a synonym for it, or recast your sentence.

Note: For the sake of clarity, you may find it necessary to establish a point of reference for acronyms and abbreviations (although they are not pronouns).

UNCLEAR This week, a special task force of the CRTC will start hearings in Ottawa on a new policy aimed at encouraging ''pirates'' to apply for licencing. [What, a reader may ask, is the CRTC? or "Pirates"?]

CLEAR This week, a special task force of the **Canadian Radio-television and Telecommunications Commission** (CRTC) will start hearings in Ottawa on a new policy aimed at encouraging ''pirate'' **broadcasters, who illegally capture U.S. television signals for rebroadcast**, to apply for licencing.

UNCLEAR The VLSI program being undertaken co-operatively by the Federal Government, the University, and several large corporations represents a significant step in interdisciplinary studies. [What is VLSI?]

CLEAR The program **designed to integrate information on a very large scale on microchips (Very Large Scale Integration—often referred to by the acronym, VLSI)** being undertaken co-operatively by the Federal Government, the University, and several large corporations represents a significant step in interdisciplinary studies.

28a

Avoid an ambiguous reference.

A pronoun, of course, may clearly refer to two or more antecedents: ''*Jack* and *Jill* met *their* Waterloo.'' Ambiguous reference, however, causes the reader to be unsure of the meaning of a pronoun because it could refer to one antecedent or to another.

AMBIGUOUS Lisa wrote to Jennifer every day when she was in the hospital.

CLEAR When Lisa was in the hospital, she wrote to Jennifer every day. OR
When Jennifer was in the hospital, Lisa wrote to her every day.

28b

Avoid a remote or an obscure reference.

Do not run the risk of your reader's momentarily losing track of the antecedent of a pronoun because you have placed the pronoun too far from its antecedent. Also avoid an obscure reference to an antecedent in the possessive case.

REMOTE A student found herself the unanimously elected president of a group of enthusiastic reformers, mostly townspeople, **who** was not a joiner of organizations. [*Who* is too far removed from the antecedent *student*. See also **25a(3)**.]

BETTER A **student who** was not a joiner of organizations found herself the unanimously elected president of a group of enthusiastic reformers, mostly townspeople.

OBSCURE When Johnson's club was organized, **he** asked Goldsmith to become a member. [reference to antecedent in the possessive case]

BETTER When **Johnson** organized his club, **he** asked Goldsmith to become a member.

Note: As a rule, writers avoid using a pronoun like *it, this*, or *he* to refer to the title of a composition or to a word in the title.

Title: Death with Dignity

AWKWARD FIRST SENTENCE How can this ever be?

BETTER How can death ever be dignified?

■ **Exercise 1** Revise each sentence below to eliminate ambiguous, remote, or obscure pronoun reference:

1. The misunderstanding between the Kemps and the Dixons did not end until they invited them over for a swim in their new pool.
2. On the dashboard the various buttons and knobs seldom cause confusion on the part of the driver that are clearly labelled.

3. After Martin's advertising campaign was launched, he had more business than he could handle.
4. The lake covers a large area. Near the shore, water lilies grow in profusion, spreading out their green leaves and sending up white blossoms on slender stems. It is well stocked with fish.
5. Elaine waved to Mrs. Edwards as she was coming down the ramp.

28c

Use broad reference only with discretion.

Pronouns such as *it, this, that, which,* and *such* may refer to a specific word or phrase or to the general idea of a whole clause, sentence, or paragraph:

SPECIFIC REFERENCE His nose was absolutely covered with warts of different sizes; it looked like a sponge, or some other kind of marine growth. —DAN JACOBSON [*It* refers to *nose.*]

BROAD REFERENCE This was One World now—and he owned a Volkswagen and a Japanese camera to prove it. —ARNOLD M. AUERBACH [*It* refers to *This was One World now.*]

When used carelessly, however, broad reference can interfere with clear communication. To ensure clarity, inexperienced writers may be advised to make each of their pronouns refer to a specific word.

(1) Avoid reference to the general idea of a preceding clause or sentence unless the meaning is clear.

VAGUE Although the story referred to James, Henry misapplied it to himself, which is true in real life.

CLEAR Although the story referred to James, Henry misapplied it to himself. Such mistakes occur in real life.

(2) As a rule, do not refer to a word or an idea not expressed but merely implied.

VAGUE Eileen said that she would stay in Victoria for at least a month. This explains her happiness. [*This* does not refer to a single stated word or idea in the preceding sentence.]

CLEAR Eileen said that she would stay in Victoria for at least a month. This remark suggests that she is happy there.

VAGUE He wanted his teachers to think he was above average, as he could have been if he had used it to advantage. [*It* has no expressed antecedent.]

CLEAR He wanted his teachers to think he was above average, as he could have been if he had used his ability to advantage.

(3) Avoid awkward use of the indefinite *you* or *it*.

AWKWARD When one cannot swim, you fear deep, stormy waters. [See also **27b**.]

BETTER The person who cannot swim fears deep, stormy waters.

AWKWARD In the book **it** says that many mushrooms are edible.

BETTER The book says that many mushrooms are edible.

Note: In some contexts, the use of the impersonal, or indefinite, *you* is both natural and acceptable. Notice in the example below that *you* is equivalent in meaning to "people in general" or "the reader."

> The study of dreams has become a significant and respectable scientific exploration, one that can directly benefit **you**.
>
> —PATRICIA GARFIELD

Some writers, however, prefer not to use *you* in a formal context.

28d

Avoid the awkward placement of *it* near another *it* with a different meaning.

AWKWARD	Although it was very hot on the beach, it was a beautiful place. [The first *it* is the indefinite or unspecified *it*. The second *it* refers to *beach*.]
BETTER	Although it was very hot on the beach, the place was beautiful.
AWKWARD	It would be unwise to buy the new model now, but it is a beautiful machine. [The first *it* is an expletive. The second *it* refers to *model*.]
BETTER	Buying the new model now would be unwise, but it is a beautiful machine.

■ **Exercise 2** Revise the following sentences as necessary to correct faults in reference. Put a checkmark after any sentence that needs no revision.

1. At the Chinese restaurant, the Meltons had a hard time eating with chopsticks, but that is their favourite food.
2. Apparently the dishwasher was out of order; it leaked all over the kitchen floor.
3. Copiers and other fine modern office machines enable business executives to accomplish more work because their assistants can manage them easily and quickly.
4. In the book it states that Mrs. Garrett can see through her fingertips.
5. Our language is rich in connectives that express fine distinctions of meaning.
6. I did not even buy a season ticket, which was very disloyal to my school.
7. Mary told Ann that she had to read *Lady Oracle*.
8. When building roads the Romans tried to detour around valleys as much as possible for fear that flood waters might cover them and make them useless.
9. The extra fees surprised many students that seemed unreasonably high.
10. In Frank's suitcase he packs only wash-and-wear clothes.

Emphasis

29

Select words and arrange the parts of the sentence to give emphasis to important ideas.

Since ideas vary in importance, expression of them should vary in emphasis. You may emphasize ideas through the use of exact diction (see Section **20**), through economy of language (see Section **21**), and through effective subordination and co-ordination (see Section **24**). You may also gain emphasis—

a by placing important words at the beginning or at the end of the sentence;
b by changing loose sentences into periodic sentences;
c by arranging ideas in the order of climax;
d by using the active voice instead of the passive voice;
e by repeating important words;
f by putting a word or phrase out of its usual order;
g by using balanced sentence construction;
h by abruptly changing sentence length.

29a

Gain emphasis by placing important words at the beginning or end of the sentence—especially at the end.

UNEMPHATIC	Total deafness is worse than total blindness, however, in many ways. [Parenthetical elements in an important position weaken the sentence.]
EMPHATIC	Total deafness, however, is in many ways worse than total blindness.
UNEMPHATIC	There was an underground blast that rocked the whole area. [Unemphatic words begin the sentence.]
EMPHATIC	An underground blast rocked the whole area.

The colon and the dash often precede an emphatic ending.

> We have developed something new in politics: the profesional amateur. —MEG GREENFIELD

> Most commercial television stations talk about helping their communities, but it is in the main just that—talk. —JEFF GREENFIELD

Since the semicolon, sometimes called a weak period, is a strong punctuation mark when used between main clauses, words placed before and after a semicolon have an important position. See also **14a**.

> A penny saved used to be a penny earned; now, after five years, it is only half a penny. —ROBERT FRIEDMAN

Note: Introductory transitional expressions do not ordinarily weaken a sentence beginning.

> Above all, the spirit of science is the spirit of progress. —HERMANN J. MULLER

■ **Exercise 1** Revise the following sentences to make them more emphatic. Change the word order when desirable, and delete unnecessary words and phrases.

1. Music has the power to hypnotize, so they say.
2. In fact, only one person could have written all these articles because of their same political slant, I am convinced.
3. There is one stunt woman who earns five thousand dollars for two hours of work.
4. Bowmanville finally decided to enforce the old ordinance; there were nearby towns that revived similar laws and began clean-up campaigns, also.
5. It had never before entered her mind to resent her husband's complacent ignorance or to ignore his unreasonable demands, however.

29b

Gain emphasis by changing loose sentences into periodic sentences.

In a *loose* sentence, the main idea (grammatically a main clause or sentence base) comes first; less important ideas or details (a subordinate clause, parenthetical phrase, an appended element) follow. In a *periodic* sentence, however, the main idea comes last, just before the period.

LOOSE Hair has always been a statement for men, variously representing strength (Samson), fashionable virtue (King Charles I of England, whose wigs were long-locked and elaborate), bravado (General Custer), and genius (Einstein).
—OWEN EDWARDS [The main idea comes first.]

PERIODIC When you die, when you get a divorce, when you buy a house, when you have an auto accident, not to mention the hundreds of times during your lifetime when you are fleeced in your role as a consumer, a lawyer either must or should be involved.
—DAVID HAPGOOD [The main idea comes last.]

Both types of sentences can be effective. The loose sentence is, and should be, the more commonly used. Although the periodic sentence is often the more emphatic, you should take care in your writing not to overuse it to the point of making your style unnatural. Variety is desirable: see Section **30**.

LOOSE Such sticky labels do not accurately describe any generation—for example, labels like *lost, beat, now, silent, unlucky,* or *found.*

PERIODIC Such sticky labels as *lost, beat, now, silent, unlucky,* or *found* do not accurately describe any generation.

LOOSE The Swiss are second only to the Americans, if the chart indicating per capita wealth is dependable.

PERIODIC If the chart indicating per capita wealth is dependable, the Swiss are second only to the Americans.

■ **Exercise 2** Convert the loose sentences to periodic sentences, and the periodic to loose. Notice how your revisions make for varying emphasis.

1. Italy remains cheerful, despite everything.
—AUBERON WAUGH
2. All things are beautiful as long as you get them in the proper order. —JOHN GRIERSON
3. The Milky Way Galaxy is entirely unremarkable, one of the billions of other galaxies strewn through the vastness of space. —CARL SAGAN
4. And then she was sweet and apologetic, as always, as she had been all her life, nervously backing away from the arguments she should have had with my father, turning aside from the talks she should have had with me.
—JOYCE CAROL OATES
5. When schemes are laid in advance, it is surprising how often the circumstances fit in with them.
—SIR WILLIAM OSLER

29c

Gain emphasis by arranging ideas in the order of climax.

Notice in the following examples that the ideas are arranged in the order of importance, with the strongest idea last:

> Urban life is unhealthy, morally corrupt, and fundamentally inhuman. —RENÉ DUBOS [adjectives in the series arranged in climactic order]

> **Every** man is wise when pursued by a mad dog; **fewer** when pursued by a mad woman; **only** the wisest survive when attacked by a mad notion. —ROBERTSON DAVIES [The three words in bold type give the sentence a climactic progression.]

> In the language of screen comedians four of the main grades of laugh are the titter, the yowl, the belly laugh and the boffo. The titter is just a titter. The yowl is a runaway titter. Anyone who has ever had the pleasure knows all about a belly laugh. The boffo is the laugh that kills. —JAMES AGEE [First, words are placed in climactic order, then sentences.]

In a sentence like the following, the order of climax depends on the writer's judgment:

> Summing up for the defence of the small diesel, one can say that it offers excellent fuel consumption, it is long-lasting, it has no ignition system to cause trouble, and its level of pollution is low. —TONY HOGG

Note: Anticlimax—an unexpected shift from the dignified to the trivial or from the serious to the comic—is sometimes used for special effect.

> When I return to Canada from time to time, what I always find most tiresome is the cultural protectionism, the anti-Americanism. No heritage is worth preserving unless it can survive the sun, the mixed marriage, or the foreign periodical. Culture cannot be legislated or budgeted or protected with tariffs. Like potatoes. —MORDECAI RICHLER

■ **Exercise 3** Arrange the ideas in the sentences below in what you consider to be the order of climax:

1. Franklin used the ant as a symbol of industry, wisdom, and efficiency.
2. Among the images in the poem are sun-drenched orchards, diamond-eyed children, and golden-flecked birds.
3. He left the city because his health was failing, his taxes were going up, and his pet dog was tired of the leash.
4. Something must be done at once. Unless we act now, the city will be bankrupt in five years. The council is faced with a deficit.
5. The would-be mayor attended a community festival, autographed books for teenagers, promised prosperity to all, and wrote letters to senior citizens.

29d

Gain emphasis by using the active voice instead of the passive voice.

UNEMPHATIC	Little attention is being paid to cheap, nutritious foods by the average shopper.
EMPHATIC	The average shopper is paying little attention to cheap, nutritious foods.

Exception: If the receiver of the action is more important than the doer, the passive voice is more effective.

> There in the tin factory, in the first moment of the atomic age, a human being was crushed by books. —JOHN HERSEY
>
> Freedom can be squashed by the tyrant or suffocated by the bureaucrat. —WILLIAM F. RICKENBACKER

■ **Exercise 4** Make each sentence below more emphatic by substituting the active for the passive voice:

1. Pennies are often thrown into the fountain by tourists.
2. Every Saturday morning, television is being watched by easily influenced children.
3. The wastebasket was being filled with illegible photocopies by a student about to run out of coins.
4. When the play was brought to an end, the actors were greeted with a loud burst of applause by the audience.
5. It is greatly feared by the citizens that adequate punishment will not be meted out by the judge.

29e

Gain emphasis by repeating important words.

> It is impossible to be simultaneously blasted by a revolution in energy, a revolution in technology, a revolution in family life, a revolution in sexual roles, and a worldwide revolution in communications without also facing—sooner or later—a potentially explosive political revolution. —ALVIN TOFFLER
>
> COMPARE
>
> It is impossible to be simultaneously blasted by a revolution in energy, in technology, in family life, in sexual roles, and in world communications without also facing—sooner or later—a potentially explosive political insurrection.

■ **Exercise 5** First make each sentence below more emphatic by substituting repetition for the use of synonyms; then write two sentences of your own using repetition for emphasis.

1. Sometimes we lie to avoid hurting someone's feelings; occasionally we prevaricate to make another person like us.
2. He gripes all the time: he complains about the weather, fusses in heavy traffic, grumbles about high prices, and is critical of his meals.

29f

Gain emphasis by occasionally inverting the word order of a sentence. See also **30b**.

> Only recently has this human deficiency been turned into law. —GERALD GRAFF [Compare "This human deficiency has only recently been turned into law."]
>
> Basic to all the Greek achievement was freedom. —EDITH HAMILTON [Compare "Freedom was basic to all the Greek achievement."]

Caution: This method of gaining emphasis, if overused, will make the style distinctly artificial. And of course the order of the parts of the sentence should never be such as to cause ambiguity: see **25a**.

29g

Gain emphasis by using balanced sentence construction.

A sentence is balanced when grammatically equal structures—usually main clauses with parallel elements—are used to express contrasted (or similar) ideas: see Section **26**. A balanced sentence emphasizes the contrast (or similarity) between parts of equal length and movement.

> For many years we had a country with little or no art; now it seems we are to have art without a country.
>
> —A.Y. JACKSON
>
> Love is positive; tolerance negative. Love involves passion; tolerance is humdrum and dull. —E.M. FORSTER

■ **Exercise 6** Write emphatic sentences using balanced construction to show the contrast between the following:

1. summer and winter
2. youth and age
3. town and city
4. hypocrisy and candour

29h

Gain emphasis by abruptly changing sentence length.

> I suppose each painter has his own way of launching into the adventures in shape, colour, texture and space that we call painting. I mostly fall into them. —DAVID MILNE [The short sentence, which abruptly follows a much longer one, is emphatic.]

■ **Exercise 7** Write a short, emphatic sentence to follow each long sentence below. Then write another pair of sentences—one long and one short—of your own.

1. According to some minor prophets of doom, the next century will be a push-button era, a computer-controlled and robot-dominated one with life dependent on the movement of a forefinger.
2. In sequined costumes the skaters glide into the huge arena, smile at the applauding spectators, strike a brief pose, and then race into a series of intricate leaps and spins, their feet perfectly balanced on thin wedges of shining steel.

■ **Exercise 8** Prepare for a class discussion of emphasis in the following passages:

1. Opportunity for purposeful activity, opportunity for self-realization, opportunity for work and rest and love and play—this is what men think of as liberty today.
   —CLINTON ROSSITER
2. The honeymoon is over, and the realization is dawning that the heavy intake of direct investment and the consequent loss of economic control has restricted Canada's freedom of action in a highly competitive world economy.
   —KEN LEVITT
3. Canada is a most horribly individualistic place, with no one thinking of anything except the amount of money that he can make, by any means, in the shortest time.
   —RUPERT BROOKE

■ **Exercise 9** Revise the following sentences for greater emphasis:

1. I think that experimenting on fetuses should stop, whether they are dead or alive.
2. These retirees fear death, illness, poverty.
3. Fields of wild flowers were all around us.
4. Fools talk about each other; ideas fill the conversations of the wise.
5. At any rate, the gun fired when the fleeing youth tripped over the officer's foot.
6. The storm broke in all its fury at the close of a hot day.
7. A quick break was made by Burns from his own end, and after the defence was outpaced by him a spectacular save was made by the goalkeeper.
8. I asked her to marry me, two years ago, in a shop on Tremont Street, late in the fall.
9. The art of the people was crude, but a great deal of originality was shown by some of them.
10. I can identify the guilty person in every Agatha Christie novel by the simple device of choosing the least likely suspect whose alibi is airtight.

Variety

30

Vary the structure and the length of your sentences to make your whole composition pleasing and effective.

Compare the two paragraphs below. Both use good sentences; both use virtually the same diction. It is varied structure and sentence length that make the difference.

> MONOTONOUS
> She picked her way toward the garden chairs beside the front porch. She poured out a customary torrent of complaint. Her eyesight was failing. She found herself swatting raisins on the kitchen table. She thought they were flies. She brought her stick down on spiders. These turned out to be scurrying tufts of lint. Her hearing was going. She suffered from head noises. She imagined she heard drums beating. [series of short, choppy sentences]
>
> VARIED
> As she picked her way toward the garden chairs beside the front porch, she poured out a customary torrent of complaint. Her eyesight was failing. She found herself swatting raisins on the kitchen table, thinking they were flies, and bringing her stick down on spiders that turned out to be scurrying tufts of lint. Her hearing was going, and she suffered from head noises. She imagined she heard drums beating.
>
> — PETER DE VRIES [Interspersed with longer sentences, the short sentences are emphatic.]

Inexperienced writers tend to rely too heavily—regardless of content or purpose—on a few comfortable, familiar structures. For that reason, Section **30** recommends sentence variety and cautions against monotonous repetition of any one type of sentence.

Note: If you have difficulty distinguishing various types of structures, review the fundamentals of the sentence treated in Section **1**, especially **1d**.

30a

As a rule, avoid a series of short simple sentences. Vary the length. See also **29h**.

Rather than present your ideas in a series of choppy, ineffective sentences, learn how to relate your ideas precisely in a longer sentence. See Section **24**.

CHOPPY An urban songwriter celebrates the simple values. These are to be found only in small towns. This songwriter probably wouldn't live in one.

EFFECTIVE The urban songwriter who celebrates the simple values to be found only in small towns probably wouldn't live in one. —THOMAS GRIFFITH

CHOPPY He was a small boy. He had to drown three newborn puppies. The blind, tiny creatures struggled for life in the bucket. This conveyed to him a vivid sense. In everything there is an "I." This "I" deserves respect.

EFFECTIVE When he was a small boy, he had to drown three newborn puppies, and the blind, tiny creatures struggling for life in the bucket conveyed to him a vivid sense that in everything there is an "I" which deserves respect. —PETER STANSKY [The conjunctions *when, and, that,* and *which* connect and relate ideas.]

CHOPPY Maybe the video revolution is not materially affecting the mass. It is at least presenting more options. The options are for those on the fringes.

EFFECTIVE If the video revolution is not materially affecting the mass, it is at least presenting more options for those on the fringes. —CHRIS WELLES

CHOPPY Some people simply put coffee in an enamel saucepan. Next, they pour very hot water over it. Then they wait until flavour develops. Finally, they add eggshell or a small amount of cold water. The idea is to get the floating grounds to settle to the bottom.

EFFECTIVE Some people simply put coffee in an enamel saucepan, pour very hot water over it, wait until flavour develops, and get the floating grounds to settle to the bottom by adding eggshell or a small amount of cold water.

Note: Occasionally, as the example below illustrates, a series of brief, subject-first sentences may be used for special effect:

> He stumbled, recovered, picked up his pace. Now he was running. He broke out of the ring. People were throwing things at him. An egg hurtled past his head. A tomato hit someone nearby and splattered onto his suit.
>
> —GERRY NADEL
>
> [The short sentences suggest staccato action.]

■ **Exercise 1** Study the structure of the sentences below, giving special attention to the variety of sentence lengths.

[1] He listened to her moving around, going from the bathroom to the kitchen. [2] Lying back, closing his eyes, he searched for something he thought he had seen in her face. [3] If he went closer to her in her stillness, would the effect be broken, the effect inside himself? [4] A girl who could give him this sudden sense of harmony—surely she had some view of her own life. [5] Something moving, something significant, must have happened to her. [6] There had to be a structure behind it. [7] How aware was she of herself? [8] Could she explain her effect on him? [9] Of course not. [10] Could he explain it himself? [11] He knew

he had always been good at measuring the achieved effects of painters and writers. [12] Information. [13] Get all the information. [14] He had the tool he trusted: analysis. [15] He had never had any patience with mysteries. [16] Everything could be explained.

— MORLEY CALLAGHAN

■ **Exercise 2** Convert each of the following series of short simple sentences to one long sentence in which ideas are carefully related:

1. Her speech had an interesting thesis. Salespersons should solve the existing problems of their customers. They should also point out new problems in order to solve them.
2. Bennett's Comet appeared in 1969. It disappeared again in 1970. It will not be visible again for thousands of years.
3. Ellen Dolan did not buy a second car. She bought a Piper. It is a cub plane. It flies at almost two hundred kilometres an hour.
4. J. Allen Boone is the author of *Kinship with All Life*. In his book Boone describes his ability to communicate with animals. He converses mentally with a dog. He orders ants to leave his home. They obey his orders. He even tames an ordinary housefly.

30b

Avoid a long series of sentences beginning with the subject. Vary the beginning.

Most writers begin about half their sentences with the subject—far more than the number of sentences begun in any other one way. But overuse of the subject-first beginning results in monotonous writing.

(1) Begin with an adverb or an adverb clause.

Suddenly a hissing and clattering came from the heights around us. —DOUGLAS LEE [adverb]

Even though baseball is essentially the same, the strategy of play then and now is different. —JAMES T. FARRELL [adverb clause]

(2) Begin with a prepositional phrase or a participial phrase.

At that moment Professor Morrison walked in. [prepositional phrase]

Waiting patiently for help, a man lay beside the road. [participial phrase]

(3) Begin with a sentence connective—a co-ordinating conjunction, a conjunctive adverb, or a transitional expression.

Notice below how each sentence connective relates the ideas in each set of sentences. See also **31c(4)**.

It's slow. **But** it's democracy, and it works. —DAVID S. BOYER [The co-ordinating conjunction *but* makes a contrast. Compare "slow but efficient."]

We cut him off. We denounce. **And**, whenever possible, we diagnose. —WALTER REICH [Compare the less emphatic "We cut him off, denounce, and diagnose."]

The nuclei of atoms become radioactive when they absorb neutrons. **That is**, they decay by giving off some kind of radiation. —ROBERT HOFSTADTER [transitional expression]

(4) Begin with an appositive or with an absolute.

A city of ancient origins, Varna lies on the Black Sea coast. —COLIN RENFREW [appositive referring to the subject]

True, we have occasional debates, but they do not tell us much. —TERRY SANFORD [single-word absolute]

His eyebrows raised high in resignation, he began to examine his hand. —LIONEL TRILLING [absolute phrase]

Note: An occasional declarative sentence with inverted word order can contribute to sentence variety. See also **29f**.

At the feet of the tallest and plushiest offices lie the crummiest slums. —E.B. WHITE [Compare "The crummiest slums lie at the feet of the tallest and plushiest offices."]

■ **Exercise 3** Prepare for a class discussion of the types of sentence beginnings in the following paragraph.

[1] Whenever the east-west context of the Canadian outlook begins to weaken, separatism, which is always there, emerges as a political force. [2] Every part of Canada has strong separatist feelings: there is separatism of the Pacific Coast, of the Prairies, of the Maritimes, of Newfoundland, as well as of Quebec. [3] Ontario, of course, began with a separatist movement from the American Revolution. [4] But since the rise of the geat ideological revolutionary movements of our time, whether communist, fascist, imperialist, Islamic or what not, separatism has been an almost wholly destructive force. [5] The successful separatings, like that of Norway and Sweden in 1905, took place before the rise of these movements. [6] In India and Pakistan, in the Arab-Jewish world, and in many other centres divided by language, colour or religion, separatism has seldom if ever stabilized the prejudices which gave rise to it, but has steadily increased them. [7] Even where there is no political affiliation, the separation of Cuba from the American sphere of influence, or of Yugoslavia from the Russian one, cannot be a politically neutral act.

— NORTHROP FRYE

■ **Exercise 4** Each of the sentences below begins with the subject. Recast each sentence twice to vary the beginning.

EXAMPLE
Two executives dropped by the dean's office and requested reasons for the inefficiency of the school's graduates.

a. *Dropping by the dean's office, two executives requested reasons for the inefficiency of the school's graduates.*
b. *In the dean's office, two executives requested reasons for the inefficiency of the school's graduates.*

1. We still need a better understanding between management and labour.
2. Reporters interviewed the newly appointed ambassador and asked him some tricky questions about world affairs.
3. Hundreds of students will line up in order to register in a floating university, the *Queen Victoria*.
4. Jesse enjoyed the course in science-fiction literature most of all.
5. The comet travelled at great speed and fascinated sky watchers throughout the country.

30c

Avoid loose, stringy compound sentences. See also **24b**.

To revise an ineffective compound sentence, try one of the following methods.

(1) Convert a compound sentence into a complex sentence.

COMPOUND The Mississippi River is one of the longest rivers in the world and in the springtime it often overflows its banks, and the lives of many people are endangered.

COMPLEX The Mississippi River, which is one of the longest rivers in the world, often overflows its banks in the springtime, endangering the lives of many people.

(2) Use a compound predicate in a simple sentence.

COMPOUND He put on his coat, and next he picked up his hat and umbrella, and then he hurried from the house.

SIMPLE He put on his coat, picked up his hat and umbrella, and hurried from the house.

(3) Use a modifier or an appositive in a simple sentence.

COMPOUND The town was north of the Red River, and a tornado struck it, and it was practically demolished.

SIMPLE The town, located north of the Red River, was struck by a tornado and practically demolished.

COMPOUND She was the mayor of the town, and she was an amiable person, and she invited the four students into her office.

SIMPLE The mayor of the town, an amiable person, invited the four students into her office.

(4) Use phrases in a simple sentence.

COMPOUND The streets were icy, and we could not drive the car.

SIMPLE Because of the icy streets, we could not drive the car.

COMPOUND He arrived in Guelph at 1:30 A.M., and then he made the toll-free call.

SIMPLE After arriving in Guelph at 1:30 A.M., he made the toll-free call.

■ **Exercise 5** Using the methods illustrated in **30c**, revise the loose, stringy compound sentences below.

1. The small car hugs the road, and it is easy to drive in traffic, but it is not comfortable.
2. The Johnsons grew tired of city smog and noise pollution, so they moved to the country, but there they had no fire department or police protection.
3. North Americans at first traded their products, and then they began to use money and bank cheques, and now they use the all-inclusive plastic credit card.
4. Harvey kept criticizing middle-class values, and he mentioned such things as marriage and two-car garages, but he did not define upper-class or lower-class values.

30d

Vary the conventional subject–verb sequence by occasionally separating subject and verb with words or phrases.

SUBJECT–VERB	**The auditorium is** across from the park, and **it is** a gift of the alumni. [compound sentence]
VARIED	**The auditorium**, across from the park, **is** a gift of the alumni. [simple sentence]
SUBJECT–VERB	**The crowd sympathized** with the visitors and **applauded** every good play.
VARIED	**The crowd**, sympathizing with the visitors, **applauded** every good play.
SUBJECT–VERB	**Her ability to listen is** an acquired skill that attracts many friends.
VARIED	**Her ability to listen**, an acquired skill, **attracts** many friends.

■ **Exercise 6** Using the methods illustrated in **30d**, vary the conventional subject–verb sequence:

1. Roger is like his mother, and he is an excellent conversationalist.
2. Joan is taller than her sister, and has an engaging smile.
3. My grandparents valued strong family ties and encouraged us young ones "to always keep in touch."
4. Margaret was racing back to the dormitory to avoid getting wet, and she fell broadside into a big puddle of water.
5. Newtown was a popular resort once, but it is a ghost town now.

30e

Occasionally, instead of the usual declarative sentence, use a question, an exclamation, or a command.

> How can anybody assert that "growth" is a good thing? If my children grow, it is a very good thing; if I should suddenly start growing, it would be a disaster. —E.F. SCHUMACHER
>
> [A rhetorical question is followed by a declarative statement.]

> Their eyes appear covered. One shudders for them. At the same time, what courage! —ALEXANDER ELIOT [The exclamation concludes a discussion of a Japanese print.]

The first and fourth sentences in the following paragraph are imperative in mood; the rest reflect the declarative:

> But wait a minute! We were quadrupeds. These statements imply that a quadruped suddenly discovered that he could move faster on two legs than on four. Try to imagine any other quadruped discovering that—a cat? a dog? a horse?—and you'll see that it's totally nonsensical. Other things being equal, four legs are bound to run faster than two. The bipedal development was violently unnatural.
>
> —ELAINE MORGAN, "The Man-Made Myth"

■ **Exercise 7** Prepare for a class discussion of sentence variety in the following paragraphs:

[1] Not life, liberty, and the pursuit of happiness, but peace, order, and good government are what the national government of Canada guarantees. [2] Under these, it is assumed, life, liberty, and happiness may be achieved, but by each according to his taste. [3] For the society of allegiance admits of a diversity the society of compact does not, and one of the blessings of Canadian life is that there is no Canadian way of life, much less two, but a unity under the Crown admitting of a thousand diversities.

[4] For this reason, it is not a matter of political concern that Canada has two major cultures and many smaller ones. [5] It would be foolish to deny that the dual culture is one of history's many harsh gifts to Canada, that the duality arose from the ordeal of conquest and suppression and that it has given rise to friction and to weakness. [6] But it is manifest that it is a gift which admits of transmutation into something rich and strange, into a political order as liberal as those which Lord Acton, by way of example, thought approached nearest the ideal. [7] The transmutation can be wrought when the two cultures are seen as variations on a common experience of the land and history of Canada, and of the common allegiance in law and spirit to the traditions and the Crown of that land.

— W.L. MORTON , "The Relevance of Canadian History"

LARGER ELEMENTS

The Paragraph 31

The Whole Composition 32

The Research Paper 33

Business Writing 34

The Paragraph

31

Write paragraphs that are coherent, adequately developed, and unified.

The paragraph is the essential unit of thought in writing. Although it may consist of a single sentence, it is usually a group of sentences that develop one main point or controlling idea. The form of a paragraph is distinctive: the first line is indented, about two and one half centimetres in handwriting and five spaces in typewritten copy.

Certain conventions or rules govern the construction of a paragraph. The reader expects a paragraph to be *coherent* (with its organization following a definite plan), *developed* (with its sentences adequately explaining or qualifying the main point), and *unified* (with all its sentences relevant to the main point). In general, most paragraphs are between 100 and 250 words long and usually consist of five to ten sentences.

Paragraph 1 observes the three conventions of coherence, development, and unity. Each of its sentences supports the controlling idea of the paragraph (called the *topic sentence*)—the fact that people have certain ‘‘curious experiences’’ when they fall asleep.

1 A number of curious experiences occur at the onset of sleep. A person just about to go to sleep may experience an electric shock, a flash of light, or a crash of thunder—but the most common sensation is that of floating or falling, which is why "falling asleep" is a scientifically valid description. A nearly universal occurrence at the beginning of sleep (although not everyone recalls it) is a sudden, unco-ordinated jerk of the head, the limbs, or even the entire body. Most people tend to think of going to sleep as a slow slippage into oblivion, but the onset of sleep is not gradual at all. It happens in an instant. One moment the individual is awake, the next moment not. —PETER FARB, *Humankind*

31a

Construct coherent paragraphs.

To construct a coherent paragraph you must have a controlling idea, usually expressed in the form of a question or statement, and a plan or pattern for organizing the supporting material.

(1) Construct a clear topic sentence and restrict it carefully.

The paragraph consists of a topic sentence (the controlling idea) and sentences that elaborate or qualify the topic sentence, much as modifiers do in a sentence. The first step in constructing a coherent paragraph is to formulate a clear, restricted topic sentence that tells the reader what the paragraph will be about.

One method of constructing a topic sentence is to put the controlling idea into the form of a question. If you wanted to write about military conscription, for example, you might ask a question like the following, which could be the topic sentence of your paragraph: Should military conscription be universal?

A second method of constructing a topic sentence is to think of your controlling idea as if it were a problem and to state the problem as clearly as possible. For example, if you wanted to write about the physics of light, you might state the idea in a topic sentence like the following:

> A problem in discussing the physics of light is that two different theories account for certain aspects of light but neither theory accounts for all the aspects of light.

A third method of constructing a topic sentence is to start with a general statement and then to restate it in a more particular way in a second sentence. These two sentences may then be combined into an introductory clause (general) and a main clause (more particular). If you wanted to write about communication, for example, you might arrive at a topic sentence as follows:

1. Many members of the animal kingdom communicate. [general statement]
   But humans communicate in the most sophisticated way. [particular statement]
2. While many members of the animal kingdom communicate, humans communicate in the most sophisticated way. [topic sentence]

This method of presenting a topic sentence has the advantage of orienting the reader in a general way and then directing the reader to the particular aspect of the general statement the writer intends to discuss.

Because paragraphs are short, the more precise or restricted the topic sentence, the better. The more general the topic sentence, the more difficulty you will have in constructing a coherent paragraph. Thus the question "What is love?" is not as good a topic sentence as "What is love among teenagers?" Although almost any statement or question can be made into a topic sentence, to be an effective topic sentence it must be precise enough to control every sentence in the paragraph.

In paragraph 2 the topic sentence begins with reasons why the author would like to know more about the yeti (the Abominable Snowman), but it concludes with the statement that the author would be saddened if the yeti were to be discovered. This topic sentence, in turn, controls all the remaining sentences. They explain why the author would be sad.

2 Even though I am intrigued with the yeti, both for its scientific importance and for what it says about our own interests and biases, I would be deeply saddened to have it discovered. If it were to be found and captured, studied and confined, we might well slay our nightmares. But the mystery and imagination it evokes would also be slain. If the yeti is an old form that we have driven into the mountains, now we would be driving it into the zoos. We would gain another possession, another ragged exhibit in the concrete world or the zoological park, another Latin name to enter on our scientific ledgers. But what about the wild creature that now roams free of man in the forests of the Himalayas? Every time man asserts his mastery over nature, he gains something in knowledge, but loses something in spirit.

—EDWARD W. CRONIN, "The Yeti"

■ **Exercise 1** Construct carefully restricted topic sentences from the following list of ideas. The more specific your topic sentences, the better.

1. Campus parking
2. Censoring television programs
3. The price of college textbooks
4. Competition for graduate school admissions
5. Reduced government spending for student aid
6. Technical education

(2) Place the topic sentence where the reader can find it.

The topic sentence is usually the first or second sentence in the paragraph. Stated immediately, it thus provides the reader with the key idea that shapes the paragraph. At times, when the controlling idea is stated early in the paragraph, it may also be restated at the end, to point up its importance. In paragraph 3 compare "the intolerable has become normal" with the final "Ugliness is accepted, no longer even noticed."

3 In the towns and cities of Ulster, the intolerable has become normal. The civic environment is scarred. In Belfast and Derry, it is hard to find a shop with windows; shopkeepers have had so many broken that they are content to leave the boards up. Burned-out houses and shops are left as abandoned hulks. The army has run out its barbed wire, concrete and corrugated iron in dozens of checkpoints, barricades and gun emplacements. Ugliness is accepted, no longer even noticed.

—PAUL HARRISON, "The Dark Age of Ulster"

Occasionally, as in paragraph 4, the topic sentence is the last sentence, especially when the writer progresses from particulars or from a specific example to a generalization.

4 Imagine waking up and glancing at your clock, which reads 8:55 a.m. This information means nothing, until you apply your perception to it. If it's a weekday, you're due at work at 9 a.m., and being punctual is important, 8:55 becomes a negative stressor. If it's Saturday, your perception of 8:55 may result in a feeling of luxurious anticipation of a lazy day. The information in both cases was the same. Your perception of it determined your response.

—JENNIFER BOLCH, "How to Manage Stress"

Note: In many paragraphs the controlling idea is not expressly stated in a topic sentence, but in a unified paragraph it is implied distinctly. The implied idea of paragraph 5 ("These are steps in the embalming process") can be clearly understood in the context of Jessica Mitford's description. (The quotations are from an embalming textbook.)

5 About three to six gallons of a dyed and perfumed solution of formaldehyde, glycerin, borax, phenol, alcohol and water is soon circulating through Mr. Jones, whose mouth has been sewn together with a "needle directed upward between the upper lip and gum and brought out through the left nostril," with the corners raised slightly "for a more pleasant expression." If he should be bucktoothed, his teeth are cleaned with Bon Ami and coated with colorless nail polish. His eyes, meanwhile, are closed with flesh-tinted eye caps and eye cement. —JESSICA MITFORD, *The American Way of Death*

■ **Exercise 2** Identify the topic sentences in paragraphs 6–8. If the topic sentence is implied, construct one.

6 If Canada is to remain a country separate from the United States it is of great importance to her that they (the United States) should not get behind us by right or by force, and intercept the route to the Pacific. . . . But in any other point of view, it seems to me that the country is of no present value to Canada. We have unoccupied land enough to absorb immigration for many years, and the opening up of the Saskatchewan would do to Canada what the Prairie lands of Illinois are doing now—drain away our youth and our strength.
—SIR JOHN A. MACDONALD, 1865

7 When we watch a person walk away from us, his image shrinks in size. But since we know for a fact that he is not shrinking, we make an unconscious correcting and "see" him as retaining his full stature. Past experience tells us what his true stature is with respect to our own. Any sane and dependable expectation of the future requires that he have the same true stature when we next encounter him. Our perception is thus a prediction; it embraces the past and the future as well as the present.
—WARREN J. WITTREICH, "Visual Perception & Personality"

8 A TV set stood close to a wall in the small living room crowded with an assortment of chairs and tables. An aquarium crowded the mantelpiece of a fake fireplace. A lighted bulb inside the tank showed many colored fish swimming about in a haze of fish food. Some of it lay scattered on the edge

of the shelf. The carpet underneath was sodden black. Old magazines and tabloids lay just about everywhere.

—BIENVENIDO SANTOS, "Immigration Blues"

(3) Organize paragraphs according to a definite pattern.

Most paragraphs are organized according to one of these three patterns: question-answer; problem-solution; topic-restriction-illustration.

a. Question-answer pattern

In this pattern the topic sentence asks a question and the supporting sentences answer it, as in paragraph 9.

9 What were Canada's "cultural" resources at the start of the second half of the twentieth century? The 1940's had brought about an astonishing increase in the nation's population, natural resources, industrial maturity, and constitutional independence. But obviously, no comparable developments had transformed the state of the arts, literature, music and scholarship. Ten years had, of course, brought some changes, but these changes had taken place chiefly in the membership of the small group of Canadian writers, artists, musicians and scholars, and in the themes and subjects which inspired them. Stephen Leacock, Emily Carr, Frederick Philip Grove, and the historian George M. Wrong had all died during the 1940's. If their deaths did not exactly signify the passing of an age, the appearance of a large number of new artists and writers definitely marked the coming of another. First novels by Hugh MacLennan, Malcolm Lowry, Gabrielle Roy, and W.O. Mitchell appeared during the 1940's. The poets Earle Birney, Irving Layton, P.K. Page, Alain Grandbois, and James Reaney published their first volumes of verse. Painters such as Alfred Pellan, Goodridge Roberts, Jacques de Tonnancour, and Cleeve Horne began to exhibit their pictures, and the work of young composers like John Weinzweig, Barbara Pentland, and Jean Papineau-Couture gained a hearing on the radio and in concert halls.

—DONALD CREIGHTON, "The Forked Road: Canada 1939–1957"

b. Problem-solution pattern

In this pattern the topic sentence states a problem, and the supporting sentences offer a solution, as in paragraph 10.

10 The trouble with the clans and tribes many of us were born into is not that they consist of meddlesome ogres but that they are too far away. [*problem*] In emergencies we rush across continents and if need be oceans to their sides, as they do to ours. Maybe we even make a habit of seeing them, once or twice a year, for the sheer pleasure of it. But blood ties seldom dictate our addresses. Our blood kin are often too remote to ease us from our Tuesdays to our Wednesdays. [*restatement of the problem*] For this we must rely on our families of friends. If our relatives are not, do not wish to be, or for whatever reasons cannot be our friends, then by some complex alchemy we must try to transform our friends into our relatives. If blood and roots don't do the job, then we must look to water and branches, and sort ourselves into new constellations, new families.

—JANE HOWARD, "All Happy Clans Are Alike"

c. Topic-restriction-illustration pattern

In this pattern, the writer announces the topic, then restricts or qualifies it in the same sentence or in the next sentence. Then the writer illustrates the restriction in the remaining sentences of the paragraph. In paragraph 11, the general topic of gaps in the study of "the whole spectrum of Canadian society" begins the paragraph. The second sentence restates the consensus "lacking in many fields," then focusses on the "more theoretical" nature of "recent Canadian social science writing." The third sentence defines the emphasis on "theory" of the restricted topic. The analogy of Rousseau and the example of jargon further explain the new emphasis on "thought."

11 This is not to say that we have now studied the whole spectrum of Canadian society, for many gaps still remain. It is fair to say, however, that although a consensus of theory and analysis is lacking in many fields, recent Canadian social science writing is rather more theoretical than in the past. The social sciences are thus reaching beyond description towards explanatory and general theory. If, as Rousseau said, "A thinking man is a depraved animal," then Canada has fallen from its state of former innocence to become "depraved" by thought. In current jargon this might be called "consciousness-raising"; or one might say that social scientists are bringing the more sophisticated tools of their disciplines to bear upon Canada data.

—HENRY B. MAYO, "Writing in the Social Sciences"

These patterns can be varied to suit your intention. The question-answer pattern, for example, can be rearranged as answer-question. Topic-restriction-illustration can be varied in a number of ways. The topic may be such that restriction is unnecessary and can be omitted. Or illustration can be first in the paragraph with the topic saved for last.

■ **Exercise 3** In paragraphs 12–15, identify the pattern of each paragraph as question-answer, problem-solution, or topic-restriction-illustration. Remember that the patterns can be rearranged.

12 What's wrong with the student-union bookshop? Everything. It's interested in selling sweatshirts and college mugs rather than good books. Its staff often is incompetent and uncivil. The manager may not be intelligent enough even to order a sufficient number of copies of required textbooks for the beginning of a term. As for more lively books—why, there are masses of paperbacks, perhaps, that could be procured at any drugstore; there are a few shelves or racks of volumes labeled "Gift Books," usually lavishly illustrated and inordinately costly, intended as presents to fond parents; but there are virtually no *book* books, of the sort that students might like to buy.

—RUSSELL KIRK, "From the Academy: Campus Bookshops"

13 Out of a thousand years of suffering, bloodshed, and contention, there has emerged in the last century the principle of common liberty. What is this liberty? It is the right of the men and women—not the men and women of the privileged classes only, but the men and women of all other classes—to live their lives, mentally, physically, morally, without interference to person or property.

—CLIFFORD SIFTON, speech in Winnipeg, July 30, 1917.

14 Beginning about 1700, Canadian officers of the colonial troops, the "Compaignies Franches de la Marine," began to have their likenesses made. These very rare paintings all have the same composition, showing a long-haired or bewigged officer wearing a cuirass over his coat. The blue-black cuirasses are presented in a fanciful manner, trimmed with gold, and some even show an opening for frills at the centre. The cuirass lining shows at the neck and arm openings as red or blue cloth edged with gold but, unlike a real cuirass lining, it often appears to be ornamental. If a cross of Saint-Louis is shown, it is sometimes pinned on steel! Obviously, neither sitter nor painter had a precise idea of what a cuirass was, and neither really cared. Their goal was a likeness indicating that the sitter was a military man. The symbol of the time was a cuirass, although none had been worn in Canada since the early 17th century. —RENE CHARTRAND, "Military Portraiture"

15 Our most important environmental problem, certainly the most urgent, is the burning of fossil fuels, which has significantly increased the carbon dioxide in the atmosphere. It is important to get rid of it because as the CO_2 concentration goes up, it acts as a sort of greenhouse. If we increase the CO_2 in the atmosphere at the rate it's been going, atmospheric warming has been predicted to be as much as a degree and a half or so over the next ten to fifteen years. This will have major consequences for the climate, and could start to melt the icecaps. —DEREK SPENCER, "Is the World Getting Warmer?"

31b

Construct well-developed paragraphs.

Once you have decided on a pattern for your paragraph (question-answer, problem-solution, topic-restriction-illustration), you must then consider how to develop the answer, the solution, or the illustrations. The method of paragraph development that you choose depends upon your purpose. Do you want to tell a story? Use a chronological order. Do you want to say how something is done? Explain a step-by-step process.

(1) Narration

Narrative paragraphs present a series of events that begin at a particular time and are organized chronologically. Narrative writing longer than a paragraph often uses a flashback (a jump back in time), but in a paragraph the reader expects that the material will be arranged in time order.

In paragraph 16, Charles Schulz's narrative begins with second grade and proceeds chronologically through high school. Often the topic sentence in a narrative paragraph is a kind of frame that pulls the various series of incidents of the paragraph together. Schulz begins his paragraph with a topic sentence that serves as such a frame. The paragraph follows the pattern of topic-restriction-illustration.

16 My scholastic career got off to a good start when I was very young. I received a special diploma in the second grade for being the outstanding boy student, and in the third and fifth grades I was moved ahead so suddenly that I was the smallest kid in the class. Somehow, I survived the early years of grade school, but when I entered junior high school, I failed everything in sight. High school proved not much better. There was no doubt that I was absolutely the worst physics student in the history of St. Paul Central High School. It was not until I became a senior that I earned any respectable grades at all. I have often felt that some semblance of maturity began to arrive at last. I saved the final report card because it was the only one that seemed to justify those long years of agony. —CHARLES M. SCHULZ, *Peanuts Jubilee*

(2) Process

Process paragraphs explain how something is done or made. For this reason, they often have a temporal element that makes a step by-step chronological arrangement both possible and natural, as in paragraph 17.

17 The best of all scientific tricks with an egg is the well-known one in which air pressure forces a peeled hard-boiled egg into a glass milk bottle and then forces it out again undamaged. The mouth of the bottle must be only slightly smaller than the egg, and so you must be careful not to use too large an egg or too small a bottle. It is impossible to push the egg into the bottle. To get the egg through the mouth you must heat the air in the bottle. That is best done by standing the bottle in boiling water for a few minutes. Put the egg upright on the mouth and take the bottle off the stove. As the air in the bottle cools it contracts, creating a partial vacuum that draws the peeled egg inside. To get the egg out again invert the bottle so that the egg falls into the neck. Place the opening of the bottle against your mouth and blow vigorously. This will compress the air in the bottle. When you stop blowing, the air expands, pushing the egg through the neck of the bottle and into your waiting hands.

—MARTIN GARDNER, "Mathematical Games"

(3) Description

Description requires a sequential arrangement of details that move in a consistent way: from near to far, from general to particular, from right to left, from top to bottom, and so forth. As the description moves in one of these ways, it provides a framework for individual details. Thus, the reader has an orderly scheme to use as he or she visualizes what you are describing.

In paragraph 18, using a near-to-far movement, Thomas Merton describes the monastery that was to become his home.

18 I looked at the rolling country, and at the pale ribbon of road in front of us, stretching out as grey as lead in the light of the moon. Then suddenly I saw a steeple that shone like silver in the moonlight, growing into sight from behind a rounded knoll. The tires sang on the empty road, and, breathless, I looked at the monastery that was revealed before me as we came over the rise. At the end of an avenue of trees was a big rectangular block of buildings, all dark, with a church crowned by a tower and a steeple and a cross: and the steeple was as bright as platinum and the whole place was as quiet as midnight and lost in the all-absorbing silence and solitude of the fields. Behind the monastery was a dark curtain of woods, and over to the west was a wooded valley, and beyond that a rampart of wooded hills, a barrier and a defence against the world.

—THOMAS MERTON, *The Seven Storey Mountain*

(4) Classification

Classification paragraphs divide a group or class of things into parts that will explain the group or class for the reader. In paragraph 19, the class is "book owners." Adler divides book owners into three types, not according to how many books they own, but according to how thoroughly they read their books.

19 There are three kinds of book owners. The first has all the standard sets and best-sellers—unread, untouched. (This deluded individual owns woodpulp and ink, not books.) The second has a great many books—a few of them read through, most of them dipped into, but all of them as clean and shiny as the day they were bought. (This person would probably like to make books his own, but is restrained by a false respect for their physical appearance.) The third has a few books or many—every one of them dog-eared and dilapidated, shaken and loosened by continual use, marked and scribbled in from front to back. (This man owns books.)

—MORTIMER J. ADLER, "How To Mark A Book"

Once you have decided on the parts of the class you are dividing, you must decide what order you want to describe them in and maintain that order throughout. Depending on the purpose of the classification, the system of ordering might be from first to last, from largest to smallest, or from least important to most important.

(5) Analysis

Analysis is similar to classification in that the subject of the analysis is divided into parts. However, the purpose of the analysis is to suggest that the parts are related as causes or effects of the thing analyzed. In paragraph 20 the authors analyze the causes of a volcanic eruption.

20 Volcanic eruptions are the final stage of a process that begins with the melting of rock in a planet's interior, the "source region." The most usual source of the heat that leads to melting is energy released by the decay of radioactive elements. The material in the source region is generally only partially molten, being made up of magma, or liquid rock, and unmelted crystals. The lighter liquid gradually rises above the denser crystals through the action of gravity and collects in magma chambers. The segregation process that drives the liquid upward can take anywhere from hundreds of years to hundreds of millions, depending primarily on the force of gravity, which varies with depth and the planet's size, on the nature of the crystals in the source region, on the amount of liquid produced by the heat available and on the viscosity of the liquid.

—HARRY Y. McSWEEN, JR. and EDWARD M. STOLPER, "Basaltic Meteorites"

(6) Definition See also **23d**.

Paragraphs of definition attempt to explain who a person is or what a place or thing is. Definitions can be formal or informal depending on your purpose. A *formal* definition is used in academic writing to explain as precisely as possible what a thing is by putting it in its class (in biology, its *genus*) and then by distinguishing it from other members of that genus. Paragraph 21 illustrates formal definition.

21 The purple martin (*Progne subis*) is locally common where proper multicelled nesting boxes or gourds are provided. No other North American swallow is dark all over. Females, young, and first-year males are light-bellied and could be confused with smaller swallows. Watch for purple iridescence on head and top of wings. Note the broad wings and more soaring flight of martins. In late summer flocks of thousands roost together in shade trees of some cities. Song and calls are a distinctive, low-pitched, liquid, rolling twitter. —*A Guide to Field Identification: Birds of North America*

Paragraph 22 illustrates an *informal* definition, which is designed to explain a term or idea for the general reader, often by providing examples or synonyms.

22 Biofeedback, Dr. Green said, means getting immediate, ongoing information about one's own biological processes or conditions—such as heart behaviour, temperature, brainwave activity, blood pressure or muscle tension—and using the information to change and control voluntarily the specific process or response being monitored. —THOMAS W. PEW JR.
"Biofeedback seeks new medical uses for concept of yoga"

A less common type of definition, but one that you may need to use from time to time, is a form of *historical* definition. In this type of definition you explain the meaning of a thing at a particular time in history. Paragraph 23 defines *English* in a historical setting.

23 English, in its original form, is Anglo-Saxon, a Low German dialect of the western sub-branch of the Germanic branch of Indo-European. Perhaps 25 per cent of our words (at least 50 per cent, however, of our words of most frequent occurrence) go back to Anglo-Saxon or to Middle English (when the dictionary describes a word as being of Middle English origin, it means that it cannot be traced all the way back to Anglo-Saxon, but also that there is no evidence that it was borrowed from any other source; this means that it is more likely to be of native, or Anglo-Saxon, origin than of any other). —MARIO PEI, *The Families of Words*

(7) Comparison/Contrast

A comparison points out the similarities of two things; a contrast points out the differences. The important thing to remember is to compare or contrast the thing with something else the reader knows better. For example, to tell the reader how large the Soviet Union is, you might say that it is larger than the entire North American continent. You can then contrast the two areas in terms of climate, population density, and so forth. Paragraph 24 is an example of contrast—the differences between two kinds of terror.

24 Most of us enjoy the gooseflesh and the tingle along the spine produced by the successful ghost story. There is something agreeable in letting our blood be chilled by bats in the moonlight, guttering candles, creaking doors, eerie shadows, piercing screams, inexplicable bloodstains, and weird noises. But the terror aroused by tricks and external "machinery" is a far cry from the terror evoked by some terrifying treatment of the human situation. The horror we experience in watching the Werewolf or Dracula or Frankenstein is far less significant than that we get from watching the bloody ambition of Macbeth or the jealousy of Othello. In the first, terror is the end-product; in the second, it is the natural accompaniment of a powerful revelation of life. In the first, we are always aware of a basic unreality; in the second, reality is terrifying.

—LAURENCE PERRINE
Literature: Structure, Sound, and Sense, 3rd edition

The comparison in paragraph 25 is between language and games.

25 The language game shares certain characteristics with all other true games. First of all, it has a minimum of two players (the private, incomprehensible speech of a schizophrenic is no more a true game than is solitaire). Second, a person within speaking distance of any stranger can be forced by social pressure to commit himself to play, in the same way that a bystander in the vicinity of any other kind of game may be asked to play or to look on. Third, something must be at stake and both players must strive to win it—whether the reward be a tangible gain like convincing an employer of the need for a raise or an intangible one like the satisfaction of besting someone in an argument. Fourth, a player of any game has a particular style that distinguishes him as well as the ability to shift styles depending upon where the game is played and who the other players are. In the case of the language game, the style might be a preference for certain expressions or a folksy way of speaking, and the style shift might be the bringing into play of different verbal strategies when speaking in the home, at the office, on the street, or in a place of worship. —PETER FARB, *Word Play*

(8) Example

A paragraph developed by example is very common. In this type of paragraph you make a statement and then supply one or more examples to illustrate it. Paragraph 26 illustrates this technique.

26 In the past decade, however, "facts" have blossomed into a fad. The sales of *Guinness Book of World Records* rival those of the Bible. The popularity of *The People's Almanac, Fascinating Facts, Isaac Asimov's Book of Facts, Easy Answers to Hard Questions, Dictionary of Misinformation, Encyclopedia of Ignorance*, as well as of television shows such as *Real People*, testifies to the public's growing appetite for mental snacks.

—CARLL TUCKER, "In the Matter of Facts"

■ **Exercise 4** Identify the pattern and the method of development in paragraphs 27–29:

27 Without doubt the most famous of all megalithic monuments is Stonehenge, on the Wiltshire plain of southern Britain. Visited by thousands yearly, it is second only to the Tower of London as a tourist attraction. It has a larger literature than any other archaeological site in the world, including the pyramids of Egypt and the great statues of Easter Island, as well as mythical sites such as Atlantis. The number of books on Stonehenge and on other megalithic monuments that have poured from the presses in the past decade or so is a measure of the continued interest in these antiquities.

—GLYN DANIEL, "Megalithic Monuments"

28 Watching a millipede crawl slowly, softly over decaying humus is like watching a symphony in movement. Children marvel that this thousand-legged worm can co-ordinate so many legs without getting them all tangled up. Of course, millipedes do not have a thousand legs, nor are they worms. Careful observation reveals that each body block, or segment, has two pairs of legs, in contrast with the one pair per body block in centipedes. Though they have more legs than centipedes, they move much more slowly, feeding mainly on decaying plant tissues.

—CECIL E. JOHNSON, "The Wild World of Compost"

29 The electronic revolution in data processing, which dominated the '70s, is anything but over. A decade ago, for instance, sixteen "bits," or pieces of information, could be packed on one chip of silicon inside a computer. Within five years, the capacity of a single chip will be 256 000 bits and rising, with no increase in price. This means that ever-smaller computers can deal with ever-larger amounts of data. Portable minicomputers may well become almost as commonplace in ten years as handheld calculators are now.

—NEWSWEEK

31c

Construct unified paragraphs.

(1) Make each sentence contribute to the main idea.

A paragraph has unity when every sentence is relevant to the main or controlling idea. Any sentence that violates this unity should be deleted. Paragraph 30 is unified beause every sentence contributes to the main idea—Canadian Nordicity.

30 Canada's Nordicity is a way for us to interpret ourselves as separate and unique. Without that fundamental perception, we cannot hope to develop the strong positions and courageous policies that are a priori conditions of self-respect and interdependence in the world community. With it, we can see our destiny within the group of nations occupying the "top of the globe." We can begin to assert ourselves in the global community. —R.D. VOYER, "Canada's Need for a Nordic Image"

Topic:
  Canada's Nordicity is a way to interpret ourselves [definition]

Restriction:
  Nordicity is a fundamental perception [definition]
    without it, no strong positions or policies [contrast]
    with it, we can assert our destiny

Caution: Do not make rambling statements that are only vaguely related to your topic. As you write a paragraph, hold to the main idea. For example, if the controlling idea of your paragraph is "My roommate Bill Jones cannot keep a secret," irrelevant sentences about Bill's sense of humour or about secrecy in general will disrupt the unity. Every sentence should pertain to Bill's inability to keep a secret.

■ **Exercise 5** Revise the following student paragraph to improve unity. Be prepared to give reasons for your revisions.

31 The expression "environmental problems" encompasses a wide range. Since the beginning of time, human beings have struggled against elements in their environment. They have always attempted to protect themselves against such natural disasters as fire and flood. As time went on, and the human population grew, abuse of land, overcrowding of cities, famine, and the extinction of various animal species became environmental problems. Human beings progressed, gaining more control over their environment and creating more problems in it. They were less dependent on environmental conditions for their lives: if it was dark, they could snap on a light, and if it was cold, they could turn up the furnace. People became very mobile, able to hop into a car and drive practically anywhere. Life was made easier by new products. But all of this "progress" had negative effects on the environment. It became increasingly more difficult to find efficient methods of disposing of waste, and air and water pollution resulted. Land, energy, and food became more scarce. Progress began as we defended ourselves against what often seemed a hostile environment, but somewhere along the way we not only gained control over—but also began to destroy—our environment.

TRANSITIONS BETWEEN SENTENCES

Sentences linked by transitional devices such as pronouns, repeated key words, transitional expressions, or parallel structure help create a unified paragraph.

(2) Link sentences by your use of pronouns.

In paragraph 32 Carin Rubenstein links her sentences by

using the pronouns *their* and *they*. Although these same two pronouns are used repeatedly, their referent, "easy victims," is always clear.

32 Several movements characterized easy victims: their strides were either very long or very short; they moved awkwardly, raising their left legs with their left arms (instead of alternating them); on each step, they tended to lift their whole foot up and then place it down (less muggable sorts took steps in which their feet rocked from heel to toe). Overall, the people rated most muggable walked as if they were in conflict with themselves; they seemed to make each move in the most difficult way possible. —CARIN RUBENSTEIN, "Body Language That Speaks to Muggers"

(3) Link sentences by repeating key words or ideas.

In paragraph 33, the repetition of the pronoun *it* and its referent *main street*, links the sentences. (The repetition also serves to provide emphasis: see **29e**.)

33 As long as *it* has existed, people have been writing about *main street*. From *its* earliest days, *main street* has been the heart of the North American town. *It* was the hub of the community where you found the town hall, the courthouse, and the railroad station. As the centre of commerce, *it* was home to the bank, the general store, and the butcher shop and, as the meeting place, *it* was the only location for the hotel, the post office, and the movie palace. Writing about *main street* meant writing about everyday life; *it* was the common thread to villages, towns, and cities that spread across the continent. As they prospered, so did *main street* until *it* became the symbol of growth that embodied the spirit of enterprise.

—DON J. LAHEY, "Heritage Authors Take a Stroll Downtown" *Canadian Heritage* (italics added)

Notice in paragraph 34 how repetition of key words binds together the sentences.

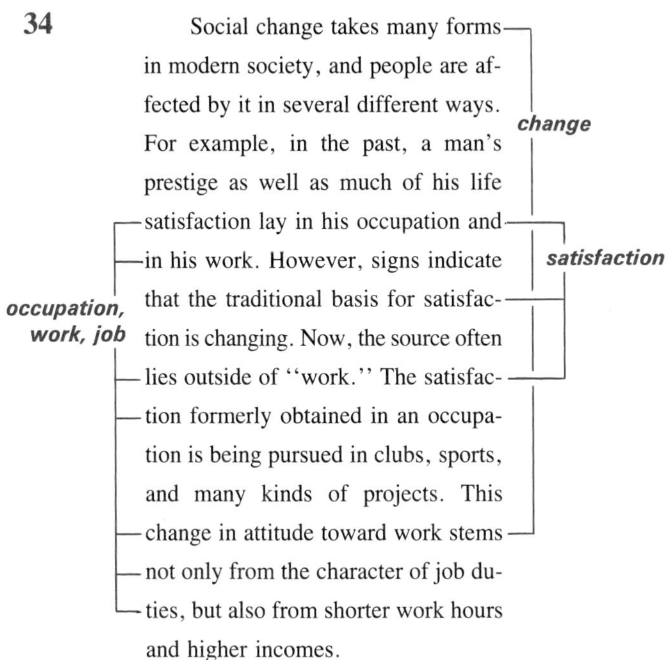

34 Social change takes many forms in modern society, and people are affected by it in several different ways. For example, in the past, a man's prestige as well as much of his life satisfaction lay in his occupation and in his work. However, signs indicate that the traditional basis for satisfaction is changing. Now, the source often lies outside of "work." The satisfaction formerly obtained in an occupation is being pursued in clubs, sports, and many kinds of projects. This change in attitude toward work stems not only from the character of job duties, but also from shorter work hours and higher incomes.

—THERON ALEXANDER, "The Individual and Social Change"

(4) Link sentences by using transitional expressions.

Below is a list of various transitional expressions:

1. *Addition*: moreover, further, furthermore, besides, and, and then, likewise, also, nor, too, again, in addition, equally important, next, first, second, third, in the first place, in the second place, finally, last.
2. *Comparison*: similarly, likewise, in like manner.

3. *Contrast*: but, yet, and yet, however, still, nevertheless, on the other hand, on the contrary, even so, notwithstanding, for all that, in contrast to this, at the same time, although this may be true, otherwise, nonetheless. (Note: Addition, comparison, and contrast are used for items of equal importance.)
4. *Place*: here, beyond, nearby, opposite to, adjacent to, on the opposite side.
5. *Purpose*: to this end, for this purpose, with this object.
6. *Result*: hence, therefore, accordingly, consequently, thus, thereupon, as a result, then.
7. *Summary, repetition, exemplification, intensification*: to sum up, in brief, on the whole, in sum, in short, as I have said, in other words, that is, to be sure, as has been noted, for example, for instance, in fact, indeed, to tell the truth, in any event.
8. *Time*: meanwhile, at length, soon, after a few days, in the meantime, afterward, later, now, in the past.

Notice the various ways that transitional expressions connect and relate ideas in the sentences of paragraphs 9 and 25.

(5) Link sentences by means of parallel structure.

Parallelism is the repetition of the sentence pattern or of other grammatical structures. See also Section **26**.

In paragraph 35 notice the parallelism in the second and third sentences, which develop the topic stated in the first sentence. The repeated pattern is *adverb clause, main clause*. This parallelism serves as a unifying force. See also **26a(3)**.

35 You must give up believing that all the riches of life will come from reaching the goals of your idealized self. If your ideal self is evidently not going to be attainable and you refuse to adjust down, you will go the route of chronic depression. On the other hand, if you recognize that you will never be president of the big-city bank, you can get on with becoming branch manager in your favourite community and maybe find your greatest pleasure in becoming a Little League coach or starting a choir. —GAIL SHEEHY, *Passages*

In the series of paragraphs below, paragraph 36 states and explains the controlling idea. Examine 37–39 for parallel structures arising from the question-answer/problem-solution pattern that serves as a unifying force. For effective variety, the final paragraph breaks the pattern by citing another writer. Consider the advantages of using this quotation, particularly in relation to the title.

36 How good is Canadian children's literature? It must be clear by now that it is of mixed quality. We all know the steady gaze of children. The best writers of children's books answer that gaze by writing directly, using their own experience of life with integrity and truthfulness. Poor writers look away from that gaze and hastily concoct soothing syrups, sugar pills, or ice-cream sundaes—none of which is a diet for life. In Canada most writers belong in the latter category, but at least there is growing recognition of the fact that children's books should be literature and that they call for genuine literary skills.

37 Many of our books, even those that are otherwise mediocre, have been informed by a deeply felt response to the land and its history; in this respect the Canadian experience has been used by our writers successfully. But success has not been achieved without cost. In concentrating on the land itself, Canadian writers have tended to slight other aspects of the country, such as city life and the mélange of ethnic backgrounds. In favouring outdoor adventure and the events of history as subjects, they have not done justice to themes of universal truth as they can be revealed in fantasy and fiction.

38 But perhaps it is not a matter of neglect. The failings in our literature for children have more to do with the imagination, intellectual resources, and motives of the writers themselves than with choice of subject. The possession of a good idea, the wish to provide facile entertainment, to use the findings of reseach, or to satisfy a school curriculum, will accomplish little in the way of giving children a genuine experience through books if the element of creativity is missing. It is therefore hard to escape the conclusion that a lack of creative power pervades our writing and that all weaknesses in content and technique stem from this.

39 Fortunately, however, enough good books have been written in Canada to persuade us that Canadian writing for children can now be taken seriously. It is the universal values of literature that matter most and they can be found in a few Canadian books that have joined the mainstream of children's books in English, and in others that are sound and worthwhile and have found a permanent place in the affection of children.

40 "Yes," Paul Hazard has written, "children's books keep alive a sense of nationality, but they also keep alive a sense of humanity. They describe their native land lovingly, but they also describe faraway lands where unknown brothers live. They understand the essential quality of their own race; but each of them is a messenger that goes beyond mountains and rivers, beyond the seas, to the very ends of the world in search of new friendships. Every country gives and every country receives—innumerable are the exchanges—and so it comes about that in our first impressionable years the universal republic of childhood is born."

—SHEILA EGOFF, *The Republic of Childhood: A Critical Guide to Canadian Children's Literature in English*

■ **Exercise 6** Prepare for a class discussion of the specific linking devices (pronouns, transitional words, repetition, parallelism) used in paragraph 41:

41 Electronic music is a new departure from orthodox, or generally accepted, music in that it is electrically originated or modified sound. This sound is the output of electric pianos, organs, synthesizers, saxophones, guitars, flutes, violins, trumpets, and many other instruments. It is the product of composers who use tape recorders and tape manipulation to distort, for better or worse, conventional sounds. Also, it is the sounds we hear in concerts and on records that use amplification to boost or alter the volume of instruments.

—MERRILL C. LEHRER, "The Electronic Music Revolution"

31d

Provide clear transitions between paragraphs.

Transitions from one paragraph to the next are just as necessary as those between sentences within the paragraph because the reader needs to be reminded of the direction of the writer's thought.

For example, read paragraph 42, which sets forth a claim made by those who promote transcendental meditation (TM). Then observe the two types of transitional devices used in the first sentence of subsequent paragraphs that refute this claim.

42 As the saying goes, "You can prove anything with statistics." TM promoters claim that the higher the meditation rate, the lower the crime rate, and specifically that in cities where one percent of the population practise TM, the crime rate is lower than in other cities.

transitional expressions | *repetition of words / ideas*

First, a correlation does not necessarily indicate a cause and effect relationship. . . .

Second, in large samples it is easy to get correlations. . . .

Third, the one per cent may not represent a cross-section of each city's populace. . . .

—RANDAL MONTGOMERY
"TM and Science: Friends or Foes?"

The closely related words in each group below are often placed at or near the beginnings of sentences to link ideas in separate paragraphs (as illustrated in paragraph 42) or within a paragraph (as in paragraph 25).

1. First. . . . Second. . . . Third. . . .
2. First. . . . Then. . . . Next. . . . Finally. . . .
3. Then. . . . Now. . . . Soon. . . . Later. . . .
4. One. . . . Another. . . . Still another. . . .
5. Some. . . . Others. . . . Still others. . . .
6. A few. . . . Many. . . . More. . . . Most . . .
7. Just as significant. . . . more important. . . . most important of all. . . .

Sometimes a transitional paragraph (usually short, often consisting of only one sentence) serves as a bridge between two paragraphs. Notice below that the first noun phrase in the transitional paragraph 44 echoes the preceding key idea and that the second noun phrase points to a fact to be explained next.

43 Indeed, instead of seeing evolution as a smooth process, many of today's life scientists and archaeologists are studying the "theory of catastrophes" to explain "gaps" and "jumps" in the multiple branches of the evolutionary record. Others are studying small changes that may have been amplified through feedback into sudden structural transformations. Heated controversies divide the scientific community over every one of these issues.

44 But all such controversies are dwarfed by a single history-changing fact.

45 One day in 1953 at Cambridge in England a young biologist, James Watson, was sitting in the Eagle pub when his college, Francis Crick, ran excitedly in and announced to "everyone within hearing distance that we had found the secret of life." They had. Watson and Crick had unraveled the structure of DNA. —ALVIN TOFFLER, *The Third Wave*

31e

Construct effective opening, concluding, and transitional paragraphs.

(1) Opening paragraphs

An opening paragraph, the one that begins an essay, functions as the writer's game plan. It must guide both writer and reader through the rest of the essay. The topic sentence of the opening paragraph is usually the thesis statement that will control all the remaining paragraphs of the essay. (See Section **32**.) The other sentences in the opening paragraph, the ones that support the topic sentence, are often used later in the essay, usually reworded, as the topic sentences of separate paragraphs.

The second function of the opening paragraph is to interest the reader. Often a writer will begin with a specific example or illustration, a quotation, an interesting statistic—whatever the writer believes will encourage the reader to read further. In magazines and newspapers, the first paragraph is often called "the hooker" because it acts like a baited hook. In academic writing, the first paragraph can be less enticing, but the writer still needs to attract the reader's attention and to focus the problem under discussion.

In paragraph 46, the opening sentences from a book review illustrate how the way the paragraph begins can attract the reader's attention (the complete review appears in exercise 9, p. 375).

46 William Coleman is a professor in the Department of Politics at McMaster University. "The independence movement," he suggests in this most readable study of Quebec separatism, "is no longer defending a unique and distinctive culture. It is seeking to preserve a community that is grasping to hold on to the skeleton of a value system and to a glimpse of its history. . . ."

(2) Concluding paragraphs

A concluding paragraph, the one that ends an essay, is the writer's final opportunity to restate the main idea of the essay. Often the concluding paragraph repeats in other words what was stated in the opening paragraph. In a short essay, the concluding paragraph may be no more than a sentence, but the longer the essay or the more complex its ideas, the more developed the concluding paragraph will need to be. The topic sentence of a concluding paragraph is usually a restatement of the main idea of the essay, and its supporting sentences are often reworded versions of the topic sentences of earlier paragraphs.

Checklist for Paragraph Revision

Coherence

1. Is the topic sentence effectively placed?
2. Is the topic sentence carefully restricted?
3. Is the paragraph pattern appropriate?

Development

4. Is the method of development appropriate?
5. Is the paragraph adequately developed?

Unity

6. Does each sentence support the main idea in the topic sentence?
7. Are the sentences smoothly linked?

Special types of paragraphs

8. If an opening paragraph, does it indicate the subject of the essay? Is it designed to interest the reader?
9. If a concluding paragraph, does it sum up the major ideas of the essay? Does it provide a convincing ending?
10. If a transitional paragraph, does it link what has gone before with what is to come?

(3) Transitional paragraphs

Paragraphs sometimes serve as transitions from one idea to another. As you saw in paragraph 44, transitional paragraphs may be as short as one sentence that sums up what went before (usually in a subordinate clause) and shows where the thought will now lead (usually in the main clause). Such a paragraph is usually short because the writer intends it to be merely a signpost.

■ **Exercise 8** Revise the following student paragraph.

47 My friend Michelle often lends her textbooks, her class notes, and even her clothes. Borrowers seldom return them. Of course, some people are luckier than Michelle. The other day, when two "hungry" boys asked my roommate for spare dimes, he quickly reached for his wallet, but they beat him to it and ran off. Again, a motorist ran out of gasoline: and when my sister Alicia stopped to help him, she parked too near the mainstream of traffic. Her brand new Honda got sideswiped.

■ **Exercise 9** The following essay appears without paragraphs. Indicate where the essay might be divided into paragraphs.

William Coleman is a professor in the Department of Politics at McMaster University. "The independence movement," he suggests in this most readable study of Québec separatism, "is no longer defending a unique and distinctive culture. It is seeking to preserve a community that is grasping to hold on to the skeleton of a value system and to a glimpse of its history. The universal pragmatism and materialism of capitalist societies have swept deep into the hearts of the Québécois. . . . Rather than acting to protect a basis for a distinctive culture, in reaching for independence they may now be pursuing a vision of a distinct culture. Visions tend to be much more ephemeral and fleeting than established foundations." In brief, that is Dr. Coleman's thesis and it has much to be said for it. "The removal of the church from the centre of education and social services and the critique of traditional values and practices carried the seeds of a crisis of identity," he also tells us. "Religion was the fundamental source of traditional French Canadian values. Removing and criticizing the theology and the system of thought that was anchored upon Catholic doctrine would inevitably force French Canadians to ask who they were and what distinguished them as a people." It is this search for a new identity which has preoccupied French Canadians throughout the tumultuous postwar period. For, the more traditional values were challenged, the more important became the values that were to replace them. The choice was not easy but it was in a sense inevitable, and successive governments, Union Nationale, Liberal and Parti Québécois have opted for it. Québec must be moved into the mainstream of North American society and to do this the structure of the state inevitably must be made, not different from, but more like the societies by which it was surrounded. The new Québécois management was to be essentially North American. The social services were to be created in the form of similar services in the rest of Canada. The education system must be changed to provide an essentially pragmatic North American outlook. There was nothing wrong with this. If Québec was to stand in the mainstream of the continent, it must, in essence, act and feel and think North American. In so doing, however, what happens to that essential and distinctive culture and how can a difference be maintained between North Americans, who speak English, and that unique group of North Americans whose language is French? "We are Québécois. . . . Being ourselves," as Premier René Lévesque said in a Toronto speech in 1968, "is essentially a matter of keeping and developing a personality that has survived for three and a half centuries. At the core of this personality is the fact that we speak French. Everything else depends on this one essential element and follows from it or leads us infallibly back to it." So language became the cultural hallmark of French Canada, which is where we are today, but language is only one aspect of culture, though a vitally important one. A modern state which believes that the faith upon which it was founded is no longer relevant must find a basis upon which to stand if it is to avoid being submerged. Hence we have the emphasis upon language, upon controlled entry into that part of the school system—the English Protestant system—which is essentially inimical to the survival of the French language, and the excesses of Bill 101. Most of these excesses, however, are necessary. The appearance of Frenchness is almost as important as Frenchness itself. The frantic attempts to maintain it in the work place, despite the overwhelming problems caused by the fundamental Englishness of the new technology, are all part of the battle, as indeed is the political challenge to a federal system which, if allowed to develop uncontested, would inevitably weaken the distinctiveness of the nation. But culture is an evolving process. In good health it is dynamic and the fact that what is evolving here is a North American French style need not destroy what is unique, if French Canada has the energy and tenacity to maintain its language in the face of such overwhelming odds. It is a heroic struggle and it is a struggle with which all Canadians should sympathize, for success in Québec essentially strengthens English-speaking Canada. It adds that special element to Canadian society which is also North American, but need not, for that reason, be American. Dr. Coleman's study follows the development of this new Québec with sympathy and understanding. He does not understate the problems nor does he lack sympathy for the effort. In one relatively short book we have here the mass of detail, the shifts and changes, the contradictions and the consistencies which have marked the struggle. If at times English-speaking Canada becomes impatient with the process, that is wrong, for what English-speaking Canada should be doing is supporting the Québec effort, which is as important to our survival as it is to the survival of French Canada. Nor need support for the attempt to protect a culture necessarily mean support for independence. There are those who feel that one must accompany the other, that "an independent and distinctive culture must rest upon an independent economy." An independent economy, however, has its obvious drawbacks and its own pressures. A proper and understanding interdependence, which recognizes the special needs of Québec, can offer a valuable security and vital room to manoeuvre. From the point of view of both Canadas this would seem the better course to follow.

—FRANK B. WALKER, review in *Chimo* of *The Independence Movement in Quebec 1945–1980* by William D. Coleman.

■ **Exercise 10** Prepare for a class discussion of the strengths and weaknesses of the following professional and student paragraphs:

48 Among the things I find hardest to do is to let a ringing telephone go unanswered. Suppose, for example, I have a good reason for not answering it. The first two rings I can easily endure, and then I start counting the rings. After I hit six, I wonder why it keeps ringing. Could it be that Dad has had another heart attack? When I finally do lift the receiver, no one is there. For the rest of the day or until it rings again and I answer it on the first ring, I have no peace of mind.

—STUDENT

49 Can hailstorms be suppressed? Attempts to modify them have been made throughout history. The Romans shot arrows toward the storm. In medieval Europe, church bells were rung—a practice that tended to increase the casualty rate because lightning often struck the unprotected belfry, electrocuting the bell ringer. With advancing technology, the hail cannon, a device that fired a ring of smoke and gas instead of a solid missile, became popular. The sound of the discharge was supposed to break up the hailstones. It at least provided some psychological comfort. Cannons were later replaced by rockets, which exploded aloft with a resounding bang. None of these remedies had any obvious success.

—JOHN HALLETT, "When Hail Breaks Loose"

50 Whatever their calling, most people spend most of their time doing chores. A chore may be defined as a somewhat disagreeable or boring task that must be done in order to accomplish one's real objective. The detective has his legwork and endless checking of details. The athlete and the musician practise what they already know. The politician makes her appearances; the lawyer prepares his briefs. Most human achievements conceal a vast, hidden background of chores, a world of routine humdrum that no one really likes but that everyone recognizes as necessary. —STUDENT

The Whole Composition

32

Arrange and express your ideas effectively.

An essay (also called a theme or paper) is a short non-fiction composition, the content and organization of which are guided by a single controlling idea, the *thesis*. Just as a topic sentence directs the development of a paragraph, the thesis, or controlling statement, limits and sums up the point of the essay. And just as a paragraph is a series of sentences developing one topic, an essay is a series of paragraphs arranged to elaborate and support the thesis. Both an essay and a paragraph contain similar parts: a controlling sentence, supporting explanation and details, logical transitions, and a conclusion. Both consist of a beginning, a middle, and an end; both are unified and coherent.

An essay has a *purpose*. Depending on what that purpose is, the writer will choose one of the four basic kinds of writing:

> *Narration*. The purpose of a narrative essay is to tell a story—to relate a sequence of events in chronological order. Usually the writer's further purpose is to make a stated or implied point about the significance of the events.
>
> *Description*. In a descriptive essay, the purpose is to evoke a mood or create a dominant impression about a

person, place, or object. Using concrete, vivid images that appeal to the reader's senses, the writer tries to make the reader see, hear, or feel what the writer saw, heard, or felt.

Exposition. Here the purpose is to inform, clarify, define, explain, or analyze. Most college writing—themes, research papers, essay examinations, lab reports—is expository, that is, students are asked to explain or clarify their ideas. Essays that explain the causes of stress, that classify types of students, that contrast solar heating and wood-burning stoves, that define the word *romantic*, or that analyze the effects of television on family meals—all are examples of exposition.

Argumentation. An argumentative essay attemps to convince, bring about an event, or move the reader to action. In an orderly way the writer analyzes a problem, offers a solution, acknowledges opposing solutions, and restates the one given in the essay. The appeal to the reader may be strictly logical or it may involve the reader's emotions.

Essays have many purposes, such as to entertain, inspire, or persuade, so the writer usually combines several kinds of writing, with one of them predominant. For example, an essay persuading legislators to require helmets for all bicycle riders might include a description of a car-bicycle collision, the story of how the accident happened, and an explanation of how helmets are designed to absorb the shock of impact.

An essay is designed for a particular *audience*. Both its content and its diction must be appropriate to the background, needs, and interests of that audience. If the topic is the pros and cons of buying a condominium in British Columbia, the audience does not want to read about the difficulties of moving from Winnipeg to Vancouver, either along with or in place of the topic. If the writer is a specialist, and the audience shares the writer's expertise, the essay can have a more sophisticated thesis and use more specialized language than an essay on the same subject written for a general audience that knows little or nothing about the subject.

Writing an essay is a *process*—a series of steps in which writers expand and organize their ideas according to their central purpose and their audience. First, they choose and limit their subject (**32a**). Then, after they have collected ideas about their subject (**32b**), they arrange the main ideas into a pattern (**32c**). Their next step is to shape the sentence that controls the entire essay—the thesis statement (**32d**)—a step in which choosing and evaluating their audience (**32e**) is a crucial factor. Finally, they prepare a rough or working outline (**32f**) as an aid in writing the various drafts of the essay (**32g-i**). As writers move through each of these steps, they may need to repeat one or more of them. For example, they may need to collect more ideas. Or they may write their essay only to discover that it does not develop the ideas announced in the thesis. They may thus have to revise their thesis, their paragraphs, or both; they may even have to choose another thesis.

No matter how much repetition of the steps is necessary, the goal is a clear statement of the thesis, developed with coherent and unified supporting information. Beginning writers sometimes think that experienced writers produce a single draft of flawless prose—that they start with the title and proceed from the introduction through the conclusion without ever stopping to rearrange the order of ideas, to eliminate wordiness, or to revise diction. The fact is that experienced writers follow the same steps described above—selecting, writing, and revising again and again—until the essay is a unified, coherent, and well-developed statement of ideas.

■ **Exercise 1** Prepare for a discussion of the following review from *Books in Canada* of these two books, *Forbidden Voice* by Alma Greene (Thomas Allen) and *Joseph Brant: A Man for His People* by

Helene Caister (Longmans), by deciding which of the four kinds of writing predominates (narration, description, exposition, argumentation), and which, if any, are secondary:

1 FORBIDDEN VOICE is both the title of this book and the Mohawk name of the writer, who is a medicine woman, a princess of the royal blood and a hereditary mother of the Turtle Clan, touched with the mysterious gift of healing and charged with keeping herself pure. As a little girl she was not allowed to have anything to do with white children:

2
> Growing up red is not the same as growing up white; for my people, the real people, the red men, think our own thoughts. We have our own magic, and our own mysteries. Magic and mysteries, medicine and stories handed down by word of mouth, and now, in this generation, in danger of being obliterated by education of Indian children in educational systems that have scant regard for Indian cultural heritage, and by the overwhelming mass culture that is North America's gift to the world.

3 That which is passed on orally is no dead and fossilized thing that stopped growing ages ago, but is a living, changing amalgam of historical commentary and contemporary dreams, old myths, ancient legends, spells, exorcisms, and a vademecum of natural medicines.

4 The format of the book and its numerous clear line drawings convey the impression that it was intended for children, and one hopes it will be read by a great many children, and by adults too. "I still have dreams," she writes, "and look for their meaning. . . . I have worked for my people, and gone many times to Ottawa to fight for them. Sometimes I have thought that I could burn the sacred tobacco and send the skeleton luck charm to cripple my people's enemies, or confuse their minds. But I have never done so."

5 Like Forbidden Voice, to use her Mohawk name, Joseph Brant was a Mohawk, although not a hereditary chief, as is popularly believed. He was just an ordinary warrior who was made a War Chief because of his fighting prowess and his education. Helene Robinson's book about him is history written for teenagers, organized like a novel with words put into the mouths of the characters. It is an easy book to follow,

and accurate as to its facts and the current historical opinion about Brant, who, as a captain in the British Army, led his people in battles against the Americans, in their War of Independence. With the war lost and the Americans wreaking vengeance on the Indians, he moved with them to the Six Nation Reserve on the Grand River.

6 Brant is an authentic Canadian hero, acknowledged as such with the town of Brantford (complete with bronze statue) named after him. It is interesting, however, that Forbidden Voice in her book has only bitter words for him. He is the one, she writes, who helped to persuade Indians to get involved with the white man's wars. He is the one who was so anxious to have the Mohawks become Christians that he destroyed the traditional longhouse.

7 Brant was without question devoted to his people, but he was also always concerned with finding favour in the eyes of whites. Ironically, he got into a serious dispute when the government prevented him from, of all things, selling reservation lands to some of his white friends.

—C. ALEXANDER BROWN, review in *Books in Canada*

■ **Exercise 1 (continued)** Examine paragraph 5, then explain the relation between the primary purpose of the review and the secondary purposes of these four groupings of ideas—(1) "Forbidden Voice," "her Mohawk name," "Helene Robinson"; (2) "Joseph Brant," "a Mohawk," "ordinary warrior," "a War Chief," "a captain in the British Army"; (3) "book," "history," "like a novel,"; (4) "fighting," "war," "vengeance."

32a

Choose a subject that interests you and limit it properly.

(1) Choosing a subject.

Whether you have been assigned a subject for an essay or

must choose one, you should ask yourself what you know about it, for writers write best about what they know best. While every writer brings a unique set of experiences to the writing task, not all of those experiences will generate a good essay. Although writers often discover what they know as they write, they are also able to gauge the extent of their knowledge as they list possible subjects.

These following questions will suggest some areas to explore as you discover what subjects you are interested in and know most about:

1. If you weren't writing an essay, what would you rather be doing? Why?
2. What things are you good at?
3. What subjects are you least interested in writing about?
4. If you could solve any one problem, what would it be? Why? How would you solve it?
5. Which of the following areas do you enjoy talking or reading about?

sports	ecology	famous people
hobbies	space exploration	marriage
politics	money	drama
religion	literature	psychology
television	careers	philosophy
advertising	movies	energy
food	music	travel

The answers to some of these questions may suggest subjects. One student, Shawn Redfield, answered as follows:

I'd rather be—sleeping, stripping that old rocking chair, drawing political cartoons, washing and waxing the car

I'm good at—finding bargains, listening to other people's problems, coaching soccer, cutting firewood

I like talking about—my favourite country-western bands, my job in the antique shop, my plans to run for political office

Ideas that occur in more than one answer are usually a logical starting point. In addition to Shawn's obvious interest in politics, the answers above suggest an essay on antiques (stripping a rocking chair, finding bargains, working in an antique shop). But what about antiques? One subject can produce many possible topics. *Antiques* names a general category, and to write one essay that treats every aspect of it is impossible—not even a whole book is sufficient for a thorough discussion.

(2) Limiting the subject.

How can an essay subject—in this case, antiques—be limited or narrowed? One way is to reduce the general category (subject) to increasingly restricted ones (topics). The more restricted the category, the more specific the idea. Shawn Redfield came up with three possible topics by limiting the general category of antiques in three different ways:

1. *Antiques*

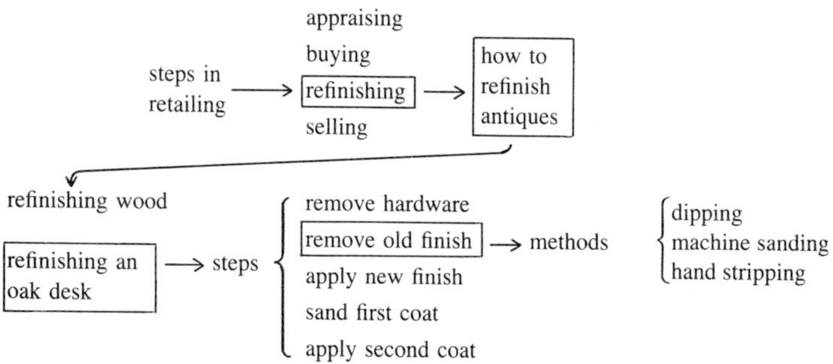

Limited topic: the factors that determine whether a refinisher uses dipping, sanding, or hand stripping to remove the finish from an old desk.

2. *Antiques*

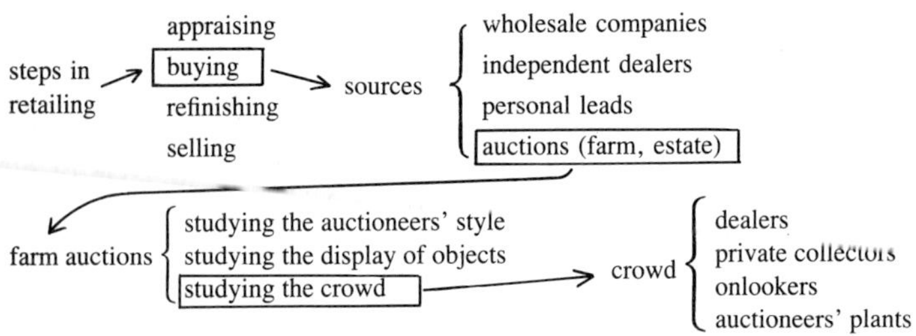

Limited topic: the motivation of bidders at farm auctions—why are they bidding? Who is most likely to drive the bidding beyond the appraised price? Why?

3. *Antiques* (Note how the two false starts below lead Shawn to his third topic.)

(a) Canadian vs. European { expense, availability, condition

all Canadian and European antiques? (no—too many to cover, and I don't know anything about European antiques)

(b) Canadian antiques

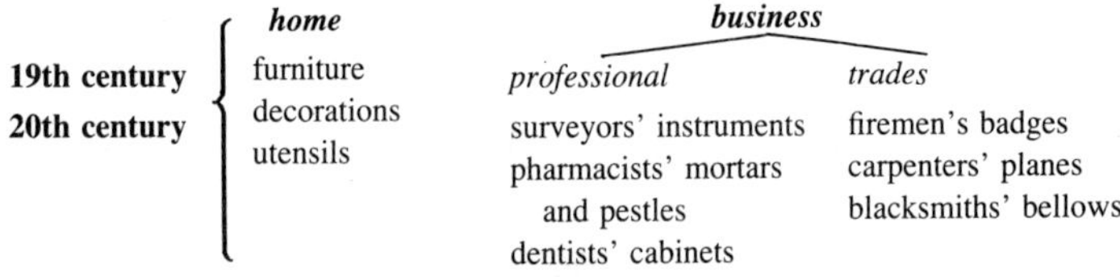

all types for both centuries?
(no—too many categories)

(c) Canadian collectibles

manufactured collectibles			*handmade collectibles*	
china	kitchen utensils	butter moulds	farm tools	wooden rakes
glassware		bowls		plows
		spatulas		wagon seats
		measuring cups		horseshoes

Limited topic: the reasons for acquiring Canadian collectibles

Another way to narrow the subject is to consider the four kinds of writing. Narration, description, exposition, argumentation—each of these is more appropriate to certain subjects than to others, and each suggests limits for an essay. When these four kinds are applied to the subject of antiques, the following topics might result:

1. *Narration*: a story relating how cleaning out an attic created an instant collection; a story about an elderly woman's preference for the objects of her youth rather than for modern things
2. *Description*: a description of an antique shop crammed with hundreds of items; a description of the apparent restraint of bidders at a formal auction
3. *Exposition*: an explanation of how to distinguish fakes and reproductions from genuine antique furniture; an explanation of the training programs for people who want to become auctioneers
4. *Argumentation*: an argument against buying antiques as a means of financial investment; an argument for developing a bidding strategy to use at auctions

■ **Exercise 2** Draw up a list of six subjects that interest you and about which you know something. Ask questions to produce two properly limited topics for one of the subjects. Apply the four kinds of writing to produce two limited topics for another subject.

32b

Collect ideas about your topic.

From his three possible topics about antiques, Shawn Redfield has decided to explore the reasons people acquire collectibles—antique handmade or manufactured objects. To generate ideas for the explanations and supporting details he needs, he may use one or all of the following methods.

(1) List-making.

Like grocery lists and lists of things to do, lists of ideas to include in an essay help you accomplish a task. Just as you jot down grocery items as they occur to you—not according to the order of the aisles at the store—you list ideas without regard to their order in the essay. And just as you delete some foods and add others during the walk through the store, you will delete some ideas and add others as you work out a plan of organization. The important thing, however, is to have ideas to organize. Write down every idea that occurs to you; save their organization for later.

Here is Shawn Redfield's list for his topic on collectibles:

antiques that are handmade, handcrafted or manufactured = collectibles
sometimes made at home, sometimes not
not very smoothly finished
practical furniture—beds, dressers, dry sinks, pie safes, rocking chairs, chests, cupboards
household things—butter moulds, bowls
functional
also handcrafted metal things (usually not homemade)
blacksmiths—candlesticks, flatirons, pots, skillets, tools, horseshoes, nails, axles
tinsmiths—pie-safe panels, candlesticks—?
pewtersmiths—such a word?—candlesticks, spoons, picture frames, mugs, plates, pitchers, ladles, porridge bowls
brassmiths(?)—pots, kettles, keys, teakettles, ladles, candlesticks, bells

copper—teakettles, pitchers, wash boilers
craftsmanship of unique pieces not all that polished
antique—defined how?
collectible—defined how?
estate or farm auctions—a good place to look
prices cheaper than really fine furniture, but prices on both keep going up
they remind me of stories Grandpa told me about using them
what did they use to mow grass—were there lawns?
go with furniture today; can still be used today
some are used for decoration, others are put to work—old dough bowl now a centrepiece, flatirons = bookends, etc.
inexpensive—lots of them around
they're popular
they'll increase in value

(2) Asking who, what, why, where, when, and how.

To be sure they have covered all aspects of a story, reporters ask the six questions above. The same questions can help you explore your topic. Here are some of the ideas Shawn came up with, asking himself the journalist's questions:

Who? Who collects handcrafted antiques? Who appraises collectibles?

What? What items appeal most to me? What's the difference between an antique and a collectible?

Why? Why is acquiring collectibles popular? Why are there more collectibles than antiques around?

Where? Where can the novice collector find out about the different kinds of collectibles? Where in Canada are older collectibles most likely to be found?

When? When is the best time, if there is one, to buy collectibles? When did the interest in collectibles start?

How? How is collectible defined? How can a collection of farm implements be displayed? How does a person begin collecting? How do I re-cane a chair or clean up a pine cupboard?

(3) Asking questions based on paragraph-developing methods (see Section 31).

The same strategies that are used to expand a paragraph may suggest some ways to approach a topic. For example:

Narration—How do I respond to something I've just added to my collection? What do I remember about starting my collection?

Process—How was a rocking chair made? How were fields plowed? How is market value determined?

Description—How can the antique shop I work in be described? What is the chief impression conveyed by a kitchen decorated with collectibles?

Classification—What types of people attend auctions? What types of collectibles can I use in my home?

Analysis—What are the parts of the collecting process? What was the function of some of the farm tools?

Definition—What does *collectible* mean? What does *antique* mean? Is the distinction of 100 years for an antique in the United States and 50 years in Canada important in collectibles?

Comparison and contrast—What's the difference between a cupboard and a hutch? How do Québec furniture and Ontario furniture differ in style?

Example—What objects represent the typical farmhouse of the mid-1800's? What objects were made at home? What objects were made by craftsmen? What objects were manufactured?

Cause and effect—What prompts people to acquire collectibles? What effect has the popularity of collectibles had on buying them? How can the popularity of collectibles be determined? What effects did daily use have on collectibles?

■ **Exercise 3** From the narrowed topics you produced in Exercise 2, select the two you know most about. Use list-making, the journalist's questions, and methods of development to collect ideas for both.

32c

Arrange your ideas into a general pattern.

To make sense out of all the information you gather, you will need to identify your main ideas. Once those are clear, you can match details, facts, examples, definitions, and explanations with the corresponding main points. Set aside anything unrelated, no matter how proud or fond of it you may be. The object is to sift through the abundance of ideas you have collected, distinguishing the main ones first, and then the supporting ones.

Shawn Redfield has decided that he will try to explain why acquiring collectibles appeals as a hobby. On his list of ideas are these eight reasons:

1. craftsmanship of unique pieces not all that polished
2. prices cheaper than larger antiques
3. reminders of Grandpa's things and stories
4. go with furniture today
5. some are used decoratively, others put to work
6. inexpensive—lots of them around
7. they're popular
8. they'll increase in value

Essentially these boil down to three main reasons:

1. moderate expense (reasons 2, 6, 8)
2. the combination of tradition and novelty (reasons 1, 3)
3. scope for individual taste—lots to choose from (reasons 4, 5, 6)

Notice that reason 7 is redundant and has been omitted, and that reason 8 is only indirectly related to expense. Working through the list and adding details suggested by the key words, Shawn now begins to supply information for each reason.

1. inexpensive
    prices of collectibles vs. prices of antiques
    produced in quantity, common in every household

Georgian mahogany desk ($5,000) vs. teakettle ($50), butter bowl ($30), tin candlestick ($15)

2. craftsmanship of pieces offers contrast of tradition and novelty

   homemade, not smoothly finished vs. polished, skilled finish of modern things

   durable

   reminders of Grandpa's stories

3. suit individual tastes

   lots to choose from, relatively little duplication—ironstone, brass, iron, tin

   appropriate for either decorative or functional use

   decorative—butter mould, spoon set

   functional then, functional now

   functional—flatirons as bookends, chests as coffee tables, quilts as tablecloths

Shawn will continue to add supporting ideas as he writes, but only if they develop the points he is making. Whether an idea was in his original list or suggested by the process of writing, he will have to discard it if it does not belong with the three main ideas.

■ **Exercise 4** For each of the following topics, identify the unrelated material:

1. arranging for house care during a two-week vacation—stopping the mail; vacuuming and dusting; locking the doors; mowing the lawn.
2. definition of *friend*—distinction between a friend and a neighbour; anecdote of someone who smuggled bacon and doughnuts through your bedroom window so you could feed unexpected visitors; titles of three essays on friendship.
3. story showing the value of budgeting money—definition of *money*; having to pass up a stereo system at 40 per cent off; peace of mind from knowing the rent is paid.

■ **Exercise 5** For one of the topics for which you have collected information, arrange your ideas into a general pattern.

32d

Shape a thesis statement.

The thesis statement is a single declarative sentence that announces the writer's attitude toward the subject and suggests the essay's overall pattern of organization. It is the single most important sentence in the entire essay. If it is lucid and precise, the essay usually is too. Although a thesis statement may be implied or delayed until the closing paragraph, as a rule it is stated as the final sentence of the introduction. If the introduction is a single paragraph, then the thesis concludes it; if the introduction is two or more paragraphs long, the thesis ends the final introductory paragraph. Placing a sentence after the thesis may weaken its emphasis, and opening the essay with the thesis seldom prepares the reader for either the topic or the writer's approach.

Like a road map showing a driver's route on major highways, a thesis statement directs the movement of ideas through an essay. An effective thesis statement is incisive, offering specific guidelines to the essay's content and organization. It limits the scope of the topic so that the thesis is appropriate for the length of the paper. An effective thesis statement does not state the obvious. Nor does it use vague, abstract terms (such as *really, things, great, nice, very*), weak verbs (*to be, to have, to seem*), or the passive voice (as in "collectibles have been called the poor person's antiques"), which weaken the force of the thesis.

Compare the following thesis statements:

1. It's really interesting to collect things.
2. There are three reasons to acquire collectibles.
3. Weekends are spent bidding against other collectors when you are in search of collectibles.
4. Bidding successfully for a sugar scoop indicates that the collector knows both the value of the prize and the limits of the competition.

5. Stripping a painted table by using ammonia and steel wool is easy, but it exposes the wood to a harsh chemical; using a power sander saves time, but it requires an even, light touch to avoid gouging the wood.

The first thesis statement gives no indication of either the topic or the approach; it is an all-purpose, say-nothing sentence that could lead to any number of different essays—which is exactly why it is useless. A thesis should suit only the essay it governs. Thesis statement 2 is weak for the same reason. It could fit several different essays with entirely different sets of reasons. Including the three reasons in the thesis would provide a more definite focus.

Thesis statement 3 provides only a general subject and no idea of the essay's organization. The reader might well ask: Who is meant by *you*? Are the other participants also after collectibles? Under what conditions are they bidding against each other? Why is the competition limited to weekends?

Just as a general subject is narrowed, a general thesis statement can also be revised to make it more specific. Thesis statement 4 is appropriate for an essay on human behaviour, while thesis statement 5 is appropriate for an essay on the advantages and disadvantages of two methods of stripping furniture.

Shawn Redfield produced the following thesis statements for his essay, and rightly decided that the fifth was the best of them all:

1. Collectibles are inexpensive and adaptable. [weak verb, inexact topic, imprecise adjectives]
2. Inexpensive collectibles are a combination of the traditional and the personal. [unclear whether all collectibles are inexpensive or only inexpensive ones combine the two features]
3. Acquiring collectibles offers an inexpensive way to express individuality. [unclear what a "way to express individuality" means]

4. There are three reasons for the popularity of collectibles. [reasons not specified]
5. Collectibles acquired will grow in popularity because collectibles are relatively inexpensive, blend well with current trends in home decorating, and adapt to individual tastes. [contains an assertion and offers supporting reasons; clearest of the five]

Once you have created a clear and precise thesis statement, you have done the most difficult part of the job, for the thesis now determines what you will discuss when, and you have simply to fulfill your announced commitment to ideas and structure.

■ **Exercise 6** Improve each of the following thesis statements:

1. Baseball and softball are different but fun.
2. My summer job taught me I could do anything as well as a man could.
3. Photography is an interesting hobby for anyone who doesn't know anything about it.
4. Many factors must be considered when deciding to become a pharmacist.
5. For a fun vacation that tests your ingenuity, try wilderness camping.

■ **Exercise 7** Create a thesis statement for your topic.

32e

Choose and evaluate your audience.

Your audience deserves your respect. Whether generalists or specialists on the topic, your readers are entitled to a clear thesis statement, coherent explanations, logical transitions, and exact diction. The more precisely you define your audience, the more you can show your respect for their intelligence and curiosity. Writers who know their audience can develop examples or draw comparisons from their shared experiences. And such writers also know which terms, if any, must be defined and how fully. Further, if they know their audience is indifferent or hostile toward the subject, they will consider that too.

In short, establishing the audience for your essay helps to determine your tone and attitude. Only after you have evaluated your audience should you decide to be witty or ironic, reverent or impudent, for an inappropriate tone will offend your readers and reduce their willingness to consider your ideas.

Use the following guidelines for evaluating your audience:

1. What does the audience already know about the topic?
2. What is the attitude of the audience toward the topic?
3. Is the audience interested in the topic? Why? Why not?
4. For what purpose is the audience likely to read about the topic?
5. What kind of information will the audience accept as convincing support?

You can assume that most of the writing you do in college is for a *general* audience—educated and intellectually curious adults with a variety of political, ethnic, religious, and social backgrounds. Such an audience is potentially interested in any subject, so it does not need to have its interest aroused. It does expect, however, that the writer will present the subject in non-technical language and will define or illustrate any specialized terms. For example, a general audience interested in the subatomic particles known as quarks wants a thorough but non-technical explanation of how they function, but it does *not* want to read an academic research report to find out. (On the other hand, a group of physicists debating the evidence for quarks would expect a thorough and highly technical argument from a colleague writing an essay for a professional journal.)

Any topic can be shaped for any audience—general or specialized—depending on the knowledge of the writer and the background of the audience. But it is not possible to write for both kinds of audience at once, since their needs and expectations are entirely different. Here, for example, are two thesis statements on the topic of opening moves in chess:

GENERAL

Having mastered the moves of the pieces, the novice chess player needs to learn several standard openings, such as Ruy Lopez, Sicilian Defence, and Queen's Gambit. [appropriate for a chess beginner, who needs to have each of these strategies described]

SPECIALIZED

Although some modern chess theorists argue that if White opens P-K4, White's game is lost, this opening provides more flexibility than P-Q3. [appropriate for a reader who knows chess notation, who understands what the two moves involve, and who is interested in a controversial defence of P-K4]

■ **Exercise 8** Prepare to discuss how to shape each of the following topics for the audiences specified:

1. rock music: college students, country-western fans, composers
2. your school: provincial taxpayers, high school seniors, alumni
3. off-campus housing: city councillors, school administrators, students, property owners
4. potatoes: home gardeners, commercial growers, nutritionists
5. changing attitudes toward marriage and the family: general audience, religious groups, sociologists

■ **Exercise 9** Read Betty S. Flowers's essay "Madman, Architect, Carpenter, Judge: Roles and the Writing Process." Be prepared to discuss her attitude toward her subject and her audience (students of writing).

**Madman, Architect, Carpenter, Judge:
Roles and the Writing Process**

''What's the hardest part of writing?'' I ask on the first day of class.

''Getting started,'' someone offers, groaning.

''No, it's not getting started,'' a voice in the back corrects. ''It's keeping on once you do get started. I can always write a sentence or two—but then I get stuck.''

''Why?'' I ask.

''I don't know. I'm writing along, and all of a sudden I realize how awful it is, and I tear it up. Then I start over again, and after two sentences, the same thing happens.''

''Let me suggest something which might help,'' I say. Turning to the board, I write four words: ''madman,'' ''architect,'' ''carpenter,'' ''judge.'' Then I explain:

''What happens when you get stuck is that two competing energies are locked horn to horn, pushing against each other. One is the energy of what I'll call your 'madman.' He's full of ideas, writes crazily and perhaps rather sloppily, gets carried away by enthusiasm or anger, and if really let loose, could turn out ten pages an hour.

''The second is a kind of critical energy—what I'll call the 'judge.' . . . He peers over your shoulder and says 'That's trash!' with such authority that the madman loses his crazy confidence and shrivels up. You know the judge is right—after all, he speaks with the voice of your most imperious English teacher. But for all his sharpness of eye, he can't create anything.

''So you're stuck. Every time your madman starts to write, your judge pounces on him.

''Of course this is to over-dramatize the writing process—but not entirely. Writing is so complex . . . that sitting down to a fresh sheet of paper can sometimes seem like 'the hardest work among those not impossible,' as Yeats put it. Whatever joy there is in the writing process can come only when the energies are flowing freely—when you're not stuck.

''And the trick to not getting stuck involves separating the energies. If you let the judge . . . come too close to the madman, . . . the ideas which form the basis for your writing will never have a chance to surface. But . . . the subjective, personal outpourings of your madman must be balanced by the objective, impersonal vision of the educated critic within you. Writing is not just self-expression; it is communication as well.

"So start by promising your judge that you'll get around to asking his opinion—but not now. And then let the madman energy flow. Find what interests you in the topic, the question or emotion that it raises in you, and respond as you might to a friend—or an enemy. Talk on paper, page after page, and don't stop to judge or correct sentences. Then, after a set amount of time, perhaps, stop and gather the paper up and wait a day.

"The next morning, ask your 'architect' to enter. She will read the wild scribblings saved from the night before and pick out maybe a tenth of the jottings as relevant or interesting. (You can see immediately that the architect is not sentimental about what the madman wrote; she's not going to save every crumb for posterity.) Her job is simply to select large chunks of material and to arrange them in a pattern that might form an argument. The thinking here is large, organizational, paragraph-level thinking—the architect doesn't worry about sentence structure.

"No, sentence structure is left for the 'carpenter' who enters after the essay has been hewn into large chunks of related ideas. The carpenter nails these ideas together in a logical sequence, making sure each sentence is clearly written, contributes to the argument of the paragraph, and leads logically and gracefully to the next sentence. When the carpenter finishes, the essay should be smooth and watertight.

"And then the judge comes around to inspect. Punctuation, spelling, grammar, tone—all the details which result in a polished essay become important only in this last stage. These details are not the concern of the madman who's come up with the ideas, or the architect who's organized them, or the carpenter who's nailed the ideas together, sentence by sentence. Save details for the judge."

The Advantages of Roles

Why all this dramatization of the writing process? What advantages does such an artificial scheme offer? . . .

1. It's easy to remember.
2. It stresses the sequential nature of the writing process—that you're likely to get better results if you work through the madman stage first rather than going back to the idea stage after you've spent three hours crafting sentences.

3. It dramatizes the need for rewriting and gives a sense of individual purpose to every draft.
4. It breaks the writing task down into manageable stages and allows the enjoyment of each stage. In other words, it shows a student how to do one thing at a time.

. . .

7. It gives a new language for correcting papers, one that doesn't shove the teacher so far into the "judge" language that most grading marks reflect. You can use the language of play for the madman, the language of design for the architect, the language of integrity for the carpenter, and the traditional language of proofreaders' marks for the judge.

. . .

—BETTY S. FLOWERS

32f

Develop a working plan or rough outline.

You will find it easier to shape an essay from all the elements discussed thus far—subject, narrowed topic, thesis, audience, tone, attitude—by preparing a rough outline that shows the pattern in which you will develop your ideas as well as the sequence in which you will arrange them. (To develop a topic or sentence outline see **33d**.)

(1) Choosing a sequence for your ideas.

One of the patterns in **31a(3)**—question-answer, problem-solution, or topic-restriction-illustration—will give you a structure for your ideas. But you must also consider the sequence of ideas and paragraphs in the essay. If you choose the problem-solution pattern, for example, you must also consider in what order to present the elements of the problem and then the steps in the solution.

Your choice of sequence depends on the subject and purpose of your essay. In a description, for example, *spatial* order is useful to create an exact and orderly picture that enables the audience to recreate the scene: details move from left to right, from foreground to background, from top to bottom, and from inside to outside.

Exposition often uses *chronological* order, which presents events or details in a time sequence—from first to last, from past to present, and so forth. A chronological sequence would be appropriate in explaining how to make sourdough bread or in recounting the events that caused the Great Depression.

The sequence of *climax* or *emphasis* moves from least important to most important. Just as the most emphatic point in a sentence occurs before the period, so the most emphatic point in an essay occurs before the conclusion. Thus, for example, a writer may choose to list the effects of a sunburn from the least dangerous to the most dangerous. Sometimes, however, when one item is of such immediate importance that it cannot be delayed, the order must be revised.

Finally, a writer may order ideas from general to specific or specific to general. An essay on the effects of the Mount St. Helens eruptions might proceed from specific, immediately recognized effects, such as volcanic ash in the streets, to general ones, such as long-term changes in weather patterns. Or an essay comparing two methods of decision-making might move from a discussion of general aims and appropriate situations for their use to the specific steps in each method.

(2) Preparing the rough outline.

In addition to listing the sequence of ideas, a rough outline should show the thesis, the audience, the purpose, and the general pattern.

Read "Do Animals Really Play?" by Eugene J. Walter, Jr., and then compare it with the rough outline that follows the essay.

Do Animals Really Play?

1 Do animals really "play"? Yes, and sometimes it's nothing more than fun and games, as when a monkey swings from a vine and tosses a stick, or when polar bears amuse themselves with stones, which they sometimes balance on their heads. Often, though, the seemingly frivolous antics we interpret as "play" are serious.

2 Play can be viewed as a pleasurable way of developing survival skills. The next time you're at a zoo, watch how the lion cubs frolic. One will crouch low against the ground, stalk slowly toward its littermate and then pounce on the surprised "victim." That usually touches off a knockabout wrestling match, with the cubs cuffing each other harmlessly. Such roughhouse sessions occur frequently among most carnivores such as wolves, tigers, cheetahs, raccoons, and coyotes. As they play, these young develop the abilities they need to become efficient predators.

3 Among monkeys and apes, playing helps lay the foundation for social order—a requirement for the survival of primate communities. Through play-fighting, a young monkey learns—in a harmless way—where it stands among its peers. The individuals that are most often victorious in the "matches" of infancy are most likely to assume a dominant role when they mature. Others that are lower on the social ladder learn their places early in life. This reduces more violent clashes among the monkeys as adults.

4 Many hoofed mammals engage in play, too. In herds of Mongolian wild horses, the breeding stallion will play-fight with his offspring, thereby helping the youngsters develop the agility they will need when confronted by predators or other stallions.

5 It appears that even whales play. A calf will perform all sorts of acrobatic gyrations on and around its mother, sliding

over her tail, standing on its head or slapping its tail or flipper against the water's surface. It's possible that such play helps cement the bond between mother and offspring.

6 And what of birds—do they play? Some ornithologists are convinced that a few of the brainier ones do. The subject needs further inquiry. At this point, it's the mammals who appear to dominate the animal playground.

—EUGENE J. WALTER, JR.

Rough outline for "Do Animals Really Play?"

Thesis: The seemingly frivolous antics of animals' "play" prepare the young for adult life.

Audience: general (no specialized knowledge of animal behaviour required)

Purpose: to explain why animals play by classifying types of play

Pattern: question-answer

1. Play develops survival skills.
   carnivores (lion cubs, wolves, tigers, cheetahs, raccoons, coyotes)
2. Play lays the foundation for social order.
   primates (monkeys)
3. Play develops agility.
   hoofed mammals (Mongolian wild horses)
4. Play develops mother-offspring bond.
   marine mammals (whales)
5. Basis for choosing examples—mammals

Before Walters could write his essay, he took the following steps: he chose a subject (animal behaviour), narrowed it (animal "play"), collected ideas (types of play and animals that engage in each type), chose a pattern (question-answer), and chose a sequence of ideas (general to specific—from a species-wide focus on survival skills to a narrow focus on the mother-offspring bond). Finally, he decided to shape his thesis for a general audience. Notice too that point

5 of the outline calls attention to the principle for choosing examples, which becomes an idea for the conclusion.

Here is Shawn Redfield's rough outline for his essay:

Rough outline for collectibles essay

Thesis: Collectibles will grow in popularity because they are relatively inexpensive, they blend well with current home decorating trends, and they adapt to individual tastes.

Audience: young couples beginning to decorate a home

Purpose: to explain the appeal of collectibles to young homemakers

Pattern: question-answer—What explains the growing popularity of collectibles?

1. collectibles = common antiques; handcrafted if not homemade or manufactured
    - furniture—chairs, tables, cupboards, dressers, chests
    - kitchen tools—spatulas, butter paddles, spoons, dough bowls, measuring cups, jars, etc.
    - farm tools—rakes, plows, scythes, axes
    - retail memorabilia
2. comparison of readily available collectibles vs. hard-to-find antiques
    - any of the above vs. paintings
    - teakettles vs. secretary desks
3. home decoration trends today
    - chrome and glass—contrasts in texture, style
    - eclectic—collectibles go with most things
    - oak and calico—the appeal of tradition
4. one person acquires collectibles
    - a unique collection possible because so many items available
        - kinds of ironstone
    - original use or invented use
        - quilt, flatiron, crock

■ **Exercise 10** Write a rough outline for your essay. (You may find that typing it rather than handwriting it helps you to see the essay's emerging structure.)

32g

Write and revise the first draft.

In this first draft Shawn Redfield concentrates on explaining each of the three parts of his thesis statement. He has kept his main ideas in mind by including the thesis and by underlining his topic sentences, and he has adhered to his outline. However, he has made no attempt to write an introduction or a conclusion nor has he supplied transitions from paragraph to paragraph. Read through the first draft and then look at Shawn's comments to himself.

FIRST DRAFT

Thesis statement: Collectibles will grow in popularity because they are relatively inexpensive, they blend well with current home-decorating trends, and they adapt to individual tastes. *awk*

1 *intro needed* <u>Collectibles</u> *weak verb* <u>are relatively inexpensive</u>. Compared to collecting art or fine furniture, collectibles are relatively inexpensive. The current *clarify* economic crunch makes this feature more important now than ever. Collectibles are the common handcrafted, homemade or manufactured utensils of the rural home. *They* ~~they~~ are priced much higher now than when they were new. *Can I prove?* These objects were produced in quantity, which makes collecting them a hobby suitable to a large number of participants. *Does it belong?* Mason

jars, a skillet, a butter mould, or a chest--compared to a silver tea service or a mahogony buffet these things are inexpensive but satisfying to collect.

[check sp.] [comparison effective?] [show $]

2 Collectibles blend well with current home-decorating trends. Whether decorators choose sleek chrome and glass contemporary or cozy oak-and-calico decors, collectibles add the contrast of tradition and the novelty of another lifestyle. The growing nostalgia infatuation is well served by collectibles. A 1929 Eaton's catalogue among magazines of the day provides a nostalgic link with days gone by. There is a certain air of security which surrounds the tools of people's ancestors. There is security in a child's toy made of cast iron, a barrel with walls of three-inch oak, or hatracks made of brass, security which is missing in today's disposable, plastic world. Besides security, collectibles provide an interesting contrast in decor. The contrast between an iron dutch oven that came to this country across the ocean and a microwave oven flown in from Japan can add character to a kitchen. A coal skuttle as a magazine holder can supply the same character of contrast to an electrically heated living room. Home-

[right word?] [right word?] [Why?]

decorating trends reflect people's needs. Tradition and novelty are two needs that will continue to be filled by the preservation of articles of past life.

3 Collectibles adapt to individual tastes. It's ~~Its~~ a hobby that allows for "mass individuality." Because of the way these objects were produced, today a lot ~~alot~~ of people could collect the same thing, say ironstone, yet no two collections would be the same. One person ~~You~~ might collect only dinnerware while a second ~~sombody else~~ collected only pitchers, and a third ~~somebody else~~ collected all white pieces. How do collectibles adapt to ~~your~~ individual tastes? They serve a function in today's home, often a function quite different from the original one. An old crock may become a planter or a magazine holder; it may even serve its original purpose. A patchwork quilt may become a cushion, a chair cover, a wall hanging, or a tablecloth. A flatiron may become a door stop, a bookend, or a paperweight. Summary needed

The first draft of Shawn Redfield's essay is a preliminary sketch of the essay under construction. Each paragraph has a topic sentence and the order of the paragraphs follows that announced in the thesis statement, but the answers to the questions implied by the topic sentences are general and the supporting examples few.

In revising this draft, Shawn needs to analyze every word—beginning with the thesis—for clarity, coherence, and adequate support. Shawn's notes to himself and your own analysis might suggest the following revisions:

OVERALL
1. creating an introduction and a conclusion
2. rewording the thesis to avoid the awkwardness of *collectibles—they*
3. revising topic sentences so that they are not mechanical restatements of sections of the thesis

PARAGRAPH 1
4. choosing a strong verb for the topic sentence
5. defining *collectibles* before beginning a discussion of their appeal
6. replacing general categories that illustrate the definition with specific examples
7. providing market values to prove the relative expense
8. omitting *satisfying* if the idea isn't proven in the paragraph

PARAGRAPH 2
9. clarifying the topic sentence by deciding whether objects blend with trends or with other objects
10. considering whether the discussions of tradition and novelty are ordered in the paragraph according to emphasis

PARAGRAPH 3
11. deciding whether collectibles adapt to one's tastes or reflect them and then, if necessary, revising the topic sentence
12. clarifying the relationship between the making of objects and their availability
13. adding a summary sentence

■ **Exercise 11** Reread the first draft of Shawn Redfield's essay, marking everything that is unclear to you or that you think needs revision. Compare your questions and comments with those of your classmates.

■ **Exercise 12** Write the first draft of your essay.

32h

Write and revise the second draft.

Shawn Redfield's notes for changes to be made in the first draft create guidelines for the writing of the second draft. Using the rough outline (but not being rigidly committed to it), the first draft, his comments on that draft, and new ideas that occur as he writes, he creates a second version, which begins to look like a conventional essay.

SECOND DRAFT

add title

weak

1 There exists an ever-growing concern about people's leisure time. With the growth of labour unions, the work week has declined steadily. What will people do with all this extra time? Photography, gardening, hiking and collecting are pasttimes that have recently grown in interest. Collecting what? Anything and everything, from the expensive to the inexpensive, from the useful to the useless--rare coins, old cars, duck decoys, mechanical banks, and Beatles albums. Yet the would-be collector with little money to spend need not feel left out, for acquiring collectibles can also be an inexpensive way to decorate an apartment or house. Collectibles include the common handcrafted, homemade, or manufactured antique utensils of the rural home; they were often considered high priced when they were

Cut - takes too long to get to thesis

prepare reader for this

new. ~~and are relatively inexpensive now~~. Because collectibles are relatively inexpensive, adapt to individual tastes, and blend with current decorating schemes, collectibles will continue to increase in popularity.

Do I prove this? No, I'm explaining the advantages of collecting.

2 Compared to collecting art or fine furniture, collectibles are very inexpensive. Because they were produced in quantity, they are now more common—and less expensive—than one-of-a-kind items or objects of limited use. A fifteen dollar vase or a potato digger does not require floating a loan, but it can make a unique addition to a collector's home. Cleaning up an old horse collar is not a major project, but it may result in a handsome frame for a mirror. Refinishing an oak keg won't necessitate cancelling the bowling league membership, but it can provide a one-of-a-kind end table. Acquiring collectibles is not a hobby of kings, but it can be one for anyone with an average income. What's average?

still weak — in terms of both time and money — awk. — effec. examples? — awk. use of *it*

3 Collectibles not only suit modest budgets but also individual tastes. In fact, they allow for "mass individuality." While today twenty international corporations may

individual taste shown by: 1. selection 2. distinctive use

manufacture the same item, in 1890 perhaps as many as one hundred small but independent companies made the same object, each company crafting a distinctive design. Thus, today hundreds of people may collect teakettles, for example, yet a high degree of duplication would be unlikely.¶ While collectors are gathering objects which say something about their likes and dislikes and their knowledge of antiques and history, they are also choosing objects which may serve a function in today's home, though often not the original function. An old crock may become a planter or a magazine holder; a patchwork quilt, a chair cover, a wall hanging or a tablecloth; a flatiron, a door stop or a bookend. A collection of collectibles is in some ways a definition of the person who has assembled them; they are chosen and used according to the tastes of their owner.

New ¶?

4 Whether the collector prefers a sleek chrome-and-glass or a cozy decor of Canadiana, collectibles add the contrast of tradition and the novelty of another lifestyle. The cover of a 1929 Eaton's catalogue among magazines of the day, for instance, provides a nostalgic

unclear

link with days gone by. The contrast between an iron dutch oven made in a nineteenth century New Brunswick foundry ~~that was brought from across the ocean by immigrants~~ and a microwave oven flown in from Japan adds character to a kitchen. A coal scuttle used as a magazine holder supplies the same character of contrast to an electrically heated living room. The preservation of these articles from the past continues to fill the need for contrast as it also reassures the need for tradition. There is security in a child's toy of cast iron, a barrel with walls of solid oak, or a hat rack made of brass--security which is missing in today's disposable, plastic world. At once removed from the present and a part of it, collectibles satisfy decorating needs and, in a large sense, family needs. → clarify

overuse of contrast

good idea

5 To sum up, assembling collectibles is a thriving, inexpensive pastime which allows collectors to be at once individuals with unique tastes and a part of the cultural tradition from which their objects come. Whether the objects are from the best of times or worst, collectors delight in their history. Even as they dust and arrange, sort and catalogue, they are making room for more.

not proven

fix ambiguous reference

After setting this second draft aside for a day or two, Shawn Redfield once again analyzes his work, checking matters of content, organization, sentence structure, paragraph unity, and diction. At this point, he is still more interested in revising (that is, rethinking the scope and shape of his ideas and how they relate to the thesis) than in proofreading (that is, looking for errors in spelling, grammar, punctuation, and mechanics).

When you revise your own work, use the checklist on pages 414-15, which will help you to evaluate all of the ideas in your essay.

■ **Exercise 13** Compare the first and second drafts of Shawn Redfield's essay to see whether the revisions have answered your questions. Are there any points that the writer made a note to revise but did not? Which questions on the checklist still need Shawn's attention?

■ **Exercise 14** Write the second draft of your essay and then answer all the questions on the revision checklist.

After using the revision checklist, Shawn makes three major decisions:

1. to begin the introduction with collecting instead of with increased leisure time
2. to revise the thesis so that it clearly defines the three points covered in the essay
3. to divide the paragraph on individual tastes and to reserve the topic sentence until the second part

He will also select a title and correct errors in spelling, punctuation, grammar, and mechanics. The result is the final draft on pages 416-19.

Reviser's Checklist

Overall considerations

1. Is every idea in the thesis stated clearly and given appropriate emphasis?
2. Does the thesis statement indicate the structure of the essay?
3. Does the sequence of paragraphs follow the order established in the thesis?
4. Do any terms require definition? If so, where should the definition(s) be introduced?
5. Do the body paragraphs prove the assertion of the thesis?
6. Are the ideas in the introduction logically related to the thesis?
7. Does the introduction attract the audience and prepare for the thesis?
8. Is there sufficient information to develop specific ideas?
9. Do the details, examples, and illustrations adequately support the ideas?
10. Is the conclusion complete without being abrupt?
11. Are all statements logically sound?
12. Is the tone consistent and appropriate for the audience?
13. Is the diction appropriate for both the content and the thesis?

Paragraphs

14. Is every paragraph controlled by a topic sentence, either stated or implied?
15. Does each paragraph explain and support its main idea? Are transitions within the paragraph clear and smooth?
16. Does each paragraph have a beginning, a middle, and an end?
17. Are the transitions between paragraphs adequate?

Sentences

18. Are the sentences varied in length? type? means of emphasis?
19. Are any words overused?
20. Are ideas within sentences given proper emphasis?
21. Are sentences grammatically correct?

Punctuation, Spelling, Mechanics

22. Are capitalization and abbreviations used correctly?
23. Have words at the ends of lines been divided correctly?
24. Are all words spelled correctly?
25. Are marks of punctuation used correctly and effectively?

32i

Prepare the final draft.

Now that Shawn Redfield has revised and proofread the second draft of his essay, he is ready to prepare a final copy. He is careful to extend the same conscientious effort that went into the writing process to the neatness and accuracy of his manuscript, for he thinks his ideas are significant, and he wants to convey that view by the appearance of his essay.

FINAL DRAFT

Collectibles for the Present

1 What are at least one third of Canadians doing with part of their leisure time? They are collecting anything and everything, from the expensive to the inexpensive, from the useful to the useless--typewriters, jukeboxes, fishing tackle, fruit-crate labels, old cars. Collecting some things, like jukeboxes or old cars, is both expensive and time-consuming. Yet the would-be collector with limited money or time need not feel left out, for collectibles offer an inexpensive and practical way to decorate a home. Collectibles include the common antique utensils associated with nineteenth-century rural life; handcrafted or homemade, imported or manufactured, collectibles may range in materials from wood or pottery to leather or metal. But kitchen tools and farm implements--butter bowls, skillets, ironstone, wooden rakes, and scythes--most often come to mind. While they are relatively inexpensive, collectibles reflect the tastes of the collector

and complement modern lifestyles.

2 Compared to collecting fine furniture, acquiring collectibles costs little in either money or time. Like pieces of furniture, collectibles were common to every household; yet they are still common--and thus less expensive than pieces of elaborate furniture. For example, a Georgian mahogany desk with inlaid panel doors may cost as much as five thousand dollars; while an iron teakettle with a porcelain finish may cost fifty. An afternoon spent cleaning great-grandmother's spoon set does not necessitate rescheduling the family vacation, but it does produce a grouping for the kitchen wall. Cleaning up an old horse collar is not a major project, but the result is a handsome mirror frame. Refinishing an oak keg won't mean cancelling the bowling league membership, but it does produce a rugged end table. Thus, collectibles provide an economical pastime for anyone with limited money and time.

3 Collectibles suit not only modest budgets but also individual tastes. In fact, they allow for mass individuality. Unlike international corporations today, the small, independent companies of yesterday relied on the skills of their craftsmen. Because many companies made the

same utensil, each company using a distinctive design (not to mention the work of self-employed craftsmen), today duplication among collections is relatively rare. Collections of ironstone, for example, may contain only a few of the same most common pieces. One person might collect only ironstone dinnerware while another collects only white ironstone and a third collects jugs and bowls of all kinds.

4 At the same time that collectors are gathering pieces which suit their taste, they are also choosing items they can use in a distinctive way, though the use is sometimes not the original one. For instance, an old crock becomes a planter or a magazine holder (it may even be used to make pickles or sauerkraut); a patchwork quilt may become a chair cover or a wall hanging; a flatiron, a door stop or a bookend. Thus, the collectibles acquired define the person who has assembled them; they are chosen and used according to the tastes of their owner.

5 Whether collectors prefer the sleekness of chrome and glass or the coziness of Canadiana, collectibles add the novelty of another lifestyle. An iron dutch oven that was manufactured in a New Brunswick foundry contrasts with a microwave flown in from Japan. A coal scuttle used as a magazine

holder emphasizes the same contrast in an electrically heated living room. As preserving these articles from past life fills a need for variety, it also fills a need for continuity and tradition. There is security in a child's toy of cast iron, a barrel with walls of solid oak, or hatracks made of brass--security which is missing in today's disposable, plastic world. At once removed from the present but a part of it, collectibles satisfy decorating and personal needs.

6 To sum up, collectibles allow collectors to be at once individuals with unique tastes and a part of the cultural tradition from which their objects came. Whether the collectibles come from the best of times or the worst, owners delight in the history of these objects and in the contrast they provide with the modern world. Even as collectors dust and arrange, sort and catalogue, they are making room for more.

■ **Exercise 15** Revise the final draft of Shawn Redfield's essay for emphasis and sentence variety. Notice, for example, that every sentence except the first is declarative, and that all but a few are either simple or complex. Try also to vary sentence lengths. What other changes would you suggest? Finally, proofread for any errors in spelling, punctuation, grammar, and mechanics.

■ **Exercise 16** Prepare the final draft of your essay.

The Research Paper

33

Learn how to prepare a research paper.

A research paper (also called a library paper or term paper) is like a short expository composition (see Section **32**) in that it is an organized series of paragraphs developing a controlling idea or thesis. A research paper differs from a short composition in that it involves the use of library sources from which facts, quotations, and the opinions of others are drawn to explain, support, or authenticate ideas in the paper. These sources are identified in the text by parenthetical citations that refer the reader to an alphabetical list of all sources cited. This list of works cited concludes the paper.

The rules in this section describe the usual steps in the preparation of a research paper:

1. Selecting and limiting the subject
2. Preparing a preliminary bibliography
3. Developing the outline
4. Taking notes
5. Writing and documenting the paper

Each of these steps is illustrated in the preparation of a sample research paper, which is then given in full at the end of the section.

33a

Choose a subject that is suitable for a research paper and then limit it appropriately. See also **32a.**

Not all subjects are suitable for a paper that relies on source materials found in the library. For example, you would probably find it difficult to document adequately a paper on your favourite childhood fantasies or on your opinions of an event so recent that little or nothing has yet been written on it.

Select a subject that you want to learn more about through reading. You might begin by selecting a general topic like literature, music, organic farming, cults, the media, or electronics.

Then start reading about your subject and decide what facets of it you could develop in a research paper. How much you limit your subject depends on the assigned length of the paper and on the availability and the adequacy of relevant books, newspapers, magazines, and so on. Below are examples of possible ways a general subject may be limited:

GENERAL literature → fiction → futuristic novels

LIMITED three futuristic novels: Orwell's *1984*, Huxley's *Brave New World*, Wells' *War of the Worlds*

MORE LIMITED Big Brother (in *1984*) and Mustapha Mond (in *Brave New World*) as world controllers

EVEN MORE LIMITED Big Brother's propaganda in the totalitarian world of *1984*

Note: You should be aware of the differences between a city or public library and a university or college library. A public library, which is designed for general use, contains mostly popular books and magazines. A university library is designed for research. It contains specialized journals, indexes, and critical works not found in a public library. For research papers, a university or college library is an indispensable tool.

■ **Exercise 1** Select a subject that would be suitable for a library paper. Then check the availability of materials. (If you cannot find enough books, periodicals, and so on, try another subject.) As you skim through the information, perhaps beginning with an encyclopedia, single out facets of the subject that you would like to investigate further. Finally, limit the subject so that you can develop it in a paper of the assigned length.

33b

Making good use of the materials in the library, prepare a preliminary bibliography. Learn an acceptable form for bibliographical entries.

A preliminary bibliography contains information (titles, authors, dates, and so on) about the materials (books, magazines, newspapers, videotapes, audiodiscs, and so on) that you are likely to use as sources. Use the main catalogue, indexes to periodicals, and reference books (as explained on the following pages) to make a preliminary bibliography by writing down the most promising titles you can find. Copy each title on a separate card (generally 12.7 cm × 7.6 cm [3 × 5 inches]) in an acceptable form: see page 432. You should keep these cards in alphabetical order until you complete your paper, adding useful titles as you find them and discarding those that prove useless. The final bibliography, to be typed at the end of your paper, will most often include only the works that help in the actual writing—usually only those cited in the text of your paper.

A computer-aided search generally saves time in preparing a preliminary bibliography. Check to see whether your library has a terminal, or "on-line" system, connected with data bases.

(1) Learn to use library catalogues.

When first established, libraries in Canada used a book catalogue as the main index to library holdings, updating it with supplements. As the number of holdings grew larger, librarians began using a file of 12.7 cm × 7.6 cm (3 × 5-inch) cards for catalogue purposes. In 1902, the U.S. Library of Congress started selling printed cards to libraries, and in time the card catalogue replaced the book catalogue.

SAMPLE CATALOGUE CARDS

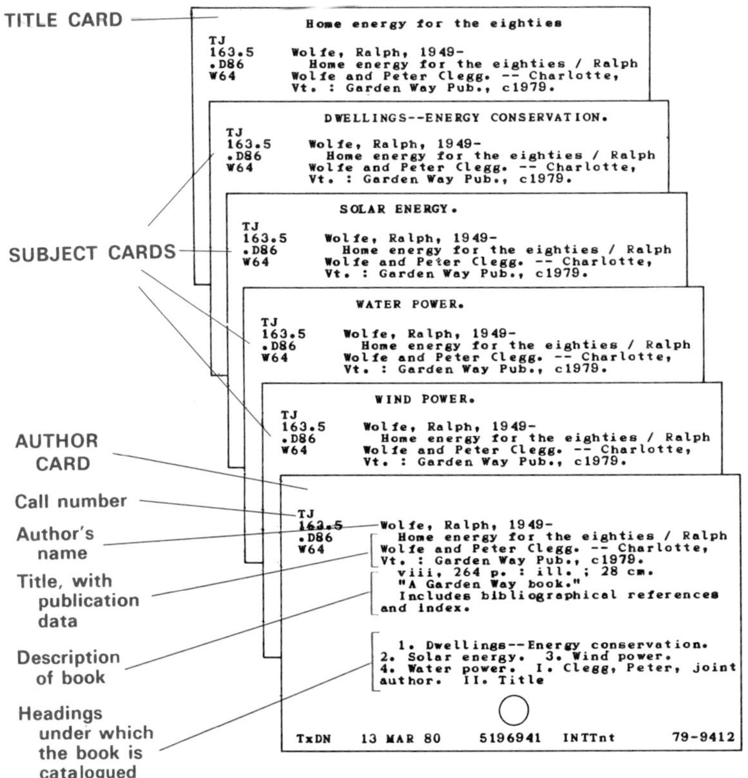

The card catalogue

Still an active file in many libraries, the card catalogue is the index to the whole library. It lists all books and all bound magazines, whether they are housed in the stacks, on the open shelves of the reference room, or in any other part of the building. In many libraries one general card catalogue lists all books owned by the college or university and shows whether the book is in the general library or in a special collection in another building.

Usually the card catalogue consists of cards arranged alphabetically in drawers. These may be "author" cards, "title" cards, or "subject" cards, for in most libraries each book is listed alphabetically in at least three places, once according to its author, again according to its title, and again according to its subject or subjects. These cards are identical except that the title card and the subject card have extra headings. As book collections in libraries mushroomed, the card catalogues became costly and cumbersome. Since 1960, many libraries have turned to the microfilm or microfiche catalogue, which photographically reproduces basically the same information found on the familiar cards.

The microfilm or microfiche catalogue

When using a microfilm catalogue housed in cartridges or cassettes, you need a microfilm viewer to read the record of library holdings. Since formats vary, you also need to find out if one alphabet covers all entries or if there are separate sections for author, title, and subject. Basically the microfiche catalogue is the microfilm entry or record arranged in rows on small 10.16 cm × 15.24 cm (4 × 6 inches) sheets. As a rule, the microfiche catalogue indexes authors, titles, and subjects separately.

A newer development in micrographics is the COM or Computer Output Microfilm catalogue. Microimages on film are exact records of output from a computer. Formatted in different ways, the COM catalogue is flexible and easy to use, although the user does need a microfilm or microfiche reader.

The computer catalogue

Today, more and more college and university libraries are computerizing their library catalogues. To query the computer, students use typewriter-like terminals (located in the library and usually elsewhere on campus). By pressing a few lettered keys, users have instant access to information about an author, a title, a subject, an editor, and so on. The computer also indicates whether the library owns a particular work. A few libraries provide printouts of the information given on the video screen. Familiarize yourself with these conveniences and useful specialized services. For example, a book important to your research but unavailable in your library may be obtained through an inter-library loan.

Note: After using the main catalogue, you may wish to refer to *Canadian Books in Print*, the *Cumulative Book Index, Books in Print,* and *Paperbound Books in Print* to find titles that are closely related to your subject. Or you may wish to read what others have written about a book, perhaps one your library does not have, in the *Book Review Digest* or in a periodical referred to by a book such as *Book Review Index*.

(2) Use indexes to periodicals.

When preparing your bibliography, remember that the periodical indexes do for articles what the main catalogue does for books in the library. You will probably find the *Social Science Index* and the *Readers' Guide to Periodical Literature* the most useful of these indexes. The front matter of each issue provides an explanation of a sample entry as well as a key to abbreviations.

Learn to distinguish the elements of a periodical index entry.

SUBJECT ENTRY
(May 10, 1980 issue)

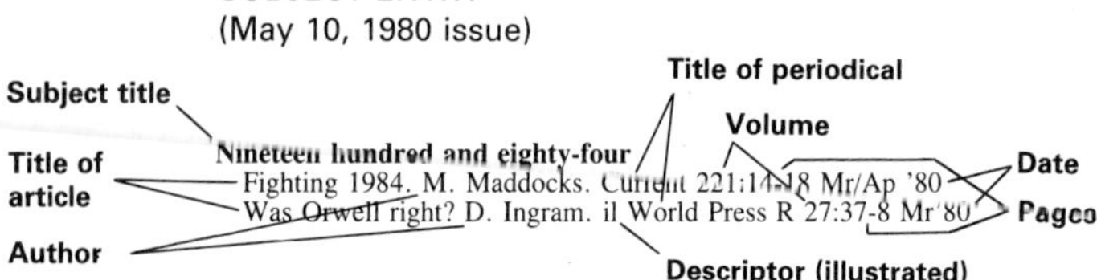

This issue contains an entry for George Orwell's *1984*: an illustrated article entitled "Was Orwell Right?" by D. Ingram—published in Vol. 27 of the *World Press Review* on pages 37-38 of the March 1980 issue.

PERSONAL NAME ENTRY
(March 1982—February 1983 issue)

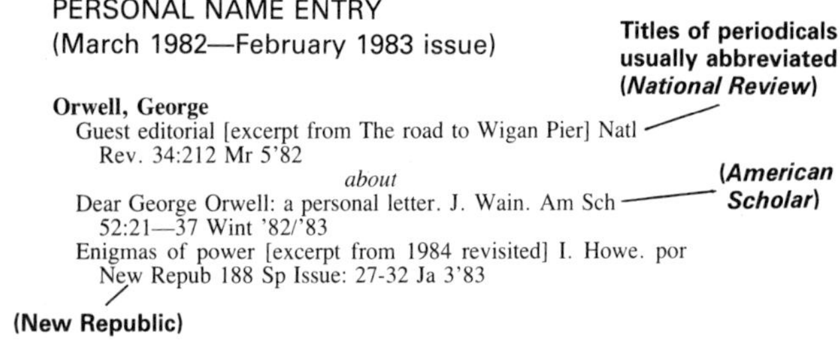

Titles of periodicals usually abbreviated (*National Review*)
Orwell, George
Guest editorial [excerpt from The road to Wigan Pier] Natl Rev. 34:212 Mr 5'82
about
(*American Scholar*)
Dear George Orwell: a personal letter. J. Wain. Am Sch 52:21—37 Wint '82/'83
Enigmas of power [excerpt from 1984 revisited] I. Howe. por New Repub 188 Sp Issue: 27-32 Ja 3'83
(New Republic)

This entry for Orwell lists first an article by Orwell and then two articles about him. The article written by Orwell is excerpted from his 1937 novel *The Road to Wigan Pier*. The excerpt appears as a guest editorial in the March 5,1982 issue of *National Review*. The volume number of this issue is 34; the page number of the excerpt is 212.

Indexes to Periodicals

General

Canadian Periodical Index. 1938–.
Poole's Index. 1802–1907. (subject index only)
Nineteenth Century Readers' Guide. 1890–99. (author, subject)
Readers' Guide. 1900–. (author, title, subject)
New York Times Index. 1913–. (a useful guide for finding the dates of important events, which can then be looked up in the *Times*, often available on microfilm, or in other newspapers)
Social Sciences Index. 1974–. Formerly *Social Sciences and Humanities Index*. 1965–73. *International Index*. 1907–65.

Special

Applied Science and Technology Index. 1958–. Formerly *Industrial Arts Index*. 1913–57.
Art Index. 1929–.
Biography Index. 1946–.
Biological and Agricultural Index. 1964–. Formerly *Agricultural Index*. 1916–64.
Business Periodicals Index. 1958–.
Canadian Business Periodicals Index. 1975–.
Canadian News Index. 1980–.
Current Index to Journals in Education. 1969–.
Education Index. 1929–.
Engineering Index. 1884–.
Humanities Index. 1974–. Formerly *Social Sciences and Humanities Index*. 1965–73. *International Index*. 1907–65.
Index to Legal Periodicals. 1908–.
Music Index. 1949–.
Public Affairs Information Service (Bulletin). 1915–.
United States Government Publications (Monthly Catalogue). 1895–.
See also the various abstracts, such as *Chemical Abstracts*, 1907–; *Abstracts of English Studies*, 1958–; *Abstracts of Popular Culture*, 1976–.

(3) Use reference books.

Learn the general location of the chief classes of reference books in order that you may turn to them without loss of time. For a detailed list of such books, with a short description of each, consult *Canadian Reference Sources: A Selective Guide* by Dorothy E. Ryder, *Guide to Reference Books* by Eugene P. Sheehy (formerly by Constance M. Winchell) and *American Reference Books Annual (ARBA)*, edited by Janet H. Littlefield. Since many reference books, especially some of the encyclopedias, are kept up to date by frequent revisions, you should remember to cite the latest copyright date of the edition you are using. A few of the more important reference books are listed on the following pages (with abbreviated bibliographical information).

Reference Books

General dictionaries (unabridged)

A Dictionary of American English on Historical Principles. 4 vols. 1938–44.

Century Dictionary and Cyclopedia. 12 vols. 1911. 3 vols. 1927–33.

Gage Canadian Dictionary. 1983.

New Standard Dictionary of the English Language. 1947, 1952, 1966.

The Oxford English Dictionary. 13 vols. 1933. Originally issued as *A New English Dictionary on Historical Principles*. 10 vols. and Supplement. 1888–1933. (Supplements)

The Random House Dictionary of the English Language. 1967.

Webster's Third New International Dictionary. 1961. (Supplement, *6000 words*, 1976)

Special dictionaries

Cowie, A.P., and R. Mackin. *Oxford Dictionary of Current Idiomatic English*. Vol. I–. 1975–.

Fowler, H.W. *Dictionary of Modern English Usage*. 2nd ed. Rev. Sir Ernest Gowers. 1965.

Hayakawa, S.I., and the Funk & Wagnalls dictionary staff. *Modern Guide to Synonyms and Related Words*. 1968.

Morris, William, and Mary Morris. *Harper Dictionary of Contemporary Usage*. 1975.
Onions, C.T. *Oxford Dictionary of English Etymology*. 1967.
Partridge, Eric. *Dictionary of Catch Phrases*. 1979.
________. *Dictionary of Slang and Unconventional English*. 7th ed. 1970.
Roget's International Thesaurus. 4th ed. 1977.
Webster's Collegiate Thesaurus. 1976.
Wentworth, Harold, and Stuart B. Flexner. *Dictionary of American Slang*. 2nd ed. 1975.

General encyclopedias

Academic American Encyclopedia. 21 vols.
The Canadian Encyclopedia. 3 vols.
Collier's Encyclopedia. 24 vols.
Encyclopedia Americana. 30 vols.
Encyclopaedia Britannica. 30 vols.

Special encyclopedias

Cambridge Encyclopaedia of Astronomy. Ed. Simon Mitton. 1977.
Dictionary of the History of Ideas. Ed. Philip P. Wierner et al. 5 vols. 1973.
Encyclopedia of Computers and Data Processing. Vol I-. 1978–.
Encyclopedia of Music in Canada. Ed. Helmut Kallmann et al. 1981.
Encyclopedia of Philosophy. Ed. Paul Edwards et al. 4 vols. 1973.
Encyclopedia of Psychology. 2nd ed. Ed. Hans Jergen Eysenck et al. 1979.
Encyclopedia of World Art. 15 vols. 1959–68.
Focal Encyclopedia of Photography. Rev. ed. 1969.
Grzimek's Animal Life Encyclopedia. 13 vols. 1972–75.
International Encyclopedia of Higher Education. Ed. Asa K. Knowles. 10 vols. 1977.
International Encyclopedia of the Social Sciences. Ed. D.E. Sills. 17 vols. 1968. Supplements.
Klein, Barry, and D. Icolari. *Reference Encyclopedia of the American Indian*. 3rd ed. 1978.
Kurian, George Thomas. *Encyclopedia of the Third World*. 2 vols. 1978.
Langer, William L. *An Encyclopedia of World History*. 5th ed. 1972.

McGraw-Hill Encyclopedia of Science & Technology. 15 vols. 4th ed. 1977. Yearbooks.

Munn, Glenn G. *Encyclopedia of Banking and Finance*. 7th rev. ed. Ed. Ferdinand L. Garcia. 1973.

The New Grove Dictionary of Music and Musicians. Ed. Stanley Sadie. 20 vols. 1980.

Stierlin, Henri. *Encyclopedia of World Architecture*. 2 vols. 2nd ed. 1979.

Story, N. *The Oxford Companion to Canadian History and Literature*. 1967. (Supplement 1973).

Thompson, Oscar. *International Cyclopedia of Music and Musicians*. 10th ed. Rev. ed. [Ed. Bruce Bohle]. 1975.

Atlases

Commercial Atlas and Marketing Guide (Rand McNally). 1981.

Cosmopolitan World Atlas (Rand McNally). Rev. ed. 1978.

Hammond Medallion World Atlas. 1977.

National Geographic Atlas of the World. 4th ed. 1975.

Oxford Economic Atlas of the World. 4th ed. 1972.

The Times (London) Atlas of the World: Comprehensive Edition. 5th ed. 1975.

The National Atlas of Canada. 4th ed. 1974.

Yearbooks—current events

Americana Annual. 1923–.

Annual Register. 1758–.

Canadian Almanac and Directory. 1847–.

Canadian News Facts. 1967–.

Facts on File. 1940–.

Reader's Digest Almanac and Yearbook. 1966–.

Statesman's Year-Book. 1864–.

Statistical Abstract of the United States. 1878–.

World Almanac and Book of Facts. 1868–.

Biography

Canadian Who's Who. 1910–.

Contemporary Authors. 1962–.

Current Biography. 1940–.

Dictionary of American Biography. 16 vols. and index. 1927–80. Supplements.

Dictionary of Canadian Biography. 1966. Vols. 1-5 and index, 9-11.
Dictionary of National Biography (British). 22 vols. 1882–1953. Supplements.
Dictionary of Scientific Biography. 16 vols. 1970–80.
International Who's Who (London). 1935–.
McGraw-Hill Encyclopedia of World Biography. 12 vols. 1973.
Webster's Biographical Dictionary. 1976.
Who's Who in America. 1899–. [See also *Marquis Who's Who Publications: Index to All Books* (revised annually).]

Literature

Bartlett's Familiar Quotations. 15th ed. 1980.
Benét, William Rose. *The Reader's Encyclopedia*. 2nd ed. 1965.
Cambridge History of American Literature. 3 vols. in 1. 1943.
Cambridge History of English Literature. 15 vols. 1907–33.
Essay and General Literature Index. 1900–.
Evans, Bergen. *Dictionary of Quotations*. 1968.
Fiction Catalog. 9th ed. 1976. Supplements.
Fleischman, W.B. *Encyclopedia of World Literature in the 20th Century*. 4 vols. 1967-75.
Granger's Index to Poetry. 6th ed. 1973.
Hart, James D. *Oxford Companion to American Literature*. 4th ed. 1965.
Harvey, Sir Paul. *Oxford Companion to Classical Literature*. 2nd. ed. 1937.
________. *Oxford Companion to English Literature*. 4th ed. 1967.
Holman, C. Hugh. *Handbook to Literature*. 4th ed. 1980.
New Cambridge Bibliography of English Literature. 4 vols. 1973. Index, 1977.
Oxford Companion to Canadian Literature. 1983.
Oxford Dictionary of Quotations. 3rd ed. 1979.
Play Index (Wilson). 1949–.
Seymour-Smith, Martin. *Funk and Wagnalls Guide to Modern World Literature*. 1975.
Short Story Index (Wilson). 1953. Supplements.
Smith, Horatio. *Columbia Dictionary of Modern European Literature*. 1947.

Spiller, Robert E., et al. *Literary History of the United States.* 4th ed. 2 vols. 1974.
Watters, Reginald Eyre. *A Checklist of Canadian Literature and Background Materials, 1628–1960.* 1972.
Watters, Reginald Eyre and Inglis Freeman Bell. *On Canadian Literature, Its Authors and Language.* 1973.

(4) Use a standard bibliographical form.

Put each item of your bibliography on a separate card (preferably 12.7 cm × 7.6 cm [3 × 5 inches]) so that you can readily drop or add a card and can arrange the list alphabetically without recopying it. Follow exactly and consistently the bibliographical form you are instructed to use. By following that style from the start of your research, you can save yourself valuable time when, later, you must compile a formal list of works cited to appear at the end of your paper. The form illustrated by the samples on pages 433-40 follows the new guidelines of the Modern Language Association (MLA).

Bibliographical entries often consist of only three units, which are separated by periods:

```
Toffler, Alvin. The Third Wave. New York: Morrow,
    1980.
```

1. *Name of the author.* Give the last name first. Your final list of works cited will be arranged alphabetically by authors' last names.
2. *Title of the book.* Underline (italicize) the title, and capitalize it in accordance with **9c**. Always include the book's subtitle.
3. *Publication data.* Include the place of publication, the publisher, and the latest copyright date as shown on the copyright page. You may give a shortened form of the publisher's name as long as it is clear.

Some entries, however, require more than three units and must be given special treatment. As you study the following MLA-style bibliographical entries, which cover most of the special problems you are likely to encounter, observe both the punctuation and the arrangement of information. See also pages 441-43 for a list of abbreviations that are permissible in bibliographies, notes, and tables. Note that the MLA style favours Arabic numbers throughout and that such abbreviations as *vol.* and *sec.* are not capitalized.

Sample Bibliographical Entries

Books

One author

Frye, Northrop. The Bush Garden: Essays on the Canadian Imagination. Toronto: Anansi, 1971.

Notice that the subtitle is always included in bibliographical entries and that the underlining of the complete title is continuous.

Rawlyk, George A. Nova Scotia's Massachusetts: A Study of Massachusetts-Nova Scotia Relations 1630 to 1784. Montreal: McGill, 1973.

The publisher's name (in this instance, McGill University Press) is shortened as much as possible while remaining clearly identifiable.

Two authors

Chapman, L. J., and D. F. Putnam. The Physiography of Southern Ontario. 2nd ed. Toronto: U of Toronto P, 1966.

Three authors

Linteau, Paul-Andre, René Durocher, and Jean-Claude Robert. Quebec: A History 1867–1929. Trans. Robert Chodos. Toronto: Lorimer, 1983.

More than three authors

Smitheram, Verner, et al. The Garden Transformed: Prince Edward Island 1945–1980. Charlottetown: Ragweed, 1982.

Corporate author

Canadian Red Cross Society. Manual for Teaching Swimming to the Disabled. Toronto: C.R.C.S., 1974.

Government publication and edition after the first

Canada. Transport Canada. Transport of Dangerous Goods Branch. Emergency Response Guide for Dangerous Goods. 2nd ed. Toronto: Copp, 1982.

Editors

MacLure, Millar and F. W. Watts, eds. Essays in English Literature from the Renaissance to the Victorian Age Presented to A. S. P. Woodhouse. Toronto: U of Toronto P, 1964.

Story or article from an anthology

Ludwig, Jack. "The Calgary Stampede." Active Voice:

An Anthology of Canadian, American and Commonwealth Prose. Eds. W. H. New and W. E. Messenger. Scarborough: Prentice, 1980. 111–20.

Translation

Tremblay, Michel. Forever Yours Marie-Lou. Trans. John Van Burek and Bill Glassco. Vancouver: Talonbooks, 1975.

Reprint

Berger, Carl. The Sense of Power: Studies in the Ideas of Canadian Imperialism. 1970. Toronto: U of Toronto P, 1971.

The original hard-cover edition was published a year earlier than this paperback version.

Collin, W. E. The White Savannahs. Introd. Germaine Warkentin. 1936. Toronto: U of Toronto P, 1975.

A work in more than one volume

Klinck, Carl F., et al., eds. Literary History of Canada: Canadian Literature in English. 2nd ed. 3 vols. Toronto: U of Toronto P, 1976.

The work consists of three volumes published in the same year.

A work in a series

Hair, Donald S. Browning's Experiments with Genre. University of Toronto Department of English

Studies and Texts 19. Toronto: U of Toronto P, 1972.

The volume number is given in Arabic numerals and without the abbreviation *vol.*

Mallea, John R., and Jonathan Young. Cultural Diversity and Canadian Education: Issues and Innovations. The Carleton Library Series. Ottawa: Carlton UP, 1984.

Magazines and Newspapers

Unsigned article

"Gretzky buys junior club." The London Free Press 9 Mar. 1985: C12.

As a rule, the names of months except May, June, and July are abbreviated. "C12" refers to the section and page number of the newspaper.

Daily Newspaper

Dwyer, Gwynn. "Tanzania paying steep price for Nyerere mismanagement." The London Free Press 9 Mar. 1985: A11.

When not part of the newspaper's name, the city's name should be given in brackets after the title. Column numbers are not used.

Weekly magazine or newspaper

Powis, Tim, and Marc Clark. "Fending Off a Takeover." Maclean's 25 Feb. 1985: 52–53.

Monthly magazine

Frohlich, Cliff. "The Physics of Somersaulting and Twisting." <u>Scientific American</u> Mar. 1980: 154–64.

Journal—continuous pagination through year

Hartwell, Patrick. "Grammar, Grammars, and the Teaching of Grammar." <u>College English</u> 47.2 (1985), 105–27.

If the pages of the journal are numbered consecutively through the year, a comma precedes the page reference. (Note that an issue number follows a volume number, separated by a period.)

Journal—separate pagination for each issue

Graham, Loren R. "Concerns about Science and Attempts to Regulate Inquiry." <u>Daedalus</u> 107 (1978): 1–21.

The pages of this journal are numbered separately for each issue, not consecutively through the year; in this case, a colon precedes the page reference.

Editorial

"Facing the Arms Dilemma." Editorial. <u>The London Free Press</u> 9 Mar. 1985: A10.

Book review

Abley, Mark. "A Chronicle of a Master Poet's Life." Rev. of <u>T. S. Eliot: A Life</u>, by Peter Ackroyd. <u>Maclean's</u> 25 Feb. 1985: 68.

Note: Sometimes a magazine article is printed on pages that are separated by other articles; for example, the first part appears on pages 137-39, the last on pages 188-203. In such a case, give only the first page number followed by a "plus" sign: 137 +.

Encyclopedia

Signed with name or initials

Thomas, Lewis H. "Riel." Dictionary of Canadian Biography. Vol. XI.

Full publication information is not required for a familiar reference work.

R[asmussen], J[ohn] O., [Jr.] "Radioactivity." Encyclopaedia Britannica: Macropaedia. 1974 ed.

Brackets enclose the added parts of the name. A list of contributors is ordinarily supplied in the index volume or in the front matter of an encyclopedia.

Unsigned

"Canadian Labour Congress." Encyclopaedia Britannica: Micropaedia. Vol. 2. 1985 ed.

In this encyclopaedia, main sections (like "Canadian Labour Congress") are arranged alphabetically in the text.

"Portsmouth, Treaty of." Columbia Encyclopedia. 1975 ed.

The title indicates that the article is listed under *P*.

Pamphlets, bulletins, and reports

Titles of pamphlets are italicized (underlined).

Canada. Department of Fisheries and Oceans.
Freshwater Fishes of Canada. Bulletin 184.
Ottawa: Canadian Government, 1979.

Notice the sequencc for a government publication: government, agency, title—each followed by a period and two spaces. The publisher in this example is the Canadian Government.

Unpublished dissertation

Benson, J. "The Evolution of Technical/Vocational
Educational Policy, 1945–1980." Diss. U of
Saskatchewan, 1981.

Micropublications

Document a book or periodical photographically reproduced in miniature form as though the work were in its original form.

Non-print sources

Motion picture

Mon Oncle Antoine. National Film Board. 1971.

Television or radio program

"The Disarmament Talks." As It Happens. CBC–CFPL
TV, London. 14 Mar. 1985.

Television interview

Wilson, Michael. Interview by Barbara Frum. The Journal. CBC–CFPL, London. 24 May 1985.

Performance of stage play

Handcuffs: The Donnellys, Part III. By James Reaney. Tarragon Theatre. Toronto. 29 Mar. 1975.

Recording

Barbeau, Dr. Marius C. "Ceremonial Chief–Songs." My Life in Recording Canadian–Indian Folk–Lore. Folkways, FG 3502, 1957.

Lecture

Kubler–Ross, Dr. Elizabeth. "Life, Death, and Transition." King's College Lecture Series. Alumni Hall, London, Ontario. 3 June 1985.

Interview

Kendall, Nancy. Personal Interview. 25 Aug. 1985.

For samples of citations of other non-print sources—such as games, globes, filmstrips, microscope slides, and transparencies—consult Eugene B. Fleischer's *A Style Manual for Citing Microform and Nonprint Media* (Chicago: American Library Association, 1978).

Note: Although the final form may not be required for preliminary-bibliography cards, it is a helpful practice to use the complete bibliographic form at this stage.

BIBLIOGRAPHY CARDS

Kanfer, Stefan. "Orwell 25 Years Later: Future Imperfect." Time 24 March 1975: 77-78.

Meyers, Jeffrey. A Reader's Guide to George Orwell. Totowa: Littlefield, 1977.

PR
6029
.R8
Z737
1977

COMMON ABBREVIATIONS

Below is a list of abbreviations commonly used in bibliographies, tables, or notes (but not the text) of research papers.

abr.	abridged, abridgment
Acad.	Academy
anon.	anonymous
app.	appendix
Apr.	April
Assn.	Association
Aug.	August
biog.	biography, biographer, biographical
bk., bks.	book, books

bull.	bulletin
c.	*circa*, "about" (for example, "c. 1966")
cf.	compare
ch., chs.	chapter, chapters
col., cols.	column, columns
Coll.	College
comp.	compiled by, compiler
cont.	contents; continued
Dec.	December
dept.	department
dir.	directed by, director
diss.	dissertation
div.	division
ed., eds.	edition(s) OR editor(s)
enl.	enlarged (as in "rev. and enl. ed.")
et al.	*et alii*, "and others"
Feb.	February
fig.	figure
fwd.	foreword, foreword by
gen. ed.	general editor
govt.	government
HMSO	Her Majesty's Stationery Office
illus.	illustrated by, illustrator, illustration
inc.	incorporated, including
Inst.	Institute, Institution
intl.	international
introd.	[author of] introduction, introduced by
Jan.	January
jour.	journal
mag.	magazine
Mar.	March
ms., mss.	manuscript, manuscripts
n, nn	note, notes (used immediately after page number: 6n3)
natl.	national
n.d.	no date [of publication]
no., nos.	number [of issue], numbers

Nov.	November
n.p.	no place [of publication], no publisher
n. pag.	no pagination
Oct.	October
P	Press (used in documentation; see "UP")
p., pp.	page, pages (omitted before page numbers unless reference would be unclear)
pref.	preface, preface by
pseud.	pseudonym
pt., pts.	part, parts
rept.	reported by, report
rev.	revision, revised, revised by OR review, reviewed by
rpt.	reprinted, reprint
sec., secs.	section, sections
Sept.	September
ser.	series
Soc.	Society
supp.	supplement
trans.	translated by, translator, translation
U	University (used in documentation; see "UP")
UP	University Press (used in documentation: Queen's UP)
vol., vols.	volume, volumes (omitted before volume numbers unless reference would be unclear)

Standard two-letter postal abbreviations for U.S. states (such as *CA* for California, *KY* for Kentucky) and standard abbreviations for countries (*Gt. Brit.* for Great Britain, *Mex.* for Mexico).

Spell out *and* rather than use &, even when the ampersand appears in the title: *U.S. News and World Report*.

■ **Exercise 2** Select a subject (the one you chose for Exercise 1 on page 422 or a different one) and prepare a preliminary bibliography. (Often you will find helpful bibliographies in the books that you consult, especially in encyclopedias and other reference works.)

Varying Styles of Documentation

Each department of a college or university ordinarily suggests a particular style for bibliographies and citations. As previously stated, the style of the Modern Language Association is used for the bibliographical and citation models on pages 433-40 and 459-66 and in the sample research paper (pages 476-511), and you may use that style unless your instructor specifies a different one. Instructors in the sciences, business, economics, and so forth, may recommend a documentation form in one of the style books listed below, which are available in most university and public libraries. If you are asked to use one of these manuals, study it carefully, and make sure your bibliography and notes correspond exactly to the examples it provides. Following the list are some examples of documentation in the style of the American Psychological Association (APA), a style commonly used in the social and behavioural sciences.

Style books and manuals

American Institute of Physics. Publications Board. *Style Manual for Guidance in the Preparation of Papers*. 3rd ed. New York: American Inst. of Physics, 1978.

American Chemical Society. *Handbook for Authors of Papers in American Chemical Society Publications*. Washington: American Chemical Soc., 1980.

American Mathematical Society. *A Manual for Authors of Mathematical Papers*. 7th ed. Providence: American Mathematical Soc., 1980.

American Psychological Association. *Publication Manual of the American Psychological Association*. 3rd ed. Washington: American Psychological Assn., 1983.

Associated Press. *The Associated Press Stylebook*. Dayton: Lorenz, 1980.

Council of Biology Editors. Style Manual Committee. *CBE Style Manual: A Guide for Authors, Editors, and Publishers in the*

Biological Sciences. 5th ed. Bethesda: Council of Biology Editors, 1983.
Gibaldi, Joseph, and Walter S. Achtert. *MLA Handbook for Writers of Research Papers*. 2nd ed. New York: Modern Language Association, 1984.
Harvard Law Review. *A Uniform System of Citation*. 12th ed. Cambridge: Harvard Law Review Assn., 1976.
Turabian, Kate L. *A Manual for Writers of Term Papers, Theses, and Dissertations*. 4th ed. Chicago: U of Chicago P, 1973.
Wiles, Roy M. *Scholarly Reporting in the Humanities*. 4th ed. Toronto: U of Toronto P, 1968.

References in APA style

In APA style, the alphabetical list of works cited is called "References." The reference entries below follow the style of the 1983 edition of the APA *Publication Manual*. Carefully observe all details of indentation, spacing, punctuation, and mechanics.

Book—one author

`Liptz, A. (1979). Prisons as social structures. Los Angeles: Scholarly Press.`

Book—two authors

`Hodge, G. and Quadeer, M. A. (1983). Towns and villages in Canada: The importance of being unimportant. Toronto: Butterworth's.`

Journal—one author

`Pinker, S. (1980). Mental imagery and the third dimension. Journal of Experimental Psychology: General, 109, 354–71.`

Journal—multiple authors

Johnson, M. K., Raye, C. L., Hasher, L., & Chromiak, W. (1979). Are there developmental differences in reality monitoring? Journal of Experimental Child Psychology, 27, 120, 128.

33c

Make a preliminary outline and develop it as you take notes on readings and as you write your research paper. See also **32f.**

After completing a preliminary bibliography and a minimum of general reading on your subject (an encyclopedia article and parts of one or two other works may suffice), make a preliminary outline that will give direction to your investigation. The outline will enable you to discard irrelevant material from your bibliography and to begin spotting valuable passages on which you will want to take notes. If you attempt to take notes without first knowing what you are looking for, your efforts will lead only to frustration.

Be careful, however, not to adhere too rigidly to your preliminary outline. For although the outline will direct your reading, your reading will almost certainly suggest ways in which the outline may be improved. No outline should be regarded as complete until the research paper has been finished. As you take notes, you will probably revise your original outline frequently, adding subheadings to it, changing subheadings to major headings, perhaps dropping some headings entirely.

You may wish to compare the form and the content of the following preliminary outline with that of the final outline on pages 474-75.

Preliminary Outline

Big Brother and His Propaganda Machine

Thesis: Used just for the sake of power, BB's propaganda is a particularly dangerous type.

George Orwell as propagandist and 1984 as propaganda

1. BB's totalitarian government related to propaganda:
   Its impact on Oceanians
   Their Leader–propagandist myth
   Pyramidal power structure
   Political machinery–the ministries
2. BB's use of propaganda to get uniformity
   Totally controls media
   History falsified
3. Newspeak–related to propaganda
   Why
   How
4. Main teachings of BB's propaganda:
   Love BB and hate his enemies.
   All else falls into place–no need to fear!

33d

Learn how to prepare a final outline.

Once you have developed and revised your preliminary outline as part of the process of organizing information, you are ready to select one of the conventional outline forms with standard notation so that your final outline shows the relationship of your main ideas and supporting information to the thesis.

First decide whether to use a topic outline, a sentence outline, or a paragraph outline. A topic outline presents information in parallel phrases or single words (see pages 474-75). A sentence outline presents the same ideas in complete grammatically parallel declarative statements (see pages 469-70). And a paragraph outline presents ideas in paragraph form.

PARAGRAPH OUTLINE

Big Brother's Propaganda

Thesis: Big Brother disseminates the most dangerous kind of propaganda.

Introduction: In *Nineteen Eighty-Four*, Orwell (a propagandist) satirizes totalitarian propaganda as he presents his vision of life--in reverse.

I. The Oceanians are propaganda targets. They act like a stupid herd, and they revere a mythical leader. They even accept the hierarchy in a "classless" society.

II. Big Brother's bureaucracy serves as a propaganda machine. Its housing is a symbol, and its parts are interrelated.

III. Big Brother has complete control of the media. He supplies all materials, and he propagates the Party's ideal.

IV. The State falsifies history to control the past and make it fit the present. Winston's use of the memory hole and the clerks' rectifying old propaganda are evidence of this efficient, systematic, frightening attack on the past.

V. Totalitarian propaganda manipulates thought and emotion. Just as the State uses Newspeak to prevent thought, it also controls love and hate by teaching love for Big Brother and hate for his enemies.

Conclusion: Much of Big Brother's propaganda is outdated, but Nineteen Eighty-Four is still widely read as a warning.

Formal outlines use a system of notation that divides ideas and ranks them according to their level of importance. In the humanities, this system consists of Roman numerals, capital letters, Arabic numerals, and lower-case letters. Thus, for instance, ideas numbered with Roman numerals are of equal rank; they are also more important than ideas lettered A and B. The equality and relative importance of ideas are also shown by indention. Major ideas are flush with the left margin with each succeeding level indented as shown below:

Thesis:
I. Major idea
  A. Supporting idea
    1. Example or illustration for supporting idea
    2. Example or illustration for supporting idea
      a. Detail for example or illustration
      b. Detail for example or illustration
  B. Supporting idea
II. Major idea

Notice that:

1. The thesis statement is not marked with a Roman numeral because it is the single most important idea in the essay; it therefore has no equal.

2. The closer to the left margin an idea is, the more important it is.

3. At least two parts are required for the division of ideas at every level used.

4. Ideas at each level are cast in grammatically parallel structures, but it is not necessary to have parallel structure between levels. (See Section **26**.)

As you can see, the form of an outline—the system of notation, the pattern of indention, and the parallel structure within ranks—emphasizes the order of and relationships among ideas.

As mentioned earlier, the system of numbers and letters discussed above is used for papers in the humanities. In the social and behavioural sciences, physical sciences, business, and engineering, a system of Arabic numerals alone is preferred:

1. Major idea
   1.1 Supporting idea
   1.2 Supporting idea
      1.2.1 Example or illustration for supporting idea
      1.2.2 Example or illustration for supporting idea
         1.2.2.1 Detail for example or illustration
         1.2.2.2 Detail for example or illustration

As you can see, both systems of notation emphasize the order of ideas and the relationships among them. Both are designed to provide a blueprint for the paper, and both serve as a table of contents for the reader.

33e

Take notes on readings (after evaluating the sources).

As you take notes on your readings, learn how to find and evaluate useful passages with a minimum of time and effort. Seldom will a whole book, or even a whole article, be of use as subject matter for any given research paper. To get what is needed for your paper, you will find that you must turn to many books and articles, rejecting most of them altogether and using from others only a section here and there. You cannot take the time to read each book completely. Use the table of contents and the index of a book, and learn to skim the pages rapidly until you find the passages you need.

One important consideration always is the reliability of the source. Do others speak of the writer as an authority? As you read, do you find evidence that the author is competent, well-informed, not prejudiced in any way? Is the work recent enough to provide up-to-date information? Is the edition the latest one available? Use your best judgment to determine the most dependable sources for your paper. You may find in the *Book Review Digest* convenient summaries of critical opinion on a book in your bibliography.

One of the best ways to take notes is on cards of uniform size, preferably 10.16 cm × 15.24 cm. (A smaller card may be used for the bibliography.) Each card must show the source of the note, including the exact page from which it is drawn. (When information is taken from more than one page, be sure to indicate in your notes exactly where one page ends and another begins.) It is a good idea to put a single note on one card (or ideas from a single source on a set of cards) with a heading keyed to a word or phrase in the outline. You can then easily arrange your note cards as you make changes in organization.

BIBLIOGRAPHY CARD WITH SOURCE

Voorhees, Richard J. The Paradox of George Orwell. Humanities Series. Lafayette: Purdue U Studies, 1961.

SOURCE (from page 87)

From the middle thirties until his death Orwell was a propagandist harping on the significance of totalitarianism because he knew that thousands upon thousands of people in democratic countries were only remotely aware of it, and still more thousands thought that there was a lot to be said for it in one form or another. *Nineteen Eighty-Four* is his fiercest piece of propaganda.

NOTE CARD

Orwell as propagandist (introduction)
(Voorhees 87)

Orwell a propagandist from mid 1930s on—
Kept "harping on" totalitarianism.

Why? He knew many people didn't know about its evils.

"Nineteen Eighty-Four is his fiercest piece of propaganda."

For other examples of note cards, see pages 484, 486, 498.

Another way to take notes is to use regular notebook paper, perhaps adding photocopies of short excerpts from materials you think you may quote directly. On a photocopy you may mark quotable material and jot down your own ideas as you study the source.

PHOTOCOPIED SOURCE WITH NOTES

from Vol. IV - Orwell's Essays

Politics and the English Language 137

covering up all the details. The great enemy of clear language is insincerity. When there is a gap between one's real and one's declared aims, one turns as it were instinctively to long words and exhausted idioms, like a cuttlefish squirting out ink. In our age there is no such thing as "keeping out of politics". All issues are political issues, and politics itself is a mass of lies, evasions, folly, hatred and schizophrenia. When the general atmosphere is bad, language must suffer. I should expect to find—this is a guess which I have not sufficient knowledge to verify—that the German, Russian and Italian languages have all deteriorated in the last ten or fifteen years, as a result of dictatorship.

[But] if thought corrupts language, language can also corrupt thought. A bad usage can spread by tradition and imitation, even among people who should and do know better. The debased language that I have been discussing is in some ways very convenient.

NEWSPEAK

1984

like Big Brother's

debatable BUT quotable

Direct quotations

Any quotations that you use in your paper should be convincing and important ones. They should be made an integral part of your text. (For examples of ways this can be done, see pages 479, 487.) When you discover a quotable passage in your reading, you should take it down verbatim—that is, copy every word, every capital letter, and every mark of punctuation exactly as in the original. Be sure to enclose the quoted passage in quotation marks. When you are quoting, quote accurately. When you are not quoting, use your own sentence structure and phraseology, not a slightly altered version of your source. Any conscious quotation (except well-known or proverbial passages) of the words of another should be placed inside quotation marks (or indented if over four lines in length), and exact sources should be cited.

In Nineteen Eighty-Four, Orwell defines doublethink as "the power of holding two contradictory beliefs in one's mind simultaneously, and accepting both of them" (215).

[Quotation marks enclose copied words, and internal documentation indicates the source.]

For other examples of the use and the documentation of direct quotations, see the sample research paper on pages 476-511.

As you write your research paper, keep a few guidelines in mind when you are quoting the exact words of another. Pay close attention to form, punctuation, and spacing: see **16a**. Use periods appropriately to indicate ellipsis: see **17i**. But do not use ellipsis periods before quotations that are only parts of sentences. To avoid these periods at the beginning of a quotation (especially one that begins a paragraph), use a word like *that* or an introductory word group before the quotation. You may use a period to end a quotation that is a grammatically complete sentence, even though the source may have a semicolon or another mark of punctuation.

Paraphrase

A paraphrase is a restatement of the source in about the same number of words. As you compare the source on the next page with the paraphrase that follows, notice differences in sentence structure and word choice.

SOURCE (from *Propaganda* by Jacques Ellul)

> The aim of modern propaganda is no longer to modify ideas, but to provoke action. It is no longer to change adherence to a doctrine, but to make the individual cling irrationally to a process of action.

PARAPHRASE

Jacques Ellul states that modern propaganda does not try any longer to change a person's ideas or loyalties to certain principles; instead, it seeks to make individuals irrationally follow a given procedure (25).

For further examples of the use and documentation of paraphrases in a research paper, see pages 500-01.

Précis

A précis is a concise summary (shorter than the source). When you make a paraphrase or write a précis, avoid copying not only the actual words but also the writer's style or sentence structure. If you cannot do this, much of the material may be worth quoting directly.

SOURCE (from *Nineteen Eighty-Four* by George Orwell)

> . . . the subtlest practitioners of *doublethink* are those who invented *doublethink* and know that it is a vast system of mental cheating. In our society, those who have the best knowledge of what is happening are also those who are furthest from seeing the world as it is. In general, the greater the understanding, the greater the delusion: the more intelligent, the less sane.

PRÉCIS

As Orwell observed in Nineteen Eighty-Four, it is the inventors of doublethink who are best at using their brand of "mental cheating." In modern times, he contends, even the best-informed do not see realities; generally speaking, "the greater the understanding, the greater the delusion: the more intelligent, the less sane" (216).

■ **Exercise 3** Carefully read paragraphs 1 (page 347) and 20 (page 359) in Section 31. First write a paraphrase of one of these paragraphs. Then write a précis of the same paragraph. Unless you are quoting directly, avoid using the sentence patterns of the source. To convey the ideas in the source exactly, choose your words carefully.

PLAGIARISM

You must acknowledge all material quoted, paraphrased, or summarized from any work. If you fail to cite a source, whether deliberately or accidentally, you are guilty of plagiarism—of presenting as your own work the words or ideas of another. As the most recent edition of the *MLA Handbook* (New York: Modern Language Assn., 1984) states:

> The most blatant form of plagiarism is to repeat as your own someone else's sentences, more or less verbatim. . . . Other forms of plagiarism include repeating someone else's particularly apt phrase without appropriate acknowledg-

ment, paraphrasing another person's argument as your own, and presenting another's line of thinking as though it were your own. (sec. 1.6)

After you have done a good deal of reading about a given subject, you will be able to distinguish between common knowledge in that field—facts, dates, and figures—and the distinctive ideas or interpretations of specific writers. When you use the ideas or information that these writers provide, be sure to cite the exact source of the material used.

NOT In *Nineteen Eighty-Four*, doublethink is defined as the power of holding two contradictory beliefs in one's mind simultaneously, and accepting both of them. [undocumented copying]

BUT In *Nineteen Eighty-Four*, Orwell defines doublethink as "the power of holding two contradictory beliefs in one's mind simultaneously, and accepting both of them" (215). [Quotation marks enclose copied words, and the page number in parentheses cites the source.]

NOT In fact, *Nineteen Eighty-Four* is Orwell's most ferocious propaganda. [an undocumented idea from the work of another writer]

BUT In fact, *Nineteen Eighty-Four* has been called Orwell's most ferocious propaganda (Voorhees 87).

OR

In fact, Richard J. Voorhees states: "*Nineteen Eighty-Four* is his [Orwell's] fiercest piece of propaganda" (87).

If you are in doubt about whether you need to cite a source, the best policy is to cite it.

33f

Using the outline, the bibliography cards, and the notes, write a properly documented research paper.

After you have made your outline as complete as possible and have taken notes on major headings and subheadings of the outline, you are ready to begin writing. Arrange your notes in the order of the outline, and then use them as the basis of your paper. Naturally you will need to expand some parts and to cut others, and you will need to provide transitional sentences—sometimes even transitional paragraphs. Write the material in the best way you can—in your own style, in your own words.

(1) Citations

Since the material in your research paper comes largely from the work of others, you will need to give proper credit by citing your sources. Traditionally, such citations took the form of notes numbered consecutively throughout the paper and placed either at the bottoms of the appropriate pages (footnotes) or all together at the end of the paper (endnotes). Beginning in 1984, however, the practice recommended by the Modern Language Association is to place citations of sources directly in the text, in parentheses. Numbered notes are now used only for supplementary or explanatory comments (as in note 1 on page 487). Parenthetical citations refer the reader to a list of works cited at the end of the paper.

The basic elements of the citation are the author's last name, a shortened but easily understood form of the title (with, if necessary, the volume number), and the page number of the material used from the source. However, only enough information to guide the reader to the appropriate source is necessary. In other words, the author's name and the title of the source can be omitted from the parenthetical citation if they are clearly identified outside the parentheses in the text of the paper. Further, if only one work by a given author is listed in "Works Cited," the work's title can be omitted from the parenthetical citation. As you study the following examples, observe that common sense rather than hard and fast rules determines the information that must be included in a parenthetical citation.

A work by one author

The following examples from the research paper on pages 476-511 provide sufficient information to refer readers to the appropriate pages of the works listed alphabetically in the list of works cited at the end of the paper.

> Nineteen Eighty-Four has been called George Orwell's most ferocious propaganda (Voorhees 87). Orwell was quick to admit that he was a propagandist. In fact, in 1940, during a BBC radio broadcast, he said that "every artist is a propagandist in the sense that he is trying, directly or indirectly, to impose a vision of life that seems to him desirable" (Essays 2: 41).

In the first citation, the author is not identified in the text and his name therefore appears within parentheses. Because only one work by Voorhees is included in the list of works cited, there is no need to use the title in the parentheses. However, the reference to a specific passage and not to the Voorhees work as a whole requires citing the page number.

In the second citation, Orwell has been identified in the text of the paper as the source of the quotation and need not be named in the citation. However, since Orwell is the author of three works appearing in the list of works cited, the title (shortened) is necessary. Further, because this work comprises four volumes, the volume number must be given as well as the specific page of the quotation.

Both citations supply only the information the reader needs to identify the source, but suppose the opening sentence were worded differently, as in the following example. Notice the information that must change for the citations to be complete.

> Nineteen Eighty-Four--unquestionably a work of art--supports the argument that "every artist is a propagandist in the sense that he is trying, directly or indirectly, to impose a vision of life that to him seems desirable" (Orwell, Essays 2: 41). The critic Richard Voorhees has called the novel Orwell's most ferocious propaganda (87), suggesting that Orwell believed in the forceful if indirect imposition of his own values.

Observe that although the same sources as before are cited, Orwell must now be identified as the author of the direct quotation, and Voorhees, now named in the actual text of the second sentence, needs no further mention in the citation.

Suppose that the text of the first sentence of this example had been written differently and provided additional information about the source, as in the following version.

> In the second volume of his Collected Essays, Orwell suggests that "every artist is a propagandist in the sense that he is trying,

```
directly or indirectly, to impose a vision of life
that to him seems desirable" (41).
```

Because author, title, and volume are clear from the context, the citation is simply a page number.

A work by two authors

```
By cleverly manipulating carefully selected facts,
propagandists today either ignore or downplay any
evidence that might effectively refute their one-
sided arguments--the old card-stacking trick
(Cantril and Hart).
```

Both authors are included in the parenthetical citation. Note, incidentally, that this citation of an encyclopedia article does not require a page reference, since encyclopedias are arranged alphabetically and a reader would have no trouble locating the source.

A work by three authors

If you are citing a source by three authors, supply the names of all three.

```
During the 1960s, economic failure was widely
blamed for social alienation and political
extremism (Aiken, Ferman, and Sheppard).
```

The absence of a page number in this citation indicates that the reference is to an entire work rather than to a specific passage.

More than three authors

If you are citing a source by more than three authors, supply the name of the first author and follow the name with *et al.*, the Latin abbreviation for "and others."

```
These arguments have occasionally been challenged
by leading historians (Bailyn et al.).
```

Works by different authors with the same last name

Occasionally your list of works cited will contain sources by two authors with the same last name—for example, Joan Johnson and Jerome Johnson (imaginary sources included here only for illustration). In such cases, whenever mention of an author's name is required, you must use the first name as well as the last.

```
At least one critic has observed that Orwell became
less bitter as he grew older (Joan Johnson 14-16).
```

```
The critic Joan Johnson has suggested that "with
age, Orwell became increasingly optimistic" (14-
16). However, others have disagreed strongly
(Jerome Johnson 286, 291).
```

Notice also in these examples the treatment of references to more than one page: 14-16 identifies continuous pages; 286, 291 indicates that the reference is to two separate pages.

Poetry, drama, and the Bible

When you refer to poetry, drama, and the Bible, you must often give numbers of lines, acts, and scenes, or of chapters and verses, rather than page numbers. This practice enables a reader to consult an edition other than the one you are using. Nonetheless, your list of works cited should still identify your edition.

Act, scene, and line numbers (all Arabic) are separated by periods with no space before or after them. Biblical chapters and verses are treated similarly. In both cases, the progression is from larger to smaller units.

The following example illustrates a typical citation of lines of poetry.

```
Emily Dickinson concludes "I'm Nobody! Who Are
You?" with a characteristically bittersweet stanza:
     How dreary to be somebody!
     How public, like a frog
     To tell your name the livelong June
     To an admiring bog! (5-8)
```

The following citation shows that Hamlet's "To be, or not to be" soliloquy appears in Act 3, Scene 1, lines 56-89 of *Hamlet*.

```
In Hamlet Shakespeare presents the most famous
soliloquy in the history of the theatre: "To be, or
not to be . . ." (3.1.56-89).
```

The following reference to the Bible indicates that the account of creation in Genesis extends from chapter 1, verse 1, through chapter 2, verse 22.

```
The Old Testament creation story (Gen. 1.1-2.22),
told with remarkable economy, culminates in the
arrival of Eve.
```

Notice that names of books of the Bible are neither underlined (italicized) nor enclosed in quotation marks and that abbreviation is desirable.

Punctuation and mechanics

Notice finally that in all the foregoing citations, punctuation is minimal. Commas are used to separate authors' names and titles (Orwell, *Essays*) and to indicate interruptions in a sequence of pages or lines (44, 47). Hyphens are used to indicate continuous sequences of pages (44–47) and lines (1–4). Colons separate volume and page numbers (*Essays* 2: 41). A space follows the colon. Periods separate acts, scenes, and lines in drama (3.1.56–89) and chapters and verses in the Bible (Gen. 1.1).

Citations should, wherever possible, appear just before punctuation in the text of the paper.

```
Joan Johnson has suggested that Orwell became less
bitter as he grew older (14-16), but Jerome Johnson
takes issue with this suggestion and argues that
the author's pessimism expanded from "personal
complaint to global despair" (286).
```

Joan Johnson's citation falls just before a comma, Jerome Johnson's just before a period. However, in the following sentence the citations cannot precede punctuation.

```
Joan Johnson (14-16) and Jerome Johnson (286, 291)
disagree over Orwell's gradually brightening
outlook.
```

In quotations set off from the text (see section **16a**), citations follow the final punctuation.

As Ralph A. Ranald has observed,

> Orwell's <u>1984</u> is about religion reversed, and above all, language reversed: not simply corrupt, but reversed. . . . [Orwell converts] all the positives of Western civilization into their negatives. (544–45)

Citations in APA style

In APA style (as in MLA style) parenthetical citations are used. The basic elements of APA citations are the author's last name, the year of publication, and the page number if the reference is to be a specific passage in the source. If the author's name is mentioned in the text of the paper, the date alone or the date and the page number are given within the parentheses. In the following examples, note the details of punctuation and the treatment of the page number.

Short quotation

One writer has stated, "Prisons can be divided into specific social groups organized by type of crime" (Liptz, 1979, p. 235), an observation with which many criminologists agree.

Long quotation (four lines or more)

Liptz (1979) has stated the following:

> Prisons can be divided into specific social groups organized by types of crime. Social

structures reflecting theft, arson, white-collar crime, and so on, were discovered within the prison walls. (p. 235)

Paraphrase

Liptz (1979) discovered that the social groups established by prisoners within a prison are organized according to the type of crime. For example, thieves tend to congregate and so do arsonists. (p. 235)

Notice that an APA citation never uses the title. The reader can easily find the title, however, by checking the references to find the entry with the same author and date.

(2) Final list of works cited or references

When you are ready to make your final revision, you will know which works from your preliminary bibliography you cite in your paper. Now eliminate the bibliography cards for the works that you do not cite, and arrange the remaining cards in alphabetical order by authors' last names. You are now ready to prepare the list of "Works Cited" or "References" that will conclude your paper. As you make your final revision, you will be checking your citations against this list to ensure that they are complete and correct.

The list of works cited or references is arranged alphabetically by author and is double-spaced throughout. In MLA style, the first line of each entry is flush with the left margin; subsequent lines are indented five spaces. If you use more than one work by the same author, list the works alphabetically by title. Give the author's name with the first title, but substitute three hyphens for the name in subsequent entries.

MLA style

Thomas, Lewis. The Lives of a Cell: Notes of a Biology Watcher. New York: Viking, 1975.

---. The Medusa and the Snail: More Notes of a Biology Watcher. New York: Viking, 1979.

APA style

If you use more than one work by the same author, list the works in order of publication date, earliest first. Repeat the author's name for each entry. The first line of each entry is flush with the left margin, and subsequent lines are indented three spaces.

Thomas, L. (1974). The lives of a cell: Notes of a biology watcher. New York: Viking.

Thomas, L. (1979). The medusa and the snail: More notes of a biology watcher. New York: Viking.

(3) Final outline

The content of your outline should have been developing steadily throughout your note-taking and writing of the paper, and you should now be ready to prepare a final copy. Before you do, however, correlate the ideas in your outline with those in your text, and make any needed revisions. Also check the form of your outline: see **33d**, pages 448-51. As you study the sample research paper on pages 476-511, notice that the arrangement of paragraphs accords with that of the divisions of the sentence outline below.

OUTLINE

Title: Big Brother's Propaganda

¶1 Introduction: In Ninteen Eighty-Four, Orwell (a propagandist) satirizes totalitarian propaganda as he presents his vision of life-- in reverse.

2 Thesis: Big Brother disseminates the most dangerous kind of propaganda.

I. The Oceanians are propaganda targets.

3 A. They act like a stupid herd.

4 B. They revere a mythical leader.

5 C. They accept the hierarchy in a "classless" society.

II. Big Brother's bureaucracy serves as a propaganda machine.

6 A. Its very housing is a symbol.

7 B. Its parts are interrelated.

III. Big Brother has complete control of the media.

8 A. He supplies all materials.

9 B. He propagates the Party's ideal.

IV. The State falsifies history.

10-11 A. The purpose is to control the past and make it fit the present.

B. The method is efficient.

12 1. Winston uses the memory hole.

13 2. Clerks "rectify" old propaganda.

14 C. The systematic attack on the past is frightening.

V. Totalitarian propaganda manipulates thought and emotion.

15 A. The state uses Newspeak to prevent thought.

16 B. Love and hate are state-controlled.

17 1. One must love Big Brother.

18 2. One must hate his enemies.

19-20 Conclusion: Much of Big Brother's propaganda is outdated, but *Nineteen Eighty-Four* is still widely read as a warning.

The outline serves primarily as a guide to writing an organized and carefully developed composition; but it can also serve, when submitted in its final state along with the finished paper, as a kind of table of contents.

(4) Final revision and proofreading

After writing and carefully documenting the first draft of your paper, make needed revisions. To make your writing as clear and effective as possible, you will probably need to rewrite some sentences, and strike out or add others. Use the Reviser's Checklist on page 414. (You may wish to review pages 405-15 of Section **32**.) Refer to **8b** as you put your paper in final form. Even when writing final copy, you will probably continue to make changes in phraseology and to correct occasional errors in spelling, mechanics, or grammar. Type or write legibly. Proofread your final revision before handing it in, using the Proofreader's Checklist on page 102.

Sample Research Paper

On pages 476-511 is a completed sample research paper whose format conforms to the new MLA (1984) guidelines. For purposes of comparison, the pages facing those of the paper contain not only selected passages from the sources but also note cards used in preparing the paper. Comments on content and form are also provided.

Note: MLA guidelines recommend the use of a title page for theses, dissertations, and books, but not for research papers. However, if you are asked to submit a separate title page and/or a formal outline along with the text of your paper, refer to the guidelines on the next four pages (472-75). Otherwise, proceed directly to page 476.

■ **Exercise 4** Prepare for a class discussion of the strengths and weaknesses of the following research paper. Give special attention to form (including whether or not a title page and outline will be used), content, organization, and documentation. Notice, as you read, how Tracy Monahan credits other authors.

COMMENTS

1. *Title page*. The title page usually gives the title of the paper, centred above the middle, with the first letter of key words capitalized (see **9c**). Place in the lower right-hand corner, with appropriate marginal spacing, your name as author, the name of the course and its section number, the instructor's name (optional), and the date (see also **8b**). Apart from the title itself, another option for this supplementary information is to centre each line of it, with appropriate spacing, on the lower half of the page.
2. *Final outline*. The final outline serves as a table of contents. If the outline occupies only one page, it is not numbered. In outlines occupying more than one page, all pages after the first are numbered with small Roman numerals in the upper right-hand corner of the page. Note that the following outline (pages 474-75) is a topic outline. If your instructor specifies a sentence outline, see the sample one on pages 469-70.
3. *Text of the paper*. The title of the paper is omitted from the first page of the text when a title page is used. Also, the first page is not numbered. All pages after the first are numbered with Arabic numerals in the upper right-hand corner of the page.

Big Brother's Propaganda

Tracy Monahan

English 131, Section 3

Professor Richards

March 12, 1985

Outline

Thesis: Big Brother disseminates the most dangerous kind of propaganda.

Introduction: In Nineteen Eighty-Four, Orwell (a propagandist) satirizes totalitarian propaganda as he presents his vision of life--in reverse.

I. The propagandized Oceanians

A. Their loss of individuality

B. Their reverence for Big Brother

C. Their use of doublethink

II. The bureaucratic propaganda machine

A. Its housing--symbolic

B. Its parts--interrelated

III. The media in a totalitarian world

A. All materials supplied

B. The Party's ideal propagated

ii

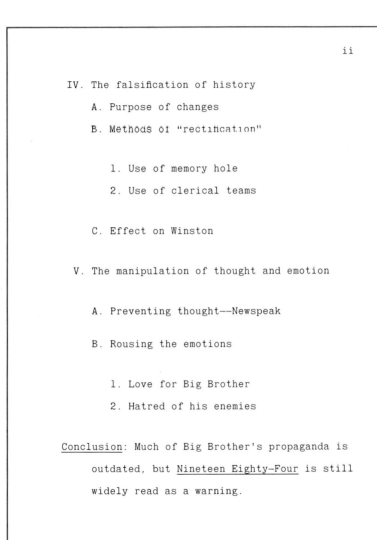

IV. The falsification of history

A. Purpose of changes

B. Methods of "rectification"

1. Use of memory hole

2. Use of clerical teams

C. Effect on Winston

V. The manipulation of thought and emotion

A. Preventing thought--Newspeak

B. Rousing the emotions

1. Love for Big Brother

2. Hatred of his enemies

Conclusion: Much of Big Brother's propaganda is outdated, but Nineteen Eighty-Four is still widely read as a warning.

Research Paper—New MLA (1984) format
COMMENTS

Using the new MLA (1984) format, this example of the research paper, with no separate title page and no outline included, consists of three parts:

1. *Text of the paper*. The identification (name, course, instructor's name, date), double spaced, begins 2.5 cm (one inch) from the top of the page and flush with the left margin. A double space precedes the title of the paper. A margin of about 2.5 cm is provided at the left, right, and bottom.

   Four spaces separate the centred title from the first line of the text. A title consisting of two or more lines is double-spaced, and each line is centred.

   All pages (including the first page) are numbered with Arabic numerals in the upper right-hand corner, about 1.5 cm (one half inch) from the top and 2.5 cm from the right. Notice that no period follows page numbers.

   In accordance with MLA style, quotations of more than four lines are indented ten spaces on the left only and are double-spaced. If the quotation consists of two or more paragraphs, indent the first line of each complete paragraph an additional three spaces.
2. *Notes*. Since references to works cited are given in parentheses in the text, numbered notes are now used to provide additional commentary or supplementary information. The notes begin on a new page, following the text and preceding the list of works cited. The page is numbered consecutively with the text pages. Superscript numbers in the body of the text signal the reader to refer to the notes page. See pages 487 and 507.
3. *Works cited*. The list of works cited begins on a new page, which is numbered consecutively with the text and notes pages.

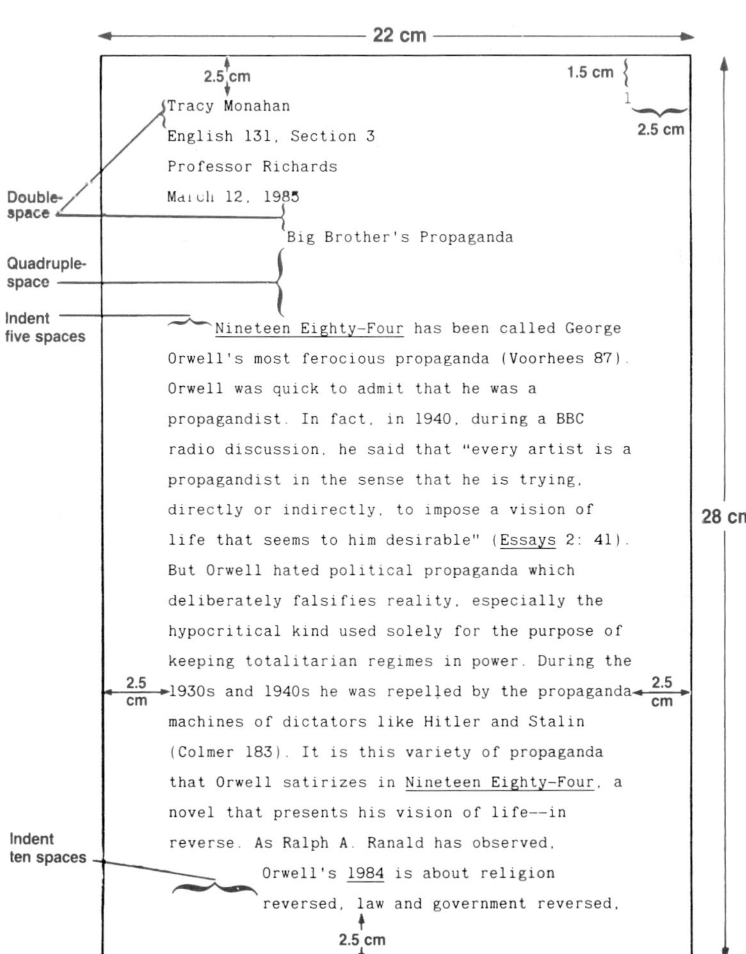

Tracy Monahan

English 131, Section 3

Professor Richards

March 12, 1985

Big Brother's Propaganda

Nineteen Eighty-Four has been called George Orwell's most ferocious propaganda (Voorhees 87). Orwell was quick to admit that he was a propagandist. In fact, in 1940, during a BBC radio discussion, he said that "every artist is a propagandist in the sense that he is trying, directly or indirectly, to impose a vision of life that seems to him desirable" (Essays 2: 41). But Orwell hated political propaganda which deliberately falsifies reality, especially the hypocritical kind used solely for the purpose of keeping totalitarian regimes in power. During the 1930s and 1940s he was repelled by the propaganda machines of dictators like Hitler and Stalin (Colmer 183). It is this variety of propaganda that Orwell satirizes in Nineteen Eighty-Four, a novel that presents his vision of life--in reverse. As Ralph A. Ranald has observed,

> Orwell's 1984 is about religion reversed, law and government reversed,

COMMENTS

1. Paragraph 1 is the introduction. (Recall that if a separate title page has been required, the first page of text will omit the page number, identification, and title.)
2. The Voorhees and Colmer citations credit the sources of ideas; the *Essays* citation credits the source of the quoted passage. See the list of works cited on pages 509 and 511.
3. Observe the way direct quotations are made an integral part of the text. The first one is introduced by *that*, the second by an introductory clause followed by a comma.
4. On the title page of the hard-cover edition of Orwell's novel is *Nineteen Eighty-Four*. On the title page of the Signet paperback edition is *1984*, the form used by Ralph Ranald and copied exactly by Tracy Monahan.

SOURCE

For Orwell quotation:

> ORWELL: "I have always maintained that every artist is a propagandist. I don't mean a political propagandist. If he has any honesty or talent at all he cannot be that. Most political propaganda is a matter of telling lies, not only about the facts but about your own feelings. But every artist is a propagandist in the sense that he is trying, directly or indirectly, to impose a vision of life that seems to him desirable. I think that we are broadly agreed about the vision of life that proletarian literature is trying to impose."

1

Tracy Monahan

English 131, Section 3

Professor Richards

March 12, 1985

Big Brother's Propaganda

1 Nineteen Eighty-Four has been called George Orwell's most ferocious propaganda (Voorhees 87). Orwell was quick to admit that he was a propagandist. In fact, in 1940, during a BBC radio discussion, he said that "every artist is a propagandist in the sense that he is trying, directly or indirectly, to impose a vision of life that seems to him desirable" (Essays 2: 41). But Orwell hated political propaganda which deliberately falsifies reality, especially the hypocritical kind used solely for the purpose of keeping totalitarian regimes in power. During the 1930s and 1940s he was repelled by the propaganda machines of dictators like Hitler and Stalin (Colmer 183). It is this variety of propaganda that Orwell satirizes in Nineteen Eighty-Four, a novel that presents his vision of life--in reverse. As Ralph A. Ranald has observed,

> Orwell's 1984 is about religion reversed, law and government reversed,

COMMENTS

1. All pages after the first page give a shortened form of the author's name (usually the last name preceded by an initial) and the page number. This information is placed in the upper right-hand corner, about 1.5 cm from the top and 2.5 cm from the right.
2. Paragraph 2 states the thesis, or central idea. Paragraph 3 begins the discussion of point I of the outline: The propagandized Oceanians.
3. In the indented quotation (over four lines in length), the interpolation in brackets supplies a subject and verb to complete the shortened sentence. See also **17g**. Notice that the citation follows the final punctuation of a quotation set off from the text.
4. Notice that the punctuation before the first ellipsis mark is retained to insure clarity. See also **17i**.

SOURCE

For Ranald quotation:

> Orwell's *1984* is about religion reversed, law and government reversed, and above all, language reversed: not simply corrupted, but reversed. In the mad world of *1984*, the mad world which Orwell sought by his writing to lead men to *avoid*—for he was a political activist not interested in simple prediction—in this world, which I call Orwell's "antiuniverse," because of his conversion of all the positives of Western civilization into their negatives, all the channels of communication are systematically being closed down, restricted to just the minimums necessary for the technical functioning of society.

> and above all, language reversed: not simply corrupted, but reversed. In the world of 1984, the mad world which Orwell sought by his writing to lead men to avoid—for he was a political activist not interested in simple prediction—in this world, which I call Orwell's "antiuniverse," . . . [Orwell converts] all the positives of Western civilization into their negatives. (544–45)

And in Orwell's crazy world, it is Big Brother's political propaganda that helps to sustain and perpetuate this reversal of values.

2 To control society, to sustain the awesome power of the State, Big Brother uses what Oliver Thompson calls the most dangerous kind of propaganda: a "steady drip, drip" of toxic, power-oriented ideas not recognized as propaganda. These ideas pollute the environment and saturate all art forms. Such propaganda deadens the awareness of its targets (132).

3 Big Brother is always watching, and his hypnotic eyes have cast a spell over the inhabitants of Oceania. Thoroughly propagandized,

COMMENTS

1. Paragraphs 4 and 5 continue point I of the outline.
2. As you read the source (below) for the last sentence of paragraph 4, observe how Tracy Monahan has combined paraphrase and direct quotation.

SOURCE

Nineteen Eighty-Four (209)

> Given this background, one could infer, if one did not know it already, the general structure of Oceanic society. At the apex of the pyramid comes Big Brother. Big Brother is infallible and all-powerful. Every success, every achievement, every victory, every scientific discovery, all knowledge, all wisdom, all happiness, all virtue, are held to issue directly from his leadership and inspiration. Nobody has ever seen Big Brother. He is a face on the hoardings, a voice on the telescreen. We may be reasonably sure that he will never die, and there is already considerable uncertainty as to when he was born. Big Brother is the guise in which the Party chooses to exhibit itself to the world. His function is to act as a focusing point for love, fear, and reverence, emotions which are more easily felt toward an individual than toward an organization.

T. Monahan 3

they act like a stupid herd. They mechanically respond to every command, no matter how illogical it is. If any person dares to act or even think like an independent human being, Big Brother resorts to liquidation or re-education. Such an individual either becomes an "unperson," one who has never existed, or a reprogramed android, one who again loves and serves the State.

4 Ironically enough, the Oceanians have never seen Big Brother--just big pictures of him. In fact, Big Brother does not exist. He is the mythical Leader so often created by propagandists. His image is projected by the Inner Party to maintain its ruling powers. Propaganda depicts Big Brother as a deity. He is omnipresent, omniscient, and omnipotent in the world of Nineteen Eighty-Four: "Every success, every achievement, every victory, every scientific discovery, all knowledge, all wisdom, all happiness, all virtue, are held to issue directly from his leadership and inspiration" (209).

5 Oceanians are programed in the art of doublethink, which the novel defines as "the power of holding two contradictory beliefs in

COMMENT

Paragraph 6 begins point II of the outline: The bureaucratic propaganda machine.

BIBLIOGRAPHY CARD FOR THOMSON

Thomson, Oliver. Mass Persuasion in History. New York: Crane, 1977.

NOTE CARD USED FOR PARAGRAPH 6

Big Brother's pyramidal power structure
(Thomson 41)

T. thinks architecture is an important propagandist medium that people don't pay much attention to.

a building can be "graphic communication."
Can inspire awe and power—with long-term impact.

". . . the pyramids projected the massive dominance of the Pharaohs."

T. Monahan 4

one's mind simultaneously, and accepting both of them" (215). The Oceanians, not aware of their loss of human rights, firmly believe that everybody is equal in their society, but they serve their king and accept the State's rigid hierarchy. The pyramidal power structure is the natural order of things in their classless society. Naturally, Big Brother sits on top of the pyramid; he represents the Inner Party, less than 2 per cent of society. Just below him or them is the Outer Party, the bureaucratic toadies, about 13 per cent. At the base of the pyramid are the proles--"the dumb masses" (209)--about 85 per cent.

6 Big Brother's bureaucracy consists of four ministries. These ministries are housed in huge white buildings, enormous pyramidal structures dominating London, the capital of Airstrip One, a province of Oceania. These towers contrast sharply with the run-down stores and shabby houses of the rest of the city. The very architecture of Big Brother's government buildings is an important propagandistic symbol because it is a "graphic communication" of awesomeness. Like the great Egyptian pyramids, they project a political image of massive, lasting power (Thomson 41).

COMMENTS

1. The discussion of point II continues. Paragraph 8 turns to point III: The media in a totalitarian world.

2. In paragraphs 7 and 8, Tracy Monahan uses superscript numbers to refer readers to endnotes that supply additional information.

3. In paragraph 8, the use of such phrases as "According to Richard S. Lambert," "knows *this*," and "Jacques Ellul writes" helps make direct quotations fit smoothly into the text.

NOTE CARD

Notice below that Tracy Monahan's own ideas are placed in brackets.

Propaganda machine

Thomson, 7 TYPES OF PROPAGANDA listed. [Five seem closely related to Big Brother's machine.]

11 political – rhetoric, subtle images
economic – promotes confidence in economy

12 war/military – concerned with morale. Uses war films, military music, etc.
ideological – "spread of complete idea systems"

12-13 escapist – media entertainment distracts, gets "social acquiescence"

[Relate this to the proles?]

T. Monahan 5

7 All four ministries are active, interrelated parts of Big Brother's massive propaganda machine. For example, they work together when grinding out materials for Hate Week. Each cog, however, has its particular job to do. The Ministry of Plenty (Miniplenty), specializes in economic propaganda; the Ministry of Peace (Minipax) in the military type. The Ministry of Love (Miniluv) reinforces or intensifies ideologic propaganda.[1] Perhaps the biggest, most responsible cog in the machine, however, is the Ministry of Truth (Minitrue). Minitrue--with its slogans WAR IS PEACE, FREEDOM IS SLAVERY, IGNORANCE IS STRENGTH--not only produces political images and rhetoric in accordance with Big Brother's input but also co-ordinates and edits the propagandistic output of Miniplenty and Minipax. The huge machine never stops its propagandizing, and its perpetual, continuous noise has a mesmerizing effect on the whole society.

8 According to Richard S. Lambert, the internal propaganda of a totalitarian government "seeks to impose complete uniformity of thought, as well as of action, upon its citizens" (138).[2] All-wise Big Brother knows this. "Where film

COMMENTS

As a rule, a comma or a colon precedes an introduced quotation. Examples from the paper:

¶1 `As Ralph A. Ranald has observed,`

¶4 `He is . . . omnipotent:`

In paragraph 8, however, are two illustrations of a different way to make a quotation an integral part of the text. Notice that the first indented quotation provides an object for the preposition *with*; the second, an object for the verb *supplies*.

Read the source, and notice the way Tracy Monahan combines paraphrase with quotation.

SOURCE

Nineteen Eighty-Four (43-44)

> And the Records Department, after all, was itself only a single branch of the Ministry of Truth, whose primary job was not to reconstruct the past but to supply the citizens of Oceania with newspapers, films, textbooks, telescreen programs, plays, novels—with every conceivable kind of information, instruction, or entertainment, from a statue to a slogan, from a lyric poem to a biological treatise and from a child's spelling book to a Newspeak dictionary. And the Ministry had not only to supply the multifarious needs of the Party, but also to repeat the whole operation at a lower level for the benefit of the proletariat. There was a whole chain of separate departments dealing with proletarian literature, music, drama, and entertainment generally. Here were produced rubbishy newspapers containing almost nothing except sport, crime, and astrology, sensational five-cent novelettes, films oozing with sex, and sentimental songs which were composed entirely by mechanical means on a special kind of kaleidoscope known as a versificator.

T. Monahan 6

production, the press, and radio transmission are not centrally controlled," Jacques Ellul writes, "no propaganda is possible" (102). Big Brother knows this too. In fact, he harnesses every channel of communication, holding tight reins on the Party specialists who run the Ministry of Truth. Minitrue provides Oceanic society with all its

> newspapers, films, textbooks, telescreen programs, plays, novels--with every conceivable kind of information, instruction, or entertainment, from a statue to a slogan, from a lyric poem to a biological treatise, and from a child's spelling book to a Newspeak dictionary. (Nineteen Eighty-Four 43-44)

Those outside the Party--the proles--have such limited intelligence that Big Brother has to adapt his communication to their level. For their benefit, Minitrue supplies

> rubbishy newspapers containing almost nothing except sport, crime, and astrology, sensational five-cent novelettes, films oozing with sex, and sentimental songs which were composed

COMMENTS

1. Observe Tracy Monahan's use of repetition as a transitional device in paragraph 9. The introduction to the long quotation ends with "the Party's ideal," and the quotation begins with "The ideal set up by the Party."
2. Paragraph 9 discusses point III(B) of the outline: Big Brother's use of the media to propagate the Party's ideal.

T. Monahan 7

> entirely by mechanical means on a special kind of kaleidoscope known as a versificator. (44)

This kind of escapist material, along with the state lottery and numerous pubs, not only contributes to the contentment of the proles but also keeps their minds busy with things other than the impact of power politics on their lives.

9 Big Brother uses the media for mass hypnosis. He disseminates misinformation (largely lies but a number of selected, twisted truths) that goes unrecognized as propaganda. His propaganda preaches only one gospel: the Party's ideal.

> The ideal set up by the Party was something huge, terrible, and glittering--a world of steel and concrete, of monstrous machines and terrifying weapons--a nation of warriors and fanatics, marching forward in perfect unity, all thinking the same thoughts and shouting the same slogans, perpetually working, fighting, triumphing, persecuting--three hundred million people all with the same face. (74)

COMMENTS

1. Paragraphs 10–14 develop point IV of the outline: The falsification of history. Observe the unified flow of Tracy Monahan's ideas as you read these paragraphs, paying special attention to the selection and arrangement of the three quotations, the first and third from Orwell, the second from Zwerdling.
2. Reread paragraphs 10–14 and carefully observe interrelations, a few of which are connected by arrows on page 494.

T. Monahan 8

With the exception of a few characters like the lovers Winston and Julia, the doublethinkers of Oceania parrot the media's message; and, putting no gods before Big Brother, they--as one body--live their religion.

10 Orwell considered "the disappearance of objective history and the willingness of individuals to work toward its elimination" as the "most frightening propagandistic achievement of the twentieth century" (Zwerdling 52). In _Nineteen Eighty-Four_, the work of the Records Department in Minitrue is the control of history. A Party slogan declares: "Who controls the past controls the future: who controls the present controls the past" (35). Always tampering with records, Big Brother distorts, recreates, or destroys the past. As Zwerdling has noted:

> No matter how intolerable the present is, the sense of alternative possibilities that objective history inevitably presents can still liberate the imagination and perhaps lead to significant change. But once the past

IV. The falsification of history

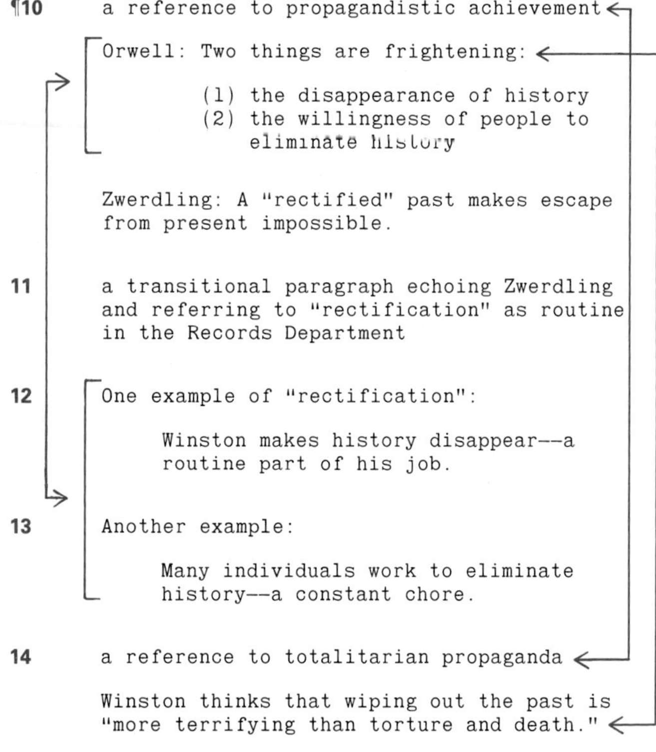

¶10 a reference to propagandistic achievement

Orwell: Two things are frightening:

(1) the disappearance of history
(2) the willingness of people to eliminate history

Zwerdling: A "rectified" past makes escape from present impossible.

11 a transitional paragraph echoing Zwerdling and referring to "rectification" as routine in the Records Department

12 One example of "rectification":

Winston makes history disappear—a routine part of his job.

13 Another example:

Many individuals work to eliminate history—a constant chore.

14 a reference to totalitarian propaganda

Winston thinks that wiping out the past is "more terrifying than torture and death."

Even Winston's thought may remind the reader of what Zwerdling said. Why this analogy? Does Winston sense, like Zwerdling, that no escape is possible except torture and death?

T. Monahan 9

> is perpetually "rectified" to
> conform to the present, this escape
> is no longer possible. (53)

11 Thousands working in the Records Department look upon such "rectification" as daily routine. This department falsifies the past to make it fit changes in present government policies.

12 False promises must be changed to suit present conditions. A clerk at the Speakwrite machine, Winston Smith "rectifies" materials sent to him through a pneumatic tube. Proficient in Newspeak (the official language), he reads a message: "times 14. 2. 84 miniplenty malquoted chocolate rectify" (39). Winston dials on the telescreen for the copy of the <u>Times</u> (February 14, 1984) that carries Miniplenty's promise not to reduce the chocolate ration in 1984. He changes the optimistic promise to a pessimistic prediction: rationing may be necessary in April. He returns the altered version for filing and destroys the original by putting it into the memory hole, a kind of incinerator for irrelevant history, outdated information about vaporized persons, and other trash.

COMMENT

"As might be expected" at the beginning of paragraph 15 provides the transition from point IV to point V. Paragraph 15 covers point V(A): Newspeak as a thought preventive.

T. Monahan 10

13 It is the state's policy to be in a constant state of war either with Eurasia or with Eastasia. Yet the Party insists that the present enemy has always been the enemy. When roles are reversed, the former enemy has never been an enemy but always an ally. Record clerks work frantically to make expedient changes in mountains of references to Eurasia and Eastasia. Minipax's military propaganda must constantly be "rectified" to protect the vital interest of the State: maintenance of power.

14 Eventually, Winston's experiences teach him to recognize totalitarian propaganda for what it is. Very disturbed by the systematic attack on the past, he thinks: "If the Party could thrust its hand into the past and say of this or that event, _it never happened_--that, surely, was more terrifying than torture and death" (35).

15 As might be expected, Big Brother manipulates language to suit his purpose. His aim is to destroy words--the material for expressing ideas--and to eventually wipe out completely the necessity for thought. The words in Newspeak are formed in various ways: for example, by compounding (_thought-crime_, _duckspeak_,

COMMENTS

1. Four paragraphs (15–18) develop point V of the outline: The manipulation of thought and emotion.
2. Of these, three (16–18) develop parts of the second sub-heading: Rousing the emotions.

NOTE CARDS

Newspeak ②

Steinhoff 166: "Newspeak is the principal intellectual means by which doublethink is transformed into a conditioned reflex."

Newspeak—doublethink ③

Zwerdling 54: from a discussion of schizophrenic thinking in 1984: "an occupational disease of propagandists that is called 'reality control' or 'doublethink.'"

Newspeak ①

In 1984— 51 AND the appendix— aim, nature, etc.

Newspeak words—compounding, adding prefixes and suffixes

bellyfeel, prolefeed, Minitrue, Pornosec, facecrime, sexcrime, crimestop, thoughtcrime—ungood, doubleplusgood, goodwise, gooder — duckspeaking

a duckspeaker, a fast talker in love with own voice, keeps quacking on and on.

prolefeed, Minipax) and by adding prefixes or suffixes (ungood, thinkful). Doubleplusgood gets rid of superlatives like best or finest and synonyms like superb or excellent. According to William Steinhoff, Newspeak is "the principal intellectual means by which doublethink is transformed into a conditioned reflex" (166). Doublethink is Big Brother's "reality control" (indeed "the occupational disease of propagandists") (Zwerdling 54). Working in the Research Department as a compiler of the Newspeak dictionary, a clerk remarks that, unlike Oldspeak, the new language has a vocabulary that grows smaller, not larger. He says, "We're destroying words--scores of them, hundreds of them every day. . . . It's a beautiful thing, the destruction of words" (Nineteen Eighty-Four 51-52).

16 Big Brother's propaganda not only straightjackets thought but also manipulates emotions. Doublethinking Oceanians know that unqualified hatred of the State's enemies is a social necessity in their kingdom of love--love for Big Brother. Though living in a police

COMMENT

Note the acknowledgment of sources of ideas that are expressed in paraphrases (rather than in the exact words of the author).

SOURCES

Below are two statements by Irving Howe that are paraphrased in paragraphs 17 and 18. Note the differences between the paraphrases and the originals.

> Oceania seeks to blot out spontaneous affection because it assumes, for good reason, that whatever is uncalculated is subversive. —IRVING HOWE

> For the faithful [in Oceania], sexual energy is transformed into political hysteria. —IRVING HOWE

T. Monahan 12

state and (except for proles) under constant surveillance by Thought Police and Junior Spies, loyal citizens have nothing to fear, for they love their Leader and hate his enemies.

17 Those who love their leader, however, must have no room in their hearts for anyone else. When affection for others rises spontaneously, that love is considered subversive, something to be eliminated (Howe 48). Though necessary for child-bearing, the sex act must be state-controlled. Winston's affair with Julia is a capital offence; the State must purify his heart in Miniluv's torture chambers.

18 Big Brother wisely turns the sex drive into political hysteria (Howe 49). The fanatical Oceanians stand ready to strike terror into the hearts of any enemies. To stimulate hatred, Big Brother not only sets up a mythical Adversary but also uses such propaganda techniques as exciting rituals, stirring military music, barbaric rhythms, noisy rallies, slogan-chanting mobs, rabble-rousing war films, staged hangings. The Two Minute Hate and Hate Week intensify the mood.

COMMENTS

1. The main discussion ends with paragraph 18. The conclusion begins with paragraph 19.
2. Reread the first paragraph of the paper. Notice there the words and ideas that are repeated in paragraph 19. References to the title of Orwell's novel and to the nature of totalitarian propaganda are two examples of repetition. Linking the ideas in the introduction and those in the conclusion contributes to the unity of the paper.

SOURCE

For first sentence of paragraph 20 (a book review):

> Orwell was never very clear about what sort of political system might work, nor was he particularly sophisticated about the peculiarities of *any* political organization. But he knew what he didn't like, and he knew why; the two short novels that emerged from this metamorphosis—*Animal Farm* and *1984*—are probably the most widely read literary/political polemics ever written in English. —ATLANTIC MONTHLY

T. Monahan 13

Like many another propagandist, Big Brother knows the unifying value of hate.

19 In Nineteen Eighty-Four, Orwell uses artistic exaggeration to help make his warning clear.[3] The reader can easily recognize Big Brother's propaganda for what it is--an obvious mixture of absurd lies and gross distortions of truth. Today's propaganda, however, is not always so easily recognized, for it tells the truth--convincing parts of it. By cleverly manipulating carefully selected facts, propagandists today either ignore or downplay any evidence that might effectively refute their one-sided arguments--the old card-stacking trick (Cantril and Hart). Modern propaganda has various names, such as government "publicity," political "advertising," or even official "communication packages." Such propaganda, like Big Brother's, often eulogizes the Leaders, hiding their mistakes and magnifying their successes (Lang 43).

20 It has been said that Orwell's Animal Farm and Nineteen Eighty-Four "are probably the most widely read literary/political polemics ever

T. Monahan 14

written in English" (Transformation 126). Of the two novels, perhaps Nineteen Eighty-Four is more likely to be remembered. It is a kind of nightmare that haunts the memory because its world looks much like our own. Readers of this novel ask questions like these: Was 1984 in 1948? Though 1984 has passed, is it still a possibility for the future? Fortunately, the nightmare has not yet become a reality, but Orwell's dystopic vision continues to challenge complacency:

> For it can be said that, so long as we can talk about 1984 and discuss whether it has come or not, then certainly it has not come: the one thing certain is that when 1984 is actually here and we are living in the kind of world that Orwell described as a warning, we shall be unconscious of it, and the very title of his book, which has become a monitory symbol for us, will have ceased to have any of its present meaning. (Small 21)

COMMENT

Three endnotes provide supplementary information that is not directly related to the thesis but that might be of interest to readers. (See page 459.)

T. Monahan 15

Notes

[1] For a description of seven types of propaganda, see Thomson (11–13).

[2] Lambert also points out that the totalitarian state is more concerned with internal propaganda than with external: "But great as have been the *external* propagandist efforts of the dictator-ruled countries, they are half-hearted an indirect as compared with their *internal* organization" (138).

[3] Orwell also warns us about "veiled censorship" in a free press. See "The Freedom of the Press."

COMMENTS

1. All (and only) works cited as sources in the paper should be included in the list of works cited.
2. Alphabetization: Initial articles (*A, An, The*) are ignored in alphabetizing. For example, Orwell's *The Collected Essays* precedes *Nineteen Eighty-Four* (*C* before *N*).
3. Punctuation: Observe the use and placement of periods and commas, especially in relation to parentheses and quotation marks. A colon separates titles from subtitles.
4. For Cantril and Hart, an encyclopedia article, page numbers are not required.
5. For Colmer, Tracy Monahan copies the title exactly as it is given on the title page of Colmer's book. For the usual treatment of titles within titles, see the Howe entry.

T. Monahan 16

Works Cited

Cantril, Hadley, and Clyde W. Hart. "Propaganda." World Book Encyclopedia. 1975 ed.

Colmer, John. Coleridge to Catch-22: Images of Society. New York: St. Martin's, 1978.

Ellul, Jacques. Propaganda: the Formation of Men's Attitudes. Trans. Konrad Kellen and Jean Lerner. New York: Knopf, 1965.

Howe, Irving. "1984: History as Nightmare." Twentieth Century Interpretations of 1984: A Collection of Critical Essays. Ed. Samuel Hynes. Englewood Cliffs: Prentice, 1971.

Lambert, Richard S. Propaganda. Discussion Books 13. London: Nelson, 1938.

Lang, John S. "The Great American Bureaucratic Propaganda Machine." U.S. News and World Report 27 Aug. 1979: 43-47.

Orwell, George. The Collected Essays, Journalism and Letters of George Orwell. Ed. Sonia Orwell and Ian Angus. 4 vols. New York: Harcourt, 1968.

COMMENTS

1. Annotation: If you are asked to submit an annotated bibliography, supply a brief description of each entry, as in this example:

Spoehr, Luther. Rev. of A People's History of the United States, by Howard Zinn. Saturday Review 2 Feb. 1980:370

Considered a radical historian, Zinn describes a kind of pyramidal power structure (the powerful elite, their servile ''guards,'' and the oppressed underclass) and advocates ''decentralized socialism that will run society from 'the bottom up'.''

2. Note that the anonymous, untitled review of Stansky and Abrahams' book *The Transformation* (cited in paragraph 20 of Tracy Monahan's paper) is alphabetized by the title of the work reviewed: *Transformation*. (The designation *Rev. of* and the article *The* are ignored for alphabetizing.)

T. Monahan 17

---. "The Freedom of the Press." New York Times Magazine 8 Oct. 1972, 12.

---. Ninotoon Eighty Four. New York: Harcourt, 1949.

Ranald, Ralph A. "George Orwell and the Mad World: The Anti-Universe of 1984." South Atlantic Quarterly 66 (1967): 544-53.

Small, Christopher. The Road to Miniluv: George Orwell, the State, and God. Pittsburgh: U of Pittsburgh P, 1975.

Steinhoff, William. George Orwell and the Origins of 1984. Ann Arbor: U of Michigan P, 1975.

Thomson, Oliver. Mass Persuasion in History: An Historical Analysis of the Development of Propaganda Techniques. New York: Crane, 1977.

Rev. of The Transformation, by Peter Stansky and William Abrahams. Atlantic Monthly Apr. 1980: 126-27.

Voorhees, Richard J. The Paradox of George Orwell. Humanities Series. Lafayette: Purdue U Studies, 1961.

Zwerdling, Alex. Orwell and the Left. New Haven: Yale UP, 1974.

Note: Some instructors prefer to receive handwritten rather than typewritten papers. Below is a sample page from a handwritten research paper.

9

"Where film production, the press, and radio transmission are not centrally controlled," writes Jacques Ellul, "no propaganda is possible" (102). Knowing this, Big Brother holds tight reins on the Party specialists who run the Ministry of Truth. Minitrue provides Oceania with all its

> newspapers, films, textbooks, telescreen programs, plays, novels — with every conceivable kind of information, instruction, or entertainment, from a statue to a slogan, from a lyric poem to a biological treatise, and from a child's spelling book to a Newspeak dictionary. (Nineteen Eighty-Four 43-44)

Those outside the Party have such limited intelligence that Big Brother has to adapt his communication to their level. For their benefit, Minitrue supplies "rubbishy newspapers" (44).

Business Writing

34

Write effective business letters and résumés.

Business letters are usually typed on only one side of white, unlined, 21.5 × 28 cm paper. Standard business envelopes measure about 9 cm × 16.5 cm or 10.16 cm × 25.4 cm. (Letterhead stationery and envelopes vary in both size and colour.)

34a

Business Letters

A business letter has six parts: (1) the heading, (2) the inside address, (3) the salutation, (4) the body of the letter, (5) the closing, which consists of the complimentary close and the signature (handwritten and then typed), and (6) any added notations.

BUSINESS LETTER FORMATS

If you work for a company, you should check to see if it has a policy about the format for business letters. Many do. Most companies use one of three styles: full block, modified block, or indented. In full block, the most formal style, all parts of the letter, including the first lines of paragraphs, are flush with the left margin. The model letter on page 517 is in full-block style. In modified-block style, shown in the letter on page 519, the heading and the complimentary close are moved to the right. The indented format (pages 521 and 523) also moves the heading and the closing to the right and uses paragraph indention. This format is the least formal, the most like a personal letter. By and large, businesses or officials use the modified block, whereas individuals use the indented format.

(1) The heading of the letter gives the full address of the writer and the date of the letter.

If letterhead stationery is used, the date is typed beneath it in the centre of the page. If plain stationery is used, the address of the writer followed by the date is put at the top of the page, flush with the right-hand margin, as in the letters on pages 521 and 523. Notice that the heading is blocked and has no end punctuation.

(2) The inside address gives the name and full address of the addressee.

Four to six lines usually separate the heading from the inside address, depending on how much space is needed to centre the body of the letter on the page.

(3) The salutation greets the addressee appropriately.

The salutation is written flush with the left margin, two spaces below the inside address, and is followed by a colon. The salutation should be consistent with the tone of the letter, the first line of the inside address, and the complimentary close.

When the surname of the addressee is known, it is used

in the salutation of a business letter, as in the following examples.

Dear Dr. Davis:
Dear Mrs. Greissman:
Dear Mayor Rodriguez:
Dear Ms. Joseph:

Note: Use *Miss* or *Mrs.* if the woman you are addressing has indicated a preference. Otherwise, use *Ms.*, which is always appropriate and which is preferred by many businesswomen, whatever their marital status.

In letters to organizations, or to persons whose name and sex are unknown, such salutations as the following are customary:

Dear Sir or Madam:
Dear Subscription Manager:
Dear L.L. Bean:
Dear Registrar:

If you do not know the name of the addressee, but you do know the sex, use either *Dear Sir* or *Dear Madam*.

For the appropriate forms of salutations and addresses in letters to government officials, military personnel, and so on, check an etiquette book or the front or back of your college dictionary.

(4) The body of the letter should follow the principles of good writing.

Typewritten letters are usually single-spaced, with double spacing between paragraphs. All paragraphs should begin flush with the left margin (in full block or modified block) or should be indented five to ten spaces (in indented format). The subject matter should be organized so that the reader can grasp immediately what is wanted, and the style should be clear and direct. Do not use stilted or abbreviated phrasing:

NOT "The aforementioned letter" BUT "Your letter"
NOT "Please send me it ASAP" BUT "Please send it to me as soon as possible."

(5) The closing ends the letter.

In full-block style, the closing is typed flush with the left-hand margin. In modified block and indented style, it is typed to the right of the letter, in alignment with the heading. The parts of the closing are as follows:

The complimentary close: This conventional ending is typed three lines below the last paragraph of the body of the letter. Among the endings commonly used in business letters are the following:

FORMAL	LESS FORMAL
Very truly yours,	Sincerely,
Sincerely yours,	Cordially,

The typed name: The name (as it will be written) is typed four lines below the closing.

Title of sender: This line, following the typed name, indicates the sender's position, if he or she is acting in an official capacity.

Manager, Employee Relations
Chairperson, Search Committee

Signature: The letter is signed between the complimentary close and the typed name.

(6) Notations supply additional information.

Notations are typed below the closing, flush with the left margin. They indicate, among other things, whether anything is enclosed with or attached to the letter (*enc.*, *att.*); to whom copies of the letter have been sent (*cc: AAW, PTN*); and the initials of the sender and the typist (*DM/cll*).

MODEL BUSINESS LETTER

CECIL STREET COMMUNITY CENTRE

10 Cecil Street Toronto, Ontario M5T 2B5

February 1, 1985

Dr. Nathan T. Swift
Community Health Centre
1420 College Street
Toronto, Ont.
M6G 2L6

INSIDE ADDRESS

Dear Dr. Swift: **SALUTATION**

We have completed our evaluation of the nutrition education program being conducted by your organization. While the results are encouraging, some aspects of the program might be modified. Awareness training for the staff, a few schedule changes, and greater involvement of the parents could significantly improve the results of the program.

We have prepared a study outlining the problems as we see them and our recommendations for improving the program. David Wong, Vice President of our community centre, has agreed to work with you, if you would like his assistance.

We look forward to hearing from you soon.

BODY

Sincerely, **Complimentary close**

Dorothy Muir **Signature**

Dorothy Muir **Typed name**
Co-ordinator, Advisory Committee **Title**

CLOSING

DM/ewl **NOTATION**

TYPES OF BUSINESS LETTERS

(1) Thank-you letter

Thank-you letters are written often in private life, but they are also used in business. If a representative of a company has been helpful or done more than you expected, a thank-you letter or note is an appropriate way of showing appreciation. A gift, recommendation, award, or prize should also be acknowledged with a letter of thanks.

Usually, thank-you letters are in the informal indented style. It is not necessary to include an inside address, and a comma replaces the colon after the salutation. There are some who think thank-you letters should be handwritten, but typewritten ones are equally correct.

THANK-YOU LETTER

1966 Hunter Street
Sudbury, Ontario
P3E 2S4
September 19, 1986

Dear Dean Smythe,

Thank you very much for recommending me for the Citizen Youth Award. Receiving this honour last Friday at the presentation banquet was a moving and memorable experience. My parents and I wish to convey to you our deepest appreciation for your kind and generous words of testimony on that occasion.

Sincerely,
Susan Gilchrist
Susan Gilchrist

(2) Claim and adjustment letter

One of the most common business letters is the letter of claim and adjustment, which should include the following information.

Your claim: Describe exactly what is wrong. The more specific your description, the easier and quicker it will be to correct the situation. If an airline has lost your suitcase, for example, describe it fully and also include the flight number, date, and your destination. If an appliance is faulty, include the model and serial numbers in addition to the brand name.

Your request: Often a company will do exactly what you suggest, as long as it is possible. Again, the more specific your request—and the more reasonable and courteous your tone—the better your chance of getting what you want.

CLAIM AND ADJUSTMENT LETTER

710–56 Mackay Street
Montreal, Quebec
H3G 2J3
February 20, 1985

Mr. Richard Weston
G & R Consulting Services
PO Box 14692, Station K
Ottawa, Ontario
K2C 4S9

Dear Mr. Weston:

Yesterday I spoke to you on the phone concerning the failure of the Tax Manager program to operate properly on my ICON computer. I tried without success the alterations in format you suggested.

Since I purchased both the computer and the program from you with the assurance problems would be unlikely, I would like you to examine the system here in my apartment, and either repair the faulty element, free of charge, or replace it to make the system operational. My telephone number is (514) 555–4140, and you can call me any day next week from noon to 5:00 p.m.

Sincerely,

Thomas McNally

Thomas McNally

(3) Order letter

In an order letter, supply the following information as exactly as possible:

Description: Indicate the name of the product, the model or stock number if you know it, the page of the catalogue from which you are ordering, the quantity of each item, and the price.

Destination: State whether you want the order shipped to the inside address at the top of your letter or to another address.

Any special circumstances: State such things as whether you need the order by a particular date, whether you want it sent a particular way (air freight, for example), or whether you will not pay more than a certain price.

Payment information: Include payment or indicate how you plan to pay for the merchandise.

Note: Traditional abbreviations for provinces in Canada and states in the United States are standard in Canadian usage, but with the increased use of computers, it is not uncommon to find the traditional abbreviation replaced by new two letter codes with no terminal punctuation as follows:

Alta.	B.C.	Man.	N.B.	Nfld.	N.S.	Ont.	P.E.I.	Que.	Sask.
AB	BC	MB	NB	NF	NS	ON	PE	PQ	SK

Computerized addresses may often show the postal code following the new abbreviation with two spaces and no punctuation marks, e.g., Edmonton, AB T2W 1Z9.

The examples in letters in this section conform to the guidelines of Canada Post by having the postal code on a separate line.

ORDER LETTER

842 Mount Joy Street
Timmins, Ontario
P4N 6Z9
February 5, 1986

Woodsmaster Ltd.
1828 Simcoe Street
Toronto, Ontario
M5J 2X3

Dear Sirs:

I wish to order the following merchandise from your February 1 Toronto Star advertisement:

1 Safari shirt, size 42, beige--	$64.00
1 Tote bag, medium, blue--	$49.50
2 Camp stools (@ $19.95)--	$39.90
	$153.50
Prov. sales tax (7%)--	10.75
Shipping & handling--	6.15
Total:	$170.40

Please ship this merchandise by surface carrier to my address as shown at the top of this letter.

I enclose a cheque for $170.40, which includes provincial sales tax, parcel post and handling charges as specified in your ordering instructions.

Sincerely,

Eric Campbell

Eric Campbell

enc.

(4) Application letter

The purpose of an application letter is to convince the reader that he or she should examine your résumé. In it you should indicate the job you want and, briefly, your qualifications. In the last paragraph you should indicate when you are available for an interview. A letter of application is usually accompanied by a résumé (page 527), which gives more information about you than your letter can. Neither your letter nor your résumé should be longer than one typed page.

BUSINESS ENVELOPES

The address that appears on the envelope is identical to the inside address. The return address regularly gives the writer's full name and address, including the postal code.

MODEL ADDRESSED ENVELOPE

```
Diane Bellows
1830 Queensway Crescent
Chatham, Ontario
N5R 6Z2

                  Mr. Aaron Navik
                  Personnel Manager
                  Echo Electronics
                  627 Southwick Street
                  St. Thomas, Ontario
                  N5R 3R7
```

APPLICATION LETTER

1830 Queensway Crescent
Chatham, Ontario
N5R 6Z2
June 8, 1985

Mr. Aaron Navik
Personnel Manager
Echo Electronics
627 Southwick Street
St. Thomas, Ontario
N5R 3R7

Dear Mr. Navik:

Please consider me for the position of Assistant Director in the Personnel Division of Echo Electronics. I was an administrative intern with Echo last summer and, now that I have graduated from the University of Western Ontario, I would like to join your company.

As you can see from the attached résumé, my major was Administrative and Commercial Studies with special emphasis in personnel management. As the chairperson of the program committee for my residence, I dealt with students, visiting guests, alumni, and faculty. The position required a sympathy for and a knowledge of the interests and capacities of my fellow university students.

As an intern with Echo, I learned a great deal about the management of a company. Through first hand experience, I was able to gain a firmer grasp of the contribution personnel management makes to the overall objectives of a company.

I would very much like to put my interests and my training to work for Echo Electronics, and I am available for an interview at your convenience.

Sincerely,

Diane Bellows

Diane Bellows

enc.

34b

The Résumé

A résumé is a list of a person's qualifications for a job and is enclosed with a letter of application. It is made up of four categories of information:

(1) Personal data: name, mailing address, telephone number
(2) Educational background
(3) Work experience
(4) Location of credentials file, which includes letters of recommendation

Like the letter of application, the résumé is a form of persuasion designed to emphasize your qualifications for a job and to get you an interview. Since there is usually more than one applicant for every job, your résumé should make the most of your qualifications. After reading all the letters and résumés received, a potential employer usually decides to interview only the three or four strongest candidates.

Writing a résumé requires the same planning and attention to detail that writing a paper does. First, make a list of the jobs you have had, the activities and clubs you have been part of, and the offices you have held. Amplify these items by adding dates, job titles and responsibilities, and a brief statement about what you learned from each of them. Arrange these items with the most recent first: March 1981–present, September 1979–February 1981. Remember that activities that do not appear to be relevant to the job you want may be explained to show that you learned important things from them. The résumés on pages 526-27 illustrate the points in the list on the opposite page.

You may find it helpful to consult one of the following books for further information on application letters, résumés, and interviews:

Juvenal L. Angel. *The Complete Resumé Book and Job-Getter's Guide*. New York: Pocket Books, 1980.

Richard N. Bolles, *What Color Is Your Parachute? A Practical Manual for Job-Hunters and Career Changers*. 5th edition. Berkeley: Ten Speed Press, 1979.

John J. Komar. *The Interview Game: Winning Strategies for the Job Seeker*. New York: Follet, 1979.

Michael H. Smith. *The Resumé Writer's Handbook*. 2nd edition. New York: Barnes and Noble, 1980.

University Career Planning Association. *The Résumé*. Toronto: U. of Toronto Career Counselling Service, 1978. Rev. 1982.

RÉSUMÉ DO'S AND DON'TS

DON'T	DO
1. Don't include personal material—age, marital status, photograph, etc.—that is not relevant to the job.	1. Do include your address and telephone number.
2. Don't mention specific courses unless they are directly relevant to the job.	2. Do mention your degree and the *areas* in which you received special training.
3. Don't include career goals. You may wish to change them or raise them.	3. Do *think* about your career goals so that you can discuss them during the interview.
4. Don't include salary unless you will not accept less.	4. Do *think* about the salary you will accept so that you can discuss it during the interview.
5. Don't mention jobs and activities unless you can make them relevant to the job.	5. Do explain briefly how each job and activity included pertains to the job you want.
6. Don't use a cluttered, sprawling format. It looks inefficient and unprofessional.	6. Do use a clear, crisp format. It shows the reader you are efficient and professional.

RÉSUMÉ 1—BEFORE

Name: Dianne Bellows	Marital Status: Single
Local Address:	Date of Birth: 3/29/60
1420 Platts Lane	Health: Excellent
Apt. 200	Height: 5.6"
Phone: 452-8600	Weight: 130
Home Address:	
180 Queensway Cres:	
Chatham, Ont.	

Education:

Sept.- May 1982-1985	University of Western Ontario Candidate for Bachelor of Arts in Administrative and Commercial Studies, Social Organization and Human Relations stream.
Sept.- June 1977-1982	Chatham District Collegiate, S.S.H.G.D.

Work History:

Oct.- April 1984-1985	Tour Guide, University of Western Ontario
May - Aug. 1984-1984	Summer Intern, Echo Instruments Inc.
May - Aug. 1983-1983	Waitress, Holly Inn Restaurant.

Extracurricular Activities:

Member of program committee for residence
Jan. 1985-March 1985
Member of Investment Club, U.W.O.
Oct. 1983-March 1984
Member of campaign committee, Joe Smith
May, 1985
Christian Education Committee, Hensall Park Baptist Church
Jan.- May, 1985

RÉSUMÉ 2—AFTER

DIANNE BELLOWS

1830 Queensway Cres.
Chatham, Ontario
N5R 6Z2
(519) 555-2220

EDUCATION

Administrative and Commercial Studies, Bachelor of Arts, University of Western Ontario (May 1985)

- concentration in social organization and human relations; courses in Business Management, Organizational Communication, Human Relations, Sociology and Psychology of Work

RELATED EXPERIENCE

Liaison Services, The University of Western Ontario, London, Ontario (part-time 1984–present, summer 1985)

- conducted campus orientation sessions and tours for prospective students and their parents
- answered inquiries about student life in orientation workshops
- wrote final report with recommendations for changes in orientation workshop

Personnel Department, Echo Electronics, Chatham, Ontario (summer 1984)

- as Student Personnel Intern, developed knowledge of benefits administration
- reorganized pension and health benefits records system
- gained knowledge of all functions of human resources operation

PERSONAL ACHIEVEMENTS

Program Committee, Saugeen-Maitland Residence, U.W.O. (1985)
- arranged evening programs for students in residence, including "Careers Night" panel of professionals from law, medicine, and business

Publicity Committee, London North riding for Provincial Election (1985)
- wrote pamphlets and press releases for MPP candidate

U.W.O. Investment Club (1983-84)
- developed personal investment portfolio for long-term growth

Note on Applications and Résumés: In preparing a résumé, Canadian students should consider consulting a career counselling and placement office in any institution near them for advice and information about improving the strategies in making application for employment, but the pamphlet, The Résumé, published by the University and College Placement Association and listed in the bibliography on page 525, makes an excellent point of departure.

Exercise

1. Prepare a résumé and then write a letter of application for a position you are competent to fill.
2. Write to the principal of the high school you graduated from, thanking her for recommending you for a summer job.
3. Call the attention of your local councillor to repairs that are needed in your neighbourhood playground.
4. Write to a national record company complaining about the technical quality of the record you ordered from them.
5. Order a particular ten-speed bicycle part from a bicycle company.

Glossary of Grammatical Terms

This glossary presents brief explanations of frequently used grammatical terms. Consult the index for references to further discussion of most of the terms and for a number of terms not listed.

absolute A parenthetical word or phrase that qualifies the rest of the sentence and is not related to it by a connective. An absolute does not modify a specific word or phrase in the sentence.

> **True**, Rome was not built in a day.
> **Considering the risks**, giving up cigarettes is sensible.

The term *absolute phrase* is often used for the type of absolute illustrated below.

> **The hostages free at last**, the nation rejoiced.
> COMPARE The hostages *were* free at last. The nation rejoiced.
>
> **The expressway jammed with rush-hour traffic**, we were delayed two hours.
> COMPARE The expressway **was** jammed with rush-hour traffic, **so** we were delayed two hours.
>
> I do not get much studying done in my dormitory room—**students running up and down the hall and yelling at one another and TV sets and stereos outblaring my FM music**.
> COMPARE I do not get much studying done in my dormitory room **because** students **run** up and down the hall and **yell**

at one another and TV sets and stereos **outblare** my FM music.

See **2a**. See also **parenthetical element, phrase** and **participle**.

abstract noun See **noun**.

acronym A word made up of the first letter or two of a series of words.

scuba [**s**elf-**c**ontained **u**nderwater **b**reathing **a**pparatus]
radar [**r**adio **d**etecting **a**nd **r**anging]
NASA [**N**ational **A**eronautics **S**pace **A**dministration]

active voice See **voice**.

adjectival Any word or word group functioning as an adjective: "*happy* people," "those *living on a fixed income*." The term is especially useful when it refers to a modifier without degrees of comparison.

this one, **subscription** TV, **its** value, **an OPEC** decision
people **on the street, Nancy's end-of-term** jitters
one **who has a good sense of humour**, films **I like best**

See also **comparison**.

adjective A part of speech regularly used to modify (describe or limit) a noun or a pronoun. Descriptive adjectives, unlike limiting adjectives, can usually be compared. See **comparison** and **adjectival**.

blue sky, **newer** car, **best** joke, **beautiful** art [descriptive]
a boy, **that** one, **its** nest, **both** men—**Whose** idea? [limiting]

Proper adjectives are capitalized. See **9a(3)**.

Christlike figure   **Irish** humour   **Victorian** styles

Predicate adjectives function as complements of linking verbs (such as *feel, look, smell, sound, taste*, and forms of *be*). See **linking verb**.

The milk tasted **sour**. They may be **lucky**. How **tall** is he?

See Section **4**.

adjective clause An adjectival containing a subject and verb. See also **adjectival** and **clause**.

We usually like the people **who like us**.

adverb A part of speech regularly used to modify (describe or limit) a verb, an adjective, or another adverb.

slowly ate, **too** tall, entered **very quietly** [*Slowly* modifies the verb *ate; too* the adjective *tall; very* the adverb *quietly; quietly* the verb *entered.*]

An adverb may also modify a verbal, or a whole phrase, clause, or sentence.

Naturally, the villain succeeds at first by **completely** outwitting the hero. [*Naturally* modifies the rest of the sentence, and *completely* modifies the gerund *outwitting*.]

See Section **4**. See also **intensifier**.

adverb clause An adverbial containing a subject and a verb. See also **adverbial** and **clause**.

The common mole is valuable **because it eats insects.**
Although it is only fifty-six kilometres long, the Niagara is one of the world's most famous rivers.
Cartoonists make at least eighteen drawings **so that Woody Woodpecker can laugh victoriously**.

adverbial A word (an adverb, but especially a noun, a conjunction, or an interjection), phrase, or clause functioning as an adverb.

Wow, I forgot to ask; **however**, I'll see him **Friday**.
When the hail started, we ran **into the library**.

adverbial conjunction See **conjunctive adverb**.

agreement The correspondence in form of one word with another to indicate number, person, or gender.

NUMBER	the boy asks, boys ask	this type, these types
PERSON	I am, you are, he is	I was, you were, he was

GENDER the man himself, the woman herself, the book itself

See Section **6**.

antecedent A word or word group that a pronoun refers to.

> Before **Ron** left, **he** paid the **man** and **woman who** delivered the firewood. [*Ron* is the antecedent of the personal pronoun *he; man* and *woman* are the antecedents of the relative pronoun *who*.]

See **6b** and Section **28**.

appositive A noun or noun substitute set beside another noun or noun substitute and identifying or explaining it.

> Davis, our **guide**, did not see the grizzly. [Compare "Davis was our guide." See also page 11.]
>
> A tasty **preservative**, salt is nutritious. [*Preservative* is in apposition with *salt*.]

See also **12d(2)**.

article *The, a,* or *an*, used adjectivally before nouns (***the** cups, **a** cup, **an** apple*). *The* is a definite article. *A* and *an* are indefinite articles: see **19i** and **indefinite**.

attributive A noun used as an adjective (***examination** questions*) or an adjective placed beside the word it modifies (***difficult** questions* OR *questions, **difficult** but **clear***). See **adjectival**; contrast **predicate adjective**.

auxiliary verb A verb (like *be, have, do*) used with a main verb in a verb phrase. An auxiliary regularly indicates tense but may also indicate voice, mood, person, number.

are eating	**will be** eating	**was** eaten
has eaten	**Do** eat with us.	**have been** eaten

Modal auxiliaries (such as *will, would, shall, may, might, must, can, could*) do not take such inflectional endings as *-s, -ing,* or *-en*.

See also **1a** and Section **7**.

case The form or position of a word that shows its use or relationship to other words in a sentence. The three cases in English are the *subjective* (or nominative), the *possessive* (or genitive), and the *objective*. Pronouns and nouns have case: see Section **5** and **15a**.

clause A group of related words that contains both a subject and a predicate and that functions as a part of a sentence. A clause is either *main* (independent) or *subordinate* (dependent).

SENTENCES
Only a few stars came out. The moon was bright.
I know Herb. He will run for office.

MAIN CLAUSES
Only a few stars came out, for **the moon was bright**.
I know Herb; he will run for office.
[sentences connected by using the co-ordinating conjunction *for* and by using a semicolon and lower case for *he*]

SUBORDINATE CLAUSES
Only a few stars came out **because the moon was bright**. [adverb clause]
I know Herb, **who will run for office**. [adjective clause]
I know **that Herb will run for office**. [noun clause—direct object]
[sentences converted to subordinate clauses by using the subordinating conjunctions *because* and *that* and the relative pronoun *who*, a subordinator]

Elliptical clauses have omitted elements that are clearly understood: see **elliptical construction**.

clipped form A shortened word like [tele]*phone*, *ad*[vertisement], or [in]*flu*[enza]. Dictionaries include no usage labels for many clipped forms; they label many others *informal* or *slang*.

collective noun See **noun**.

comma splice Misuse of a comma between main clauses not connected by a co-ordinating conjunction. See Section **3**.

common noun See **noun**.

comparative See **comparison**.

comparison The inflection or modification of an adjective or adverb to indicate degrees in quality, quantity, or manner. There are three degrees: positive, comparative, and superlative.

POSITIVE	COMPARATIVE	SUPERLATIVE
good, well	better	best
high	higher	highest
quickly	more quickly	most quickly
active	less active	least active

See **4c**.

complement A word or words used to complete the sense of a verb. Although the term may refer to a direct or an indirect object, it usually refers to a subject complement, an object complement, or the complement of a verbal like *to be*.

The lasagna tasted **delicious**. [subject complement]
We made the ferret our **mascot**. [object complement]
To be a good **leader**, one must learn how to follow. [complement of the infinitive *to be*]

complete predicate See **predicate**.

complete subject See **subject**.

complex sentence See **sentence**.

compound A word or word group with two or more parts that function as a unit.

COMPOUND NOUNS dropout, hunger strike, sister-in-law
COMPOUND SUBJECT **Tories, Liberals,** and **New Democrats** are working together.
COMPOUND PREDICATE Kate **has tried** but **has** not **succeeded**.

See also **sentence**.

compound-complex sentence See **sentence**.

compound predicate See **compound**.

compound sentence See **sentence**.

compound subject See **compound**.

concrete noun See **noun**.

conjugation A set or table of the inflected forms of a verb that indicate tense, person, number, voice, and mood.

PRINCIPAL PARTS

see *saw* *seen*

Active voice	*Passive voice*
INDICATIVE MOOD	
PRESENT TENSE	
I / you / we / they *see* he / she / it *sees*	I *am seen* he / she / it *is seen* you / we / they *are seen*
PAST TENSE	
I / he / you / we / they *saw*	I / he *was seen* you / we / they *were seen*
FUTURE TENSE	
I / he / you / we / they *will* (OR *shall*) *see*	I / he / you / we / they *will* (OR *shall*) *be seen*
PRESENT PERFECT TENSE	
I / you / we / they *have seen* he *has seen*	I / you / we / they *have been seen* he *has been seen*
PAST PERFECT TENSE	
I / he / you / we / they *had seen*	I / he / you / we / they *had been seen*
FUTURE PERFECT TENSE	
I / he / you / we / they *will* (OR *shall*) *have seen*	I / he / you / we / they *will* (OR *shall*) *have been seen*

Active voice	*Passive voice*
SUBJUNCTIVE MOOD	
PRESENT TENSE	
that he / I / you / we / they *see*	that he / I you / we / they *be seen*
PAST TENSE	
that he / I / you / we / they *saw*	that he / I / you / we / they *were seen*
PRESENT PERFECT TENSE	
that he / I / you / we / they *have seen*	that he / I / you / we / they *have been seen*
PAST PERFECT TENSE	
(same as the indicative)	
IMPERATIVE MOOD	
PRESENT TENSE	
see	*be seen*

See pages 80-81 for a synopsis of the progressive forms.

conjunction A part of speech used to connect and relate words, phrases, clauses, or sentences. There are two kinds of conjunctions: co-ordinating and subordinating.

Co-ordinating conjunctions connect words and word groups of equal grammatical rank: *and, but, or, nor, for, so,* and *yet.*

> Dick **and** Mario will go into politics **or** social work.
> Not only did the temperature fall below zero, **but** the wind was blowing.

See also Section **26** and **correlatives**.

Subordinating conjunctions mark a dependent clause and connect it with a main clause: *after, although, as, as if, because, before, if, since, unless, until, when, while*, and so forth.

> **When** Frank does not wish to hear, he acts **as if** he were deaf.

conjunctive adverb An adverbial connective, such as *consequently, then, nonetheless.* See the list on page 45.

> Inflation and recession affect the purchasing power of the dollar; **moreover**, they have an impact on the consumer's buying habits.

connective A word or phrase that links and relates words, phrases, clauses, or sentences, such as *and, although, otherwise, finally, on the contrary, which, not only . . . but also.* Conjunctions, conjunctive adverbs, transitional expressions, relative pronouns, and correlatives function as connectives. See also **31c(4)**.

construction A grammatical unit (such as a sentence, clause, or phrase) or the arrangement of related words in a grammatical unit.

contact clause One clause, usually subordinate, attached to another clause without the use of a connective. A contact clause that functions as an adjective is restrictive.

> Luke did not have a friend **he could fully trust**. [*whom* or *that* omitted after *friend*]
> The trivia **I am interested in** can be found in newspaper fillers. [*which* or *that* omitted after *trivia*]

See also **restrictive**.

co-ordinating conjunction See **conjunction**.

correlatives Connectives used in pairs: *both . . . and; either . . . or; neither . . . nor; not only . . . but also; whether . . . or*. See also **26c** and **co-ordinating conjunctions**.

count noun See **noun**.

dangling modifier A word or word group that does not modify (or modify clearly) another word or word group in the sentence. An absolute expression is not a dangling modifier.

DANGLING **Racing to class**, that open manhole went unnoticed. [*Racing* modifies nothing in the sentence. The reader expects *racing* to modify the subject—which is *manhole*.]

REVISED **Racing** to class, **I** did not notice that open manhole. [*Racing* clearly modifies the subject *I*.]

See also **25b**.

declension A set or table of inflected forms of nouns or pronouns. As the following table shows, nouns are inflected only in the possessive case. The personal pronouns and the relative/interrogative pronoun *who* are inflected in all three cases.

NOUN

	Subjective	*Possessive*	*Objective*
SINGULAR	day	day's	day
PLURAL	days	days'	days

PRONOUNS

	Subjective	*Possessive*	*Objective*
		Singular	
FIRST PERSON	I	my, mine	me
SECOND PERSON	you	your, yours	you
THIRD PERSON	he, she, it	his, her, hers, its	him, her, it
		Plural	
FIRST PERSON	we	our, ours	us
SECOND PERSON	you	your, yours	you
THIRD PERSON	they	their, theirs	them
	Subjective	*Possessive*	*Objective*
		Singular and Plural	
	who	whose	whom

demonstrative pronoun One of the four pronouns that point out: *this, that, these, those.* These words often function in sentences as adjectives.

> **This** brand is as good as **that**.

dependent clause A subordinate clause: see **clause**.

descriptive adjective See **adjective**.

determiner A word (such as *a, an, the, my, their,* or *our*) which signals the approach of a noun.

diagraming A graphic means of showing relationships within the sentence. Various forms are used; any form is serviceable if it helps to show how the sentence works. Illustrations of three kinds of diagrams follow:

The dark clouds on the horizon had appeared suddenly.

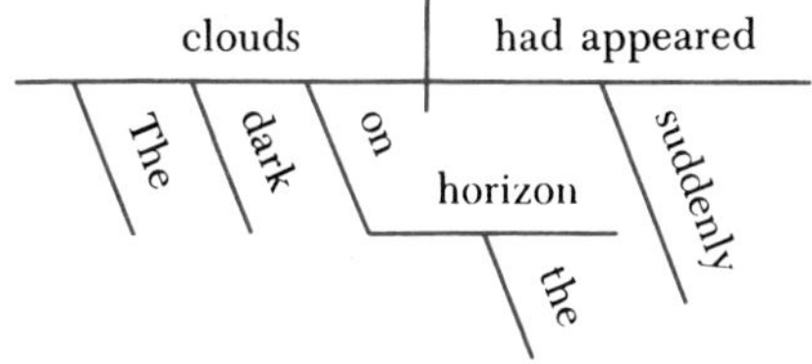

The key to the diagram:

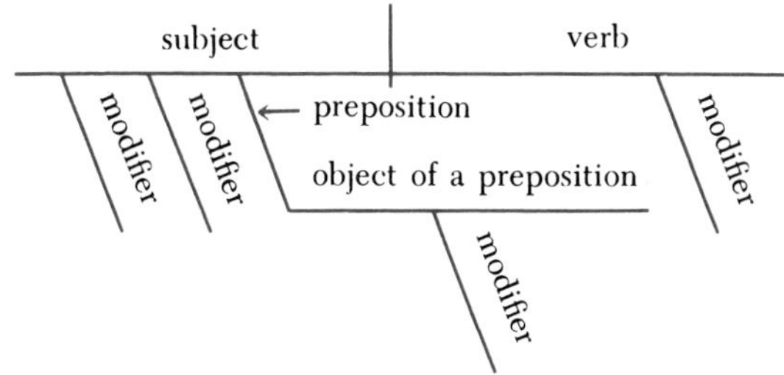

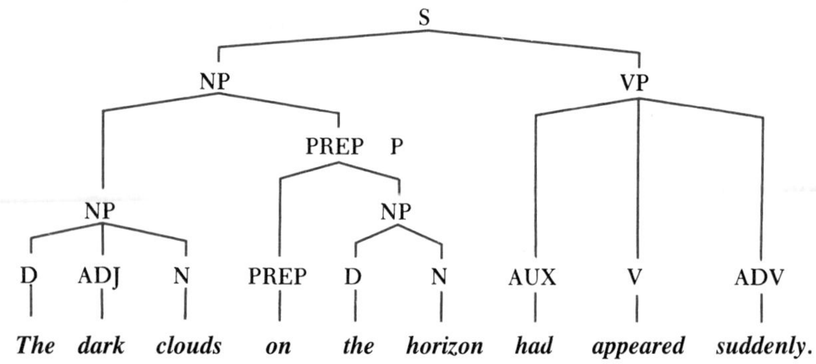

The key to the abbreviations:

ADJ	Adjective	PREP	Preposition
ADV	Adverb	PREP P	Prepositional Phrase
AUX	Auxiliary	S	Sentence
D	Determiner	V	Verb
N	Noun	VP	Verb Phrase
NP	Noun Phrase		

A key to the diagram below (which shows the layers of structure) is not provided. Terminology is left to the analyst's choice. (For example, one analyst might write *complete subject* on the line connecting *on the horizon* with *The dark clouds*, but another might prefer *noun phrase*.)

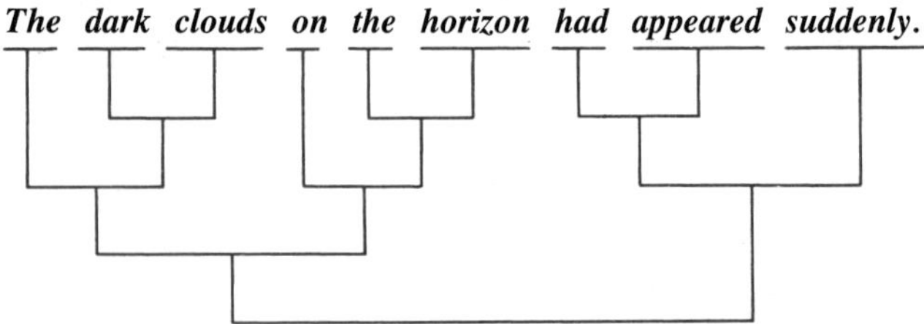

direct address A parenthetical word or phrase naming or denoting the person(s) spoken to.

Falstaff enters and exclaims, "Well said, **Hal**!"
Don't forget, **backseat passengers**, to use those seatbelts.

direct object See **object**.

direct quotation The exact spoken or written words of others.

DIRECT QUOTATION John asked, "Why haven't you joined the group, Martha?"
INDIRECT QUOTATION John asked Martha why she had not joined the group.

See also **16a**.

double negative A non-standard construction containing two negatives and having a negative meaning, such as *I didn't have no change with me*. See **not . . . no**, page 239.

elliptical construction A construction in which words are omitted but clearly understood.

The curtains are newer than the carpet [is].
Whenever [it is] possible, get a full night's sleep.
His hair is black; his face [is] deeply tanned.

expletive The word *there* or *it* used as a structural filler and not adding to the meaning of the sentence.

There were only a few ballet tickets left. [Compare "Only a few ballet tickets were left."]
It is obvious that they do not like us. [Compare "That they do not like us is obvious."]

finite verb The principal verb of a sentence or a clause. A finite verb can serve as the only verb of a sentence. Verb forms classified as gerunds, infinitives, and participles (verbals) are non-finite verbs.

One prisoner **escaped**. Clyde **will read** the book.

See also **non-finite verb**.

form change See **inflection**.

fragment See **sentence fragment**.

function words Words (such as prepositions, conjunctions, auxiliaries, and articles) that indicate the functions of other words (*vocabulary words*) in a sentence and the grammatical relationships between them. See also **vocabulary words**.

fused sentence Two sentences run together without any punctuation or a co-ordinating conjunction. See Section **3**.

gerund A verbal (non-finite verb) that ends in *-ing* and functions as a noun. Gerunds may take objects, complements, or modifiers.

> He escaped by ***swimming* rapidly**. [The gerund *swimming* is the object of the preposition *by* and is modified by the adverb *rapidly*.]
>
> ***Borrowing* money** is a mistake. [The gerund phrase—the gerund *borrowing* and its object, *money*—serves as the subject of the sentence.]

A possessive noun or pronoun before a gerund may be classified either as an adjectival (modifying the noun element of the verbal) or as the subject of the gerund.

> **His borrowing** money is a mistake. [Compare "*his* action" and "*He borrowed* the money."]

See also **non-finite verb**.

idiom An expression in good use that is characteristic of or peculiar to a language. Perfectly acceptable idioms may seem illogical if taken literally or may violate established rules of grammar.

> He **gave himself away** by smiling.
> I have known him for **many a year**.

imperative See **mood**.

indefinite An article (*a, an*), a pronoun (*anybody, everyone*, and so on) or an adjective (*any* book, a *few* friends, *several* replies, and so on) that does not specify distinct limits.

independent clause A main clause: see **clause**.

indicative See **mood**.

indirect object See **object**.

indirect quotation See **direct quotation**.

infinitive A verbal (non-finite verb) used chiefly as a noun, less frequently as an adjective or an adverb. The infinitive is usually made up of the word *to* plus the present form of a verb (called the *stem* of the infinitive), but the *to* may be omitted after such verbs as *let, make*, and *dare*. Infinitives may have subjects, objects, complements, or modifiers.

> Hal wanted ***to open* the present**. [*Present* is the object of the infinitive *to open*; the whole infinitive phrase is the object of the verb *wanted*.]
>
> The work ***to be done*** overwhelms me. [The infinitive is used adjectivally to modify the noun *work*.]
>
> ***To tell* the truth**, our team almost lost. [The infinitive phrase is used adverbially to modify the rest of the sentence.]

See also **non-finite verb**.

inflection A change in the form of a word to show a specific meaning or grammatical relationship to some other word or group of words.

> VERBS drink, drinks, drank, drunk; grasp, grasps, grasped
> PRONOUNS **I, my** life, a gift for **me**
> NOUNS dog, dogs; dog's, dogs'
> ADJECTIVES a **good** one, a **better** one, the **best** one
> ADVERBS carefully, **more** carefully, **most** carefully

See also **conjugation, declension,** and **comparison**.

intensifier (intensive) A modifier used for emphasis. Such adverbs as "*very* boring," "*certainly* did," and "*so* pleased" are intensifiers. See also **qualifier**.

intensive pronoun A *-self* pronoun used to emphasize another word in the sentence.

> The premier **himself** answered my letter. [The pronoun *himself* refers to and emphasizes *premier*.]

interjection A part of speech used for simple exclamations: *Oh! Ouch! Whew!* When used in sentences, mild interjections are set off by commas.

intransitive See **verb**.

interrogative pronoun A pronoun (*which, what, who, whom, whose*) used to ask a question. An interrogative pronoun may function as a noun or as an adjective.

> **What** happened? **Which** did he choose? **Whose** car is it?

inversion A change in the usual word order of a sentence.

> Up go the referee's hands.
> In the middle of the lake is a small island.

irregular verb A verb that does not form its past tense and past participle in the standard way—that is, by the addition of *-d* or *-ed* to the stem of the infinitive (as with the regular verbs *hope, hoped; look, looked*). The principal parts of five common types of irregular verbs are given below.

> swim, swam, swum [vowels changed]
> beat, beat, beaten [*-en* added]
> feel, felt, felt [vowel shortened, *ee* changed to *e*]
> send, sent, sent [*-d* changed to *-t*]
> set, set, set [no change]

lexical words See **vocabulary words**.

linking verb A verb which relates the subject to the subject complement. Words commonly used as linking verbs are *become, seem, appear, feel, look, taste, smell, sound*, and the forms of the verb *be*.

> She **is** a pharmacist. The panels **feel** rough.

main clause An independent clause: see **clause**.

mass noun See **noun**.

misplaced modifier An adjectival or adverbial in an awkward position—usually, far away from what it modifies. Sometimes a misplaced modifier confuses the reader because it could qualify either of two words.

MISPLACED	I heard how to make catsup flow out of the bottle **on the radio**.
REVISED	I heard **on the radio** how to make catsup flow out of the bottle.
MISPLACED	To do one's best **sometimes** is not enough.
REVISED	To do one's best is **sometimes** not enough. OR It is not enough to do one's best **sometimes**.

See also **25a**.

modal auxiliary See **auxiliary verb**.

modifier An adjective or adverb (adjectival or adverbial), which describes, limits, or qualifies another word or word group: see Section **4**.

mood (mode) The way a speaker or writer regards an assertion—that is, as a declarative statement or a question (*indicative* mood), as a command or request (*imperative*), or as a supposition, hypothesis, recommendation, or condition contrary to fact (*subjunctive*). Verb forms indicate mood.

INDICATIVE	Joe **was** a winner.	**Does** he drop by?
IMPERATIVE	**Be** a winner.	**Do** drop by!
SUBJUNCTIVE	Joe talked as though he **were** a loser.	
	I recommend that he **do** this soon.	

See Section **7**.

nominal A word (such as a pronoun or gerund), phrase, or clause used as a noun.

Repairing that machine was not easy.
He contends **that selfless love is power**.

nominative See **case**.

non-finite verb A verbal functioning as a noun, an adjective, or an adverb. A non-finite verb cannot stand as the only verb in a sentence.

NON-FINITE VERBS IN PHRASES
to take a vacation together
shoppers **milling** around
by just **remaining** silent

NON-FINITE VERBS IN SENTENCES
My family wanted **to take** a vacation together.
Shoppers **milling** around did not buy much.
Some people win arguments by just **remaining** silent.

See also **verbal** and **finite verb**.

non-restrictive Non-essential to the meaning of a sentence. A phrase or clause is non-restrictive (parenthetical) when it is not necessary to the meaning of the main clause and may be omitted: see **12d**.

The old horse, **slow but confident**, plodded on. [phrase]
The airplane, **now being manufactured in large numbers**, is of immense commercial value. [phrase]
The airplane, **which is now being manufactured in large numbers**, is of immense commercial value. [clause]

See also **restrictive**.

noun A part of speech that names a person, place, thing, idea, animal, quality, or action: *Mary, Canada, apples, justice, goose, strength, departure*. A noun usually changes form to indicate the plural and the possessive case, as in *man, men; man's, men's*.

Types of nouns

COMMON	a **man**, the **cities**, some **trout** [general classes]
PROPER	**Mr. Ford**, in **Regina**, the **Forum** [capitalized, specific names]
COLLECTIVE	a **flock**, the **jury**, my **family** [groups]
CONCRETE	an **egg**, the **bus**, his **ear**, two **trees** [tangibles]
ABSTRACT	**honour, jealousy, pity, hatred** [ideas, qualities]

COUNT — One **dime**, ten **dollars**, a **job**, many **times** [singular or plural—often preceded by adjectivals telling how many]

MASS — much **money**, more **work**, less **time** [singular in meaning—often preceded by adjectivals telling how much]

Functions of nouns

SUBJECT OF FINITE VERB **Dogs** barked.
OBJECT OF FINITE VERB OR OF PREPOSITION He gave **Jane** the **key** to the **house**.
SUBJECT COMPLEMENT (PREDICATE NOUN) She is a **nurse**.
OBJECT COMPLEMENT They named him **Jonathan**.
SUBJECT OF NON-FINITE VERB I want **Ed** to be here.
OBJECT OF NON-FINITE VERB **I** prefer to drive a **truck**.
APPOSITIVE Moses, a **prophet**, saw the promised land.
ADVERBIAL **Yesterday** they went **home**.
ADJECTIVAL The **dogwood** is the **provincial** flower of British Columbia.
DIRECT ADDRESS What do you think, **Angela**?
KEY WORD OF ABSOLUTE PHRASE The **food** being cold, no one really enjoyed the meal.

noun clause A subordinate clause used as a noun.

Whoever comes will be welcome. [subject]
I hope **that he will recover**. [direct object]
I will give **whoever comes first** the best seat. [indirect object]
Spend it for **whatever seems best**. [object of a preposition]
This is **what you need**. [subject complement]
I loved it, **whatever it was**. [appositive]
Whoever you are, show yourself! [direct address]

See also **nominal** and **clause**.

noun phrase See **phrase**.

number The inflectional form of a noun, a pronoun, a demonstrative adjective, or a verb that indicates number, either singular (one) or plural (more than one). See Section **6** and **18e**.

object A noun or noun substitute governed by a transitive active verb, by a non-finite verb, or by a preposition.

A *direct object*, or the *object of a finite verb*, is any noun or noun substitute that answers the question *What?* or *Whom?* after a transitive active verb. A direct object frequently receives, or is in some way affected by, the action of the verb.

William raked **leaves**. **What** did he say?
The Andersons do not know **where we live**.

As a rule, a direct object may be converted into a subject with a passive verb: see **voice**.

An *object of a non-finite verb* is any noun or its equivalent that follows and completes the meaning of a participle, a gerund, or an infinitive.

Washing a **car** takes time. He likes to wear a **tie**.
Following the **truck**, a bus rounded the bend.

An *indirect object* is any noun or noun substitute that states *to whom* or *for whom* (or *to what* or *for what*) something is done. An indirect object ordinarily precedes a direct object.

He bought **her** a watch.
I gave the **floor** a second coat of varnish.

It is usually possible to substitute a prepositional phrase beginning with *to* or *for* for the indirect object.

He bought a watch for her.

An *object of a preposition* is any noun or noun substitute which a preposition relates to another word or word group.

Pines grow tall in these **hills**. [*Hills* is the object of *in*.]
What am I responsible for? [*What* is the object of *for*.]

object complement See **complement**.

objective See **case**.

parenthetical element Non-essential matter (such as an aside or interpolation) that is set off by commas, dashes, or parentheses to mark pauses and intonation. A word, phrase, clause, or sentence may be parenthetical.

> **Granted**, over eighty million people, **according to that estimate**, did watch one episode.
> **In fact**, the parachute ride—**believe it or not**—is as safe as the ferris wheel.

See also **12d, 17e,** and **17f**.

participle A verb form that may function as part of a verb phrase (was *laughing*, had *finished*), as an adjective (the *laughing* children, the *finished* product), or as a non-finite verb (The children, *laughing* loudly, left).

The present participle ends in *-ing* (the form also used for verbal nouns: see **gerund**. The past participle of regular verbs ends in *-d* or *-ed*; for a list of past participles of irregular verbs, see pages 83-84.

Functioning as non-finite verbs in *participial phrases*, participles may take objects, complements, modifiers:

> The prisoner ***carrying*** **the heaviest load** toppled forward. [The participle *carrying* takes the object *load*; the whole participial phrase modifies *prisoner*.]
>
> The telephone operator, **very *confused* by my request**, suggested that I place the call later. [The participle *confused* is modified by the adverb *very* and by the prepositional phrase *by my request*; the participial phrase modifies *telephone operator*.]

See also **non-finite verb**.

particle with verb A phrasal unit consisting of a verb plus one or two uninflected words like *after, in, up, off,* or *out* and having the force of a single-word verb.

> We **ran out on** them. [Compare "We deserted them."]
> He **cut** me **off** without a cent. [Compare "He disinherited me."]

parts of speech The eight classes into which most grammarians group words according to their form changes and their position, meaning, and use in the sentence: *verbs, nouns, pronouns, adjectives, adverbs, prepositions, conjunctions,* and *interjections.* Each of these is discussed separately in this glossary. See also **1c**.

passive voice See **voice**.

person Changes in the form of pronouns and verbs denoting or indicating whether one is speaking (*I am*—first person), spoken to (*you are*—second person), or spoken about (*it is*—third person). In the present tense, a verb changes its form to agree grammatically with a third-person singular object (*a bird eats, everybody does*). See **6a** and **27b**.

personal pronoun Any one of a group of pronouns—*I, you, he, she, it* and their inflected forms—referring to the one (or ones) speaking, spoken to, or spoken about. See **declension**.

phrase A group of related words without both a subject and a (finite) verb.

NOUN PHRASE A **young stranger** stepped forward.
VERB PHRASE All day long they **had been worrying**.
PREPOSITIONAL PHRASES **By seven o'clock**, the lines stretched **from the box office to the corner**.
GERUND PHRASE **Building a sun deck** can be fun.
INFINITIVE PHRASE Do you want **to use your time that way**?
PARTICIPIAL PHRASE My friends **travelling in Italy** felt the earthquake.
APPOSITIVE PHRASE I introduced her to Bob, **my roommate**.
ABSOLUTE PHRASE **The game over**, we shook hands.

positive See **comparison**.

possessive See **case**.

predicate A basic grammatical division of a sentence. A predicate is the part of the sentence comprising what is said about the subject. The *complete predicate* consists of the main verb along with its auxiliaries (the *simple predicate*) and any complements and modifiers.

The town ***used*** **a unity theme for its annual fair that year**. [*Used* is the simple predicate, the headword of the complete predicate.]

Had the team **already** ***been preparing*** **themselves psychologically**? [The simple predicate is the verb phrase *had been preparing*.]

predicate adjective An adjective functioning as a subject complement: see **complement** and **linking verb**

predicate noun A noun functioning as a subject complement: see **complement** and **linking verb**.

prefix An added syllable or group of syllables attached to the beginning of a base or root (or another prefix). A prefix changes the meaning or creates a new word: *meditated, premeditated, unpremeditated*. See **18c**. See also **suffix**.

preposition A part of speech (a function word) that links and relates a vocabulary word to some other word in the sentence. See pages 17-18 for a list of words commonly used as prepositions.

These paintings hung **in** the hall. [The preposition *in* connects and relates *hall* (the object of the preposition *in*) to the verb *hung*.]

prepositional phrase See **phrase**.

principal parts The forms of any verb from which the various tenses are derived: the present infinitive (*take, laugh*), the past (*took, laughed*), and the past participle (*taken, laughed*).

See also Section **7**.

progressive verb A verb phrase consisting of a present participle (ending in *-ing*) used with a form of *be* and denoting continuous action.

I have been playing tennis all afternoon.

See also pages 80-81.

pronoun One of the eight parts of speech. Pronouns take the position of nouns and function as nouns do.

NOUNS	The old **house** was sold to Fred's aunt.
PRONOUNS	**It** was sold to **his** aunt. OR **That** was sold to **her**.

Types of pronouns

PERSONAL	**She** and **I** will see **him** in Medicine Hat.
INTERROGATIVE	**Who** are they? **What** is right? **Which** car is better?
RELATIVE	Leslie is the one **who** likes to bowl. A dog **that** barks may bite.
DEMONSTRATIVE	**This** is better than **that**.
INDEFINITE	**Each** of you should help **someone**.
RECIPROCAL	Help **each other**. They like **one another**.
REFLEXIVE	Carl blames **himself**. Did you injure **yourself**?
INTENSIVE	We need a vacation **ourselves**. I **myself** saw the crash.

See Sections **5, 6,** and **28**.

See also the separate entry for each type of pronoun: **personal pronoun, interrogative pronoun,** and so on.

proper adjective A capitalized adjective (*a* ***Scottish*** *tune*) derived from a proper noun (*Scotland*).

See also **adjective**.

proper noun See **noun**.

qualifier Any modifier, descriptive or limiting. Frequently, however, the term refers only to those modifiers that restrict or intensify the meaning of other words.

> **Many** thieves lie. **Almost** all of them do. [Compare "Thieves lie."]
>
> **Sometimes** children are **too** selfish to share.

See also **intensifier**.

quotation See **direct quotation**.

reciprocal pronoun A compound pronoun expressing an interchangeable or mutual action or relationship: *each other* or *one another*.

> They compete with **each other**.
> We respect **one another**.

reflexive pronoun A *-self* pronoun used as an object or a complement and referring to the individual or individuals named by the subject.

> They denied **themselves** nothing. I am not **myself** today.

regular verb A verb that forms its past tense and past participle by adding *-d* or *-ed* to the stem of the infinitive: *love, loved; laugh, laughed*.

relative pronoun One of a small group of noun substitutes (*who, whom, whose, that, which, what, whoever, whomever, whichever, whatever*) used to introduce subordinate clauses.

> He has a son ***who* is a genius**. [adjective clause introduced by the relative pronoun *who*]
> ***Whoever* wins the prize** must have talent. [noun clause introduced by the relative pronoun *whoever*]

restrictive Essential to sentence meaning. A phrase or clause is restrictive when it is necessary to the meaning of the main clause and cannot be omitted: see **12d**.

> Every drug **condemned by doctors** should be taken off the market. [restrictive phrase]
> Every drug **that doctors condemn** should be taken off the market. [restrictive clause]

See also **non-restrictive**.

sentence An independent unit of expression. A simple sentence follows the pattern **SUBJECT—PREDICATE**. Sentences are often classified according to structure as *simple, compound, complex*, or *compound-complex*.

SIMPLE We won. [subject—predicate]

COMPOUND They outplayed us, but we won. [two main clauses]

COMPLEX Although we did win, they outplayed us. [subordinate clause, main clause]

COMPOUND-COMPLEX I know that they outplayed us, but we did win. [two main clauses—the first of which contains a subordinate clause]

Sentences are also classified according to their purpose.

DECLARATIVE	We will fly to Yellowknife.	[statement]
IMPERATIVE	Fly to Yellowknife.	[command]
INTERROGATIVE	Shall we fly to Yellowknife?	[question]
EXCLAMATORY	Would we like to fly to Yellowknife!	[exclamation]

See Section **1**.

sentence fragment A non-sentence written as though it were a sentence. The term generally refers to a grammatically incomplete declarative sentence. See Section **2**.

sentence modifier A word or word group that modifies the rest of the sentence.

Yes, the bus arrived late.
Fortunately, no one was hurt.
The best professional teams win important games, **as a rule**.

subject A basic grammatical division of a sentence. The subject is a noun or noun substitute about which something is asserted or asked in the predicate. It usually precedes the predicate. (Imperative sentences have subjects that are not stated but are implied.) The *complete subject* consists of the *simple subject* and the words associated with it.

The dog locked in the hot car needed air. [*Dog* is the simple subject. *The dog locked in the hot car* is the complete subject.]

See also **1a**.

subject complement See **complement**.

subjective See **case**.

subjunctive Scc **mood**.

subordinating conjunction See **conjunction**.

subordinate clause A dependent clause: see **clause**.

subordinator A word that marks a dependent, or subordinate, clause: see page 25.

suffix An added sound, syllable, or group of syllables attached to the end of a base or root (or another suffix). Suffixes change meanings, create new words, and indicate grammatical functions.

the play**s**	play**er**	play**er's**	play**ing**
play**ed**	play**ful**	play**fully**	play**fulness**

See also **inflection** and **18c**.

superlative See **comparison**.

syntax Sentence structure. The grammatical arrangement of words, phrases, and clauses. See **word order**.

tense The form of the verb which indicates its relation to time. Inflection (*eat, eats, eating, ate, eaten*) and the use of auxiliaries (*will* eat, *have* eaten, *had* eaten, *will have* eaten, and so on) show the tense of a verb. See **conjugation** and Section **7**.

transitive See **verb**.

verb A part of speech denoting action, occurrence, or existence (state of being). Inflections indicate tense (and sometimes person and number) and mood of a verb: see **inflection, mood, voice,** and Section **7**.

A *transitive verb* is a verb that requires an object to complete its meaning. Transitive verbs can usually be changed from the active to the passive voice: see **object** and **voice**.

Sid **hung** a wreath on his door. [direct object: *wreath*]

An *intransitive verb* is a verb (such as *go* or *sit*) that does not have an object to complete its meaning. Linking verbs, which take subject complements, are intransitive.

She **has been waiting** patiently for hours.
I **was** sick last Christmas.

The same verb may be transitive in one sentence and intransitive in another.

TRANSITIVE Dee **reads** novels. [direct object: *novels*]
INTRANSITIVE Dee **reads** well.

verb phrase See **phrase**.

verbal A non-finite verb used as a noun, an adjective, or an adverb. Infinitives, participles, and gerunds are verbals. Verbals (like finite verbs) may take objects, complements, modifiers, and sometimes subjects.

Mr. Nelson went ***to see*** **his daughter**. [*To see*, an infinitive, functions as an adverb modifying the verb *went*. The object of the infinitive is *daughter*.]

Cars ***parked*** **in the loading zone** will be towed away. [*Parked*, a participle, modifies cars.]

Studying **dialects in our area** was fun. [*Studying*, a gerund, heads the phrase that is the subject of the verb *was*.]

See also **non-finite verb** and **gerund, infinitive, participle**.

vocabulary (lexical) words Nouns, verbs, and most modifiers—those words found in vocabulary-building lists. See also **function words**.

voice The form of a transitive verb that indicates whether or not the subject performs the action denoted by the verb. A verb with a direct object is in the *active voice*. When the direct object is converted into a subject, the verb is in the *passive voice*. A passive verb is always a verb phrase consisting of a form of the verb *be* (or sometimes *get*) followed by a past participle.

ACTIVE Priscilla **chose** John. [The subject (*Priscilla*) acts.]
PASSIVE John **was chosen** by Priscilla. [The subject (John) does not act.]

Speakers and writers often omit the *by*-phrase after a passive verb, especially when the performer of the action is not known or is not the focus of attention.

Those flowers **were picked** yesterday.
The guilty ones **should be punished** severely.
We just heard that a new secretary **was hired**.

See also **29d**.

word order The arrangement of words in sentences. Because of lost inflections, modern English depends heavily on word order to convey meaning. See **syntax**.

Nancy gave Henry $14 000.
Henry gave Nancy $14 000.

Tony had built a barbecue pit.
Tony had a barbecue pit built.

Index

Numbers in **boldface** refer to rules; other numbers refer to pages. A colon is used after each boldface number to indicate that the following pages refer to the rule or the part of the rule concerned. The **boldface** rule is given in detail—**9a(4)** or **20a(3)**, for example—in order to pinpoint a needed correction, but a less detailed reference **(9** or **9a)** will usually be sufficient for the student.

A

a
before common nouns, **9f:** 113
before consonant sound, **19i:** 225
See also *article*.
abbreviations, **11:** 120–23, 520
acronyms formed from, 110
as shown in dictionary, 108
capitalization of, **9a(4):** 110
common, 441–43
distinguished from clipped forms, 123
division of, **8d(7):** 100
Mr., Mrs., Dr., etc., **11a:** 120–21
Ms., Miss, Mrs., in business letters, 515
names of courses, **11d:** 122
names of organizations, 122
names of provinces, months, days of week, etc., **11b:** 121
point of reference for, **28:** 319–20
periods after, **17a(2):** 174–75
provinces, **34a:** 520
Street, Company, etc., **11c:** 121–22
titles and degrees, with proper names, **11a:** 121, 122
volume, chapter, page, **11d:** 122
with dates or figures, 122
absolute, defined, 529
absolute meaning, comparison of modifier with, **4c:** 54
absolute phrase
defined, 529
introductory, comma after, **12b** : 133
misused as sentence, **2a:** 35
parenthetical, commas with, **12d(3):** 143
use of, for variety, **30b(4):** 339
abstract and concrete words, **20a(3)** : 250–53
abstract noun, defined, 546
accept, except, **19i:** 233
accidentally, **19i:** 225
acronyms
capitalization of, **9a(4):** 110
defined, 530
division of, **8d(7):** 100
periods not used with, 123
point of reference for, **28:** 319
active voice
defined, 79, 557
use of, for emphasis, **29d:** 330
adapt, adopt, **19i:** 225
addresses
commas with, **12d(2):** 141

numbers in, **11**: 124–25
of business letters, 522
ad hominem argument, **23f(9)**: 289
adjectival, defined, 530
adjective clause
defined, 26–27, 531
position of, **25a(3)**: 303
restrictive and non-restrictive, **12d(1)**: 137–40
without connective (contact), 537
adjective-forming suffixes, 16, 50
adjective phrase
recognition of, 23
restrictive and non-restrictive, **12d(1)**: 137–40
adjectives, **4**: 50–55
among parts of speech, 16
as complements, 11–12, **4b**: 52–53
attributive, 532
comparison of, **4c**: 53–54
compound, hyphens with, **18f(1)** : 207–08
co-ordinate, commas with, **12c** : 135–36
defined and classified, 530
distinguished from adverbs, **4** : 50–53
indefinite, 542
nouns as, **4d**: 54–55, 547
participles as, **4**: 51, 549
proper, capitalized, **9a(3)**: 110, 552
adopt, adapt, **19i**: 225
ad populum argument, **23f(10)** : 289–90
adverb clause
dangling, **25b(3)**: 305–06
defined, 27, 531
elliptical, 27, 133
punctuation of, **12b(1)**: 132–33
subordinating conjunctions in, 25, 132
to begin sentence, for variety, **30b(1)**: 338
adverb phrase, 23–24
adverbial, defined, 531
adverbial conjunction, See *conjunctive adverbs.*
adverbs, **4**: 50–55
among parts of speech, 17
comparison of, **4c**: 53–54
conjunctive, 45
defined, 531
distinguished from adjectives, **4**: 50–53
misused as complements, **4b**: 52–53
modifying verbs, adjectives, and other adverbs, **4a**: 51–52
to begin sentence, for variety, **30b(1)**: 338
advice, advise, **19i**: 225
affect, effect, **19i**: 225–26
aggravate, **19i**: 226
agreement, **6**: 66–77, 531
agreement of pronoun and antecedent, **6b**: 74–77
collective nouns, **6b(3)**: 75
compound antecedents, **6b(2)**: 75
person, each, etc., **6b(1)**: 74–75
agreement of subject and verb, **6a** : 68–74
subjects joined by *and*, **6a(2)** : 68–69
subjects joined by *or*, **6a(3)**: 69–70
collective nouns, **6a(7)**: 71–72
each, one, etc., **6a(6)**: 71
intervening nouns or pronouns, **6a(1)**: 68
inverted order, **6a(4)**: 70
news, physics, etc., **6a(9)**: 72–73
some, none, etc. **6a**: 71
pronunciation as cause of error in, **6a(1)**: 68
quantity-denoting phrases, **6a(7)** : 71–72
-s (or *-es*) suffix, 66–67
subject complement, verb form not affected by, **6a(8)**: 72
there—verb—subject, **6a(4)**: 70
title of a work, etc., **6a(10)**: 73

who, which, that, **6a(5)**: 70–71
a half a, **19i**: 226
ain't, **19i**: 226
all, agreement of verb with, **6a**: 71
all-, hyphen with, **18f(4)**: 209
all ready, already, **19i**: 226
all right, alright, **19i**: 226
all the farther, all the faster, **19i**: 226
alliteration, overuse of, **19h**: 223
allude, elude, **19i**: 232
allusion, illusion, **19i**: 226
almanacs
form for "Works Cited," 438–439
almost, most, **19i**: 238
a lot, **19i**: 226
already, all ready, **19i**: 226
alright, **19i**: 226
also, as conjunctive adverb, **3b**: 45
altogether, all together, **19i**: 226
A.M., P.M. **11**: 122; **19i**: 227
ambiguity, in argument, **23f(13)**: 290
ambiguous reference, **28a**: 320
American, British, and Canadian usage, 191
among, between, **19i**: 227
amount of, number of, **19i**: 227
ampersand, in titles, **11c**: 122
an
before common nouns, **9f**: 113
before vowel sound, **19i**: 225
See also *article*.
analogy. See *comparison or contrast*.
analogy, false, **23f(7)**: 289
analysis
in essay, **32b(3)**: 390
in paragraph, **31b(5)**: 359
and
as co-ordinating conjunction, 18
beginning sentences with, **30b(3)**: 339
excessive use of, **24b**: 296–97
omission of in a series, **12c**: 136
punctuation with, **3a**: 41; **12a**: 129–30; **12c**: 135–36
spelled out, **11c**: 122
unstressed, **18a**: 192–93
and etc., **19i**: 227
and who, etc., in parallel structures, **26d**: 312
annotated bibliography, 510
ante-, anti-, **19i**: 227
antecedent
agreement of pronoun with, **6b**: 74–77
ambiguous reference to, **28a**: 320
anyone, person, etc. **6b(1)**: 74–75
collective noun as, **6b(3)**: 75
compound, **6b(2)**: 75
defined, 532
implied, **28c(2)**: 323
in possessive case, **28b**: 321
of relative pronoun, **6a(5)**: 70–71
reference of pronoun to, **28**: 319–24
remote, **28b**: 321
word group or general idea as, **28c(1)**: 322
anticlimax, 329
antonyms, 213
a number, the number, **19i**: 227
any, agreement of verb with, **6a**: 71
anyone
agreement of verb, with, **6a(6)**: 71
distinguished from *any one*, **19i**: 227
reference of pronoun to, **6b(1)**: 74–75
anyway, as conjunctive adverb, **3b**: 45
anyways, anywheres, **19i**: 228
APA documentation style, 445–446, 466–467, 468
apostrophe, **15**: 159–63
in contractions, **15b**: 161–62
misuse of, with pronouns and plurals, **15d**: 163
to form possessive case
of compounds, **15a(3)**: 160
of nouns denoting joint/individual ownership, **15a(4)**: 160–61

of plural nouns, **15a(2)**: 160
of singular nouns and indefinite pronouns, **15a(1)**: 160
to indicate plurals of letters, abbreviations, etc., **15c**: 162
to mark omissions, **15b**: 161–62
variation in use of, 161
appeal to authority or prestige, **23f(12)**: 290
appositives
as sentence fragments, **2c**: 37–38
beginning sentences with, for variety, **30b(4)**: 339
compound, case of, **5a**: 59
defined, 532
non-restrictive, **12d(2)**: 140
preceded by colon, **17d(1)**: 177
related to complement, 11
restrictive, **12d(2)**: 140; **13d**: 148–49
use of in combining sentences, **24a**: 295
archaic words, **19f**: 222
argument, deductive and inductive, **23e**: 285–86
See also *fallacies* and *logical thinking*.
argumentative essay, 380, 387
article
capitalization of, in titles, **9c**: 111
choice of *a* or *an*, **19i**: 225
defined, 532
italics for, in titles, **10a**: 115–16
omission of, **22a**: 272
repetition of, **26b**: 310–11
as
case after, **5b(3)**: 61
for *like, if*, or *since*, **19i**: 228
as a result, as transitional phrase, **3b**: 45
as follows, idiomatic use of, 179
at, after *where*, **19i**: 228
atlases, list of, 430
attributive, defined, 532
audience
and tone, 396
choice and evaluation of, **32e**: 395–400
general vs. specialized, 395–97
use of diction appropriate to, **19**: 220–22
authority, appeal to, **23f(12)**: 290
auxiliary verbs
defined, 532
list of, 6
modal, 532
omission of, **22b**: 274
awful, **19i**: 228
awhile, a while, **19i**: 228
awkward or obscure sentences, **23c(3)**: 282–83

B

bad, badly, **4b**: 53; **19i**: 228
balanced sentence, for emphasis, **29g**: 332
See also *parallel structure*.
bandwagon appeal, **23f(11)**: 290
be
as auxiliary, 6
as linking verb, 11
forms of, **7**: 81
in the subjunctive, **7c**: 91–92
used to form passive, 10, 79
with *-ing* verbs, 80–81
because, after *reason is*, **19i**: 241
begging the question, **23f(3)**: 287
beginning of paper, **31e**: 373
beginning of sentences, varying the, **30b**: 338–41
being as, being that, **19i**: 229
beside, besides, **19i**: 229
besides, as conjunctive adverb, **3b**: 45
be sure and, for *be sure to*, **19i**: 228
better, had better, **19i**: 229
between, among, **19i**: 227
between you and me, **5a**: 59
Bible
capitalization of, **9a(1)**: 109
citation of, 463–464

italics or quotation marks not used for, **10a**: 116
use of colon in references to, **17d(2)**: 178
bibliography for research paper, **33b(4)**: 432–46
APA "References," 467–468
cards for preliminary, 441
MLA "Works Cited," 467–468
sample entries, 433–40, 445–46
specimen, MLA style, 509, 511
use of sources for, 422–32
indexes, 426–27
library catalogues, 422–25
reference books, 428–32
biographical dictionaries, list of, 430
book reviews
form for "Works Cited," 437
books, titles of
capitalization of, **9c**: 111–12
in APA references, 445
in citations, 459–465
in MLA list of works cited, 433–438
italicized, **10a**: 115–16
both . . . and, parallel structure with, **26c**: 311
boys, girls, **19i**: 234
British, American, and Canadian usage, 191
broad reference, **28c**: 322–23
broke, for *broken*, **19i**: 229
bug, **19i**: 229
bulletins
form for "Works Cited," 439
bunch, **19i**: 229
business letters, **34a**: 513–23
envelopes for, 522
formats of, 513–14
parts of, 514–16
types of, 518–23
application, 522–23
claim and adjustment, 519
order, 521
thank-you, 518
bust, busted, bursted, **19i**: 229
but
as co-ordinating conjunction, 18
beginning sentences with, **30b(3)**: 339
excessive use of, **24b**: 296–97
in contrasted element, **12d(2)**: 140–41
linking main clauses with, **3a**: 41–43; **12a**: 129–32
but what, **19i**: 229
by-phrase, after passive verb, 79, 557

C

call numbers, in library, 423
can, may, **19i**: 230
can't hardly, can't scarcely, **19i**: 230
capitalization
after a colon, **9e**: 112; **17d**: 178
dictionary as guide to use of, 108
of abbreviations, **9a(4)**: 110
of acronyms, **9a(4)**: 110
of calendar designations, **9a(1)**: 109
of derivatives, **9a(3)**: 110
of first word of sentence, **9e**: 112
of fragment in dialogue, **9e**: 112
of geographical names, **9a(1)**: 109
of historical documents, periods, events, **9a(1)**: 109
of holy books, **9a(1)**: 109, 464
of hyphenated words in titles, 111–12
of *I* and *O*, **9d**: 112
of languages, **9a(1)**: 109
of members of groups, **9a(1)**: 109
of names of persons, **9a(1)**: 109
of organizations, **9a(1)**: 109
of personification, 110
of proper names, **9a(1)**: 109
of *River, Street*, etc., **9a(2)**: 110
of Supreme Being, words denoting, **9a(1)**: 109
of titles of books, papers, etc., **9c**:

111–12
of titles of persons, **9b**: 111
of trademarks, **9a(1)**: 109
overuse of, **9f**: 113
style sheet for, 113
card catalogue, in library, 423–24
caret, for insertions, **8e**: 103
case, **5**: 56–65
after *than* or *as*, **5b(3)**: 61
defined, 532–33
forms of nouns and pronouns, 56–57, 538
in combined sentences, 58–59
in compound constructions, **5a**: 59–60
objective: uses of, 57; with infinitive, **5e**: 64
possessive
apostrophe with, **15a**: 159–61
before gerund, **5d**: 64
subjective for complement of *be*, **5f**: 65
subjective, uses of, 56–57
who as subject of clause used as object, **5b(1)**: 60
who/whom before *I think, he says*, etc., **5b(2)**: 61
whom, for objects, **5c**: 62–63
case, line, **19i**: 230
cause and effect, analysis of, **31b(5)**: 359; **32b(3)**: 390
cause of . . . on account of, due to, **19i**: 230
central idea. See *thesis statement; topic sentence*.
centre on, revolve around, **19i**: 230
checklists
for proofreading, 102
for revising, 374, 414–15
choppy sentences, **24a**: 295–96
chronological order, **31b**: 356–57; **32f(1)**: 401
circular reasoning, **23f(3)**: 287
citations, in research papers, 459–467
classification, use of
in definition, 284, 360
in essay, **32b(3)**: 390
in paragraph, **31b(4)**: 358–59
clauses
adjective, 26–27, 531
adverb, 27, 531
as sentence fragments, **2b**: 36–37
contact, 537
dangling, **25b(3)**: 305–06
defined and classified, 25, 533
elliptical, 27, **25b(3)**: 305–06
introductory, punctuation of **12b(1)**: 132–33
main (independent), punctuation between, **3**: 40–49; **12a**: 129–30; **14a**: 152–54
misplaced, **25a(3)**: 303
non-restrictive, commas with, **12d(1)**: 137–40
noun, 26, 547
recognition of, 25–29
restrictive, **12d(1)**: 137–40
subordinate (dependent), 25–28, 533
clichés, **20c**: 257
climax
in essay, 401
in sentence, **29c**: 329
clipped form
defined, 533
no period after, **11**: 123
coherence in sentences, marred by
dangling modifiers, **25b**: 304–06
excessive detail, **23b**: 280
faulty parallelism, **26**: 308–13
misplaced parts, **25a**: 301–04
unrelated parts, **23a**: 279–80
coherent paragraphs, **31a**: 347–55
collective noun
defined, 546
number of pronoun referring to, **6b(3)**: 75
number of verb agreeing with, **6a(7)**: 71–72

colloquial English, **19b:** 219–20
colon
after salutation in business letter, **34a(3):** 514–15
before appositive, **17d(1):** 177
before explanation, **17d(1):** 177–78
before series, **17d(1):** 177
before summary, **17d(1):** 177
between main clauses, **17d(1):** 178
between title and subtitle, **17d(2):** 178
capitalization after, **9e:** 112; **17d(1):** 178
distinguished from semicolon, **14:** 154
in scriptural references, **17d(2):** 178
in time references, **17d(2):** 178
position of, with quotation marks, **16e(2):** 171
superfluous, **17d(3):** 178–79
comma
after conjunctive adverbs, **14a:** 153
after introductory adverb clauses, **12b(1):** 132–33
after introductory transitional expressions, interjections, etc., **12b(3):** 134
after long introductory phrases, **12b(2):** 133–34
before co-ordinating conjunctions joining main clauses, **12a:** 129–32
between co-ordinate adjectives, **12c(2):** 136
between items in series, **12c(1):** 135–36
between short, parallel main clauses, **3a:** 43
between statement and tag question, **3a:** 43
pause and voice variation in guide to use of, **12:** 128; **13:** 147; **14:** 151
position of, with quotation marks, **16e(1):** 171
superfluous, **13:** 147–50
to mark omissions, **21c:** 269; **22a(2):** 273
to prevent misreading, **12e:** 143–44
to set off contrasted elements **12d(2):** 140–41
to set off geographical names and items in dates and addresses, **12d(2):** 141
to set off non-restrictive appositives, **12d(2):** 140
to set off non-restrictive clauses or phrases, **12d(1):** 137–40
to set off parenthetical elements, **12d(3):** 142–43
comma splice, **3:** 40–49
between main clauses not linked by *and, but*, etc. **3a:** 41–44
defined, 533
in divided quotations, 46
revision of, 41
with conjunctive adverb or transitional phrase, **3b:** 45–47
common gender, 68, 74
common noun, defined, 546
comparative degree, use of, **4c:** 54
compare to, compare with, **19i:** 230
comparison
completion of, **22c:** 274–75
defined, 534
double, **4c:** 54; **21a:** 263
elliptical, case with, **5b(3):** 61
faulty, in argument, **23f(7):** 289
forms for, adjectives and adverbs, **4c:** 53–54
metaphor as, 253–54, **23c(1):** 282
of absolute modifiers, **4c:** 54
other in, **22c:** 275
simile as, 253–54
comparison or contrast
in balanced sentence, **29g:** 332
to develop paragraph, **31b(7):** 361–62

to develop thesis, **32b(3)**: 390
complementary, complimentary, **19i**: 230
complements
and subject-verb agreement, **6a(8)**: 72
defined and classified, 534
recognition of, 11–13
object, 11–13, **4b**: 52–53
subject, 11–13, **4b**: 52–53; **5**: 65
complete subjects and predicates, 3, 550–51, 554–55
complex sentence
defined, 29
for variety, **30c(1)**: 341
complimentary close, in business letters, **34a(5)**: 516
composition
asking *who, what*, etc., **32b(2)**: 389
audience, **32e**: 395–97
ideas
arranging, **32c**: 391–92
collecting and listing, **32b**: 388–90
sequence of, **32f(1)**: 400
outline, rough, **32f**: 400–04
paragraph-development methods, **32b(3)**: 390
purpose, **32**: 379–80
Reviser's Checklist, 414–15
subject
choosing, **32a(1)**: 383–85
limiting, **32a(2)**: 385–87
thesis statement, **32d**: 393–95
writing and revising
first draft, **32g**
second draft, **32h**: 409–15
final draft, **32i**: 415–19
See also *paragraphs; research paper*.
compound-complex sentence, defined, 29
compound constructions
case of pronoun in, **5a**: 59–60
defined, 534
compound predicate
defined, 534
part of, as fragment, **2c**: 37–38
use of, for variety, **30c(2)**: 341
compound sentence, defined, 29
See also *sentences*.
compound subject
agreement of verb with, **6a**: 68–70
defined, 534
compound words
apostrophe with, **15a(3)**: 160
co-ordinate adjective before, **12c(2)**: 136
division of, **8d(4)** 100
hyphenation of, **18f**: 207–09
nouns as, 16
numbers as, **18f(2)**: 208
computerized library catalogue, 425
conciseness, **21**: 261–70
concluding paragraph, **31e**: 374
conclusions, valid and invalid, **23e**: 285–86
concrete noun, defined, 546
concrete and abstract words, **20a(3)**: 250–53
conjugation, defined and illustrated, 535–36
conjunctions
among parts of speech, 18
co-ordinating, defined and listed, 18, 536
correlative, parallel structure with, **26c**: 311–12
defined and classified, 536–37
omission of, **22a**: 272–73
repetition of, **26b**: 310–11
subordinating, lists of, 18, 25, 132
to begin sentence, for variety, **30b(3)**: 339
conjunctive adverbs
between main clauses, punctuation with, **3b**: 45–47; **14a**: 152–53
defined, 537
list of, 45
position of, 46

to begin sentence, for variety, **30b(3):** 339
connectives, defined, 537
connotation, **20a(2):** 249–50
conscious, conscience, **19i:** 230–31
consequently, as conjunctive adverb, **3b:** 45
construction, defined, 537
contact clause
defined, 537
restrictive, **12d(1):** 139
contractions
apostrophe in, **15b:** 161–62
appropriate use of, **15b:** 162
avoided in formal writing, **19b:** 219–20
distinguished from possessive pronouns, **18b:** 193
contradiction, in argument, **23f(2):** 287
contrast. See *comparison or contrast.*
contrasted elements, set off by commas, **12d(2):** 140–41
controlling idea. See *topic sentence.*
co-ordinate adjectives, punctuation of, **12c(2):** 136
co-ordinating conjunctions
at beginning of sentence, for variety, **30b(3):** 339
defined and listed, 18, 536
meanings of, **12a:** 131
punctuation with, **12a:** 129–32; **12c:** 135–36
co-ordination
distinguished from subordination, **24:** 293–95
excessive, in choppy sentences, **24a:** 295–96
revising, for variety, **30c:** 341–42
unemphatic, in stringy compound sentences, **24b:** 296–97
use of in parallel structures, **26:** 308–13
corrections, manuscripts, **8e(1):** 101–03
correlatives
defined and listed, 537
parallel structure with, **26c:** 311–12
could of, **19i:** 231
count noun, 547
couple, couple of, **19i:** 231
criteria, **19i:** 231
Cumulative Book Index, 426

D

-d, -ed, omission of, **4:** 51; **7a:** 82–83
dangling modifiers, **25b:** 304–07
defined, 537
elliptical, **25b(3):** 305–06
gerund or infinitive, **25b(2):** 305
participial, **25b(1):** 304–05
dash
after introductory series, **17e(4):** 181–82
distinguished from comma and parentheses, 183
formation of, in typing and in handwriting, 180
to mark sudden break in thought or change in tone, **17e(1):** 180
to set off explanation or illustration, **17e(2):** 180–81
to set off parenthetical element, **17e(3):** 181
data, **19i:** 231
dates
commas with, **12d(2):** 141
numbers in, **11e:** 124
days of week, capitalization of, **9a(1):** 109
decimals, figures for, **11e:** 125
declarative sentences
containing questions, **17b:** 175
distinguished from commands, questions, etc., 29, 554
declension, defined and illustrated, 538
deduction, fallacies of, **23f:** 287
deductive logic, **23e:** 285–86
definition

classification in, 284, 360
connotative, 285
differentiation in, 284, 360
formal, 284, 360
formulation of, **23d**: 283–85
historical, 360–61
informal, 285, 360
in paragraph development, **31b(6)**: 360–61
is when, is where, avoided in, **19i**: 236; **23c(3)**: 282–83
use of examples or synonyms in, 285, 360
degrees of comparison, **4c**: 53–54
Deity, capitalization of references to, **9a(1)**: 109
demonstrative pronoun, defined, 539
denotation, **20a(1)**: 247–49
dependent clauses, 25–28, 533
See also *subordinate clauses.*
description
in paragraph development, **31b(3)**: 357–58
related to purpose, **32**: 379–80
descriptive adjective, 530
descriptive essay, 379–80, 387, 401
detail, excessive, **23b**: 280–81
details, specific
in description, **31b(3)**: 357–58; **32f**: 401
in sentences, **20a(3)**: 252
determiner, 539
development
of paragraph, **31b**: 356–63
of plan or outline, **32f**: 400–04; **33c**: 445
diagraming, defined and illustrated, 539–40
dialectal words, **19d**: 221
dialogue
contractions in, **15b**: 162
fragments in, **9e**: 112
informal words in, **19b**: 219–20
paragraphing of, **16a(3)**: 167–68
punctuation of, **16a(4)**: 168–69
diction
abstract and concrete words, **20a(3)**: 250–53
archaic, **19f**: 222
big words, **19c**: 221
clichés, **20c**: 257–59
colloquial, **19b**: 219–20
connotations, **20a(2)**: 249–50
defined, 246
denotations, **20a(1)**: 247–49
direct, economical, **21**: 261–70
euphemisms, **20c**: 257
exact words, **20a**: 247–55
figurative language, **20a(4)**: 253–55
formal English, **19b**: 219–20
general English, **19a(6)**: 218–19
Glossary of Usage, **19i**: 224–45
idiomatic usage, **20b**: 255–56, 542
informal English, **19b**: 219–20
jargon, **19c**: 220–21
non-standard English, **19e**: 222
obsolete, **19f**: 222
omission of necessary words, **22**: 271–76
ornate, **19h**: 223–24
regional, **19d**: 221
repetition of words, **21c**: 267–70; **29e**: 331
slang, **19c**: 220–21
specific and general, **20a(3)**: 250–53
standard English, defined, 225
tautology, **21a(1)**: 262–63
technical words, **19g**: 222
trite expressions, **20c**: 257–59
unpleasing combinations of sounds, **19h**: 223
varieties of usage, 218–19, 224–25
wordiness, **21**: 261–70
dictionaries
lists of, 210, 428–29
sample entry from, 211
use of, 210–19
differ from, differ with, **19i**: 231
differentiation, in definition, **23d**: 284

direct address
commas with, **12d(3):** 142
defined, 541
direct diction, **21:** 261–70
direct object
defined, 9, 548
recognition of, 9–10
direct quotations
accuracy of, 452–53
brackets with, **17g:** 183–84
capitalization in, **9e:** 112
colon before, **17d(1):** 177, 486
commas with, **12d(3):** 143
defined, 541
divided, 46
documentation of, 454–455, 457–58
ellipsis mark in, **17i:** 185–86
introduction of, 453, 476, 484, 486
in note-taking, 452–53
poetry as, **16a(2):** 166–67
prose passages as, **16a(1):** 165–66
quotation marks with, **16a:** 165–69
slash with, **16a(2):** 166; **17h:** 184
discourse, shifts from indirect to direct, **27c:** 316
disinterested, uninterested, **19i:** 231
dissertations, unpublished
form for bibliography, 439
forms for notes, 465, 467
divided quotations, comma splice in, 46
division, false, **23f(16):** 291
division of words at end of line, **8d:** 99–101
do, as auxiliary, 6, 78, 87–88
documented paper. See *Research Paper*.
done, misuse of, **19i:** 231
don't, for *doesn't*, **19i:** 231
double comparative or superlative, **4c:** 54; **21a:** 263
double negative
defined, 541
modifiers in, **4:** 51
neither in, **19i:** 239
not . . . no/none/nothing, **19i:** 239
double possessive, **15:** 159
double subject, **21a(1):** 263
due to, after *cause of*, **19i:** 230

E

each
as antecedent, **6b(1):** 74–75
as subject, **6a(6):** 71
with subject, **6a(2):** 69
each and every, **19i:** 231
economical diction, **21:** 261–70
-ed, omission of, **4:** 51; **7:** 82–83
editorials
form for "Works Cited," 437
effect, affect, **19i:** 225–26
effect and cause, analysis of, **31b(5):** 359; **32b(3):** 390
ei/ie, in spelling, **18d:** 198
either, number of
as antecedent, **6b(1):** 74
as subject, **6a(6):** 71
either . . . or
parallel structure with, **26c:** 311–12
subjects joined by, **6a(3):** 69–70
either-or fallacy, **23f(16):** 291
-elect, hyphen with, **18f(4):** 209
elicit, illicit, **19i:** 232
ellipsis mark
to indicate omission, **17i:** 185–86
to mark pause, **17i:** 187
elliptical constructions
case with, **5b(3):** 61
comma with, 269, 273
dangling, **25b(3):** 305–06
defined, 541
use of, to avoid repetition, **21c:** 269
elude, allude, **19i:** 232
emigrate from, immigrate to, **19i:** 232
eminent, imminent, **19i:** 232
emotions, appeal to, **23f(10):** 289–90
emphasis, **29:** 325–34
abrupt change in sentence length for, **29h:** 333

active voice for, **29d**: 330–31
balanced sentence for, **29g**: 332
climactic order for, **29c**: 329–30; **32f(1)**: 401
conciseness for, **21**: 261–70
exact diction for, **20**: 246–60
inverted word order for, **29f**: 332
italics for, **10e**: 118
periodic sentence for, **29b**: 327–28
placement of words for, **29a**: 326–27
punctuation for
colon, **17d(1)**: 177–78
dash, **17e**: 180–81
semicolon, **14b**: 155
repetition for, **29e**: 331
emphatic verb form, 87–88
encyclopedias, 429–30
form for "Works Cited," 438
end marks, **17**: 173–77
ending, of paper, **31e(3)**: 373–74
endnotes. See *notes*.
English language, origin and development of, 214–18
enthuse, enthused, **19i**: 232
envelope for business letter, 522
equivocation, **23f(14)**: 290–91
errors, record of, 105
essay, defined, 379
See *composition*.
etc., **11**: 123; **19i**: 232–33
etymology, 214–15
euphemisms, **20c**: 257
evaluating the audience, **32e**: 395–97
even, position of, **25a(1)**: 301
ever so often, every so often, **19i**: 233
every, before singular compound subject, **6a(2)**: 69
everyday, every day, **18b**: 193
everyone, every one, **19i**: 227
everyone, everybody
as antecedent, **6b(1)**: 74–75
as subject, **6a(6)**: 71
evidence
exceptional or unusual, **23f(5)**: 288
sufficient and relevant, **23e**: 286
ex-, hyphen with, **18f(4)**: 209
exact word choice, **20**: 246–60
See also *diction*.
example
in definition, **23d**: 285
in essay, **32b(3)**: 390
in paragraph development, **31b(8)**: 362
except, accept, **19i**: 233
excessive co-ordination, **24b**: 296–97
excessive detail, **23b**: 280–81
exclamation point, **17c**: 176–77
overuse of, **17c**: 176
position of, with quotation marks, **16e(3)**: 171–72
uses of, **17c**: 176
exclamatory sentence, 23, **17c**: 176
expansion of simple sentence, 3–4
expletive
defined, 541
there—verb—subject, **6a(4)**: 70
explicit, implicit, **19i**: 233
expository essay, 380, 387

F

fact and value judgment, **23f(4)**: 288
fallacies, **23f**: 287–92
ad hominem, **23f(9)**: 289
ad populum, **23f(10)**: 289–90
ambiguity, **23f(13)**: 290
appeal to authority, **23f(12)**: 290
bandwagon, **23f(11)**: 290
circular reasoning, **23f(3)**: 287
confusion of fact and value judgment, **23f(4)**: 288
equivocation, **23f(14)**: 290–91
false analogy, **23f(7)**: 289
false division, **23f(16)**: 291
hasty generalization, **23f(5)**: 288
ignoring the question, **23f(8)**: 289
non sequitur, **23f(1)**: 287
of deduction or inference, **23f**: 287
of imprecision, **23f**: 290–91

of induction, **23f**: 287–89
of irrelevance, **23f**: 289–90
of misrepresentation, **23f**: 291
oversimplification, **23f(15)**: 291
post hoc, ergo propter hoc, **23f(6)**: 288–89
self-contradiction, **23f(2)**: 287
false analogy, **23f(7)**: 289
false division, **23f(16)**: 291
false premise, **23e**: 285–86
farther, further, **19i**: 233
faulty logic, **23f**: 287–92
See also *fallacies*.
faulty parallelism, **26**: 308–13
See also *parallel structure*.
feel, modifier after, **4b**: 52–53
fewer, less, **19i**: 233
figurative language
effective use of, **20a(4)**: 253–55
mixed metaphors, **23c(1)**: 282
figures
for numbers, **11e**: 124–25
forming the plural of, **15c**: 162
when to italicize, **10d**: 117
figures of speech, 253–55
final consonant, when doubled before suffix, **18c(3)**: 197
final *e*, when dropped before suffix, **18c(2)**: 196–97
final *y*, in spelling, **18c(4)**: 197
finally, as conjunctive adverb, **3b**: 45
fine, **19i**: 233
finite verb, defined, 541
fit, fitted, **19i**: 233
folks, **19i**: 233
footnotes. See *notes*.
for
as conjunction, comma before, **12a**: 129–32
as preposition, case with, **5a**: 59
for example, as transitional phrase, **3b**: 45
foreign spellings, retention of, 200
foreign words, italicized, **10b**: 116–17
form of argument, **23e**: 285–86
formal definition, **23d**: 283–85; **31b(6)**: 360
formal English, **19b**: 219–20
former, **19i**: 234
fractions
hyphen with, **18f(2)**: 208
use of figures for, **11**: 125
fragment, sentence, **2**: 32–39
appositive as, **2c**: 37–38
defined, 32, 554
in dialogue, **9e**: 112
part of predicate as, **2c**: 37–38
phrase as, **2a**: 35
recognition of, 32–34
revision of, 34
fun, **19i**: 234
function words, 14, 542
further, farther, **19i**: 233
furthermore, as conjunctive adverb, **3b**: 45
fused sentence, **3**: 40–49
defined, 542
revision of, 41
future and future perfect tenses, 79, 88–89

G

gender, 68, 74
general vs. specialized audience, 395–97
general English, defined, 224
general and specific words, **20a(3)**: 250–53
generalizations
hasty, **23f(5)**: 288
in inductive argument, **23e**: 286
genitive case, 532
See also *possessive case*.
geographical names
capitalization of, **9a(1)**: 109
commas with, **12d(2)**: 141
use of apostrophe with, 161
gerund
defined, 542
in dangling phrases, **25b(2)**: 305

in noun phrase, 22
possessive before, **5d**: 64
get, **19i**: 234
girls, boys, **19i**: 234
Glossary of Grammatical Terms, 529–57
Glossary of Usage, 224–45
good, for *well*, **4a**: 51; **19i**: 234
Grammatical Terms, Glossary of, 529–57
great, **19i**: 234
guy(s), **19i**: 234

H

hackneyed phrases, **20c** ; 257–59
had better, better, **19i**: 229
had of, had have, **19i**: 234
had ought, hadn't ought, **19i**: 234
half, agreement of verb with, **6a**: 71
handwritten paper
legibility of, **8c(1)**: 98
manuscript form for, **8a-b**: 96–98
revision of, **8e**: 101–05
sample page from, 512
hang, **19i**: 234
hanged, hung, **19i**: 234
hardly
position of, **25a(1)**: 301
with negative, **19i**: 235
hasty generalization, **23f(5)**: 288
have, of, **19i**: 239
heading of business letter, **34a(1)**: 514
hence, as conjunctive adverb, **3b**: 45
here, after *this*, **19i**: 244
himself, not *hisself*, **5**: 57; **19i**: 235
historical definition, **31b(6)**: 360–61
historical present, **7**: 87
hooked on, **19i**: 235
hopefully, **19i**: 235
how come, **19i**: 235
however, as conjunctive adverb, **3b**: 45
hung, hanged, **19i**: 234
hyperbole, 254
hyphen, **18f**: 207–09
at end of line, **8d**: 99–100
in adjectival before noun, **18f(1)**: 207–08
in compound nouns, **18f**: 207
in numbers and fractions, **18f(2)**: 208
suspension, **18f(1)**: 208
to avoid ambiguity, **18f(3)**: 209
with figures or letters, **18f(4)**: 209
with prefixes, **18f(4)**: 209
with suffix *-elect*, **18f(4)**: 209
hyphenated words in titles, capitalization of, **9c**: 111–12

I

I and *O*, **9d**: 112
identifying a paper, **8b(7)**: 98
idioms, **20b**: 255–56
ie/ei, in spelling, **18d**: 198
ignoring the question, **23f(8)**: 289
illicit, elicit, **19i**: 232
illiteracies, **19e**: 222
illusion, allusion, **19i**: 226
illustration, in paragraph pattern, **31a(3)**: 353–54
immigrate to, emigrate from, **19i**: 232
imperative mood, 80, 545
imperative sentence, **17a**: 174, 554
implicit, explicit, **19i**: 233
imply, infer, **19i**: 235
imprecision, fallacies of, **23f**: 290–91
in to, into, **18b**: 193
in regards to, **19i**: 236
incidentally, **19i**: 225
incomplete comparisons, **22c**: 274–75
incomplete constructions, **22**: 271–76; **23c(3)**: 282–83
incomplete sentence, **2**: 32–39
See also *fragment*.
incredible, incredulous, **19i**: 235
indeed, as conjunctive adverb, **3b**: 45
indefinite, defined, 542
indefinite pronouns
defined, 542

number of, **6a(6):** 71; **6b(1):** 74–75
possessive case of, **15a:** 159–60
indefinite *you*, awkward use of, **28c(3):** 323
indention
for paragraphs, **31:** 346
for quotations, **16a:** 165–67
in APA "References," 468
in business letters, 514
in MLA "Works Cited," 467–468
in outlines, 449–451
independent clauses, 28, 533
See also *clauses; main clauses.*
indexes to periodicals, 425–27
indicative mood, 80, 545
indirect object, 9–10, 548
indirect question, **17a(1):** 174
indirect quotation, **16a:** 165, 541
Indo-European languages, 214–15
infer, imply, **19i:** 235
inference, fallacies of, **23f:** 287
inferior than, **19i:** 235
infinitive
and repetition of *to*, **26b:** 310–11
case with, **5e:** 64
defined, 543
split, **25a(5):** 303
tense forms of, 81, **7b(2):** 90
infinitive phrases
dangling, **25b(2):** 305
uses of, 22–23
inflection, defined, 543
informal definition, **23d:** 285; **31b(6):** 360
informal English
avoided in formal writing, **19b:** 219–20
contractions in, **15b:** 162
defined, 225
ingenious, ingenuous, **19i:** 235
insertions
in quotations, brackets with, **17g:** 183–84
in revision of paper, **8e:** 101–03
inside address, **34a:** 514
instead, as conjunctive adverb, **3b:** 45
intensifiers (intensives)
defined, 543
so, such, too as, **22d:** 275–76
intensive pronoun, defined, 544
interjections
among parts of speech, 19
commas with, **12b(3):** 134; **12d(3):** 142
exclamation points with, **17c:** 176
interrogative pronoun, 544
interrogative sentence, 554
interrupters, set off by commas, **12d(3):** 142
interview
form for "Works Cited," 440
into, in to, **18b:** 193
intransitive verb, 12, 556
introductory elements, punctuation of, **12b:** 132–35
introductory or opening paragraph, **31e:** 373
inversion
defined, 544
for emphasis, **29f:** 332
subject-verb agreement and, **6a(4):** 70
irregardless, **19i:** 236
irregular verb, defined, 544
irrelevance, fallacies of, **23f:** 289–90
is when, is where, in definitions, **19i:** 236; **23c(3):** 282
it, awkward use of, **28c(3):** 323; **28d:** 324
italics
for emphasis, **10e:** 118
for foreign words, **10b:** 116–17
for names of ships, airplanes, etc., **10c:** 117
for titles of books, newspapers, films, etc., **10a:** 115–16
for titles of works of art, **10c:** 117
for words, etc., as such, **10d:** 117

overuse or misuse of, **10e**: 118
underlining as indication of, **10**: 115
its, it's, **15d**: 163; **19i**: 236

J

jargon, **19c**: 220–21
joint ownership, possessive to indicate, **15a(4)**: 161
journals
forms for APA "References," 445–446
forms for MLA "Works Cited," 437
just, position of, **25a(1)**: 301

K

kick, **19i**: 236
kind, with *that* or *this*, **19i**: 236
kind of, sort of, **19i**: 236
kind of a, **19i**: 236

L

later, latter, **19i**: 236
lay, lie, **7a(2)**: 85–87; **19i**: 237
learn, for *teach*, **19i**: 237
lectures
form for "Works Cited," 440
legibility, **8c**: 98
less, fewer, **19i**: 233
letter of alphabet
forming plural of, **15c**: 162
italics for, **10d**: 117
letters, business
See *business letters*.
let's us, **19i**: 237
let's you and me, **5a**: 59
lexical words, 556
liable to, **19i**: 237
libraries, **33**: 422–32
catalogues in, 422–25
indexes in, 426–27
reference books in, 428–32
lie, lay, **7a(2)**: 85–87, **19i**: 237
like, for *as, as if*, **19i**: 237–38
likewise, as conjunctive adverb, **3b**: 45
limiting adjective, 530
limiting the subject
of a composition, **32a(2)**: 385–87
of a research paper, **33a**: 421–22
line, case, **19i**: 230
linking verbs, 11–12, **4b**: 52–53
list-making, in planning essay, 388–89
lists of works cited, in research papers, 467–468
literary present, **27a**: 315
literature, guides to, 431–32
logical thinking
deduction and induction, **23e**: 285–86
formulating definitions, **23d**: 283–85
mistakes in, **23f**: 287–92
See also *fallacies*.
look, modifier after, **4b**: 52–53
loose, lose, **19i**: 238
loose sentences
distinguished from periodic, **29b**: 327–28
revision of, for variety, **30c**: 341–42
lousy, **19i**: 238
-ly
as suffix of modifiers, **4**: 50
hyphen not used after, **18f(1)**: 208
when added to a final *l*, in spelling, **18c(5)**: 198

M

magazines
form for "Works Cited," 436–437
italics for titles of, **10a**: 115–16
main clauses
defined, 28, 533
linked by *and, but*, etc., **12a**: 129–32
linked by conjunctive adverbial, **3b**: 45–47; **14a**: 152–53
recognition of, 28–29
separated by colon, **17d(1)**: 178
separated by semicolon, **14a**: 152–54
main idea. See *thesis statement; topic*

sentence.
main verb, after auxiliary, 6
manuscript
arrangement of, on page, **8b**: 97–98
division of words in **8d**: 99–101
handwritten, **8a(1)**: 96; **8c(1)**: 98
identification on, **8b(7)**: 98
indention in, **8b(2)**: 97
legibility of, **8c**: 98
margins in, **8b(1)**: 97
paging of, **8b(3)**: 97
proofreading of, **8e(1)**: 101–03
punctuation in, **8b(6)**: 98
quoted material in, **8b(5)**: 97; **16a**: 165–67
research paper, **33**, 420–512
revision of
after marked by instructor, **8e(2)**: 103–05
before handed in, **8e(1)**: 101–03; **32**: 405–15
title of, **8b(4)**: 97
title page, specimen of, 473
typewritten, **8a(2)**: 96; **8c(2)**: 98
margins of manuscript, **8b(1)**: 97
mass noun, 547
may, can, **19i**: 230
may be, maybe, **19i**: 238
me and, **19i**: 238
meaning, of words
connotative, **20a(2)**: 249–50
denotative, **20a(1)**: 247–49
metaphorical, 254
meanwhile, as conjunctive adverb, **3b**: 45
merely, position of, **25a(1)**: 301
metaphors
effective use of, **20a(4)**: 253–55
mixed, **23c(1)**: 282
microfilm or microfiche catalogue, in library, 424–25
micropublications, citation of, 439
Middle English, 216
mighty, **19i**: 238
misplaced modifier, defined, 545
misplaced parts, **25a**: 301–04
clauses, **25a(3)**: 303
phrases, **25a(2)**: 302
single-word modifiers, **25a(1)**: 301
split infinitives, **25a(5)**: 303
squinting modifiers, **25a(4)**: 303
misrepresentation, fallacies of, **23f**: 291
misspelling, **18**: 190–209
See also *spelling*.
mixed constructions, **23c(2)**: 282
mixed metaphors, **23c(1)**: 282
MLA style of documentation
in citations, 460–466
in lists of works cited, 433–40, 467–68
modal auxiliaries, 532
mode, defined, 545
See also *mood*.
modifiers
adjectives and adverbs, **4**: 50–55
after *feel, look*, etc., **4b**: 52–53
co-ordinate, **12c(2)**: 136
dangling, **25b**: 304–07
defined, 50, 545
hyphenated, **18f(1)**: 207–08
misplaced, **25a**: 301–04, 545
non-restrictive, **12d(1)**: 137–40
position of, 300–01
restrictive, **12d(1)**: 137–40
squinting, **25a(4)**: 303
mood
defined, 80, 545
imperative, **7**: 80, 545
indicated by verb form, **7**: 80
indicative, **7**: 80, 545
shift in, **7d**: 92–93, **27a**: 314–15
subjunctive, **7**: 80; **7c**: 91–92
moral, morale, **19i**: 238
moreover, as conjunctive adverb, **3b**: 45
most
agreement of verb with, **6a**: 71
for *almost*, **19i**: 238

motion pictures
  form for "Works Cited," 439
  italics for titles of, **10a:** 115–16
Mr., Dr., etc., **11a:** 120–21
Mrs., Miss, Ms., use of in business letters, 515
myself, for *I* or *me,* **19i:** 238

N

narration
  in essay, 379, 387, 390
  in paragraph development, 356
nce, nts, in spelling, **18b:** 193
nearly, position of, **25a(1):** 301
negative. See *double negative.*
neither
  in double negative, **19i:** 239
  pronoun with, **6b(1):** 74–75
  verb with, **6a(6):** 71
neither . . . nor
  linking antecedents, **6b(2):** 75
  linking subjects, **6a(3):** 69–70
  parallel structure with, **26c:** 311–12
nevertheless, as conjunctive adverb, **3b:** 45
newspapers
  form for "Works Cited," 436
  italics for titles of, **10a:** 115–16
nicknames, avoiding quotation marks with, **16d:** 170
no
  in double negative, **19i:** 239
  introductory, comma after, **12b(3):** 134
no such a, **19i:** 239
no-account, no-count, no-good, **19i:** 239
nobody, no body, **18b:** 193
nohow, **19i:** 239
nominal, defined, 545
nominative case, 532
  See also *subjective case.*
none
  agreement of verb with, **6a:** 71
  in double negative, **19i:** 239
nonetheless, as conjunctive adverb, **3b:** 45
non-finite verb, defined, 546
non-print sources
  forms for "Works Cited," 439–440
non-restrictive elements
  appositives, **12d(2):** 140
  defined, 546
  modifiers, **12d(1):** 137–40
non sequitur, **23f(1):** 287
non-standard English, **19e:** 222
nor
  antecedents joined by, **6b(2):** 75
  as co-ordinating conjunction, 18
  main clauses linked by, **12a:** 129, 131
  subjects joined by, **6a(3):** 69
not . . . no/ none/ nothing, **19i:** 239
not only . . . but also, parallel structure with, **26c:** 311–12
notation
  in business letters, 516
  in outlines, 448–49
notes (endnotes/footnotes), 460
note-taking
  evaluation of sources for, 451–52
  keyed to outline, 452
  on cards, 452–53
  on photocopies, 453–54
  paraphrasing in, 455–56
  précis in, 456–57
  quoting directly in, 454–55
  selection of material for, 451–53
noun clause
  defined, 25, 533
  recognition of, 25–26
noun phrase
  defined, 22, 550
  denoting quantity, agreement of verb with, **6a(7):** 71–72
  recognition of, 22–23
nouns

among parts of speech, 15–16
attributive, 532
case of, 56, **15a**: 159–61
collective, number of, **6a(7)**: 71–72
compound, 16
declension of, 538
defined and classified, 546–47
functions of, 15, 547
plural forms of, **18e**: 199–200
proper, capitalized, **9a**: 109–10
nowheres, **19i**: 239
nts, nce, in spelling, **18b**: 193
number
agreement in, **6**: 66–77
defined, 547
shifts in, **27b**: 315–16
number
abbreviation of, 110
distinguished from *amount*, **19i**: 227
preceded by *a* or *the*, verb agreement with, **19i**: 227
numbers
as figures or words, **11e**: 124
compound, hyphenated, **18f(2)**: 208
plural form of, **15c**: 162
special usage of, **11e**: 124–25
when to use italics for, **10d**: 117

O

O, oh, **9d**: 112
object
defined, 548
direct, 9–10, 548
indirect, 9–10, 548
of preposition, 17, 548
of verbal, 57, 548, 556
object complement
adjective as, **4b**: 52
defined, 11, 534
recognition of, 11–13
objective case
after *than* or *as*, **5b(3)**: 61
defined, 56–57
in compound constructions, **5a**: 59
uses of, **5**: 57
whom, **5b(2)**: 61; **5c**: 62
with infinitive, **5e**: 64
obscurity
awkward construction, **23c(3)**: 282–83
excessive detail, **23b**: 280
obsolete words, **19f**: 222
of, for *have*, **19i**: 239
off of, **19i**: 239
OK, O.K., okay, **19i**: 240
Old English, 216–17
omissions, **22**: 271–76
indicated by apostrophe, **15b**: 161–62
indicated by comma, 269, 273
indicated by ellipsis mark, **17i**: 185–86
of completing phrases or clauses after *so, such, too*, **22d**: 275–76
of necessary articles, pronouns, conjunctions, or prepositions, **22a**: 272–73
of necessary verbs, **22b**: 274
of words needed to complete comparisons, **22c**: 274–75
of words needed to make parallels clear, **26b**: 310–11
on the contrary, on the other hand, as transitional phrases, **3b**: 45
one
pronoun with, **6b(1)**: 74–75
verb with, **6a(6)**: 71
only, position of, **25a(1)**: 301
opening paragraph, **31e**: 373
or
antecedents joined by, **6b(2)**: 75
as co-ordinating conjunction, 18
main clauses linked by, **12a**: 129–31
subjects joined by, **6a(3)**: 69–70
order of ideas
in essay, **32f**: 401
in outline, **32f**: 402–04, **33d**: 450–

51
in paragraph, **31b**: 356–63
order of words. See *word order*.
organization
of the essay, **32f**: 400–04
of the paragraph, **31a(3)**: 352–55
See also *outlines*.
ornate style, **19h**: 223–24
other, omission of, **22c**: 275
otherwise, as conjunctive adverb, **3b**: 45
ought, **19i**: 234
outlines
final, 468–70
headings and subheadings, **33d**: 448–51
in relation to paragraphing, 468–70
indention and notation, **33d**: 448–51
preliminary, **33c**: 446–47
rough (working plan), **32f**: 400–04
types of
paragraph, 448–49
sentence, 448, 469–70
topic, 448, 475–77
overlapping subordination, **24c**: 297–98
oversimplification, **23f(15)**: 291
overwriting, **19h**: 223–24

P

page numbers
figures for, **11e**: 122
in citations, 459–467
in "Works Cited," 434, 436–438
of manuscript, **8b(3)**: 97
pamphlets
form for "Works Cited," 439
paper. See *compositions*.
paperback edition as source, 435
paragraph outline, 448–49
paragraphs, **31**: 346–78
checklist for revising, 374
coherence in, **31a**: 347–55
concluding, **31e(2)**: 374
defined, 346
in dialogue, **16a(3)**: 167–68
indention of, **8b(2)**: 97
length of, 346
methods of development of, **31b**: 356–63
analysis, 359
classification, 358–59
comparison/contrast, 361–62
definition, 360–61
description, 357–58
example, 362
narration, 356–57
process, 357
opening, **31e(1)**: 373
organization according to pattern, **31a(3)**: 352–55
problem-solution, 352–53
question-answer, 352
topic-restriction-illustration, 353–54
topic sentences in, **31a**: 347–52
placement of, 349–50
restriction of, 347–49
transitional, 375
transitions between, **31d**: 371–72
transitions within, **31c**: 365–70
unity in, **31c**: 364–70
parallel structure
in balanced sentence, **29g**: 332
in paragraphs, 368–70
in outlines, **33d**: 448
of clauses, **26a(2)**: 309
of sentences, **26a(3)**: 309
of words and phrases, **26a(1)**: 309
repetition of article, preposition, etc., in, **26b**: 310–11
with *and who, and which*, **26d**: 312
with co-ordinating conjunctions, 293, 308
with correlatives, **26c**: 311–12
parallelism, defined, 308, 368
See also *parallel structure*.
paraphrase, 455–56
parentheses

compared with dashes and commas, 183
position of, with other punctuation, **17f:** 182
replaced by brackets, **17g:** 183–84
to set off parenthetical or supplementary matter, **17f:** 182–83
with figures or letters in enumeration, **17f:** 182
with question mark, to express uncertainty, **17b:** 176
with repeated numbers, **11e:** 125
parenthetical citation, **16e(1):** 171, 443
parenthetical elements
brackets with, **17g:** 183–84
commas with, **12d:** 142–43
dashes with, **17e(3):** 181
defined, 548–49
parentheses with, **17f:** 182–83
participial phrase
as adjectival, 23
dangling, **25b(1):** 304–05
defined, 21, 549
in sentence patterns, 304–05
introductory, for variety, **30b(2):** 338–39
misused as sentence, **2a:** 35
non-restrictive and restrictive, punctuation of, **12d(1):** 137–38
participle
as adjectival, form of, **4:** 51
defined, 549
distinguished from gerund, 21
in verb phrase
present, **7:** 80–81
past, **7a(1):** 82–85
tense forms
in sequence, **7b(2):** 90
list of, 81
particle, with verb, 6–7, 549
parts of speech
defined, 549–50
functions of, 14
labelled in dictionary, 19, 212
recognition of, 13–19
passive voice
defined, 79, 557
formation of, 10, **7:** 79
of verb *see*, 535–36
unemphatic use of, **29d:** 330–31
past and past perfect tenses, **7b:** 87–88
past participle, as principal part of verb, **7a:** 82
See also *participle*.
patterns of paragraphs
problem-solution, 353
question-answer, 352
topic-restriction-illustration, 353–54
per, **19i:** 240
percentages, figures for, **11e:** 125
perfect infinitive, use of, **7b(2):** 90
perfect tenses, **7:** 79, 88–89
period, **17a:** 174–75
after abbreviations, **17a(2):** 174
at end of sentences, **17a(1):** 174
with ellipsis mark, **17i:** 186, 187
with quotation marks, **16e(1):** 171
periodic sentence, for emphasis, **29b:** 227–28
periodicals
forms for APA "References," 445–46
forms for MLA "Works Cited," 436–439
indexes to, 425–27
person
agreement in, **6:** 66–67, 70
defined, 550
shift in, **27b:** 315–16
personal pronoun
apostrophe misused with, **15d:** 163; **18b:** 193
case of, **5:** 56–57
classification as, 550, 552
declension of, 538
personification
capitalization with, **9a(1):** 110
defined, 254

perspective, shift in, **27e**: 317
phenomena, **19i**: 231
photocopies, annotated, 452
phrasal prepositions, list of, 18
phrases
  absolute, commas with, **12d(3)**: 143
  appositive, punctuation of, **12d(2)**: 140
  dangling, **25b**: 304–05
  defined and classified, 20–24, 550
  introductory, punctuation of, **12b(2)**: 133–34
  misplaced, **25a(2)**: 302
  misused as sentences, **2a**: 35–36
  restrictive and non-restrictive, punctuation of, **12d(1)**: 137–40
  transitional, punctuation of, **3b**: 45–46
  use of, for variety, **30b**: 338–39; **30d**: 343
plagiarism, **33e**: 457–458
planning the composition. See *composition.*
plays, titles of
  capitalization of, **9c**: 111
  italics for, **10a**: 115–16
plenty, for *very*, **19i**: 240
plurals
  of letters, figures, etc., **15c**: 162
  spelling of, **18e**: 199–200
plus, for *and*, *moreover*, **19i**: 240
P.M., A.M., **11**: 122; **19i**: 227
poetry, quoting, **16a(2)**: 166–67
position of modifiers, **25a**: 301–04
  See also *word order.*
positive degree, 534
possessive case
  apostrophe to indicate, **15a**: 159–61
  before gerund, **5d**: 64
  defined, 159, 532
  of-phrase and *'s* to indicate, **15**: 159
  of pronouns, **5**: 57; **15d**: 163
post hoc, ergo propter hoc, **23f(6)**: 288–89
practical, practicable, **19i**: 240
précis, 454–55
predicate, defined, 550–51
predicate adjective
  after linking verb, **4b**: 52–53
  as subject complement, 11
  defined, 551
predicate noun, defined, 551
prefix
  defined, 551
  hyphen after, **18f**: 209
  meaning of, 214
  spelling of, with root, **18c(1)**: 195
preliminary outline, 445–46
premises in argument, **23e**: 285–86
prepositional phrase
  defined, 17, 550
  introductory, punctuation of, **12b(2)**: 133–34
  misused as a sentence, **2a**: 35
  position of, **25a(2)**: 302
  to begin sentence, for variety, **30b**: 338–39
  uses of, 22–23
prepositions
  among parts of speech, 17–18
  case of objects of, **5**: 57, 59
  defined, 551
  idiomatic use of, **20b**: 256
  omission of, **22a(2)**: 272
  phrasal, 18
  position of, 17
  repeated in parallel structure, **26b**: 310
present and present perfect infinitive, **7b(2)**: 90
present and present perfect participle, **7b(2)**: 90
present tense, **7**: 78–79, 87
prestige, appeal to, **23f(12)**: 290
principal, principle, **19i**: 240–41
principal parts of verbs, 82–85
  defined, 551
  functions of, **7a**: 82–85
  lie, lay, sit, set, **7a(2)**: 85

spelling of, **7a**: 84
printout of computerized catalogue, 425
problem-solution pattern, 353, 401
process, in paragraph development, 357
progressive verbs
defined, 80, 551
forms of *see*, 80–81
pronouns
agreement with antecedent, **6b**: 74–77
among parts of speech, 16
as subjects, agreement of verb with, **6a**: 70–71
case of, **5**: 56–65
declension of, 538
defined and classified, 552
demonstrative, 539
forms of, 7, **5**: 56–57, 538
indefinite, 542
intensive, 544
interrogative, 544
omission of, **22a(1)**: 272
personal, 538, 550
reciprocal, 553
reference of, **28**: 319–24
referring to Deity, **9a(1)**: 109
referring to title of composition, **28b**: 321
reflexive, 553
relative, 553
use of, for coherence, **31c(2)**: 365
pronunciation
related to spelling, **18a**: 191–93
shown in dictionary, 211–12
Proofreader's Checklist, 102
proofreading, 101–02, 190, 412, 415
proper adjective, **9a(3)**: 110, 552
proper names (nouns), **9a**: 109–10
proposition in argument, 285
public library, resources of, 421
punctuation
apostrophe, **15**: 159–63
brackets, **17g**: 183–84
colon, **17d**: 177–79
comma, **12**: 128–46
dash, **17e**: 180–82
ellipsis mark, **17i**: 185–88
exclamation point, **17c**: 176–77
parentheses, **17f**: 182–83
period, **17a**: 174–75
question mark, **17b**: 175–76
quotation marks, **16**: 164–72
semicolon, **14**: 151–58
slash, **17h**: 184–85
purpose, related to types of writing, **32**: 379–80

Q

qualifier, defined, 552
question mark, **17b**: 175–76
after direct question, **17b**: 175
position of, with quotation marks, **16e(3)**: 171
to show uncertainty, 176
question-answer pattern, 352, 401
questions
direct, question mark after, **17b**: 175–76
indirect, period after, **17a**: 174
tag, comma before, 43
use of, for variety, 343–44
quotation marks, **16**: 164–72
double and single, **16a**: 165
for dialogue, **16a(3)**: 167–68
for direct quotations, **16a**: 165–69
for quotations within quotations, **16a**: 165
for titles, **16b**: 169
for words with special senses, **16c**: 169–70
misuse of
for emphasis, **16d**: 170
for indirect quotations, **16a**:165
for theme titles, **8b(4)**: 97
overuse of, **16d**: 170
position of, with other punctuation marks, **16e**: 170–71
quotations

capitalization of first word of, **9e**: 112
colon before, **17d(1)**: 177
direct and indirect, **16a**: 165–69
divided, a cause of comma splice, **3**: 46
documentation of, 452–53
insertions in, brackets for, **17g**: 183–84
introduction of, in research paper, 453, 476, 484, 486
omissions in, ellipsis mark for, **17i**: 185–86
poetry, form for, **16a(2)**: 166–67; **17h**: 184
prose, form for, **16a(1)**: 165–66
within other quotations, **16a**: 165
quote, for *quotation*, **19i**: 241

R

radio programs
form for "Works Cited," 440
italics for titles of, **10a**: 115–16
quotations for titles of episodes of, **16b**: 169
raise, rise, **19i**: 241
rap, for *chat*, **19i**: 241
rarely ever, **19i**: 241
Reader's Guide, sample entry from, 426–27
real, for *very*, **19i**: 241
reason . . . because, **19i**: 241
reasoning. See *logical thinking*.
reciprocal pronouns, 553
reckon, **19i**: 241
record of errors, 105
recordings
form for "Works Cited," 440
reduction, 4
redundancy. See *wordiness*.
reference books
atlases, 430
biographical dictionaries, 430
dictionaries, 210, 428–29
encyclopedias, 429–30
literature, guides to, 431–32
yearbooks, 430
reference lists. See *"References," APA style*.
reference of pronouns, **28**: 319–24
agreement with antecedent, **6b**: 74–77
ambiguous, **28a**: 320
awkward use of indefinite *you* or *it*, **28c(3)**: 323
broad, **28c**: 322–23
it, confusing use of near another *it*, **28d**: 324
to antecedent in possessive case, **28b**: 321
to clause or sentence, **28c(1)**: 322
to implied word or idea, **28c(2)**: 323
to remote antecedent, **28b**: 321
to title of paper, **28b**: 321
"References," APA style, 445–46, 467–68
reflexive pronoun, defined, 553
regional words, **19d**: 221
regular verb, defined, 553
relating ideas
for clarity or sentence unity, **28a**: 279–80
use of parallel structure in, **26**: 308–13
use of subordination in, **24**: 293–95
relative pronouns
as subjects, agreement of verb with, **6a(5)**: 70–71
case of, **5**: 60–63
defined, 553
list of, 25, 553
remote reference of pronoun, **28b**: 321
repetition
as transitional device, **31c(3)**: 366–67
careless or needless, **21c**: 267–70
for emphasis, **29e**: 331
for parallel structure, **26b**: 310–11
research paper
handwritten, specimen page, 512

list of works cited for, 467–68
notes (footnotes/endnotes), 459
note-taking for, **33e**: 451–57
outline for
final, **33d**: 448–51
preliminary, **33c**: 457–58
preliminary bibliography of, **33b**: 422–44
sample of, 472–511
subject for, selection and limitation of, **33a**: 421–22
title page of, 472–73
use of library resources for, 422–32
writing of, with documentation, **33f**: 459–512
See also *composition.*
respectfully, respectively, **19i**: 241
restriction
of topic sentence, **31a(1)**: 347–49
in paragraph pattern, **31a(3)**: 352–55
restrictive appositives, **12d(2)**: 140
restrictive modifiers
defined, 553
distinguished from non-restrictive modifiers, **12d(1)**: 137–40
misuse of commas with, **13d**: 148–49
résumés, **34b**: 524–27
reviews, source of, 426
Reviser's Checklist, 414–15
revision of a paper
after marked by instructor, 103–05
checklists for, 374, 413–14
of first draft, 405–08
of paragraphs, 374
of second draft, 409–412
right, for *very*, **19i**: 242
rise, raise, **19i**: 241
root, distinguished from prefix in spelling, **18c**: 195
round numbers, large, **11e**: 125
run-together sentences, **3**: 40–49

S
-s (or *-es*)
in spelling, **18e**: 199–200
in subject-verb agreement, **6**: 66–67
said, for *this* or *these*, **19i**: 242
salutation of business letter, **34a**: 514–15
same, for *it, this*, **19i**: 242
says, for *said*, **19i**: 242
scarcely, with negative, **19i**: 235
schwa, in spelling, 192
seldom ever, **19i**: 242
self-, hyphen with, **18f(4)**: 209
self-contradiction fallacy, **23f(2)**: 287
semicolon
between items in series, **14b**: 155
between main clauses not linked by *and, but*, etc., **14a**: 152–54
distinguished from colon, **14a**: 154
misuse of, **14c**: 156
position of, with quotation marks, **16e(2)**: 171
with *therefore, for example*, etc. between main clauses, **3b**: 45–46
with *yet, so, and*, etc., linking main clauses, 153
sentence fragment, **2**: 32–39
See also *fragment, sentence.*
sentence modifier, defined, 554
sentence outline, 448, 469–70
sentences
balanced, **29g**: 332
choppy, **24a**: 295–96
classified, 28–29, 554
combined, case in, **5**: 58
compound
comma before *and, but*, etc., in, **12a**: 129–32
defined, 29
overuse of, **24b**: 296–97
revision of, for variety, **30c**: 341–42
semicolon in, **14a**: 152–54

compound-complex, defined, 29
defined, 553–54
diagramed, 539–40
effective, 278–344
fragmentary, **2**: 32–39
fused (run-on), **3**: 40–49
grammar of, **1**: 2–31
loose, **29b**: 327–28; **30c**: 341–42
parallel, **26a(3)**: 309
periodic, **29b**: 327–28
run-on, (fused/run-together), **3**: 40–49
simple, defined, 29, 553–54
stringy, **30c**: 341–42
topic, **31**: 347–52
unity in, **23a-c**: 278–83
variety in, **30**: 335–44
See also *co-ordination; subordination.*
sequence of tenses, **7b(2)**: 89–90
series
colon introducing, **17d(1)**: 177
commas with, **12c**: 135–36
introductory, dash after, **17e(4)**: 181–82
parallel form for items in, **26**: 308
question mark with, **17b**: 175
semicolon with, **14b**: 155
set, sit, **7a(2)**: 85–86; **19i**: 242
shifts
from indirect to direct discourse, **27c**: 316
in number or person, **27b**: 315
in perspective, **27e**: 317
in tense or mood, **7d**: 92–93; **27a**: 314–15
in tone or style, **27d**: 316–17
in voice, **27a**: 314–15
should and *would*, use of, **7e**: 94
show up, **19i**: 242
sic, 183
signature on business letter, **34a**: 516
simile, 253–55
simple predicate, defined, 550–51
simple sentence, defined, 29, 553–54
simple subject, defined, 554–55
single quotation marks, **16a**: 165
sit, set, **7a(2)**: 85–87; **19i**: 242
slang
overuse of quotation marks with, **16d**: 170
restricted use of, **19c**: 220–21
slash, use of, **17h**: 184
slow, slowly, **4**: 51
smell, modifier after, **4b**: 52–53
so
comma before, between main clauses, **12a**: 129, 131
overuse of, as intensive, **19i**: 242
semicolon before, between main clauses, 153
without completing clause, **22d**: 275–76
some
agreement of verb with, **6a**: 71
for *remarkable, somewhat*, **19i**: 242
someone, some one, **19i**: 227
somewheres, **19i**: 243
sort, kind, **19i**: 236
sort of a, **19i**: 243
sound, modifier after, **4b**: 52–53
sounds, distracting combination of, **19h**: 223
sources for research paper
acknowledgment of, 455–56
evaluation of, 450
spacecraft, names of, **10c**: 117
spatial order, 357–58, 401
specialized audience, 395–97
specific and general words, **20a(3)**: 250–53
spelling, **18**: 190–209
British, American and Canadian usage, **18**: 191
in dictionary, 190–91, 211
of words with similar sound, **18b**: 193–95
of troublesome verb forms, **7a**: 84
proofreading for errors in, 190
pronunciation as guide to, **18a**:

191–93
rules of
ei or *ie*, **18d**: 198
final *e* before suffix, **18c(2)**: 196–97
final *l* before *-ly*, **18c(5)**: 198
final *y* before suffix, **18c(4)**: 197
prefix and root, **18c(1)**: 195
-s or *-es*, for plural, **18e**: 199–200
single or double consonant before suffix, **18c(3)**: 197
words often confused, 194–95
words often misspelled, 200–06
split infinitive, **25a(5)**: 303
squinting modifier, **25a(4)**: 303
stage plays
form for ''Works Cited,'' 440
standard English, defined, 225
stationary, stationery, **19i**: 243
statistics, figures used for, **11e**: 125
still, as conjunctive adverb, **3b**: 45
style books, list of, 444–45
styles of documentation, 444–46
subject
agreement of verb with, **6a**: 68–73
and predicate, 3
complete, 3, 554–55
compound, **6a**: 68–70, 534
defined, 11, 554–55
double, **21a(1)**: 263
of infinitive, case of, **5e**: 64
of verb, recognition of, 5–8
of verbal, 21, 556
simple, 3, 554–55
subject complement
adjective as, 11, **4b**: 52–53
defined, 11, 534
pronoun as, **5f**: 65
recognition of, 11–12
subjective case
after *be*, **5f**: 65
after *than* or *as*, **5b(3)**: 61
defined, 56–57, 532–33
for appositives, **5a**: 59
in compound constructions, **5a**: 59
uses of, **5**: 56–57
who, in clause, **5b**: 60–61
subjects for papers, choice and limitation of, **32a**: 383–87; **33a**: 421–22
subjunctive mood, **7c**: 91–92, 545
subordinate clauses
defined and classified, 25–27, 533
markers of, 25, 132
misused as sentences, **2b**: 36
subordinating conjunctions, defined, 25
subordination
distinguished from co-ordination, 293–94
excessive or overlapping, **24c**: 297–98
to combine short sentences, **24a**: 295–96
to revise faulty compound sentences, **24b**: 296–97; **30c**: 341–42
subordinators
defined, 555
lists of, 25, 132
subtitle of book
in ''Works Cited,'' 433
use of colon with, **17d(2)**: 178
such, without completing clause, **22d**: 275–76
such as, needless colon after, **17d(3)**: 178
suffixes
adjective-forming, 16, 50
adverb-forming, 17, 50
-d or *-ed*, omission of, **4**: 51; **7**: 82–83
defined, 555
-elect, hyphen with, **18f(4)**: 209
noun-forming, 15
-s or *-es*
in forming plurals, **18e**: 199–200

in subject-verb agreement, **6**: 66–67
spelling rules for adding, **18c**: 196–98; **18e**: 199–200
verb-forming, 5, 15
summary, distinguished from paraphrase, 456–57
superfluous commas before or after a series, **13e**: 149
separating subject from verb or verb from object, **13a**: 147–48
setting off non-parenthetical words or phrases, **13c**: 148
setting off restrictive elements, **13d**: 148–49
with co-ordinating conjunctions **13b**: 148
superior than, **19i**: 243
superlative degree, **4c**: 53–54, 534
supposed to, **19i**: 243
sure, for *surely*, **19i**: 243
sure and, for *sure to*, **19i**: 228
suspension hyphen, **18f(1)**: 208
syllabication, **8d**: 99, 211
synonyms
awkward use of, to avoid repetition, **21c**: 267, 268
in definition, **23d**: 285
in dictionary and thesaurus, 213–14
syntax, defined, 555

T

tag question, comma with, 43
taking notes. See *note-taking*.
taste, modifier after, **4b**: 52–53
tautology, **21a(1)**: 262–63
teach, learn, **19i**: 237
technical terms, **19g**: 222
television programs
form for "Works Cited," 440
italics for titles of, **10a**: 115–16
quotation marks for titles of episodes of, **16b**: 169
tense
and time, **7b(1)**: 87–89
classification of, 78–79
conjugation illustrating, 535–36
defined, 78, 555
sequence of, **7b(2)**: 89–91
shifts in, **7d**: 92–93; **27a**: 314–15
than, case of pronoun after, **5b(3)**: 61
then, for *than*, **19i**: 243
that, which, in restrictive clauses, **12d(1)**: 139
that is, as conjunctive adverbial, **3b**: 46
that there, this here, **19i**: 244
the number, a number, **19i**: 227
their, there, they're, **19i**: 243
theirselves, **5**: 57; **19i**: 243
them, for *those*, **19i**: 243
theme. See *composition*.
then
as conjunctive adverb, **3b**: 45
for *than*, **18**: 192; **19i**: 243
there—verb—subject, agreement in, **6a(4)**: 70
therefore, as conjunctive adverb, **3b**: 45
thesaurus, use of, 213–14
these kind, these sort, **19i**: 236
thesis statement, **32d**: 393–95
thing, **19i**: 243
this here, that there, **19i**: 244
thus, as conjunctive adverb, **3b**: 45
thusly, **19i**: 244
time, related to tense, **7b**: 87–89
title of a composition
manuscript form for, **8b(4)**: 97
reference of pronoun to, **28b**: 321
title page of paper, 472–73
titles of books, plays, etc.
agreement of verb with, **6a(10)**: 73
capitalization of, **9c**: 111–12
italics for, **10a**: 115–16
quotation marks for, **16b**: 169
titles of persons
abbreviations of, **11a**: 120–21, 122
capitalization of, **9b**: 111

in business letters, **34a(3)**: 515
redundant use of, **11a**: 121
to, too, two, **19i**: 244
tone
and audience, 396
shift in, **27d**: 316–17
too, without completing phrase, **22d**: 275–76
topic outline, 446, 475–77
topic-restriction-illustration pattern, 353–54, 401
topic sentence
construction of, 347–49
implied, 350–51
placement of, **31a(2)**: 349–52
restriction of, **31a(1)**: 347–49
trademarks, 108
transitional expressions
commas with, **12b(3)**: 134; **12d(3)**: 142
list of, 367–68
to begin sentence, for variety, **30b(3)**: 339
transitional paragraph, **31e**: 375
transitional phrases, connecting main clauses, **3b**: 45–47
transitions
between paragraphs, **31d**: 371–72
within the paragraph, **31c**: 365–70
transitive verb, defined, 556
triteness, **20c**: 257–59
try and, for *try to*, **19i**: 244
type, for *type of*, **19i**: 244
typewritten papers, form of, **8a(2)**: 96
typing, legibility of, **8c(2)**: 98

U

underlining, to indicate italics, **10**: 115
See also *italics*.
uninterested, disinterested, **19i**: 231
unique, absolute meaning of, **4c**: 54
unity
in essays, **32f**: 400–04
in paragraphs, **31c**: 364–70
in sentences, **23a-c**: 278–83
See also *coherence*.
unpublished works
form for bibliography, 439
forms for notes, 465, 467
Usage, Glossary of, **19i**: 224–45
usage labels in dictionaries, 218–19
use to, used to, **19i**: 244
used to could, **19i**: 244

V

vague reference of pronouns, **28**: 319–24
valid argument, **23e**: 285–86
value judgment, distinguished from fact, **23f(4)**: 288
variety in sentence structure, **30**: 335–44
of beginning, **30b**: 338–41
of length, **30a**: 336–38
of sentence types, **30c**: 341–42; **30e**: 343–44
of subject-verb sequence, **30d**: 343
verb phrase, 6, 550
verbals
dangling, **25b**: 304–05
defined, 556
in sentence fragments, **2a**: 35
recognition of, 21
tenses of, 81, 90
See also *gerund, infinitive* and *participle*.
verbs
agreement with subject, **6a**: 68–74
among parts of speech, 15
auxiliary, 6, 78, 532
conjugation of, 535–36
defined and classified, 556
finite and non-finite, 541, 546
intransitive, 12, 556
irregular, 544
linking, 11–12, **4b**: 52–53, 544
mood of, 80, 545
particles with, 6–7, 549

principal parts of, **7a**: 82–85, 551
progressive, 80–81, 551
recognition of, 5–8
regular, 553
tense of, 78–79, **7b**: 87–91, 555
transitive, 12, 556
voice of, 79–80, 557
very, overuse of, **19i**: 244
viewpoint, shift in, **27e**: 317
vocabulary, **20**: 246–60
See also *diction*.
vocabulary (lexical) words, 556
voice of verbs
active, for emphasis, **29d**: 330–31
defined, 79–80, 557
shift in, **27a**: 314–15
vowel sounds, related to spelling, **18**: 192

W

wait on, for *wait for*, **19i**: 244
want for, **19i**: 244
want in, want out, **19i**: 244
want that, **19i**: 244
ways, for *way*, **19i**: 245
what, for *who* or *that*, **19i**: 245
what-clause, and subject-verb agreement, **6a(8)**: 72
what is more, as adverbial connective, **3b**: 46
when or *where*, in definitions, **19i**: 236; **23c(3)**: 282
where . . . at/to, **19i**: 245
where, for *that*, **19i**: 245
whether . . . or, parallel structure with, **26c**: 311–12
which, for *who* or *that*, **19i**: 245
which, that, in restrictive clause, **12d(1)**: 139
while, overuse of, **19i**: 245
who, whose, whom, **5**: 56–58, 60–62
whose, who's, **15d**: 163
word division, **8d**: 99–101
wordiness, **21**: 261–70
meaningless words as, **21a**: 262–65
restructuring sentences to avoid, **21b**: 265–67
tautology, **21a(1)**: 262–63
uneconomical diction, **21a(2)**: 263–65
words, choice of. See *diction*.
words referred to as words
agreement of verb with, **6a(10)**: 73
italics for, **10b**: 116–17
plural forms of, **15c**: 162
working plan for a composition, **32f**: 400–04
"Works Cited," list of, MLA style, 433–40, 467
would and *should*, use of, **7e**: 94
would have, for *had*, **7**: 94
would of, **19i**: 245

X

Xmas, **19i**: 245

Y

yearbooks, list of, 430
yes, introductory, **12b(3)**: 134
yet, between main clauses, **12a**: 129–32
you, awkward use of, **28c(3)**: 323
you were, **6**: 67
your, you're, **18b**: 193; **19i**: 245

Acknowledgments

The author and publisher wish to thank the following for permission to reprint the material below:

C. ALEXANDER BROWN for his review of *Forbidden Voice* by Alma Green and *Joseph Brant: A Man for His People* by Helene Caister; reprinted from the December 1971 issue of *Books in Canada*.

CANADIAN HERITAGE MAGAZINE for the excerpt from "Heritage authors take a stroll downtown" by Don J. Lahey; reprinted from the May/June 1983 issue of *Canadian Heritage Magazine* with the permission of the publisher.

RENE CHARTRAND for the excerpt from his article "Military Portraiture"; reprinted from the January/February 1985 issue of *Canadian Collector* magazine.

CHIMO! MAGAZINE for the review by Frank B. Walker of *The Independence Movement in Quebec 1945–1980* by William D. Coleman. Reprinted from the November/December 1984 issue with the courtesy of CHIMO! *Magazine*.

BETTY S. FLOWERS for her essay "Madman, Architect, Carpenter, Judge: Roles and the Writing Process," copyright © 1979. Reprinted from *Proceedings* of the Conference of College Teachers of English of Texas 44 (September 1979).

HARCOURT BRACE JOVANOVICH, INC. for the excerpt from *Power of Words* by Stuart Chase.

McCLELLAND AND STEWART LIMITED for the excerpt from *The Forked Road* by Donald Creighton. Used by permission of The Canadian Publishers, McClelland and Stewart Limited, Toronto.

MERRIAM-WEBSTER INC. for the thesaurus entry *empty*. From *Webster's Collegiate Thesaurus*; © 1976 by Merriam-Webster Inc., publisher of the Merriam-Webster® Dictionaries.

NATIONAL WILDLIFE FEDERATION for the essay "Do Animals Really Play?" by Eugene J. Walter, Jr.; © 1979 by the National Wildlife Federation. Reprinted from the September/October 1979 issue of *International Wildlife Magazine*.

THE ESTATE OF THE LATE SONIA BROWNELL ORWELL AND MARTIN SECKER & WARBURG LTD. for the photocopied excerpt from *The Collected Essays, Journalism and Letters of George Orwell, Volume 4*.

OXFORD UNIVERSITY PRESS for the excerpt from *The Republic of Childhood: A Critical Guide to Canadian Children's Literature in English* by Sheila Egoff; © Oxford University Press Canada 1967. Reprinted by permission.

SHAWN REDFIELD for his essay "Primitives for the Present," appearing in this book under the title "Collectibles for the Present."

SIMON & SCHUSTER, INC. for the dictionary entry *empty*. From *Webster's New World Dictionary of the American Language*, Second College Edition; copyright © 1980 by Simon & Schuster, Inc.

Acknowledgments

THE UNIVERSITY OF CHICAGO PRESS for the excerpt from the essay "The Relevance of Canadian History" by W.L. Morton; reprinted from *Contexts of Canadian Criticism* edited by Eli Mandel; copyright © 1971 by the University of Chicago Press.

UNIVERSITY OF TORONTO PRESS for the excerpt from the essay "Writing in the Social Sciences" by Henry B. Mayo; reprinted from *Literary History in Canada, Volume 3*, Second Edition, edited by Carl F. Klink and published by the University of Toronto Press.

ROGER D. VOYER for the excerpt from his essay "Canada's Need for a Nordic Image"; reprinted from the November 23, 1977 issue of the *Globe & Mail*.

RUDY WIEBE for the excerpt from "The Naming of Albert Johnson" in *Where is the Voice Coming From?* by Rudy Wiebe.

THE H.W. WILSON COMPANY for the excerpts from the *Reader's Guide to Periodical Literature*; copyright © 1980, 1982, 1983 by The H.W. Wilson Company. Material reproduced by permission of the publisher.

Every reasonable effort has been made to acquire permission for copyright material used in this book, and to acknowledge all such indebtedness accurately. All errors and omissions called to our attention will be corrected in future printings.

A LIST OF LISTS

Abbreviations: 441–43
Adverb clauses, introductory: 132
Adverbs, conjunctive: 45
Bibliography samples: 433–40
Conjunctions, co-ordinating: 18
Conjunctions, correlative: 18
Conjunctions, subordinating: 25
Glossary of Grammatical Terms: 529–57
Glossary of Usage: 224–45
Prepositions: 17–18
Pronouns, personal: 538
Pronouns, relative: 25
Proofreader's checklist: 102
Reviser's checklists: 374, 414–15
Transitional expressions: 45, 367–68, 372
Trite expressions: 258–59
Verbs, auxiliary: 6
Verbs, tenses of: 79
Verbs, linking: 11
Verbs, progressive forms of: 80–81
Verbs, principal parts of: 83–84
Words frequently confused: 194–95
Words frequently misspelled: 200–06

Other Correction Symbols	